AF553286

NUCLEAR POLITICS IN SOUTH ASIA

NUCLEAR POLITICS IN SOUTH ASIA

SURESH DHANDA

REGAL PUBLICATIONS
New Delhi - 110 027

NUCLEAR POLITICS IN SOUTH ASIA

ISBN 978-81-8484-064-3

Typeset by
RAHUL COMPOSERS
358, Pocket-B, Phase-II, Sector-16 B, Dwarka, New Delhi - 110 075

Printed in India at
NEW ELEGANT ENTERPRISES
A-49/1, Mayapuri, Phase-I, New Delhi - 110 064

Published by
REGAL PUBLICATIONS
F-159, Rajouri Garden, New Delhi - 110 027 • Phone : 45546396
E-mail : regalbookspub@yahoo.com

Contents

Preface

The nuclearisation of South Asia brought a qualitative change in the power potential of the sub-continent. Simultaneously, it trapped both India and Pakistan into an unaffordable and dangerous tit for tat kind of arms race that can lead to a nuclear holocaust. Both are obsessive for weapons of mass destruction, and undermining the risks of nuclear and missile proliferation. Consequently, the region is being described by many as the most dangerous place in the world. Conventional conflict at any level is a big challenge for deterrence in the region as it carries the potential for escalation from one level to another and then ultimately to the grim prospects of nuclear exchange. Both of them also lack assured second-strike capability, a necessary condition for a successful deterrence which was prevailed during the cold war between super powers. Lack of effective command and control system further makes the situation complicated which increases the possibility of accidental nuclear war. The safety and security of nuclear facilities, material and weapons is also a cause of serious concern as there are various terrorist organizations active in the region. There is a real threat from insiders and outsiders that nuclear weapons and facilities could fall into the hands of terrorists.

The risk of nuclear escalation is further increased by the fact both are deeply involved in developing various kinds of missiles to deliver their nuclear weapons. These missile programmes have serious security implications at regional and global level. Mobility of missiles during the period of crisis may lead to escalation between the two countries. Due to lack of comprehensive and accurate intelligence one side may misread the passive dispersal of weapons, and can interpret the defensive moves of other as threatening, and initiate a chain of reaction regarding deployment of such missiles. As a result, both could enter into a spiral of escalation. India's quest to establish ballistic missile defence system will further stimulate the arms race and debilitate the security scenario in the region. What is needed is that both the countries as responsible nuclear neighbours should carefully evaluate the overall security situation in the region. The issues should be addressed through both short and long-term measures. Present volume aims at tracing politics behind all these issues and suggesting some measures to establish peace and security in the sub-continent.

In the accomplishment of this task I have received help from number of institutions, individuals, friends, colleagues and well-wishers in one or another way, I am indebted to them. I owe my sincere gratitude to my teacher Professor R.S. Yadav, who has been kind and considerate enough in extending his full support, learned guidance and valuable suggestions during the course of present study despite his extremely busy schedule. Working with him has been a great learning experience for me. His constant guidance, strong motivation and encouraging attitude always inspired me to work sincerely. I also express my regards to my teachers in the department, Professor Leela Yadav and Saroj Malik for their valuable comments and suggestions. My friend, Anil Gautam, also deserves special thanks for his co-operation regarding computational work.

I sincerely pay my thanks to the staff of American Centre Library, British Council Library, Indian Council of World Affairs, Institute for Defence Studies and Analysis, JNU Library, United Nations Information Centre, Indian Council of Social Science Research, Delhi University Library and India International Centre Library, New Delhi for helping me in collecting necessary information, data and research material. I am also thankful to Carnegie Endowment for International

Peace, Washington, D.C. for their regular e-mails on nuclear security issues which have been of great relevance for me to keep myself update. I am also obliged to various scholars and analysts whose prestigious works I have read and cited in my work.

SURESH DHANDA

Abbreviations

AAM	:	Air-to-Air Missile
ABM	:	Anti Ballistic Missile
AEC	:	Atomic Energy Commission
AI	:	Artificial Intelligence
ALH	:	Advanced Light Helicopter
ARDE	:	Armament Research and Development Establishment
ASPL	:	Akash Self Propelled Launcher
ATBM	:	Anti Tactical Ballistic Missile
ATGM	:	Anti Tank Guided Missile
ATV	:	Advanced Technology Vessel
BARC	:	Bhabha Atomic Research Center
BDL	:	Bharat Dynamics Limited
BMD	:	Ballistic Missile Defence
BSRBM	:	Battlefield Short Range Ballistic Missile
BVRAAM	:	Beyond Visual Range Air-to-Air Missile
C^4I	:	Command, Control, Communication, Computers and Intelligence
CCS	:	Cabinet Committee on Security
CDS	:	Chief of Defence Staff
CEP	:	Circular Error Probability
CIA	:	Central Intelligence Agency
CIP	:	Continuous Improvement Programme
CISF	:	Central Industrial Security Force
CPPNM	:	Convention on Physical Protection of Nuclear Material

DAE	:	Department of Atomic Energy
DESTO	:	Defence Science and Technology Organisation
DND	:	Draft Nuclear Doctrine
DRDL	:	Defence Research and Development Laboratory
DRDO	:	Defence Research and Development Organisation
DSTO	:	Database on Nuclear Smuggling, Theft and Orphan Radiation
EC	:	Executive Council
EMP	:	Electromagnetic Pulse
ERA	:	Explosive Reactor Armour
ERDE	:	Electronic Research and Development Establishment
FMCT	:	Fissile Material Cut-off Treaty
FSB	:	Federal Security Services
GCC	:	Gulf Cooperation Council
GLONESS	:	Global Navigation Satellite System
GPS	:	Global Positioning System
GUC	:	Gas Ultracentrifuge
HAM	:	High Altitude Motor
HE	:	High Explosive
HEAT	:	High Explosive Anti Tank
HEU	:	Highly Enriched Uranium
IAEA	:	International Atomic Energy Agency
IAF	:	Indian Air Force
ICBM	:	Inter-Continental Ballistic Missile
IDSA	:	Institute for Defence Studies and Analysis
IGMDP	:	Integrated Guided Missile Development Programme
IIR	:	Imaging Infra Red
IIS	:	Institute for International Studies
IN	:	Indian Navy
INS	:	Inertial Navigation System
IRBM	:	Intermediate Range Ballistic Missile
IRFNA	:	Inhibited Red Fuming Nitric Acid
IRS	:	Indian Remote Sensing
ISI	:	Inter-Service Intelligence
ISIS	:	Institute for Science and International Security
ISP	:	Integrated Sensing and Processing
ISPR	:	Inter-Services Public Relations

ISRO	:	Indian Space Research Organisation
ITR	:	Integrated Test Range
KRL	:	Khan Research Laboratory
KT	:	Kilo Ton
LCA	:	Light Combat Aircraft
LEU	:	Low Enriched Uranium
LIC	:	Low Intensity Conflict
LOC	:	Line of Control
LOS	:	Line of Sight
MAL	:	Mobile Autonomous Launchers
MIRV	:	Multiple Independently Re-entry Vehicle
MRBM	:	Medium Range Ballistic Missile
MRCP	:	Multi-Directionally Reinforced Carbon-fiber Perform
MTCR	:	Missile Technology Control Regime
MVRDE	:	Military Vehicle Research and Development Establishment
NCA	:	National Command Authority
NCA	:	Nuclear Command Authority
NDA	:	National Democratic Alliance
NDC	:	National Defence Complex
NESCOM	:	National Engineering and Scientific Commission
NORAD	:	North American Aerospace Defense Command
NPT	:	Non-Proliferation Treaty
NRDC	:	Natural Resource Development Council
NSAB	:	National Security Advisory Board
PAEC	:	Pakistani Atomic Energy Commission
PAF	:	Pakistani Air Force
PAL	:	Permissive Action Link
PC	:	Political Council
PMO	:	Prime Minister Office
PNE	:	Peaceful Nuclear Explosion
PRP	:	Personnel Reliability Programme
PSLV	:	Polar Satellite Launch Vehicle
PTA	:	Pilot-less Target Aircraft
PTV	:	Pakistan Television
R&D	:	Research and Development
RAW	:	Research and Analysis Wing
RCI	:	Research Center Imarat

RDD	:	Radiological Dispersal Device
RPY	:	Remotely Piloted Vehicle
RV	:	Re-entry Vehicle
SAM	:	Surface-to-Air Missile
SFC	:	Strategic Force Command
SINS	:	Strap-down Inertial Navigation System
SLMC	:	Submarine Launched Cruise Missile
SLV	:	Satellite Launch Vehicle
SRBM	:	Short Range Ballistic Missile
SSM	:	Surface-to-Surface Missile
SSPL	:	Solid State Physics Laboratory
SUPARCO	:	Space and Upper Atmosphere Research Commission
TBM	:	Tactical Ballistic Missile
TBM	:	Theatre Ballistic Missile
TCV	:	Trishul Combat Vehicle
TD	:	Technology Demonstrator
TDOA	:	Time Delay of Arrival
TEL	:	Tractor Erector Launcher
TES	:	Technology Experiment Satellite
THAAD	:	Theatre High Altitude Area Defence
TLC	:	Transport Launch Canister
TTB	:	Technology Test Bed
UAV	:	Unmanned Air Vehicle
WMD	:	Weapons of Mass Destruction

1

Introduction

South Asia is a region in which three rival nations—India, Pakistan and China[1]—share disputed frontiers. They are torn by deep-rooted animosities, and face each other with nuclear and missile capabilities. The hostilities between India and Pakistan, on the one hand, and between India and China, on the other, are spurring the costly arms race and creating serious security problems in the region. The growing domestic, political, ethnic and sectarian strife in India and Pakistan directly influence the security of the sub-continent. Both these countries of the region remain trapped in an antagonism that has changed very little since their independence in 1947. The terms of their disputes and the accompanying images remain largely fixed. Perceptions that are steeped in history and the emotional trauma of partition have always been a dominating factor in the psyche of the people in both the countries. Opinions in Pakistan widely hold that India is intent upon undermining and humiliating Pakistan, and would reabsorb all of the sub-continent's Muslims. Indians feel that Pakistan is fanatical in its determination to repay India for past defeats, including the loss of East Pakistan, and would like to seize Kashmir in a proxy war. Authorities in New Delhi also view Pakistan as responsible for making efforts to set Islamic

World against India, in order to create a hostile political, military and economic bloc. In turn, Pakistan points to what it sees as evidence of India's hegemonic ambitions and expansionism at the expense of all its smaller neighbours. The failure of India and Pakistan to create confidence building measures (CBMs) and a normalization of relations reflect prevailing high degree of mistrust, and reveal the existence of suspicions between them. Thus, both the countries are locked into an increasingly expensive political and security competition that ignores the opportunity of utilizing the scarce resources for welfare purposes.[2]

The perpetual cold war between India and Pakistan has also turned into full-scale hot wars in 1948, 1965 and 1971. Besides these full-scale wars, they have indulged once in a limited confrontation at *Kargil* in 1999. During all the three full-scale wars neither India nor Pakistan was having any missile or nuclear capability, but now the situation is not only different, but also dangerous. Both are now nuclear weapon states after the successful nuclear tests of 1998. Since then both are engaged seriously in revising and developing their nuclear weapons and delivery systems. Now they possess nuclear weapons, weapon usable material, and civil and military nuclear infrastructure up to a significant extent. Though, India is uppermost in the field of civil nuclear energy production but on the military side, both have produced significant nuclear weapons usable material. India is supposed to have between 60-105 warheads and Pakistan 35-90.[3] Both of them have adopted different methods and routes to make nuclear weapons. India's programme is plutonium-based while Pakistan has adopted uranium-based route. This is particularly because of different histories of their nuclear developments. India started on weapons course via its civilian routes through nuclear energy research. On the other side, Pakistan adopted the clandestine route by stealing and begging the nuclear technology from abroad.[4] China and North Korea provided the maximum help in this direction.[5] National self-expression, long-term geo-political factors, Chinese nuclear threat, desire to play the role in world politics have been the main factors to motivate India's programme. On the other side, Pakistan has a simple reason, e.g. cost-effective reaction to India's overwhelming military capabilities. India's nuclear weapons programme is limited and it does not utilize the entire capability available to produce weapons-grade material. Pakistan's nuclear programme is "bomb centric" e.g., it makes weapons-grade material using almost the entire nuclear infrastructure and uses them to build nuclear weapons. India has a declared "no-first-use" nuclear doctrine while Pakistan lacks it. But unofficially it has declared some "red-lines", and crossing of these would compel Pakistan to think seriously for using nuclear weapons.

These developments have led to a new strategic situation that is bound to have long-lasting implications for both the countries of South Asia in particular and for the international community in general. Moreover, since 2001 both the countries have accelerated their missile programmes, which is likely to have grave implications not only at the regional level but also at global level. The fact that missiles ideally suited to deliver weapons of mass destruction, which both the countries already possess, has further accentuated the seriousness of the problem. Technology control regimes, particularly MTCR, because of their selective application and duplicity of approach, have succeeded only in slowing the pace of development of missiles but failed to prevent their spread in South Asia. However, by now no missile has been used by them during conflicts but both have operational missiles in their inventories, and the numbers are progressively increasing. The expanding capabilities, marked by significant improvements in payload, range, reliability and accuracy, are not only threatening to push the region towards a debilitating arms race, but also have the potential to bring the nuclear armed adversaries a step closer towards the deployment of their strategic arsenals.[6]

Besides aircrafts, both these countries now rely on various kinds of missiles as delivery systems.[7] India has an extensive, largely indigenous ballistic missile programme, including infrastructure for both solid and liquid fuelled missiles. India's existing missiles are of *Prithvi* and *Agni* series. India has *Prithvi*-I with a range of 150 km capable of having payload of 1000 kg., *Prithvi*-II with a range of 250 km capable of having a payload of 500 kg and *Prithvi*-III (reportedly under development) with a range of 350 km.[8] India's second family of ballistic missiles is the *Agni*-I, II and III. The *Agni* missiles are designed to extend the reach of Indian nuclear capabilities, particularly to China.

However, one more variant of *Agni*, now officially referred to as *Agni*-I is specifically designed for missions against Pakistan and was tested with a capacity of 1000 kg payload on January 8, 2003 to a range of 700 km.[9] India reportedly intends to retrofit its *Brahmos* adaptation of Russian supplied *Yakhont* anti-ship, cruise missile so that it can be fired either from naval ships or from SU-30 MKI attack aircraft. This cruise missile apparently could be used as a stand-off system with either conventional or nuclear weapons.[10]

Pakistan also has an active missile acquisition and development program since the early 1980s. This includes indigenous missile development (based in part on foreign design) as well as the reported purchase of M-11 missiles from China in the early 1990s although Pakistan and China denied these reports. Pakistan has several types of road mobile, nuclear capable ballistic missiles with shorter and longer ranges, solid and liquid fueled. The *Hatf*-I is an indigenous single stage solid propellant missile with a range of 60 to 80 km carrying a 500 kg payload.[11] Then there are *Hatf*-II (*Abdali*), single stage solid fueled missile with a range of 280-300 km and *Hatf*-III (*Ghazani)* single stage solid fueled (300 km) and *Hatf*-IV (*Shaheen*) single stage solid fueled with a range of 600 km.[12] Pakistan's longer range *Ghauri*-I, single stage with 1000-1500 km range and *Ghauri*-II, two stage with 2500 km range (still in development testing) are liquid fueled missiles that are believed to be based on the North Korean "No-Dong" and "*Taepo-Dong*" missiles, derived originally from Soviet scud technology.[13]

However, both the countries have entered into the production mode in case of short and medium range missiles, but overall missile programmes still appears to be largely in the development phase. India's missile programme is deeply linked with its space programme while Pakistan's programme is linked with its space programme peripherally. Missiles of both the countries have sufficient range to cover all the important targets deep inside each other's territory. As far as organizational infrastructure is concerned, India has a wide base and coalition of various indigenous organizations and actors involved in the task of development of various missile components while Pakistan has a limited base and mainly dependent on foreign assistance. India is also pursuing seriously the option of ballistic missile defence with the help of USA, Israel and Russia, and simultaneously developing indigenous system. Pakistan's response in this direction depends upon the type, size and shape of an Indian BMD. It could go either for its own defence systems or build up its offensive forces to overwhelm India's defences. Since Pakistan's ability to produce its own missile defence systems is extremely limited both from technological and economic point of view, so it could go for qualitative and quantitative improvement in its nuclear and missile forces and its strategy. The future plans of India is to develop a nuclear triad to have a second-strike capability for which it is working on intermediate and intercontinental *Agni* ballistic missiles, Brahmos cruise missile, *Avatar* and SLBM *Sagarika*. Pakistan is also working seriously on *Shaheen*-I, *Ghauri*-II and *Ghazanvi* ballistic and *Babar* cruise missiles.

Keeping in view the developments in the field of nuclear weapons and missile systems it seems that deterrence is not likely to work in the region. Rather vertical and horizontal proliferations have increased the possibility of nuclear war if not by design then by accident/miscalculation. The region does not seem to fulfil the prerequisites of a successful deterrence. Success of nuclear deterrence depends upon: (i) prevention of conventional war, (ii) second-strike capability; (iii) avoidance of accidental nuclear war, and (iv) safety of nuclear weapons. These four prerequisites seem to be missing in the context of South Asia. First, the prevailing India-Pakistan hostilities and suspicion are sufficient reasons for the beginning of conventional war between them. As long as such possibilities exist, the chances of nuclear exchange can not be ruled out. Second, the lack of second-strike capability between them also creates the fear of pre-emptive attack. This fear can be overcome through defence measures like hardening, mobility, dispersal and concealment of nuclear weapons. But in this manner India and Pakistan will increase the susceptibility of their forces due to failure of connectivity. As a result, development of nuclear triad in the form of long range bombers, land-based and submarine-based missiles will be required. But India and Pakistan lack this nuclear triad. Third, command and control of the strategic forces, known as command, control, communication, computers and intelligence (C^4I), is an extremely crucial factor in the use of such weapons. It provides a link between the national command authority and the personnel who have physical control of the weapons. In case of Indian and Pakistani lack of requisite nuclear command and control system, nuclear safety and related technical issues enhance the possibility of accidental nuclear war. Besides, inadequate warning systems, short flight times, false alarms and non-institution of Personnel Reliability Programmes (PRPs) by both of them may increase the chances of such warfare. Missile test launch during a crisis could also be misperceived as the start of a nuclear attack. Finally, the political and social turmoil in the region increases the threat from both insiders and outsiders to nuclear facilities, material and weapons, and fear that nuclear weapons and facilities could fall into the hands of terrorists. Presence and threats from terrorist outfits like Al Qaeda in this region further escalate such threat scenarios. Delegation of authority to field operations may further complicate the problem of providing security.

Apart from these operational problems regarding the success of deterrence, these nuclear and missile developments in South Asia have serious security implications on regional as well as global level. At regional level, the inventory and types of missiles increase an escalation of tension between the relations of India and Pakistan on the one hand, and between India and China on the other. At global level, the developments in the South Asia have serious rather negative implications on the non-proliferation regime, and encouraging the other states to pursue nuclear and missile programmes.

Potential operational problems regarding the mobility of missiles during the period of crisis may lead to escalation between the two countries. Besides, due to the lack of comprehensive and accurate intelligence one side may misread passive dispersal of weapons, and can interpret the defensive moves of other as threatening, and initiate a chain reaction regarding deployment of such missiles. Consequently, India and Pakistan could enter into a spiral of escalation. Moreover, these delivery systems themselves could become a source of tension and could by their nature and disposition increase the incentive to attack first in a crisis. In South Asia, short range missiles can easily attack on national capitals of adversaries within a span of less than five minutes leaving little time for warning and protective measures due to the close geographical proximity. An accidental or even authorized test launch during period of tension may precipitate a conflict and hence affects the stability of the region in a serious way. Ambiguity regarding type of warhead mounted on a missile launched also creates the confusion among decision-makers because government statements frequently describe a missile system as nuclear capable. The assumption on the receiving end may likely to read any missile launched as a missile carrying a nuclear warhead.

Introduction of ballistic missile defence (BMD) has further complicated the already surcharged scenario in the region. Response to an Indian BMD may bring quantitative and qualitative change in Pakistan's nuclear force structure, deployment postures, and decisions to go for its own missile defence. This action-reaction spiral is likely to give boost to the phenomenon of arms race in South Asia which will increase the chances of conflict between India and Pakistan. Even these BMDs could create a false sense of security among political and military leadership and are likely to invite military adventurism or even a pre-emptive strike against adversary.

These missile development programmes may also have negative fallouts on global arms control efforts. Transfer of BMD technologies from Washington or Tel Aviv to New Delhi would violate Missile Technology Control Regime (MTCR). It may reverse the process of reducing the number of warheads in nuclear stockpiles. It would also weaken the support for the CTBT, MTCR, and Fissile Material Cut-off Treaty (FMCT) negotiations. Improvement of warhead designs by Pakistan might necessitate nuclear testing, disturbing the nuclear test ban between India and Pakistan in the short-run, and likely to weaken their support for non-proliferation efforts in the region. Deployment of missile defences by India may also jeopardize the ongoing peace process with Pakistan and China. Moreover, increased spending on offensive and defensive weapons would further retard developmental activities in this poverty-ridden region of South Asia. This process is tantamount to enhance the unnecessary burden on economies of both the countries and lead to the diversion of their resources from much-needed developmental tasks. Hence, this study is very much relevant and important as it tries to examine the various issues regarding the nuclear politics prevailed in the South Asian region.

The present volume is divided into the seven chapters. First chapter deals with the introduction of the main theme of the book. Second chapter highlights the nuclear weapon programmes of both the countries. It also explains the motivations and justifications behind their nuclear programmes. Then it takes the possible scenarios in which deterrence may collapse and the risk of nuclear escalation increases in the South Asian region. An assessment of four pre-requisites for a stable and sound deterrence—prevention of war, formation of second-strike capability, avoidance of accidental nuclear war and checking the nuclear terrorism and nuclear accidents—in the context of South Asia, has also been done. Third chapter presents a comprehensive study of India's missile development programme. Historical background, motivations, issue of foreign assistance, organizational infrastructure and future plans of Indian missile programme has been discussed. The technical description of all the missile systems of India, whether operational or underdevelopment, has been given in detail. Forth chapter deals with the Pakistan's missile programme in which evolution, motivation, route, issue of foreign assistance, organizational infrastructure and future plans have been discussed in detail. The technical description of all the missile systems of Pakistan has also been provided. In the fifth chapter a comparative assessment of nuclear and missile programmes of India and Pakistan has been made by taking into consideration various issues like evolution, motivation, weapon inventories, current capabilities, doctrinal level, strategy, target and range, foreign assistance, missile defence systems and future trends. Security implications of these missile programmes at bilateral, regional and international level have been examined in greater detail in chapter six. Findings of the study have been recorded in the conclusion. It is followed by appendices and bibliography related to the main theme of the study.

Notes and References

1. Though China is not a part of South Asia but has serious implications for South Asian Security. The South Asian security equation cannot be realistically assessed without taking China into account. China sees itself as an emerging economic, political and military superpower, with real and expanding interests in South and Southeast Asia. As such China challenges India's pre-eminence, and their relationship has settled into a protracted rivalry. In the absence of a strategic buffer, competing territorial claims have long brought China into India's security planning. Since the mid 1960s, China has lent its political weight and transferred arms to Pakistan to create a counterweight to Indian position. But Indian policy-makers insisted that Chinese aims—directed at securing port facilities and economic dependencies, and generally, in seeking to project its influence over the Indian Ocean—indicated a broader design. As further evidence, they cited arms transfers to Bangladesh, Sri Lanka and Myanmar. Above all, India believes that the power balance in South Asia is affected by the fact that China is a nuclear power. Indian leaders express concern that China is likely to use its quantitative and qualitative superiority in nuclear weapons to intimidate the sub-continent and control the region's future. Indian policy-makers believe that in the long-term China is likely to develop highly aggressive tendencies, pushing ahead vigorously with the development of tactical, strategic and theatre nuclear weapons.
2. At present, neither India nor Pakistan has the physical or human infrastructure to support a modern economy for most of its citizens, although India has achieved some progress. However, Pakistan and India have been slow to realize their economic potential. India has taken an enormous effort to extricate itself from a largely centralized economy, while Pakistan, having started at a material disadvantage, has policies that remain hostage in the hands of feudal elites and corrupt bureaucracy. In this context, investments in nuclear weapons and an assured second-strike capability would increase total annual defence expenditure manifold in South Asia.
3. This estimation is given by David Albrght, President of Institute for Science and International Security Washington D.C. (ISIS). *Times of India,* September 9, 2005. The report is available at isis-online.org/publications/southasia/ch-indpak.html Also see, Duncan Lennox. "Comparing India's and Pakistan's Strategic Nuclear Weapons Capabilities", *Jane's Strategic Weapon Systems,* May 30, 2002.http://www.janes.com/security/international_security/news/jsws/jsws020530_1_n.shtml
4. Pakistan is still relying largely on illicit sources and smuggling routes to maintain its nuclear weapons making capability. *The Tribune,* 7 May, 2007. Also see, Jyotirmoy Banerjee, "Pokharan-II: Fallout and Implications", *World Affairs,* Vol. 3, No. 3, July-September 1999, p. 120.

5. J.N. Dixit, *India-Pakistan in War and Peace,* Books Today, New Delhi, 2002, p. 337. Chinese assistance to Pakistan's nuclear programme is known to have commenced in 1976. In the years that followed China supplied fissile material, nuclear weapons designs and ring magnets for Pakistan's nuclear programme. Gary Milholtin, director of the Wisconsin Project on Arms control has aptly commented: "If you subtract China's help from the Pakistani nuclear programme, there is no Pakistani nuclear programme." Even today China is actively involved in constructing unsafeguarded plutonium processing facilities for Pakistan in Khushab and Chasma, G. Parthasarathy, "Missile and N-Proliferation Axis" *The Tribune,* 28 August, 2003.
6. The dangers of ballistic missiles stem from their capabilities. First, ballistic missiles can attack distant targets with a rapidity that may preclude warning. This is especially true of the India-Pakistan situation where, due to geographical proximity, the time interval between launch and impact is less than seven minutes. Second, unlike aircraft, missiles once launched are impossible to recall and very difficult to destroy once in flight. Third, ballistic missiles can carry a variety of destructive munitions, including chemical and nuclear ordnance. Because of these attributes, ballistic missiles make crises more difficult to control and conflict deadlier than ever. Martin Navias, "Ballistic Missile Proliferation in the Third World", *Adelphi Papers,* No. 252, The International Institute for Strategic Studies, London, 1990, p. 3.
7. Since the early 1990s India and Pakistan have been steadily moving their nuclear deterrence from aircraft based to ballistic missile based with potentially devastating results for the South Asian stability. The introduction of nuclear capable ballistic missiles on a significant scale adds to the negative variables that collectively raise the risk of an inadvertent nuclear war breaking out in a region that is unstable principally due to the Kashmir territorial dispute. Ben Sheppard, "Ballistic Missiles: Complicating the Nuclear Quagmire", in D.R. Sardesai and Raju, G.C. Thomas, eds., *Nuclear India in the Twenty-first Century,* Palgave-Macmillan, New York, 2002, p. 189.
8. The *Prithvi* class of missiles is a road mobile, single stage, liquid fuelled, short range missile that employs propulsion technology from the Soviet SA-2 surface to air (SAM) missile. The *Prithvi* is otherwise Indian in design. The *Prithvi* program began in 1983 and was test fired in 1988. Three basic types *Prithvis* currently exit. The *Prithvi*-I has a range sufficient to strike any significant target if deployed anywhere along the Indian border. The Indian army has reportedly ordered 100 of these missiles, which entered into serial production in 1997 and reportedly can be equipped with 5 types of warheads. A longer range variant of *Prithvi*-I, the *Prithvi*-II (SS-250), an air force version has also been developed. Underdevelopment is a *Prithvi*-III (SS-350), which will be used for naval purposes. This third variant also known as Dhanush, may be solid fueled. It is believed to be derived from the Russian SA-2. Published reports in September 2000 indicated an Indian government decision to proceed with production

of 300 Prithvi missiles. "India to Make 300 Prithvi Missiles", *The Hindu,* 8 September 2000.

9. The *Agni* missiles have been developed, reportedly with distant China as well as nearby Pakistan in mind, and have been tested in three versions, with a forth, intended to be of longer range, underdevelopment. The first variant, *Agni*-I, was demonstrated in various tests to ranges between 900 and 1200 km, and the second variant, *Agni*-II, to ranges between 1200 and 2000 km., each with notional payloads of 1000 kg. A third variant referred as again *Agni*-I, is Pakistan specific with a range of 700 km. This Pakistan specific missile reportedly weighs twelve tons and evidently uses only solid fuel propulsion. It presumably lighter in weight than the variants with the liquid fuel engines, and easier to mount on road-mobile transport-erector-launchers (TELs) or on the rail road launch cars, India reportedly has been developing. A forth variant, *Agni*-III intended for ranges closer to 3000 km (using three sold fuel stages) with a 1000 kg payload has been tested, and is underdevelopment. See *The Military Balance, 2003-04,* IISS, London, 2003, p. 131.
10. Brahmos missile is a product of an Indo-Russian joint venture. Brahmos is a cruise missile which cruises horizontally and travels only in the atmosphere. It is a two stage vehicle that has a solid propellant booster and liquid propellant ramjet system. The Brahmos is the first and the only supersonic cruise missile that uses liquid ramjet technology. It cruises in the atmosphere at the speed faster than sound. It has been rated at 290 km. in range when surface launched using the supersonic boost state, it may be capable of longer ranges if used only in sub-sonic mode or when launched from aircraft. It has been configured to launch from ground including silos and ships, submarines and aircrafts. Besides, it can blast-off from a mobile platform on land, that is, from a vehicle. One may assume it as a nuclear capable, if equipped with a small enough nuclear warhead. For details, see Rahul Datta, "India to Go in for Cruise Missiles", *The Pioneer,* 15 June 2001. "Brahmos Launch a Big Breakthrough", *The Hindu,* October 30, 2003. "Before You Can Say Brahmos", *Hindustan Times,* 30 October 2003, "Brahmos Flight Tested", *The Hindu,* 30 October 2003, "Anti-ship Version of Brahmos Proves it Mettle", *The Hindu,* 3 December 2003, and R. Prasanam, "India Enters The Cruise Missile Race; Hyplane Avatar Reaches Planning State", available at http://www.google.com
11. *Hatf*-I theoretically could be nuclear capable but there are no credible reports that it is a nuclear equipped missile. *Federation of American Scientists,* Washington D.C., 9 March 2000, available at http://www.fas.org/nuke/guide/pakistan/missile/hatf-I.htm.
12. *Hatf*-III and *Hatf*-IV resemble to the Chinese export type designated M-11 and M-9 respectively. The Chinese designation of M-9 is DF-15 and of M-11 is DF-11. Here is a point to be noted that some confusion exists in the various published sources regarding the Pakistani designations of its own missiles (e.g. on *Hatf* sequence numbers, and on the names *Shaheen*-II, *Shadoz, Abdali* and *Ghaznavi*). See the *Federation of American Scientists* Website for characteristics of Chinese

missile systems and what is believed to have been exported to Pakistan. http://www.fas.org/nuke/guide/china/theater/df-11.htm.

13. The name *'Ghauri'* is highly symbolic and taken from a Muslim historical figure, Sultan Muhammed (Shahubiddin) *Ghauri* who defeated the Hindu ruler Prithvi Raj in the last decade of 12th century. *"Prithvi"* is the name India has assigned to its short range ballistic missile. Thus Pakistan is attempting to manipulate public perceptions and show that it has developed a credible response to Indian missile capabilities. http;//www.pakmilitary.com/army/missles/ghauri.html.

2

Nuclear Security in South Asia

In May 1998, India and Pakistan, both the countries of South Asia, have crossed the nuclear rubicon, embarking on a journey that can only bring greater insecurity, tension, arms race and mal-development to the region.[1] Since then both the countries have been continuously engaging themselves in revising their plans and developing their nuclear systems, and little real progress has been made to reduce the danger.[2] Threat making, provocative military maneuvers, display of offensive force capabilities and large military exercises on borders have been common in the region. Moreover, missile flight tests at present have also raised the concerns of nuclear security and stability more seriously.[3]

For the past three decades, India and Pakistan have been engaged in a nuclear rivalry, that is, both as a symptom and a cause of their bilateral discord and both these countries have a long history of conflicts including three full-scale wars, and one small scale war of Kargil in 1999.[4] As the nuclear weapons capability of the two states grew, so did their mutual suspicion and animosity, and in 1999 they came perilously close to a major war that had potential of escalating into a nuclear exchange.[5] These two countries have been involved in constant conflict since their independence and even the periods of peace between the two have been characterized as "ugly stability". Now, when the existence of nuclear weapons in the region is the hard reality and both the countries provide little information about the security of their nuclear capabilities, the paradigm of nuclear security needs to be closely examined.

NUCLEAR PROGRAMMES OF INDIA AND PAKISTAN

Before analyzing the nuclear security problems in the region, it is pertinent to have a look on the nuclear programmes and weapon inventories of both the countries. After the 1998 tests, they possess nuclear weapons, weapon usable material, and civilian and military nuclear infrastructure up to a significant extent. India is uppermost in the field of civilian nuclear energy production, and during the year 2001-02 its production was ten times than that of Pakistan, which is comparable to that of China.[6] On the military side, both the countries have produced significant nuclear weapons usable material. India is supposed to have between 60-105 warheads and Pakistan 55-90.[7]

India's quest for nuclear capability had begun with Prime Minister Nehru and Atomic Energy Commission (AEC) chairman Hommi Bhabha. India's nuclear posture can be traced back to the 1950s, when it procured a candu-type CIRUS reactor from Canada for its atomic energy programme, which went critical in 1960 and provided India with access to unsafeguarded plutonium.[8] The other important plant was constructed at Trambay and commissioned in mid-1964.[9] These two facilities allowed India to acquire the fissile material to construct a nuclear explosive device.

India took ten years to make an ambiguous response to China's maiden nuclear test of 1964. The *Pokharan*-I test in 1974 was officially declared as peaceful nuclear explosion (PNE) but there has always been doubts and nobody believed it to be PNE.[10] But the *Pokharan*-II ultimately washed away all the doubts about India's capability to build the nuclear weapons.

While Indian nuclear programme has been a bi-product of its civilian nuclear programme but Pakistan has adopted a different route which selected to steal and beg nuclear technology abroad in order to build its own bomb. Abdul Quadir Khan, the father of Pakistani nuclear weapons programme, while working in civilian nuclear programme in Europe in mid-1970s, sneaked out gas ultracentrifuge (guc) secrets from Urenco, a German-British-Dutch consortium.[11] He took the blueprints while working at the enrichment plant, Almelo, in Holland and shifted to Pakistan. With non-proliferation measures tightening after *Pokharan*-I in 1974, Pakistan set-up a circuitous network of high-tech acquisition which spread its clandestine tentacles in advanced countries.[12] Abdul Quadir Khan and Munir Ahmad Khan, who headed the Pakistani Atomic Energy Commission (PAEC), continued to maintain contacts with some European businessmen even after some clandestine deals were detected in late 1980s.[13] During 1970s and 1980s Pakistan made impressive strides towards acquiring its own nuclear capability through clandestine means. Pakistan was helped in its nuclear weapons programme by France, UK, US, Holland, Germany, Italy and Scandanavian countries indirectly, and China directly.[14] Pakistan has single-mindedly followed a nuclear weaponization process for 20 years which culminated in its tests of May 1998.[15] Even during 1972-1979 Pakistan had persuaded Libya, Saudi Arabia, and Iraq also to fund its nuclear weapons programme in the name of Islamic bomb.[16] However, there is no incontrovertible evidence to suggest that muslim countries like Libya and Saudi Arabia have specifically funded Pakistan's nuclear weapons programme. But it can be mentioned that as late as October 1978, Premier Jalloud of Libya was reported to visit Pakistan to renew the Libyan offer to finance Pakistani nuclear energy projects.[17] It is also reported that a Pakistani nuclear device was tested at the Chinese testing site at Lop Nor in Sinkiang in 1987 eleven years back to its open test in 1998.[18] By 1992, Pakistan started claiming through Abdul Quadir Khan and other senior officers like Pakistani foreign secretary Shahryar Khan that Pakistan is a nuclear weapons capable state.[19] If it was true then the events of May 1998 at *Chagai* hills have only formalized the existing situation.

Both the countries have different rationales for acquisition of nuclear weapons. Pakistan's rationale is that India has them, but India's motivations relate to Pakistan only peripherally. The Chinese detonation of an atomic device in 1964 led India to seek nuclear umbrella for its security as India was humiliated by China in 1962 war. After the failure of security guarantees from US and erstwhile USSR, India adopted the policy of keeping its nuclear options open.[20]

The *Pokharan*-I was percieved by Pakistan as India acquiring nuclear capability. Even before *Pokharan*-I, Pakistan received a humiliating defeat in Indo-Pak war of 1971. And as a natural reaction, Pakistan too sought to acquire nuclear umbrella for its security. It also failed to get one. The option for Pakistan was thus limited to acquiring the capability to make the bomb. The political will to acquire nuclear weapons was thus strengthened. Even the issue raised the public sentiments in both the countries. The bomb debate in India since 1965 led to the arousal of public sentiments within the country. The official stand against NPT, against the IAEA safeguards and in favour of PNEs became synonymous with national honour. Similar story was repeated in Pakistan during Z.A. Bhutto's regime. He raised the nuclear issue in Pakistani politics to such an extent that it was difficult for successive governments to reverse the policy.[21]

In fact, in the beginning Pakistan has sought nuclear weapons essentially to neutralize India's conventional military superiority, which hangs over Pakistan like a permanent sword of Democles.[22] It is generally said in Pakistan that there has been peace in South Asia since 1987 due to the acquisition of nuclear weapons by Pakistan[23] inspite of serious tensions between two countries on various issues.[24] India, on the other hand, visualized its nuclear weapons programme in relation to the larger framework of an inequitable international order, that is, predominance of nuclear five members of the world. Within this larger scenario, the issue of India's national security has to be addressed in the context of either global nuclear disarmament or acquisition of nuclear weapons. On the whole, India's nuclear weapons programme seems to be justified on the grounds of national security requirements, technological self-reliance, strategic balance in its neighbourhood, powers' role in the region, discriminative international regimes regarding non-nuclear weapon states, global politics of non-proliferation and arms control and disarmament.[25]

Neither India nor Pakistan is a member of NPT but both are members of IAEA[26] and parties to the Convention on the Physical Protection of Nuclear Material (CPPNM).[27] However, some of the nuclear facilities in each country are under voluntary IAEA safeguards. In India only 4 of its operating 14 power reactors are under IAEA safeguards, and IAEA safeguards are intended for only 2 of 12 reactors in the planning or construction stage. None of the research reactors, breeder reactors, uranium enrichment facilities, reprocessing facilities, or uranium processing facilities is safeguarded by the IAEA. In Pakistan, both of its operating power reactors and 2 of 3 research reactors are under IAEA safeguards, but other facilities remain outside IAEA safeguards.[28]

In India the department of atomic energy (DAE) has overall responsibility for nuclear safety and regulation of civilian and military facilities. Security is provided by Central Industrial Security Force (CISF), but other details are not available.[29] Though India's chain of decisions command could reduce the chances of inadvertent or accidental use, yet its role in physical security of nuclear weapons is not clearly known.[30] In Pakistan, the National Command Authority (NCA) oversees civilian nuclear operations, and military nuclear facilities are under tight military control. Little information is available about security procedures. Though most facilities in the region are not under IAEA safeguards, yet membership in IAEA has provided both countries with training in physical security of nuclear facilities.[31]

DETERRENCE IN SOUTH ASIA

The nuclear weapon states have been developing and refining their nuclear facilities over the decades on the basis that weapons of mass destruction provide security.[32] Nuclear weapons are considered essential for their own security but they are being denied to non-nuclear states. As a result, possession of these weapons has been justified in terms of deterrence. Historically, justification for deterrence is provided on the basis of their non-use. But non-use can't be considered only criterion to prove that deterrence has actually worked. Besides, it also failed to explain that possession of nuclear weapons has prevented war.

Theoretically speaking, there are two camps of deterrence theorists regarding whether the nuclear weapons will prevent a major conflict or foster escalation control.[33] The one camp is of scholars and defense analysts who argue that the spread of nuclear weapons in South Asia will significantly reduce, or even eliminate the risk of future wars between India and Pakistan. These proliferation optimists argue that statesmen and soldiers in India and Pakistan know that a nuclear exchange in South Asia will create devastating damage and, therefore, will prevent military escalation using nuclear weapons. These nuclear optimists cite Western experiences to bolster their case.[34] Former national security advisor to Prime Minister of India, J.N. Dixit clearly mentioned that a certain parity in nuclear weapons and missile capabilities with Pakistan will put in place structured and mutual deterrents and could persuade the governments of both the countries to discuss the bilateral disputes in a more rational manner[35] Former army chief of India, K. Sunderji also strongly predicted that nuclear deterrence would add stability and peace in Indo-Pak relations and the chances of conventional war between the two will be less likely than before.[36] Similar views were expressed by Raj Chengappa and Jasjit Singh. Raj Chengappa says that nuclear testing by India and Pakistan would mean an end to war on the sub-continent.[37] Jasjit Singh, former director of IDSA has argued that with the advent of offsetting nuclear capabilities deterrence will continue, but on a higher level. He said that I don't think we are going to see a slide towards instability. I don't think anybody will allow it to happen.[38]

Similar views were also expressed even in Pakistan when General K.M. Arif in 1995 declared that the nuclear option will promote regional peace and create stability.[39] Air Marshal Zulfikar Ali Khan also opined that nuclear weapons make wars hard to start.[40] Former Pakistani foreign minister Abdul Sattar also appreciated the nuclear capabilities and argued that it has increased stability and prevented the dangers of war.[41] Similarly, the former chief of the Army Staff General Aslam Beg and father of Pakistan's nuclear bomb, Abdul Quadir Khan also declared nuclear weapons as the weapons of peace.[42]

The other camp of scholars and defense analysts which may be called proliferation/deterrence pessimists, however, argue that nuclear weapons are likely to increase the crises, accidents, terrorism and nuclear war. They say that history has proved that deterrence is not going to work in future. The continuing vertical and horizontal proliferation increases the possibility that nuclear weapons may be used by design, accident or miscalculation. The corresponding reliance on deterrence policy reveals that it is likely to fail and its assumptions are not going to prove correct.

The proliferation pessimist Devin T. Hegerty concludes that there is no more ironclad law in international relations that nuclear weapon states do not fight wars with each other.[43] Ashley J. Tellis is also of the same opinion when he remarked that there is no guarantee that deterrence will not breakdown in the future in South Asia.[44] Among Indian scholars and defense analysts V.R. Raghvan, while referring to the Kargil experience, stressed on the fact that instead of seeking a stable relationship on the basis of nuclear capabilities, Pakistan has used nuclear deterrence to support aggression. Nuclear weapons increased the confidence of Pakistan that it could raise the conflict thresholds with India.[45] P.R. Chari also belongs to the camp of proliferation pessimists. According to him the combination of harsh rhetoric, provocative action and the absence of trust and communication channels between India and Pakistan on leadership levels invites destabilizing actions and escalation.[46]

The nuclear pessimists are present not only in India but are there in Pakistan as well. Pakistani analyst Talat Masood writes that it would be dangerous for either country to presume that its nuclear capability provides a cover for high risk strategies or gives immunity from an all-out conventional war.[47] M.B. Naqvi commented on the nuclear weapons by saying that the mere presence of them have actually proved to be a deeply destabilizing factor.[48] Beside these South Asian nuclear pessimists, there are many other analysts worldwide who strongly supported the view that nuclear weapons do not stop the war and enhance the security.

At practical level, these two theoretical perspectives thus lead to different predictions about the consequences of nuclear proliferation in South Asia. Unfortunately, the emerging evidence strongly supports the pessimistic observations of the organizational theorists.

Generally speaking, for successful deterrence there is need for three components—(a) capability, (b) communication, and (c) credibility. (a) The country bearing attack must have the capability to use nuclear weapons against an aggressor. This capability should be of such a degree that adversary is unwilling to risk further provocations. Deterrence optimists, such as Kenneth Waltz, argue that this condition has been facilitated by the addition of nuclear weapons into the arsenals of various states.[49] It is pointed out that lack of war between nuclear powers is proof of this concept. This concept attracted many supporters during the cold war period as they believed that the mission of the military in the nuclear age had changed from winning wars to preventive wars. However, nuclear weapon states have been involved in wars with non-nuclear weapon states, and limited conflicts have been fought between nuclear powers. (b) The threat of retaliation must be clearly communicated to the potential aggressor by a reliable source. For deterrence it is important to communicate capability to adversaries. There can be significant problems with communicating a threat intended to deter an adversary. The threat can be lost in a crises situation due to competing signals and information overload, and the adversary may not be able to pick it up. (c) Lastly, for deterrence, the adversary must believe that the threat is real, i.e. there is willingness to carry through with the threatened action. This means that for the success of nuclear deterrence, the adversary must believe that nuclear weapons will be used if it continues with its actions. This is the most complex of above three components. It is based upon the existence of the first two components. A nuclear response must appear to be credible, not a bluff. This third component is however very difficult to establish. Consequently, nuclear weapon states have not been able to use it in combat since the end of world war-II.

In case of South Asia, the component 'capability' is an ambiguous term as it has various dimensions. Although both, India and Pakistan, have tested and declared their nuclear capabilities, yet there exit some asymmetries in regard to nuclear weapons stockpiles and forces among the two, which can affect the second-strike capabilities. The component of 'communication' is active only during the crises period in the region. Both the countries use to give nuclear signals particularly during the crises periods by means of flight tests of ballistic missiles, speeches to the public and to the armed forces, and press briefings. These signals have been conveyed at multiple levels by the political, military and bureaucratic leadership. Finally, credibility is also doubtful because it is exclusively based upon capability without which a stable nuclear deterrence can not be established. Hence, all the three components of deterrence are doubtful in context of South Asia.

A stable nuclear deterrence, however, can be obtained when the following four requirements are met, and all these requirements can be considered as part of the 'capability' portion of the deterrence. These are—(i) prevention of conventional war, (ii) the development of survivable second-strike forces, (iii) the avoidance of accidental nuclear war, and (iv) prevention of nuclear accidents and safety of nuclear weapons from going in the hands of terrorists. In South Asian context, each of these requirements needs an in-depth examination.

Prevention of Conventional War

The problem related to the prevention of war is linked with the decision-making systems in each country, and the perception that adversaries also have system of decision-making. An adversary would contemplate a preventive or pre-emptive first strike if it believes that it could destroy opponent's strategic arsenals, decapitate its command authority and thus prevent the opponent from launching a retaliatory strike. Military officers often have biases in favour of preventive war because they believe that war is inevitable in the long-run, and thus it is advantageous to strike first when one has a strong advantage and the other side is catching up. Pakistan has been under direct military rule for almost half of its existence, and the military runs nuclear weapons programme even during the periods in which civilian Prime Ministers have held the reins of the governments. Many scholars, therefore, worried about Pakistani military officers making unwanted decisions about the initiation of war. Even in India, evidence suggests that military influences produced serious risks of preventive war in 1980s despite the strong institutionalized civilian control.

The distinction between prevention and pre-emption is notable here. A preventive strike is one, which is used to forestall the acquisition of weapons of mass destruction (WMD) by an opponent while pre-emption pertains narrowly to military action when actual use of WMD by an adversary is imminent.[50] Israel's destruction of Osiraq reactor in 1981 may fall under the example of preventive strike, but there has been no example of a pre-emptive strike against nuclear deployment so far.

In case of South Asia, though the potential for nuclear pre-emption remains uncertain yet serious risks of preventive war situations in 1980s can't be ruled out. In 1982, it is being alleged that following the occupation of the Siachin glacier by Pakistan, India considered the option of using nuclear capability so as to prevent Pakistan to becoming strong nuclear power.[51] Another incident of both India and Pakistan considering the use of nuclear arsenal has been the Brasstacks crises of 1986-87. It is believed that large-scale provocative Indian troop exercises were a part of a masked plan for a preventive war.[52] The Brasstacks crises began when the Indian army initiated a massive military exercise in Rajasthan. The Pakistani military, fearing that the exercise might turn into a large scale attack, alerted military forces and conducted its own exercise called *Zerb-e-Momin* along the border which led Indian military to counter movements closer to the border and an operational Indian Air Force alert.

The former Indian chief of the army staff, K. Sunderji believed that India's security would be greatly eroded by Pakistani development of a usable nuclear arsenal and thus deliberately designed the Brasstacks exercises in the hope of provoking Pakistani military response. This in turn could then provide Indian government with an excuse to implement existing contingency plans to go on the offensive against Pakistan and take out the nuclear programme in a preventive strike.

George Perkovich is of the view that considerations of an attack on Pakistani nuclear facilities by New Delhi went all the way up to the most senior decision-makers as "Prime Minister Rajiv Gandhi now considered the possibility that Pakistan might initiate war with India. In a meeting with a handful of senior bureaucrats and General Sunderji, he contemplated beating Pakistan to the draw by launching pre-emptive attack on the Army Reserve South".[53] This preventive war problem may emerge again if either side develops ballistic missile defenses. The Indian government has already expressed interest in eventually procuring or developing its own missile defense capability. Given the relatively small number of nuclear warheads and missiles in Pakistan, however, such Indian defenses would inevitably reopen the window of opportunity for preventive war considerations.

Although the "bolt out of the blue" nuclear attack seems implausible in the foreseeable future in South Asia for political as well as technical reasons but there are three levels of conventional conflict that recent events make entirely plausible which could sow the seeds of nuclear escalation: (i) an all out conventional war, (ii) limited conventional war for circumscribed purposes, and (iii) unconventional or low intensity war employing guerilla warfare through clandestine methods. An unconventional or low intensity conflict may escalate into a limited conventional conflict, as did Kargil through India's response in 1999, and a war that opens as a circumscribed conventional operation may escalate to one that broadens into a major conventional war—the potential manifested in India's "*Prakram*" mobilization in 2002, and in Pakistan's counter-mobilization.

As long as the Indo-Pak relations remain hostile and mutual suspicion exists, war may reoccur, and the terrorist activities have more potential in this direction. This war, at any level, carry the potential for escalation from one level to another and then ultimately to the grim prospects of nuclear exchange. Pakistan, despite its overall size, is strategically vulnerable to a fully mobilized Indian conventional invasion mounted simultaneously in separate corridors along its north-south axis, and also vulnerable to naval action that could embargo traffic into and out of its port. Pakistan's geographically confined main lines of communication between the main port of Karachi in Sindh province to the South and the Punjab heartland in the north could be severed by a large scale, air supported armored incursion. The vulnerability is further accentuated by the proximity of Pakistan's key urban centers in Punjab, particularly Lahore, just few kilometers from the border and potential subject to long range artillery from Indian soil. On the other side, Southern Punjab and Sindh of Pakistan are just fifty to sixty miles from Rajasthan border mainly a desert terrain. Traversing this with armored columns given close air support, Indian forces could sever Pakistan's North-South main railway and road links between Rahimyar Khan and Sukkur. Such operations have been the part of Indian military force planning, doctrine and exercises since the tenure of General K. Sunderji in mid-1980s. This major conventional war scenario of cutting Pakistan in two could be amplified by an Indian naval blockade of Karachi and Gwadar. Such action was hinted at by Indian naval preparations and movements in the Kargil war in 1999, and on a larger scale during the full military mobilization of 2001-02. A major conventional war, unfolded on these lines, will put an intense international pressure on India to stand down and withdraw its forces behind the international border. This international pressure may work, but it might fail. If India were to set aside international pressure and continues its operation to achieve quick results, which may cause a Pakistani loss of territory, its military defeat or political submission, which will be the crossing of "red-lines" in Pakistani perception, then its leadership almost certainly would deploy combat ready nuclear forces and seriously consider how to apply its nuclear option.[54] Similarly, if India deploys its nuclear weapons in response then Pakistan's reaction could be very stark. It could either seek help from abroad, if possible, or fire a nuclear weapon in an uninhabited area as warning shot or devise a tactical nuclear attack on Indian conventional military to break its momentum. Once any nuclear strike is carried out, then it will be almost impossible to halt the conflict without further nuclear attack. Even high profile terrorist action would create much more intense pressure on decision-makers if it is to occur when the opposing armed forces are already mobilized and ready for conventional war. There would be a temptation to assume that terrorist act was a covert extension of the other side's military campaign, even though this act could be quite independent and different.

It is also possible that during the conventional warfare both Indian and Pakistani military planners would feel compelled to take precautions against the other side escalating to the nuclear level. Pakistan is also apprehensive of an Indian conventional pre-emptive campaign to destroy nuclear assets before they could be used.[55] Similarly India would be worried about Pakistani leaders contemplating a nuclear decapitation attack.[56] And if either side becomes convinced that its opponent is preparing a nuclear decapitation attack, howsoever remote it may be both sides might feel compelled to strike first.

It is not necessary that future Indian pre-emptive or disarming strike will only be nuclear. A conventional disarming strike based on initial surprise, and then on an extended air campaign against those Pakistani strategic nuclear assets that may be stored in fixed sites is at least theoretically conceivable. Such a campaign probably could not quickly find and target mobile nuclear missiles already dispersed in the field or even camouflaged nuclear capable aircraft at dispersed air-strips. But such a campaign might be aimed at destroying strategic nuclear weapon components in storage sites, if all those sites are known or can be identified early in the course of operations. The objective would be to prevent nuclear weapon assembly and mating with strategic delivery systems. Indian conventional air strikes against air bases and other high value military facilities in Pakistan are part of its military planning and could be unleashed as punitive measures to a severe provocation, as prelude to a punitive invasion on the ground, or as further retaliation for a Pakistani conventional response to an Indian punitive attack. Pakistan's efforts in recent years to augment its anti-aircraft defenses could make a difference, but it is not clear they could blunt a determined offensive air campaign. Air defense systems would also be early targets for suppression in an air campaign. This scenario is not only theoretically conceivable but also conforms to India's military air mission during a full-scale conventional war. How successful India would be in this faces a number of imponderables. Pakistan's nuclear storage facilities presumably are below ground and well camouflaged, and probably concentrated in Northern Punjab amidst ground forces that could be mobilized quickly to counter commando raids. In addition, Indian intelligence means might be successful over time in identifying critical sites that have distinctive signatures associated with nuclear weapons. For Pakistan to be sure it can defeat this Indian objective, it presumably had emergency dispersal procedures for dedicated aircraft and missile delivery systems, and may be prepared, even under attack, to keep moving nuclear weapon assets and delivery systems out of harmful way. But movement of these systems under such duress could shorten their fuse. If these Pakistani efforts of dispersal and concealment of aircraft and mobile missile systems were only partially successful and significant attrition of these strategic assets occurred, it could lead Pakistan to "use it or lose it" mentality, and Pakistani leadership would almost certainly consider threatening to use surviving strategic assets for retaliation before all were lost. Even if India contemplates conventional pre-emptive attacks on air bases and other ground-based military facilities, Pakistani strategic nuclear assets are likely to come under attack as well. For its part Pakistan could launch long-range air attacks on Indian airfields or logistical infrastructure similar to the events during 1965 and 1971 wars, or even use ballistic missiles. Its aircrafts and longer-range ballistic missiles have sufficient range to hit many targets in India's Western region where India may have strategic forces stationed. Such air attacks could be in the form of pre-emptive attacks or interdiction to limit the support for Indian ground forces.

If a scenario of limited war is considered, the chances of nuclear escalation would be much less than from a major or all-out conventional conflict mentioned above. But there is hardly a chance that limited conventional war may not convert into a major and all-out conventional war. Rather later probability is stronger. After the *Kargil* crises of 1999, India announced the doctrine of "limited war" to avoid the dangers of nuclear escalation during the all-out conventional war. The doctrine was presented by the then Indian Defense Minister in a seminar on January 24, 2000.[57] This doctrine of limited war under the nuclear umbrella was to be waged in the strategic space between Low Intensity Conflict (LIC) and full-scale conventional war. In response, Pakistan also announced the creation of a nuclear command apparatus on February 2, 2000, and delineated the roles and responsibilities of all organs of the state. But it avoided making any formal comment on doctrinal use aspects, perhaps deliberately to deter against aggression, conventional or nuclear.[58] Periodically, however, Pakistani officials have declared informally the parameters and factors that would be considered by the employment committee of the national command authority.

Theoretically, a war can be limited through various measures adopted by concerned parties or adversaries. First, limits can be set on political and military objectives, which will certainly limit the war up to a significant extent. Second, geographical limits on the war zone can limit the war on specific areas. Third, some restrictions can be placed on the type of weapons to be used during the warfare. Such a limit would reassure the adversary about controlling possible escalation. Fourth, a time limit can be placed on the war by stating that military operations can be called-off when the adversary complies with certain demands.

In case of South Asia, it is worth noting that past wars between India and Pakistan have exhibited none of these limits, with one exception. And the exception was India's terminating of 1971 war immediately after Pakistan's forces laid down arms in Bangladesh. In previous wars India has reserved and exercised the right to take the battle into Pakistani territory in response to an attack on Jammu and Kashmir.[59] All available resources, including the navy, were employed in previous Indo-Pak wars, and all weapon systems available were utilized. Neither country imposed a time ceiling on the war. Neither side threatened civilian populations during the wars. A significant factor in these conflicts, however, was that neither side posed an existential threat to the survival of the other. But now the overt acquisition of nuclear weapons by both the countries has altered the context of military conflicts between them. It has substantially raised the threat of a nuclear conflict if another war is fought, whether full-scale or limited, between the two countries.

The Indian analyst Major General Ashok Krishna explained four basic options of limited war for India: first option is to attack across the international boundary or line of control (LOC), but to keep the objective limited. The second option is to attack the selected points along the LOC, presenting Pakistan with the option of escalating by responding with a riposte. The third option is to capture and hold a critical area along the LOC. The final option is to carry out the surgical strikes across the border and then return.[60] In fact, the main focus of limited war option, at the time of its inception in 1999, was along the LOC region of *Kashmir,* with effects of the *Kargil* war fresh in mind. The main thrust was on the feasibility of using limited military strikes to interdict infiltration from Pakistan, and to attempt to destroy or shut down so called terrorist training camps believed to be located around Mujaffarabad in the western and most heavily populated part of Pakistan- held Kashmir, adjoining Punjab province. The operational concept for such strikes apparently involved combined fighter aircraft, ground attack sorties and helicopter- borne special force operations intruding across the LOC without warning.[61] These strikes might be accompanied by artillery barrages immediately across the LOC, ostensibly attacking infiltration routes but also tying down opposition infantry forces locally. The primary objective of these strikes may be political to draw world attention to the problem of terrorist infiltration into India and to force Pakistan to clamp down *jihadi* organizations. But Pakistan would retaliate with some form of artillery and air strikes at least on Indian military posts near the LOC, and perhaps with fighter air craft sorties against Indian security forces staging areas deeper in *Kashmir*, to satisfy its own public that it has means and the will to retaliate against India. And this retaliatory action of Pakistan, which is quite natural, may lead the limited war to all-out war.

In fact, the concept of Indian surprise air attacks on terrorist training camps in *Azad Kashmir* assumed a far higher sensitivity after certain serious incidents like operation *Prakram*, September 11 and particularly the incident of 13 December 2001. If India conducts surprise air attacks on localities near Mujaffarabad, while working on its limited war concept, it would bring Indian aircrafts or copters only minutes away from such sensitive defence related facilities in Pakistan as the Kathua uranium enrichment plant or nearby nuclear storage facilities. Pakistan may perceive it in the sense that these Indian attacks directed ostensibly against terrorist targets might cover expended strategic attacks on Pakistan's nuclear assets. So there is a high risk of escalation in limited war doctrine as it did not regard inadvertence to be of any significance.[62]

The doctrine of limited war is ambiguous and uncertain in South Asia because it leaves many questions unanswered.For example, how would the political and military leadership in India and Pakistan plan and conduct limited war against each other? Can they ultimately limit political and operational objectives? The answers to these questions remain uncertain; as one side's limited political and military objectives could be viewed as unlimited and unacceptable by the other. If a nuclear first strike from Pakistan is to be avoided after a limited war is started, how will Indian political and military saliencies be conveyed? If Pakistan wishes to avoid escalating a limited conflict with a nuclear strike how would it cope with an outcome which is militarily or politically unfavourable? Indicating the geographical limits of war would detract greatly from operational needs, while identifying political limits will allow the adversary to better plan its response. Under these circumstances, how victory would be quantified in political and military terms? In *Kargil* war, which was on much smaller scale than a limited war, India was able to define its geographic salience by announcing that its forces would not cross the LOC in Jammu and Kashmir. That immediately placed serious limits on operational plans and forced a high casualty rate on the Indian army. A number of former senior military officers started criticizing publicly the government's self- imposed limitations at the cost of military casualties. This criticism placed the government under pressure and it started moving its major combat forces to operational locations, as preparations for widening the conflict, if necessary. That in turn placed the Pakistani military leadership under pressure and forced it to think about the nuclear weapons option. Fortunately, the *Kargil* conflict ended but it left a burning question behind it that future wars between India and Pakistan, whether limited or full scale have a potential threat of nuclear exchange. So at the moment, both official pronouncements and published doctrine fail to clarify how the two sides will limit a future conventional war. There is also no perceptible change from past patterns in Indian and Pakistani approaches of fighting a conventional war. The way the two countries fought previous wars throws some light on how they could escalate to the nuclear threshold.[63]

Although, nuclear forces are not kept on an alert status during peace-time as compared to those of cold war period, but in an unfolding crisis, as it is clear from above discussion, the imminent possibility of conventional war could compel India and Pakistan to keep nuclear weapons in as close to a "ready state" as possible without being visible. The state of preparation of weapons thus would be directly proportional to the state of tension and crisis. To avoid being caught unprepared, in the event that a conventional war begins to go badly, both sides are likely to begin their nuclear forces to alert state at virtually the same time that they assemble their conventional forces. From this point on, the danger of inadvertence would become very real. In this situation, Indian declaration of no first use would become practically irrelevant.

The Indian declaration of "no first use" of nuclear weapons becomes irrelevant even in certain likely scenarios as observed by Indian defense analyst Jyotirmoy Banerjee.[64] Scenario one, suppose India is loosing heavily in a conventional war with either Pakistan or china or both. Can India stop itself from using battlefield nuclear weapons? Scenario two, if India uses the doctrine of "launches-on-warning", it will be highly relevant in the event that Indian radars detect incoming hostile missiles or bombers or both. What will India do? Will it wait till they devastated it or let fly its second-strike forces at once? If India waits in order to stick its pledge of "no-first-use", it may suffer an unacceptable damage even to its second-strike capability. If, on the other hand, India launches on warning, this will be cutting its pledge too thin. There will remain not even seconds to properly asses the threat under "launch-on warning". India's hair trigger reaction will undergo the risk of an enormously avoidable spasmodic nuclear war, in case the warning on incoming hostile missiles turns out to be false. Radar and other sensors are, after all machines. Like all machines, they can go, and have gone wrong.[65] Scenario three, if India receives information that the enemy is about to launch, then India launches its own strike to pre-empt the enemy's first strike. This doctrine of pre-emption is also dangerous. While under normal political circumstances this scenario may seem a bit far-fetched especially given India's "no-first-use", but under crisis conditions fact has a tendency to overtake fiction. Again massive time constraints upon assessing a threat and pondering will dominate. In this way, all the three scenarios make the Indian "no-first-use" doctrine irrelevant and raise the issue of nuclear dangers in the sub-continent.

After the doctrine of "limited war" a new concept characterized as "cold start operation" is also emerging in India since its withdrawal from operation *Prakram* in 2002 without launching even limited strikes.[66] The concept trades on the value of having mobilized operational forces always ready to conduct limited punitive strikes against Pakistan under the threshold of

Pakistan's red lines. In the case of cold start, however, focus was no longer on striking terrorist training camps in Pakistan held Kashmir but rather on high value Pakistani military facilities in Pakistan itself. The cold start strategy calls for a rapid deployment of integrated battle groups comprising of army, air force and, if needed, navy to conduct high intensity operations. The objective is to reach across, or circle around, the Pakistan's concentrated defensive positions and firepower on selected targets deeper in the Pakistan's territory, and to do so quickly. After achieving their initial objectives, the intruding forces would either secure, hold and facilitate reinforcement of a band of occupied territory, or withdraw before the main conventional ground forces could move to engage. So a rapid deployment and quick securing of limited objectives can be used to achieve limited political objectives before international interference kicks in or before the conflict spirals out hand into a nuclear exchange. The proponent of this doctrine perhaps hopes that this new operational level doctrine will have the strategic outcome of deterring Pakistan from pursuing its proxy war agenda. Although there has been no official response on this cold start type of strategy from Pakistani side, but it is certain that Pakistan will not ignore India's decision to achieve limited war objectives through this new strategy. Pakistani military will definitely prepare for an appropriate response. It will consider any action taken by India based on this strategy as an act of aggression and open war. Because of the element of surprise at the strategic level, it will also reduce the time for diplomacy to work. Therefore, this concept of cold start will straightway invite full-scale conventional war between the two forces. And this full-scale conventional war has potential to turn into nuclear exchange at certain points or in certain situations as discussed earlier.

Second-Strike Capability

Nuclear retaliation is another dimension to be considered for deterrence. Stability with nuclear weapons could be attained by the development of second-strike capability.[67] This means that the nuclear forces must be able to survive to retaliate if attacked first. The establishment of survivability of nuclear forces for second-strike demands a deployment doctrine, a plan about the way weapons are stored and readied for use during war time. If opponent is able to prevent the use of those weapons during the war time, the effect of the deterrent would be nullified. In order to keep the deterrent intact, therefore, weapons must be protected from a pre-emptive attack. Moreover, the adversary must be convinced that pre-emption is not feasible.

There are two basic ways to protect any asset: active defense and passive defense. Active defense means destroying any attacking force before it can destroy its target, while passive involves limiting the effects of an attack without actually stopping it. Given the current rudimentary air defence capability on both sides in South Asia, active defense is currently unlikely; a protection scheme based on passive defence measures is more likely to provide for robust defense. Because Indian and Pakistani arsenals are still fairly limited in size, so focus will be on those passive defence measures most likely to complement the advantages of a small arsenal : hardening, dispersal, and mobility.

Hardening is a technically straightforward way of a passive defense measure. But a hardened facility is fixed and immovable, and is likely to attract attention to whatever is being held there[68] Hardening may minimize the destructive effects of an attack, but it does little to prevent an attacker from locating a target in actual sense; it may even have the perverse effect of encouraging a more ferocious attack, if the value of the target is high enough.

In this way, more likely passive measures are those that make it most difficult for an attacker to pinpoint the heart of other side's arsenal. Two such methods are—dispersal and concealment. Dispersal places the weapons in a variety of locations rather than on one location. Dispersal also capitalizes on the ease of moving mobile weapons from place to place, making it more difficult for an attacker to know where these weapons are presently, and thus reducing the possibility thatall weapons could be destroyed in a pre-emptive attack.

To conceal the weapons is another way to protect them. In case when an attacker can't find its enemy's weapons, it can't attack and destroy them. For this purpose, multiple hiding places can be used or weapons could be made mobile continually to move them around. In such a mobile configuration, weapons are both dispersed and concealed. But while using these two methods of dispersal and concealment in deployment of forces, it in turn affects a critical aspect of command and control: the connectivity. It means the ability of political leadership to maintain constant communications with its nuclear forces. It includes the measures that may be taken to ensure that nuclear forces are always in position to receive timely instructions from the institutions designated to authorize alerting, launch, or recall of nuclear forces. The potential for connectivity failure raises issues of execution and pre-delegation, if leadership can't talk to the forces, how should those forces respond?

In this way, the measures taken to make the arsenals survivable affect the issue of connectivity, which is of high importance during the wartime. The first option for these measures is hardening, which requires buried phone lines that provide the greatest chance of continued connectivity but this option is unlikely choice for both India and Pakistan because it is likely to attract the attention of adversary. In this situation, mobility, which combines the benefits of dispersal with the benefits of concealment, is a more likely option. But by increasing their survivability in this manner, India and Pakistan will also increase the susceptibility of these forces to broken connectivity, since forces on the move are more difficult to talk than forces at a fixed and known location. Thus in trying to ensure survivability through mobility, a country trades one strategic problem for another. In fact, the kinds of connectivity challenges a country faces depend on the delivery vehicles it deploy. This requirement led both the USA and erstwhile USSR to develop nuclear triads, made up of long-range bombers, land-based missiles and submarine-based missiles. But India and Pakistan lack this nuclear triad. So it is very pertinent here to have a look on delivery vehicles in the region because survivability of nuclear forces highly depends on delivery vehicles through dispersal and concealment of nuclear weapons.

Although, the fragmentary information about India's and Pakistan's nuclear forces, operational capacity and elements of command and control have emerged but the numbers, readiness status, and employment plans for these nuclear delivery capabilities remain murky in many respects.[69] Currently one can assume that India has stockpile between 60 to 105, with a median estimate of 80, and Pakistan 55 to 90, with a median estimate of 70.[70] It is now generally accepted that both India and Pakistan initially developed airborne nuclear weapons suitable for external carriage by tactical ground-attack aircraft, while pursuing missile programmes. By 1998 both evidently were developing nuclear warheads shaped to fit the cylindrical confines of the front sections of short and medium range ballistic missiles, and these designs may have been validated in the May 1998 nuclear tests conducted by both the countries.

India has configured its nuclear devices as aerial bombs or missile warheads. While a precise breakdown of number of bombs versus missile warheads is unknown, a senior Pakistani military official reportedly claimed that the majority of India's nuclear weapons were configured as aerial bombs. While India reportedly has a number of different types of aircrafts but it apparently chose Soviet built Mig-27 M Flogger aircraft with a range of 800 km and the Anglo-French Jaguar aircraft with a 1600 km range to deliver nuclear aerial bombs.[71] The Sukhoi 30 MKI aircraft with a capacity to carry an 800 kg payload and with a normal range of 3200 km and air-to-air refueling range of about 7000 km, gives India a nuclear deep strike capability and some experts believe that India acquired the Sukhoi to counter China's deep strike capability.[72] Mirage-2000 H can also be equipped with nuclear bombs but is more likely to be used for air defense missions.[73]

On the other hand, while Pakistan has obtained a variety of combat aircrafts from different nations, many experts believe that the most likely aircraft to be used to deliver nuclear weapons would be the US F-16 fighters. F-16 is believed to be capable of delivering a 1000 kg nuclear bomb to the range of 1600 km.[74] Pakistan has also option to employ the older Mirage-5 for bomb delivery.

But aircrafts have several disadvantages as delivery vehicles. An aircraft may be destroyed on the ground in a conventional or a nuclear attack, or an airbase runway may be destroyed, preventing take-off. Protection from a conventional attack may be possible by hardening shelters for airplanes, putting them under cover to hide them, or dispersing them to a number of bases to complicate the targeting problem for a potential attacker. Even so, aircrafts have several weaknesses as a secure second-strike delivery vehicle. They may be vulnerable to both nuclear and conventional attacks, and because of their reliance on runways, may not be able to respond if the runway is destroyed. Moreover, connectivity with flying aircraft, through two-way radio communication, is not as assured as is landline communication with a fixed and hardened facility. However, assuming surviving command posts and the absence of communications degradation from prior atmospheric nuclear blasts, connectivity with aircraft can be maintained with moderate effectiveness.

Besides aircrafts, India and Pakistan have also developed nuclear capable ballistic missiles as delivery systems.[75] India has an extensive, largely indigenous ballistic missile programme, including infrastructure for both solid and liquid fuelled missiles. India's existing missiles for mission against Pakistan are of *Prithvi* and *Agni* series. India has *Prithvi*-I with a range of 150 km capable of having payload of 1000 kg, *Prithvi*-II with a range of 250 km capable of having a payload of 500 kg and *Prithvi*-III (reportedly under development) with a range of 350 km.[76] India probably has deployed only one type of short range ballistic missile (SRBM) *Prithvi*-I (SS-150). Some experts insist that both *Prithvi*-I and II are nuclear capable. Other analysts believe only the Prithvi-II can carry nuclear warheads and express doubts that the *Prithvi*-I would be nuclear tipped, given its short range, mobility and liquid fuel supply. But the CIA has assessed only *Prithvi*-I as having a nuclear role.[77]

India's second family of ballistic missiles is the *Agni*-I, II and III. The *Agni* missiles are designed to extend the reach of Indian nuclear capabilities, particularly to China. However, one more variant of *Agni,* now officially (and confusingly) referred to as *Agni*-I is specifically designed for missions against Pakistan and was tested with a capacity of 1000 kg payload on January 8, 2003 to a range of 700 km.[78] India reportedly intends to retrofit its *Brahmos* adaptation of Russian supplied *Yakhont* anti-ship, cruise missile so that it can be fired either from naval ships or from SU-30 MKI attack aircraft. This cruise missile apparently could be used as a stand-off system with either conventional or nuclear weapons.[79]

Pakistan also has an active missile acquisition and development program since the early 1980s. This includes indigenous missile development (based in part on foreign design) as well as the reported purchase of M-11 missiles from China in the early 1990s although Pakistan and China denied these reports. Pakistan has several types of road mobile, nuclear capable ballistic missiles with shorter and longer ranges, solid and liquid fueled. The *Hatf*-I is an indigenous single stage solid propellant missile with a range of 60 to 80 km carrying a 500 kg payload.[80] Then there are *Hatf*-II (*Abdali*), single stage solid fueled missile with a range of 280-300 km and *Hatf*-III (*Ghazani)* single stage solid fueled (300 km) and *Hatf*-IV (*Shaheen*) single stage solid fueled with a range of 600 km.[81] Pakistan's longer range *Ghauri*-I, single stage with 1000-1500 km range and *Ghauri*-II, two stage with 2500 km range (still in development testing) are liquid fueled missiles that are believed to be based on the North Korean "No-Dong" and "*Taepo-Dong*" missiles, derived originally from Soviet scud technology.[82]

Although a mobile ballistic missile escapes some of the disadvantages of aircrafts necessary for the establishment of secure second-strike capability as it is not tied to a run way and may simply be moved and readied for launch miles away from its home base but field deployment presents a challenge to continued connectivity. At an established base, hardened landlines provide the assurance that national leaders can talk to their forces. But once these forces start deploying to other locations, where they can take advantage of concealment, established landlines become fewer, and continued connectivity becomes problematic.

Submarines, finally, have the built-in-advantage of dispersal and concealment. But communication with submerged submarines is extremely difficult and this option virtually guarantees poor connectivity. Moreover, at least for the time being, completed development of a submarine and associated missiles is years away for both India and Pakistan.

Strategic depth or the lack of it also plays a major role in the potential for ground and air operations to threaten the survival of the strategic weapons, and cause inadvertent escalation. In this case India has all advantages of strategic depth, which allows it to disperse strategic forces widely among numerous sites, installations and airfields. On the other hand, Pakistan lacks this strategic depth, which means many of its airfields and strategic assets are closer to India. There are very few Pakistani aircrafts, which are able to perform the nuclear delivery role as compared to those of India. However, Pakistan has offset this disadvantage by vigorously pursuing ballistic missiles. The *Hatf*-III and *Hatf*-IV use solid fuel, which make for a very reliable delivery option. Solid fueled missiles have a much smaller logistical support train and corresponding signature compared to liquid fueled, representing a major advance in military technology. The small signature of these systems may play a major role in their survivability for Pakistan. But *Agni's* longer range combined with India's strategic depth would probably make it invulnerable to Pakistani attack and enhances the survivability. Moreover, doctrinal separation of the nuclear weapons from the delivery systems, and the civilian control of the weapons themselves is another factor, which enhances the survivability of Indian nuclear forces. But the negative factor with Indian *Prithvi* and current stage-II version of *Agni* is that these are liquid fueled missiles and require intense logistical support to operate, and moreover, have a corresponding large signature, which leads to the easy detection. That is why, despite all the efforts, both the countries are not well successful in maintaining the secure second-strike capability, and a lot of confusion prevails there in calculating the other sides capabilities and strategies.

According to classical strategic deterrence theory a robust level of nuclear deterrent stability between nuclear rivals would depend upon two interrelated conditions. First, each must have a credible capability for delivering nuclear weapons against valued targets in the opponent's homeland in sufficient numbers to dissuade the opponent from believing it could gain critical advantage by initiating nuclear war. Second, each must be able to count on the survivability of sufficient strategic nuclear assets in the event of a hypothetical preemptive strike by the opponent to be able to conduct a retaliatory strike that inflicts unacceptable damage. This nuclear reasoning evolved from superpower experience during the cold war. It also rested, in part, on extensive tactical nuclear weapons deployments and the credibility of extended deterrence protecting allies. But the conditions of cold war were quiet different from the situation that prevails in South Asia. While the East-West strategic confrontation was essentially bipolar, the India-Pakistan nuclear relationship is not isolated, at least in Indian perceptions, from China as a major Asian nuclear power. Another key difference between nuclear South Asia and former superpower nuclear relationship is that a rough parity was established between the latter at both strategic nuclear and conventional levels. In South Asia, conventional military relationship between Pakistan and India is asymmetrical and likely to become more so over time.[83] Consequently, whatever tolerance each side may believe it has for experimentation with limited conventional conflict, this practice is exceedingly dangerous from the standpoint of nuclear stability, and absence of normalization of relations, it is likely to become more so. In a context in which limited conventional war is considered acceptable, it would seem likely that deployment of tactical and battlefield nuclear weapons in South Asia would further contribute to crisis instability.

Indian and Pakistani weapon systems, deployment procedures and force structures are also sources of instability. India relies mainly on calculated ambiguity regarding the warheads of its short range *Prithvi* missiles.[84] Pakistan's ballistic missiles are inherently dual capable as well, particularly the solid-fueled types with ranges between 200 and 600 km. The Indian *Prithvi* was developed as a platform for both conventional and nuclear warheads by civilian technologists and imposed on the military, rather than designed or procured to support objective military requirements.[85] As far as India's army and air force were concerned in 1980s, the *Prithvi* would be militarily useful as an offensive bombardment missile for air base suppression, using conventional sub-munition warheads to destroy exposed aircraft, blast through hangars, and disrupt runways. But *Prithvi* has also been reported as having been tested and weaponized as a nuclear delivery system. When nuclear capable *Prithvis* are launched with conventional ordnance against air bases, how would Pakistan know from its ground-based radar system that nuclear weapons are not on the way, or would not immediately follow? If Pakistan launches one or more M-11s or M-9s in the general direction of cities as well as military facilities in India, will Indian operators hold back action until they land to see if they are conventional or nuclear? *Prithvi's* inclusion in Indian nuclear force structure as a short range, dual capable, ballistic missile is inherently destabilizing. It has doubtful military utility unless equipped with a nuclear warhead and it has poor survivability characteristics. *Prithvi* must be positioned fairly close to the borders to be able to target air bases in Pakistan, but is, when so deployed, visible to air surveillance. It could easily be targeted and destroyed at its launch site by any state-of-the-art, ground attack aircraft. Being liquid fueled, it is slow to move to a pre-surveyed site and to prepare for a launch. Its liquid fuel makes the system highly combustible under attack. Although described as a mobile system, it is not easy to hide or move in a "shoot-and-scoot" mode because of its ungainly design and large retinue of about a dozen support vehicles. Once in the field, it is a lucrative and vulnerable target for conventional attack.[86]

If *Prithvi's* commonly advertised mission is suppressing air bases with conventional munition, then Pakistan's Air Force would be virtually compelled, in the event India begins hostilities, to attack any *Prithvi* batteries it discovers near the border. Would such a strike cross an internally determined but never explicitly announced Indian red lines? What if one or more *Prithvi* missiles were nuclear tipped, and the bombing discharged a *Prithvi* nuclear warhead on Indian soil?

Addition of Israeli supplied Phalcon airborne warning and surveillance system, and Arrow ballistic missile defense system are likely to create balance in favour of India.[87] The Arrow-2 missile system is designed to provide terminal phase intercept against short and medium range ballistic missiles which can detect and track up to 14 imbound missiles at distances of 500 km and intercept them as close as 16 to 48 km from the missile system.[88] Some experts believe that India would deploy the Arrow system along the LOC to protect population and military centers.[89] Since 1995 India is also reported to be negotiating with Russia to acquire either the S-300 PMU-I or S-300 V anti-tactical ballistic missile system.[90] In May 2003, India had discussed purchase of the US Patriot advanced capabilities-3 or PAC-3 air and missile defense system with US Deputy Secretary of State Richard Armitage. But the US government has not given clearance for such acquisitions.[91] However, given the nature of indo-US ties, India is likely to get this system very soon.

Such deployments by India could erode Pakistan's confidence that its F-16s can provide a credible nuclear deterrent against India.[92] Besides, it can break the current state of mutual non-weaponized deterrence[93] and lead Pakistan to mount nuclear warheads on deployed missiles. This can give birth to serious destabilizing effects in the region. Pakistan may also adopt "use it or lose it" policy whereby nuclear forces can be deployed early in the conflict situations with India.[94] It could also boost Pakistan's development of large number of missiles and nuclear warheads in order to saturate and overwhelm India's ballistic missile defenses.

The *phalcon* system would enable India to detect and track flights of Pakistani aircraft within a radius of up to 400 Kms from its flight position, providing warning of Pakistani air attack and intercept data for Indian fighter aircraft.[95] Pakistan has no comparable capability on border *vis-à-vis* India, although both fly unmanned air vehicles (UAVs) for surveillance close to the border. At the very least, India's Phalcon capability would be seen in Pakistan as increasing its uncertainty about the penetration rate of its nuclear delivery aircraft in the event they are called upon, and a strong incentive to acquire long range surface-to-air missiles.

Additionally, India's acquisition of theatre anti-ballistic defense system could reduce Pakistani missile penetration rates and thus could erode, at least, marginally, the credibility of its missile deterrent. Depending on what missile interceptor systems India actually acquires and whether they could be used in ascent-phase and in area defense, their deployment could shrink Pakistan's maneuvering towards India. Pakistan could perceive that these technology transfers can open the door for India's, acquisition for both offensive and defensive technologies in the field. Pakistan, on the other hand, in response, could increase its inventory of offensive missiles, diversify the areas mobile missile dispersal, develop penetration aids, procure sea-based launch platforms, as India already plans, and probably add cruise missiles as nuclear delivery platforms. If a competitive dynamic persists between India and Pakistan under these conditions, deterrent stability calculations would become more complex, the demands on command and control more severe, and the chances of accident and miscalculation greater.

Accidental Nuclear War

Issue of accidental nuclear war is another important factor in the politics of South Asia. This problem is directly related to command and control systems of nuclear rivals. Command and control of strategic forces, known as command, control, communication, computers and intelligence (C^4I), is an extremely important process. It is the link between the national command authority, the decision makers who ultimately control the release of the nuclear weapons, and the personnel who have physical control of the weapons themselves. Command and control has been defined as an arrangement of the facilities, personnel, procedures, and means of information acquisition, processing and dissemination used by a commander in playing, directing and controlling military operations.[96] A robust command and control system is one that has built in buffers to review and confirm intelligence assessments, redundant and hardened communication channels, protection against communication intercepts, methods to verify that communications are functioning throughout the system, and procedure to ensure safe and secure nuclear weapons custody and operation of delivery systems. But command and control centers may themselves be designated targets of nuclear attack, and vulnerable to both conventional and nuclear effects. No modern nuclear command and control system has ever been tested under realistic conditions. Over the time, new technologies and hardware are invented to help prevent unauthorized access or arming of nuclear weapons, to make nuclear weapons less sensitive to shock and fire, to ensure reliable communications over long distances, and to improve the survivability of weapons and communication links under attack.[97]

There has been an anxiety in the Western World about the Indian and Pakistani nuclear command and control system, nuclear safety, and other technical and procedural issues, coupled with uncertainty as to whether these generic difficulties are recognized and are being addressed effectively to avoid the accidental nuclear war.

There also exit some potential structural challenges to escalation control under current command and control arrangements in South Asia, which can lead to accidental nuclear war. First is the limited geographical space for operation, especially for Pakistan. The short flight times of delivery systems to targets also place tremendous stress on intelligence and early warning. Second derives from existing limitations on national technical means of intelligence and surveillance that deprives both of adequate early warning. Third arises from the likelihood that the reported low readiness status of nuclear weapons in both the countries would be transformed into permanently deployed systems at higher levels of readiness. The fourth arises from the potential temptation to deploy tactical and battlefield nuclear weapons, the strategic forces that are presumably reserved for deterrence.

Although, the current South Asian nuclear deterrence system is both smaller and less complex today than those of the USA or former Soviet Union during the cold war yet South Asian nuclear relationship is inherently more tightly coupled because of geographical proximity of the states. Inadequate warning systems and short flight times provide highly compressed time lines for decision-making, and the danger that one accident could lead to another and then lead to a catastrophic accidental war is high and growing. The geographical proximity of potential adversaries poses particular concerns about rapid "decapitation" attacks on National capitals.

The small sizes of India and Pakistan's nuclear arsenals, however, provide a reason for the proliferation optimists to be less worried about the problem. But the key from a normal accidents perspective is not the numbers, rather the structure of the arsenal. But there are some positive and negative developments in this context. Positively speaking, under normal peacetime conditions, India, and Pakistan are not likely to deploy nuclear forces mated with delivery systems in the field. Negatively speaking, Indian intelligence reports reveal that Pakistan had begun initial nuclear alert operations during the *Kargil* conflict. Hence, possibility of such accidental warfare can't be ruled out completely.

Geographical proximity is an important factor in the missile deployment in the sub-continent. Ballistic missile flight times between India and Pakistan has serious consequences for the feasibility and utility of possible early warning systems. It is assessed that the flight time is as little as 300 seconds. The study of use of radars and geo-stationary satellites with infrared detectors indicate that the warning times, including the estimates of missile transit time, are at best enough for confirming the signals as genuine. But no time will be left for consultations or deliberation by decision-makers. Any response would have to be pre-determined and automatic. If such an automatic response involves a launch on warning posture, as is the case with the U.S.A and Russia, there is a significant likelihood of accidental nuclear war from false alarms. Moreover, the location of major cities in India and Pakistan, including their capitals, close to the shared border necessarily implies that missile flight times and possible warning times in South Asia will be much shorter than the times available to the United States and Soviet Union during the Cold War.

In Indian Draft Nuclear Doctrine (DND), it has been proposed to set up an "effective intelligence and early warning capabilities", that would use "space-based and other assets" to provide "early warning, communications, damage/detonation assessment."[98] As a result, it has started acquiring key components of such an early warning network, including the Green Pine radar from Israel.[99] The Green Pine is also part of the Israeli Arrow anti-ballistic missile system in which India has expressed its interests.[100] India is also engaged in the development of a capability to launch geo-synchronous satellites, which could serve to provide infra-red detection of missile launches (as is done by the United States' Defense Support Program early warning satellites). In late 2001, India also launched a Technology Experiment Satellite (TES) with a high resolution imaging camera reportedly capable of "sensitive defense surveillance applications."[101] New Delhi is in the process of purchasing a Phalcon airborne early warning system also from Israel, however, the Phalcon system is primarily used to track aircraft.

Pakistan has not declared a formal nuclear doctrine but three leading statesmen warned of the "dangers of pre-emption and interception" and recommended that a "high state of alert will become more necessary as India proceeds with deployment of nuclear weapons."[102] Pakistan's then Minister for Science and Technology hinted at matching Indian plans for early warning when he announced that the government was preparing to launch a geo-stationary satellite "to meet its strategic and communication needs."[103]

An early warning system is an important step in the deployment and use of missiles in South Asia as it is more than the set of detectors and platforms for monitoring missile launches. It includes the procedures for evaluating, assessing and interpreting the "warning" data. To understand how the initial signal may translate into a meaningful warning and response, the procedures adopted by the United States and the erstwhile Soviet Union, to assess missile warnings are hereby relevant.[104] However, the flight times between the missile fields and targets of those two states are about thirty minutes. So it becomes important to look at whether analogous procedures could be practicable in case of South Asia given the much shorter warning time.

It is, however, also to be noted that an early warning system is not infallible and can create false alerts as it is evident from the history of the cold war itself.In the U.S.A., during 1977 to 1984, the only period for which official information has been released, the early warning systems gave on an average of 2,598 warnings each year of potential incoming missiles attacks. Of these about 5% required further evaluation.[105] Senate report on false alerts from the early warning system noted that all 3,703-missile display conferences from January 1, 1979 to June 30, 1980, resulted from "actual pickup by warning sensors of some physical phenomena or reconfiguration of warning sensors." It is further observed that computers and communications systems also transmitted false information. In a notable 1980 case, the North American Aerospace Defense Command (NORAD) director was given evidence for an attack from the early warning satellites and radars, but ground station operators reported the sensors were gathering no such data. Strategic warning also suggested no credible threat. Faced with this, NORAD was unable to give its assessment within the required 3 minutes. It took 8 minutes to determine that there was no substance in the warning. Similarly, in 1995 a Norwegian scientific rocket launch was detected and the matter went all the way up the command chain to President Yeltsin before it was recognized not to be the precursor to an attack.

In this way, the early warning systems in India and Pakistan will, of course, also be prone to false alarms. The shorter flight times in South Asia will limit the opportunities available to decision-makers to assess the data from their early warning systems. Thus, the risk posed by false alarms is greater than was the case during Cold War between super powers. It is because in South Asia, the estimated total missile flight times range from

8-13 minutes for distances of 600 km to 2000 km, respectively. Factually this time is less than the estimated one. It could be as low as 5 minute for a 600 km missile flight in case when a depressed missile trajectory is adopted.[106] These missile flight times of 5-13 minutes encompass paths from missile launch points at airbases in both countries to the national capitals and to major military facilities, including possible locations of the nuclear arsenals or their command posts, in the other country. The earliest that a missile on a depressed trajectory could be detected might be about half a minute to a minute after launch, provided India or Pakistan had the appropriate infrared sensors on early warning satellites in geosynchronous orbit. Neither country has this capability at present; given the experience of Russia/Soviet Union, one would expect that the development of the necessary infra-red sensors would be a significant challenge. In fact, the early warning radars (such as Green Pine), if deployed in South Asia, would have sufficient range to see a missile, side-on, soon after launch—once the missile rises above the radar horizon. This detection would come within approximately half a minute after detection by a geosynchronous satellite. This is markedly different from the case of the U.S.A. and former U.S.S.R/ Russia, where satellites provided several additional minutes of warning.

If the satellites truly provide an independent way of observing missile launches it would reduce the risk of false alarms. However, this depends strongly on the architecture of the system. Because the warnings from the two systems would have to be evaluated together, there is a possibility of a common mode failure.[107] Extra components also add to the complexity of the system making it more opaque and harder to foresee ways by which the system may not perform as designed.[108] Redundancies also produce a false sense of security that may prompt decision-makers to trust the system more than warranted.[109] In the light of above arguments, the use of early warning satellites in South Asia is questionable.

Even the use of information of a missile launch is detected by a satellite or radar, or both, can be appropriately assessed is a matter of doubt in case of India and Pakistan. It is because it require a very efficient system where information be received, processed and decision be taken within at the most 4-7 minutes.

Such a short period places much more stringent constraint on procedures for evaluation and verification of any warning, and decision-making. In the case of the depressed trajectory, missiles launched towards capital cities leave no time for consultation or deliberation after receiving this warning. Any action would, therefore, have to rely entirely on prior planning, i.e., automatic action, which may cause a serious threat of missile launch by mistake.

Warning coming out of the system could be used in two ways. One is to feed it directly into a missile defense system. Its response could be automatic and not require human decision-making. The second use is to pass the warning to the military and political leadership so that they would have time only to put in motion some predetermined response. This predetermined response may be of two kinds. The first is to ride-out the possible attack and then determine the further course of action. In this case, early warning would not have served to inform decision-making in any meaningful way. The second class would be to retaliate immediately upon receipt of a warning (i.e., a launch on warning posture), which in turn requires keeping weapons on high alert. Indeed, it could be argued that organizational biases would predispose decision-makers to use the acquisition of an early warning system for adopting a launch on warning posture.[110] And with a launch on warning posture, the risks of accidental nuclear war are even graver in South Asia than it was there in case of super power confrontation.

The false warning incident that occurred just prior to the Pakistani nuclear tests in May 1998 is an important case demonstrating the dangers of accidental war in South Asia. During the crucial days just prior to Prime Minister Sharif's decision to order the tests of Pakistani nuclear weapons, senior military intelligence officers informed him that the Indian and Israeli air forces were about to launch a preventive strike on the test site. The incident is shrouded in mystery, and neither the cause nor the consequences of this warning message are clear. Some press reports claim that Pakistani intelligence officers, fearing an Israeli raid like the attack on Osirak in 1981, misidentified an F-16 aircraft that strayed into or near Pakistani territory.[111] Other reports state that the warning message was triggered by an Israeli cargo plane carrying Prime Minister

Benjamin Netanyahu's armored Cadillacs enroute to a state visit. A third possibility is that the ISI officials did not believe there was any threat of an imminent Indian-Israeli attack in 1998, but deliberately concocted (or exaggerated) the warning of a preventive strike to force the Prime Minister, who was wavering under U.S. pressure, to test the weapons immediately. There is not authenticity about these but the thing is more worrisome that false warnings could be catastrophic in a crisis whether they are deliberate or genuinely believed.

Though the possibility of a false warning producing an accidental nuclear war in South Asia is reduced by India's adoption of a nuclear no-first use policy, yet it by no means eliminated the possibilities of such threats. Not only might the Pakistani government, following its stated first-use doctrine, respond to intelligence (in this case false) that India was about to attack successfully a large portion of Pakistani nuclear forces, but either government could misidentify an accidental nuclear detonation, occurring during transport and alert activities at one of their own military bases, as the start of a counterforce attack by the other state. Pakistan has to be sensitive to this possibility because of the memory of the 1988 Ojheri incident near Rawalpindi as it has caused false fears among its decision-makers regarding Indian attack.[112] This kind of accident producing a false warning of an attack cannot, however, be ruled out in India as well, as long as the government plans to alert forces, or mate nuclear weapons to delivery vehicles during crisis.[113]

There are some problems with organizational structures and incentives also, which exist in both countries to fix safety problems once they occur. Unfortunately, there is a lack of independent regulatory systems in both countries. In both states, learning from past mistakes is limited because the organizations in charge are not forced by regulatory agencies to scrutinize their operations or adjust after errors are detected. In Pakistan, there is no independent group to provide checks and balances to the military planners or scientists. In India, a nuclear regulatory body exists, but it lacks sufficient independence to work effectively. For example, when nuclear reactor safety problems were identified by the chairman of the Atomic Energy Regulatory Board, he was dismissed from his position.[114]

In addition, there is need of serious concern about the maintenance of centralized authority over nuclear use decisions. Though government policies in this regard are kept classified, yet the need for some form of pre-delegation is recognized by serious analysts in both countries. Some Pakistani observers are aware of this issue, consequently they have advocated pre-delegation of nuclear authority to lower level military officers.[115] The Indian Draft Nuclear Doctrine simply states that "the authority to release nuclear weapons for use resides in the person of the Prime Minister of India, or the designated successor(s)." But some Indian analysts also recognize that in crisis or war, nuclear weapons' control may pass to the professional military personnel by design or default.[116]

The risk of accidental war in South Asia is exacerbated by the fact that governments have not instituted a Personnel Reliability Program (PRP), safety training, and drug use and mental health monitoring programmes as used in the United States to reduce the risk that an unstable civilian or military officer would be involved in critical nuclear weapons or command and control duties.[117] This personnel reliability problem is serious in India, where civilian custodians maintain custody of the nuclear weapons. It is more serious in case of Pakistan where the weapons are controlled by a professional military organization facing the difficult challenge of maintaining discipline in the midst a society facing a failing economy, serious social problems, and growing religious fundamentalism.[118]

Finally, there is evidence that neither Indian nor Pakistani military has focused sufficiently on the danger that a missile test launch during a crisis could be misperceived as the start of a nuclear attack. There is an agreement, as part of the Lahore accords in January 1999, to provide missile test advance notification, but even such an agreement is not a fool-proof solution. Moreover, both Pakistan and India appear to be planning to use their missile test facilities for actual nuclear weapons launches during war which further enhances the risk of misperception about the test launch of a missile.

Nuclear Terrorism and Accidents

The fourth challenge to the nuclear security in the region is nuclear terrorism and nuclear accidents. Both these propositions are very dangerous for the region. Nuclear terrorism usually subsumes a wide range of malevolent activities in order to blackmail the targeted state to accede to the demands of the terrorists threatened or actual use of a nuclear device, targeting nuclear facilities like nuclear power stations, breeder reactors, reprocessing and enrichment plants, cooling ponds of spent fuel or dispersal of radioactive substances called a dirty bomb. Nuclear facilities and complex may be the most preferred targets of terrorists. The fuel laden planes or explosives laden vehicles crashing into nuclear installations may result in a nuclear disaster. The objectives of such attacks may not only be restricted to demolition of nuclear facilities but massive casualties also. Even an ordinary suicide attack or a strong car bomb explosion against the nuclear materials storage facility would cause radiological dispersion. The same kind of attacks could cause explosion at the transporting facilities of nuclear materials or equipments. Terrorists may also use nuclear material as radiological weapons, and can disperse them in crowded habitations by using a conventional bomb explosion. Detonation of suitcase bombs pilfered from erstwhile Soviet Union may also pose a treat.

However it seems difficult for non-state actors or terrorist entities to develop either crude or sophisticated nuclear weapons as it require necessary infrastructural facilities like technology, components and scientists which is not possible without the help of nuclear capable state or agency, but readymade nuclear warheads may possibly whisked away by wrong hands during the transportation of equipments from place of production to storage or deployment sites. In case of South Asia, the political and social turmoil increases the threat from both insiders and outsiders to nuclear facilities, material and weapons, and fear that nuclear weapons and facilities could fall into the hands of terrorists. Perceptions of greater political volatility and ambivalent attitude toward terrorist organizations further heighten the concerns about nuclear security in the region. In addition, Pakistan's lack of a "no first use" nuclear doctrine could imply greater dispersal of nuclear weapons. Delegation of authority to field operations may further complicate the problem of providing security.

There is an anxiety and fear in the Western world about the Indian and Pakistani nuclear security. One well publicized Western fear after September 11, 2001 has been that Al Qaeda or other such terrorist networks might penetrate Pakistan's nuclear establishments and steal nuclear weapons or nuclear material. Another stems from the extraordinary doubts raised about the reliability of Pakistani physical security and personnel reliability procedures following the disclosures in 2003-04 of Abdul Qadeer Khan's black market sales of Pakistani nuclear technology to Libya, Iran and North Korea. While sensational disclosures of this kind have not arisen in the Indian context, concerns also exist about the generic integrity of Indian nuclear security measures against insider threats.

After the tragic events of September 11, 2001, no one doubts that terrorists might be interested in killing a lot of people. It is evident from the US Attorny General John Ashcrof's sensational report about the "dirty bomb" or a radiological dispersal device (RDD) after the arrest of alleged Al-Qaeda terrorist Jose Padilla at Chicage's O' Hare Airport on June 10, 2002. Such a weapon "spreads radioactive material that is highly toxic to humans and can cause mass death and injury."[119] Earlier, on March 6, 2002, the US Senate Foreign Relations Committee held hearings on the potential for acts of terrorism involving radioactive materials. Though there was an agreement among experts within and outside the US government that a dirty bomb would not cause large loss of life as on September 11, 2001, yet it could create widespread panic and economic damage.

A scenario of radiological dispersal, in which low levels of radiation are quietly spread around a city, has been discussed by a nuclear expert before the Senate committee.[120] It is described that an anonymous tip alerts to the police, confirm the attack with radiation detectors. While no one in the contaminated area would die or even get ill as a result of short-term exposure to the radiation, evacuation and cleanup of part of the city would be required. Exposure to such low levels of radioactive material over many years would cause an increased risk of cancer. Potentially whole buildings would have to be torn down and disposed of as radioactive waste, and the heart of the city might be abandoned for years and rehabilitated only at great expense.

In fact, problem from the dispersal of radioactive material have occurred in past are similar in to those of an RDD attack as happened in Goiania, Brazil in 1987-1988.[121] The records of these events suggest that, depending on the type and amount of radioactive material involved in an RDD attack, tens or hundreds could die and potentially thousands grow ill from radiation poisoning. Furthermore, the US Department of Homeland Security believes that the threat of RDD attacks against the United States is not only credible, but also a near-term threat. On New Year's Eve in 2003, nuclear experts mingled with holiday crowds in major cities with radiation detectors hidden in briefcases and golf bags during the elevated terrorist alert level "Code Orange". The threat of nuclear radiological terrorism is not limited to the confines of the United States only but South Asia continues to be a volatile region that hosts many militant groups and sources of radioactive material. Nuclear and radiological terrorism remains a frightening possibility in India and Pakistan. The source material for nuclear terrorism could come from illicit transactions of poorly protected materials originating outside the region, as well as material from within the region used for military or civilian purposes. Though India and Pakistan have established regulatory bodies and agencies to deal with the safety and security of their nuclear materials, yet they may not protect against every potential threat.

However, the possibility of a deliberate nuclear exchange between India and Pakistan has receded with the efforts by both the governments to engineer improved relations but some other types of events could prompt unintended escalation in South Asia. These scenarios are: a terrorist use of RDDs, a terrorist detonation of a nuclear weapon and the accidental explosion of nuclear arms at military bases in either country. These three events, none of which involve the deliberate use of nuclear assets by India or Pakistan, could have horrific consequences ranging from the significant loss of life and long-lasting contamination. Though the nuclear weapons have not been used in warfare since 1945 yet many accidents have occurred involving military and non-military nuclear programmes so far. In this context highest security arrangements have been made to protect nuclear weapons and their infrastructure, but what about radioacti materials usually found at many research laborat hospitals? Despite extra vigilance on the part of both the states of South Asia, possibilities of accidents can not be ruled out. Moreover, terrorist groups in India and Pakistan, as elsewhere, might seek to produce casualties or massive disruption by means of radioactive materials.

Nuclear terrorism, in the form of Radiological dispersal or a dirty bomb, poses a substantial threat to the security partially because of the relative abundance of radioactive sources. Unlike the fissile materials used to produce nuclear weapons that are stored in comparatively few locations, radiological materials are widely used in medicine and industry. These radiological materials may not be well guarded and are susceptible to theft from individuals who work inside, or outside, the facility. Security regulations associated with these materials are not so sound and vary greatly among countries and even within a single country.

In fact, these radiological dispersal devices are not nuclear weapons, nor do they produce similar weapons effects. There is no nuclear yield, and the amount of destruction and damage caused by an RDD in many orders of magnitude are less when compared to a nuclear detonation. The greatest threats posed by an RDD lie in its capacity to wreak psychological and economic havoc on a city, as well as its potential to produce escalation. The common man might not know the distinctions between a radiological weapon and a nuclear weapon, and may think a radiological weapon as a nuclear weapon. The mass media might inflame public reaction and contribute to confusion, panic and pressure on national leaders to retaliate and escalate. In this way, the radiological contamination of any kind strikes fear into the surrounding community.

Radioactive materials can be categorized in terms of the strictness of controls, as tight and loose, governing their access and disposition. Material used for nuclear weapons and nuclear power plants are tightly regulated, making it difficult, but not impossible, to gain unauthorized access to these sites while radioactive materials that have industrial and medicinal uses, ranging from the treatment of cancer to the sterilization of food and spices, typically are subject to minimal security, making them far more susceptible to unauthorized access and use. Radioactive material is available worldwide, which makes the threat of radiological terrorism plausible.[122] The use of radioactive materials in medicine and industry has become globalized. Radioactive materials are stored and used throughout India and Pakistan for cancer therapy, food irradiation, and medical product sterilization. The same materials that save or improve lives on a daily basis can threaten the public well-being, if used by terrorist groups. They are spread throughout both countries and have varying levels of security. Many of these sources have been produced in the region, but some are imported from abroad. There are many private and public suppliers of radioactive materials, and each year many of these sources are lost and can no longer be tracked. In the United States and European Union, over 370 sources are lost on an annual basis. Thousands have been lost from countries that were once part of the Soviet Union and have yet to be recovered. Additionally, there have been 643-recorded incidents of nuclear smuggling, 80 of which involved the use of radioactive materials with malevolent intent, such as extortion, bribery, and murder.[123]

In case of India, IAEA data reveals that India has reported several cases of stolen and lost sources over the last few years. There have been twenty-five reported cases of missing radioactive materials. Of these, thirteen have never been recovered and 52 percent have occurred by theft.[124] Nearly 10,000 radioactive sources are used throughout India of which about 400 are particularly worrisome. Comparable data from Pakistan are not publicly available. The efficacy of existing radiological regulatory practices in India and Pakistan remains opaque to outside analysts. Typically, only one or two radiation safety officers control each source in hospitals, research laboratories, and industrial plants. Security practices are sometimes deficient. On August 17, 2003, the *Times of India* reported that individuals in Jamshedpur, India, stole small gauges filled with Co-60.[125] These deficiencies are by no means confined to India or Pakistan but are worldwide.

Various types of radioactive material commonly used in industry and medicine have characteristics that would make them effective RDD weapons. Sealed radioactive sources are produced in nuclear reactors as by-products of nuclear fission or via target irradiation. For any particular radioactive material, knowing the type of ionizing radiation it emits is essential for protection, detection, storage, transport, and cleanup. Ionizing radiation, which causes damage to human cells, comes in the form of alpha, beta and gamma radiation. These three types of radiation differ in their ability to penetrate materials.[126] So the exposure to radiation on human health has different effects.[127] The severity of these effects depends on the level of dose."[128] Possible effects include "damage to body tissues such as the red bone marrow, gastrointestinal tract,[129] central nervous system, lung and skin; and at very high doses, these effects may lead to death within a short period."[130] Stochastic effects include increased incidence of cancer as well as the possibility of hereditary mutations seen in later generations.[131]

Beside the terrorist use of RDDs, there is another scenario, which can cause damage and casualties on a large scale and may prompt unintended escalation in the region. It is the detonation of a low-yield nuclear weapon by the terrorists. There are five basic nuclear weapons effects. "Blast and shock effects are the primary damage producing mechanisms for soft targets such as cities and are often the only effective mechanism for destroying underground structures such as missile silos."[132] Immediately after a nuclear explosion, a high-pressure wave moves from ground zero outwards. This wave is usually reflected off the ground creating a secondary blast wave.[133] Thermal effects are responsible for producing burns and eye injuries and could also lead to the ignition of combustible materials. Fire damage from a nuclear detonation has historically been viewed by the United States military as difficult to quantify but may result in up to five times the amount of damage from nuclear blast. The fourth effect is radiation.[134] Finally, there is the electromagnetic pulse (EMP) effect. This effect occurs at the moment of nuclear detonation. It can be thought of as a very strong electrical disturbance akin to an extremely powerful, fast, and expansive bolt of lightning.[135] This effect disables electronics and communications equipment almost instantaneously. It has two primary modes of damage: physical damage, such as shorts and burnouts, and temporary operational instabilities, such as power loss and fluctuation. The EMP is particularly devastating to advanced electronics, such as computers, servers, avionics equipment, and other technologies. Older technologies, such as motors and vacuum tubes, are less susceptible. EMP effects can devastate civilian infrastructure.

EMP effects can also severely hamper military command, control, communications and intelligence.[136] In this situation the generals and their staff will not be able to talk to their front line troops and they will not be able to receive instructions from higher headquarters.

The severe damage caused by a nuclear weapon necessitates an examination of how non-state actors might acquire such a capability. Although estimates vary, the production of a functional nuclear weapon may require only a few kilograms of plutonium or about fifteen to twenty-five kg of uranium. Reports of theft or unaccounted for nuclear material are widespread and have recently been compiled by Stanford University's Institute for International Studies (IIS). The Database on Nuclear Smuggling, Theft and Orphan Radiation Sources (DSTO) has reported that about "forty kilograms of weapons—usable uranium and plutonium have been stolen from poorly protected nuclear facilities in the former Soviet Union during the last decade."[137] Although most of this material has since been retrieved, there still remains two kilograms of highly enriched uranium that is unaccounted for. A researcher at the IIS argues that "this is the tip of the iceberg" and that more than ten times that amount might actually be missing. In 1998, the Russian Federal Security Services (FSB) thwarted a plan by nuclear facility employees to divert 18.5 kg of HEU.[138] Had this not occurred, there would have been almost enough fissile material to produce a nuclear weapon. There are no binding IAEA standards of protection, accountancy, and security for weapon-grade material, and most states would be reluctant to accept intrusive foreign assistance to upgrade existing practices. Stolen nuclear material can reach its destination by many different routes. Stanford University's DSTO monitors trafficking routes, and these routes snake through Central Asia toward South Asia. An instance of nuclear terrorism involving HEU or plutonium would have very grave consequences. The likelihood of this eventuality is perhaps less than the likelihood of radiological terrorism involving the use of a dirty bomb, but the consequences would obviously be far greater. More scientific skills would be needed to produce a nuclear weapon utilizing stolen HEU, and the material handling challenges associated with a plutonium bomb would be quite severe. Nonetheless, the possibility of nuclear terrorism using HEU or plutonium cannot be discounted in South Asia.

The possibility of nuclear accidents is another proposition, which can cause serious dangers in the region for nuclear security. Apart from the command and control issues, accidents could occur as a result of a weapon-handling incident, a fire, a conventional attack against a nuclear target, a ground transportation accident, a malfunction of an aircraft carrying a nuclear device, or by other means. Though it is believed that neither India nor Pakistan has deployed their nuclear weapons, yet the possibility of accidents still can not be ruled out. More importantly, the likelihood of accidents occurring will increase in the event of deployment, or during movement of nuclear assets in a crisis environment.

Ever since the beginning of the nuclear age, there have been accidents involving nuclear weapons and their delivery vehicles. Information of such accidents is scarce and not possible to list all of them. It is claimed that there have been at least 230 nuclear weapons accidents involving the U.S.A, former U.S.S.R., and the U.K. between 1950 and 1980.[139] In the United States alone, there are more than ten documented cases where the high explosives surrounding the fissile cores have detonated. Of these, two produced a dispersal of nuclear material over an expansive area—Palamores, Spain in 1966 and Thule, Greenland in 1968.[140] During 1945-51, nuclear arsenal of U.S.A. consisted of aircraft delivered fission bombs, which were designed in the manner that the nuclear capsule had to be manually inserted. This was done while the aircraft was in flight, and removed before landing. It was only in 1952, the warheads were designed to permit the capsules to be inserted mechanically, allowing aircraft to carry bombs externally and the development of ballistic missile warheads. It was only in the mid-1950s that the USA developed "sealed pits" which allowed the weapons to remain assembled at all times, with the fissile material pit enclosed inside the high explosive lenses. This allowed for reductions in weapon size and weight and increased operational readiness. These designs however increased the risk of accidental detonation of the high explosive in the weapons leading to either the dispersal of the fissile material or a nuclear explosion.[141]

A nuclear weapon could detonate because of a failure of its safety mechanisms. The United States was successful in developing safety mechanisms for its nuclear weapons. As a result, safety devices and policy guidelines minimize the probability of a chain reaction in the event of an accident. These risks were recognized and attempts were made over the years to reduce the likelihood of such accidents. The United States conducted 88 nuclear detonation safety tests from 1945-90 with the explicit purpose of confirming that "a nuclear explosion will not occur in case of an accidental detonation of the explosive associated with the device."[142] The erstwhile Soviet Union conducted forty-two such tests.[143] New nuclear powers might find it difficult to ensure such high levels of safety due to the limitations of technology, research, and nuclear testing. Consequently, these states might face difficulty preventing detonations in the event of nuclear accidents. Despite these attempts, accidents continued to occur. An official summary released by the Department of Defense of USA in 1981 lists 32 accidents involving its nuclear weapons between 1950 and 1980. These include a number of instances where the high explosive in nuclear weapons has burned or detonated and led to contamination.[144]

Different types of accidents can produce different effects. One possible accident scenario involves the burning of a weapon's high explosives around the fissile core, which could cause the fissile material in the core to melt. In this event, radioactive contamination would occur without a nuclear detonation. Cleanup would be expensive but manageable. Another scenario involving a plutonium bomb would entail a detonation of high explosives that does not produce a nuclear yield, but instead disperses radioactive plutonium in the surrounding region. This scenario can be described as a "very dirty bomb" and would be similar to RDDs using alpha sources. A far more alarming accident scenario would entail the detonation of a weapon's high explosives triggering a nuclear yield. This nuclear yield could range from being a very small fraction of the intended yield to the total intended yield of the weapon. The span of potential yields is important because in the lowest fractional yields it might initially be difficult to differentiate between a nuclear blast and a conventional one.

The accidents typically involve delivery vehicles, either aircraft or missiles. Most notable among missile accidents is the 1960 accident involving a U.S. BOMARC missile at the McGuire Air Force base in New Jersey which suffered an explosion and a fire involving the missile's fuel tanks.[145] The significance of this accident is that it happened when the missile was in a "ready storage" condition (permitting launch in two minutes).[146] A related example is the September 1980 Titan II ICBM fuel explosion at Damascus, Arkansas, which did not, however, result in plutonium dispersal.

There have been many less severe accidents involving missiles and missile silos, fortunately. The US Air Force has revealed that in a period of four years, during 1975 to 1979, there were 125 accidents at its missile sites, and a further ten from March 1979 to September 1980. In case of aircrafts, the most famous accidents have been of Palomares, Spain, and near Thule, Greenland. In both cases, aircraft carrying nuclear weapons crashed and the high explosive surrounding the nuclear core detonated which led to dispersal of plutonium over a large region.[147]

There have been accidents involving U.S. naval nuclear weapons as well. One assessment lists 383 accidents during 1945 to 1988.[148] These included a number of instances in which nuclear weapons were lost at sea as a result of the sinking of submarines and ships. Information about accidents in the erstwhile Soviet Union is harder to obtain, but one source lists over 25 serious nuclear weapon accidents there.[149] These included a 1977 accident in which, reportedly, fuel leaked from a nuclear missile in its silo and subsequently exploded.[150] Such accidents continue to happen. A recent example is the ballistic missile explosion at Vladivostok that occurred as the missile was being unloaded from a transport ship on June 16, 2000.[151] According to preliminary information the missile caught on the pier railing, which led to a leak of approximately 3 tons of the oxidizing agent. A number of people were injured and villages had to be evacuated.

Though it is believed that neither India nor Pakistan has deployed nuclear weapons by now, but If they deploy, they too shall face the risk of accidents involving nuclear weapons and their delivery systems. Experience suggests that the possibilities of such risks of aircraft and missile accidents can not be ruled out. India's Comptroller and Auditor General reported in 1997 that there had been 187 accidents and 2729 "incidents" involving Indian Air Force (IAF) aircraft during April 1991 to March 1997, in which it lost 147 aircraft and 63 pilots.[152] Data on Pakistan Air Force (PAF) accidents are not easily available. However, Pakistan Institute for Air Defence Studies reveals that there were 11 major PAF accidents during January 1997 to August 1998.[153]

Besides aircrafts, both India and Pakistan have been developing and testing a number of ballistic missiles as delivery systems for nuclear weapons. There have been no reports of accidents involving ballistic missiles in South Asia. But experience elsewhere suggests possibility of accidents can not be ruled out completely. Of particular concern are the liquid fuelled missiles, India's Prithvi and Pakistan's Ghauri, which may have significant risks.

If we see India's *Prithvi* missile, it is fuelled by a liquid propellant, and according to most reports the oxidizer is inhibited red fuming nitric acid (IRFNA)[154] and the fuel is a 50:50 combination of xylidine and triethylamine.[155] This combination is hypergolic, i.e., self-igniting when mixed, and highly volatile and has to be loaded just prior to launch. In this way it is an accident-prone missile.

In case of Pakistan, its *Ghauri* missile is reportedly based on the North Korean No-Dong missile.[156] This is claimed to have a cluster of four North Korean Scud Mod B engines. The fuel is given as unsymmetrical dimethylhydrazine with inhibited red fuming nitric acid as an oxidiser.[157] There have been only a few tests of this missile. Consequently, lack of adequate testing can create problems in its use. For example, it has been reported that during the fourth test of Prithvi, the missile engine did not fire because of faulty wiring.[158] Similarly, the first of three user trials by the Indian Army was postponed because of a faulty nozzle in the fuel feed mechanism, allowing fuel to leak into the engine casing.[159]

Apart from the delivery systems, nuclear weapons themselves are also accident-prone.The consequences of nuclear weapons accidents create severe damages. A fire or fuel explosion near a nuclear weapon could lead to a range of consequences depending on the source and intensity of the fire, as well as the design of the weapon and its high explosive. Several hundreds of thousands of people could die due to the occurrence of accidental nuclear explosion. In addition, such explosions might be assumed to be a nuclear attack and can lead to a nuclear response. Thus an accidental nuclear explosion may even initiate a nuclear war. Even if such a catastrophic accidental nuclear explosion does not occur, the dispersal of plutonium due to a high explosive detonation could lead to several thousand fatalities. Thus, prudence dictates that India and Pakistan should not deploy nuclear weapons. They should also store them far away from missiles and aircraft carrying potentially explosive fuel. A further level of safety may be gained by keeping the weapons disassembled, so that the HE is not close to the fissile material pit. All these steps would not only reduce the danger of accidental explosions, but also reduce the risk of a nuclear weapon being launched through error, panic or miscalculation.

In this way all the four requirements for an effective deterrence are doubtful in case of South Asia. As long as the Indo-Pak relations remain hostile and suspicion exists, prevention of war is a difficult task. Conventional conflict, at any level, carry the potential for escalation from one level to another and then ultimately to the grim prospects of nuclear exchange. The criterion of second-strike capability also fails in the region. Neither India nor Pakistan has survivable second-strike capability. The lack of effective command and control system further makes the situation complicated which increases the possibility of accidental nuclear war. Finally, the political and social turmoil in the region increases the threat from both insiders and outsiders to nuclear facilities, material and weapons, and fear that nuclear weapons and facilities could fall into the hands of terrorists. The risk of nuclear escalation further increases by the fact that both the countries of the region are deeply involved in developing missiles to deliver their nuclear weapons.

Notes and References

1. For details see, Praful Bidwai and Achin Vanaik, South Asia on A Short Fuse, Oxford University Press, New Delhi, 2002.
2. For details see, Robert E. Rehbein, "Managing Proliferation in South Asia : A Case for Assistance to Unsafe Nuclear Arsenals", *The Non-proliferation Review,* Vol. 9, No. 1, Spring 2002. Also see, Andrew

Coach, "India, Pakistan : Nuclear Arms Race Gets Off to a Slow Start", *Jane's Intelligence Review,* 13, January 2001, pp. 36-40; David Albright, "India's and Pakistan's Fissile Materials and Nuclear Weapons Inventories, end of 1999",*Institute for Science and International Security,* October 11, 2000, http://www.isis-online.org/ Duncal Lenox, "Comparing India's and Pakistan's Strategic Weapons capabilities", Jane's Strategic Weapon Systems, May 30, 2002; http://www.janes.com/security/international_security/ new/janes/janes020530_1_n.shtml

SIPRI Year Books, 1998-2006, Stockholm International Peace Research Institute, Oxford University Press, Oxford; and "India's Nuclear Weapons Update 2003", *The Risk Report,* prepared by Wisconsin Project on Nuclear Arms Control, Vol. 9, No. 5, September-October 2003.

3. Feroz Hasan Khan, "Nuclear Signaling, Missiles and Escalation Control in South Asia", in Michel Krepon, *et. al.* eds., *Escalation Control and Nuclear Option in South Asia,* The Henry L. Stimson Center, Washington D.C., November 2004, p. 75.
4. India and Pakistan have fought three full scale wars in 1947-48 in Jammu and Kashmir, in 1965 in Kutch, Punjab and Jammu and Kashmir, in 1971 during the East Pakistan crises, and one limited war at Kargil in 1999. Former Foreign Secretary Late J.N. Dixit was of the opinion that out of the four conflicts, it is only during the 1965 and 1971 conflicts that New Delhi formally declared that a state of war existed between India and Pakistan. Otherwise there has been reluctance to accept the fact that all the major conflicts between India and Pakistan were in fact regular wars in which the armed forces of the two countries engaged in military operations against each other. The military conflict of 1999 in Kargil was certainly not a skirmish, border incident or marginal intrusion but it was a war which was launched by Pakistan with a definite and clear strategic territorial and political motives with premeditated planning and detailed preparations. For detail See, J.N. Dixit, *India's Foreign Policy, 1947-2003,* Picus Books, New Delhi, 2003; and his, *India-Pakistan in War and Peace,* Book's Today, New Delhi, 2002. For historical perspective on Kashmir see, Maroof Raza, *Three Wars and No Peace Over Kashmir,* Lancers, New Delhi, 1996. For 1965 war see, Lt. Gen. Harbaksh Singh, *War Dispatches : Indo-Pak Conflict 1965,* Lancers, New Delhi, 1991. For 1971 war see, Lt. Gen. J.F.R. Jacob, *Surrender at Dacca: Birth of a Nation,* Manohar, New Delhi, 1997. For Kargil crises see, Lt. Gen. V.K. Sood and Pravin Sawhney, *Operation Prakram : The War Unfinished,* Sage, New Delhi, 2003. Also see, *Kargil Review Committee Report,* Tabled in Parliament on February 23, 2000; Jasjit Singh, ed., *Kargil 1999: Pakistan's Fourth War For Kashmir,* Knowledge World, New Delhi, 1999; and Ashok Krishna and P.R. Chari, ed., *Kargil : The Tables Turned,* Manohar, New Delhi, 2001.
5. It has been reported that the Pakistani military had prepared their nuclear tipped missiles to fight back a possible Indian attack during the Kargil crises. The then US President Bill Clinton had conveyed this news to the Pakistani Prime Minister Nawaz Sharif during a meeting

of both the leaders. It is quoted by Hussain Haqqani in his forthcoming book titled *Pakistan Between Mosque and Military* through Bruce Riedel, a special assistant to Clinton and a senior director of "Near East and South Asian Affairs" at the National Security Council during Clinton's tenure, who was present in the meeting of July 4, 1999 between the two leaders. Reidel recalls that during the meeting Clinton asked Sharif, "Did he order Pakistani nuclear missile force to prepare for action? Did he realize how crazy that was? You have put me in middle today, set the US fail and I won't let it happen. Pakistan is messing with nuclear war?" At the end of the meeting, Sharif agreed to announce a Pakistani withdrawal from Kargil and restoration of the sanctity of LOC in return for Clinton taking a personal interest in resumption of the Indo-Pak dialogue, *Times of India,* 21 June 2005. Also see, Samina Ahmad and David Cotright, *South Asia at Nuclear Crossroad,* Fourth Freedom Forum, Joan B. Kroach Institute for International Peace Studies, Managing the project at Harvard University, March 2001.

6. "World Nuclear Power Reactors 2001-2002 and Uranium Requirements", *Information and Issue Brief,* World Nuclear Organization, December 2002. http://www.world-nuclear.org/info/reactors.htm. Also see, Ashley J Tellis, *Stability in South Asia,* Santa Monica, CA: RAND, 1997.
7. This estimation is given by David Albrght, President of Institute for Science and International Security Washington, D.C. (ISIS). *Times of India,* September 9, 2005. The report is available at isis-online.org/publications/southasia/ch-indpak.html
   Also see, Duncan Lennox. "Comparing India's and Pakistan's Strategic Nuclear Weapons Capabilities", *Jane's Strategic Weapon Systems,* May 30, 2002. http://www.janes.com/security/international_security/news/jsws/jsws020530_1_n.shtml
8. CIRUS (Canadian-Indian, US), a 40 mwt research reactor that was offered to build by Canada in 1955 as part of the "Colombo Plan"(Colombo plan was an initiative by the rich commonwealth nations to help the poor commonwealth nations of South and South-East Asia. The US contribution in this direction was the heavy water to moderate the reactor). US agreed to supply 21 tonnes heavy water for this reactor in February 1956 under the Eisenhower's plan "Atoms for Peace". The acquisition of CIRUS was a watershed event in nuclear proliferation and was specifically intended by India to provide herself with a weapons option, and this reactor produced the plutonium which was used in the PNE of 1974.
9. Prime Minister Nehru in July 1958, authorized the project "phoenix" to build a plant with a capacity of 20 tonnes of fuel a year sized to match the production capacity of CIRUS. The plant was based on the US developed purex process, and an American firm "vitro international" prepared the plan for it.
10. Jyotirmoy Banerjee, "Pokharan-II: Fallout and Implications", *World Affairs,* Vol. 3, No. 3, July-September 1999, p. 120.
11. *Ibid.*
12. *Ibid.*

13. Jyotirmoy Banerjee, *Nuclear World : Defence and Politics of Major Powers*, Manas, New Delhi, 2002, p. 197.
14. J.N. Dixit, *India's Foreign Policy : 1947-2003*, Picus Books, New Delhi, 2003, p. 438.
15. *Ibid.*
16. For details see, D.K. Palit and P.K.S. Namboodri, *Pakistan's Islamic Bomb*, Vikas, New Delhi, 1979.
17. *Times of India*, New Delhi, 11 June 1979, cited in Brij Mohan Kaushik and O.N. Mehrotra, Pakistan's Nuclear Bomb, Sopan, New Delhi, 1980, p. 138.
18. Dixit, n. 14., p. 439.
19. *Ibid.*
20. For a good account of negotiations for security guarantees see, Joyce Battle, *India and Pakistan on Nuclear Threshold*, US documents, Electronic Book No. 6, National Security Archive, Washington D.C., 1998. www.gwu.edu/~nsarchiv/NSAEBB/NSAEBB6/index.html
21. Kaushik and Mehrotra, n. 17, p. 61.
22. Agha Shahi, cited inFashar H. Syed, ed., *Nuclear Disarmament and Conventional Arms Control Including Light Weapons*, Friends, Rawalpindi, 1997, p. 421.
23. A. Pakistani nuclear device was reportedly tested at the Chinese testing site at Lop Nor in Sinkiang in 1987. Dixit, n. 14, p. 439. In an interview in 1987, the Pakistani scientist Abdul Quadir Khan claimed that Pakistan had already made nuclear weapons. He dismissed such a thing as a peaceful nuclear programme, and boasted that whereas India took twelve years to assemble the bomb, Pakistan had done it in seven. *The Observer*, London, 1 March 1987.
24. General Aslam Beg, cited in Jasjit Singh, "Nuclearization and Regional Security : Indian Perspective", *The Balance of Power in South Asia*, Emirates Center for Strategic Studies and Research, Abu Dhabi, 2002, p. 46.
25. The NPT recognized only those five countries as nuclear weapon states which had manufactured and exploded a nuclear weapon or other nuclear device prior to 1 January 1967. India refused to sign NPT by saying that it has a discriminatory character as it stops only the horizontal and not vertical proliferation. India, therefore urges the nuclear powers that they ought to effect vertical non-proliferation, which in turn might induce others not to engage in nuclear proliferation. But, paradoxically, seeds of nuclear proliferation are inherent in the clause of NPT itself. For instance, under article iv of the treaty, signatories become automatically entitled to acquire nuclear capability under the guise of peaceful intent of nuclear energy. India, *Rajya Sabha Debates*, Vol. CLXXIII, No. 36, May 26, 1997, cols. 290-91. For details on NPT, see, MahmedI. Shaker, *The Nuclear Non-Proliferation Treaty : Origin and Implementation* 1959-79, 3 Vols., Oceana, New York, 1980.
26. *Ibid.*
27. Pakistan acceded to the CPPNM in 2000 and India in 2002.

28. Joseph Cirincione, *Deadly arsenals : Tracking Weapons of Mass Destruction,* Carnegie Endowment for International Peace, Washington D.C., 2002, pp. 201-09 and 217-18.
29. For details see, Rajesh M. Basrur and Hasan-Askari Rizvi, "Nuclear Terrorism and South Asia", *Occasional Paper SAND 98-0505/25,* Cooperative Monitoring Centre, Sandia National Laboratories, Albuquerque, 2003.
30. Unni Krishan, "India Sets Up Nuclear Weapons Command Chain", ABS-CBN.COM, January 5, 2003, http://www.abs-cbnnews.com
31. Since 1998 a number of experts from India and Pakistan have participated in the IAEA sponsored international training courses on physical protection of nuclear facilities and materials conducted by Sandia National Laboratories in Albuquerque, New Mexico. See, http://www.iaea.org.at/worldatom/About/Policy/GC/GC39/Documents/gc3919.html
32. It is estimated that up to 2002, USA, Russia, France, UK, China, India and Pakistan have conducted the number of nuclear tests—1032, 715, 210, 45, 45, 6, 6 respectively and stockpiles of nuclear weapons is estimated up to 2002, with USA-7600, Russia-8331, France-348, UK-185, China-402, India-30-35 and Pakistan-24-28. The stockpiles of India and Pakistan are thought to be only partly deployed. This estimation is by number of deployed warheads. *SIPRI Year Book,* OUP, Oxford, 2002, p. 526.
33. For a detailed exposition of these views see, Scott D. Sagan and Kenneth N. Waltz, *The Spread of Nuclear Weapons : A Debate,* W.W. Norton, New York. 1995.
34. For example, the then external affairs minister of India, Jaswant Singh observed that if deterrence works in West than why not in South Asia? Jaswant Singh, "Against Nuclear Aparthied", *Foreign Affairs,* Vol. 77, No. 5, 1998, p. 43. Similarly, Vijay Nair, an early advocate of Indian nuclear weapons argues that there has been no direct conflict between states of the western world while conflict has been the order of the day in non-nuclear third world. Vijay Nair, Nuclear India, Spencer and Lancer, Hartford, WI, 1992, p. 79.
35. J.N. Dixit, *India-Pakistan in War and Peace,* Routledge, London, 2002, p. 338.
36. K. Sunderji, "Proliferation of WMD and the Security Dimensions in South Asia : An Indian View", in William H. Lewis and Stuart E. Johnson, eds., *Weapons of Mass Destruction : New Perspective on Counter-proliferation,* National Defence University Press, Washington D.C., 1995, p. 59.
37. Raj Chengappa, *Weapons of Peace : The secret Story of India's Quest to be a Nuclear Power,* Harper Collins, New Delhi, 2000, p. 8.
38. Jasjit Singh, "One on One", *Defence News,* 27 July-2 August 1998, p. 22.
39. K.M. Arif, "Retaining the Nuclear Option", in Tariq Jain, ed., *Pakistan's Security and the Nuclear Option,* Institute of Policy Studies, Islamabad, 1995, p. 123.
40. *Ibid.,* p. 138.
41. *Ibid.,* p. 189.

42. Beg said that it is the nuclear deterrent which has kept wars in South Asia at bay. Aslam Beg, *India and Pakistan Security Perspective,* Foundation for Research on National Development and Security, Rawalpindi, 1994, p. 73. While Abdul Quadir Khan is reported to have told to *The Times of Oman* that anyone will have to think hundred times before try to indulge in any misadventure against Pakistan. I don't care if somebody disagrees but I consider nuclear weapons as weapons of peace. *The Hindu,* 26 August 2002.
43. Hegerty argues that nuclear weapons on sub-continent deter nuclear and conventional aggression but not the unconventional military operations such as guerrilla warfare. Devin T. Hegerty, *The Consequences of Nuclear Proliferation : Lessons from South Asia,* The MIT Press, Cambridge MA, 1998, p. 184.
44. Ashley J. Tellis, *India's Emerging Nuclear Posture : Between Recessed Deterrent and Ready Arsenal,* RAND Project, Santa Monica, 2001, p. 743.
45. Raghvan concludes that the probability of nuclear war between India and Pakistan is high in the event the two countries engage in direct military conflict. V. R. Raghvan, "Limited War and Nuclear Escalation in South Asia", *The Nonproliferation Review,* Vol. 8, No. 3, Fall-Winter 2001, p. 83.
46. Chari argues that the nuclearized environment in South Asia has not informed the leadership in both the countries to observe the restraint in making provocative and inflammatory public declarations. P.R. Chari, in Michael Krepon and Chris Gagne, eds., *The Stability-Instability Paradox : Nuclear Weapons and Brinkmanship in South Asia,* The Henry L Stimson Centre, Washington, D.C., June 2001, p. 20.
47. Talat Masood, "Our Multiple Challenges", *DAWN,* June 22, 2002. http://www.dawn.com /2002/06/22/op.htm.
48. M.B. Naqvi, "Facts about Indo-Pak Impasse", *The News,* June 3, 2002. http://www.jang.com. pk/thenehes/mar2002-daily/06-03-2002/oped/04.htm.
49. See, Sagan and Waltz, n. 33.
50. Robert, S. Litwak, "The New Calculus for Pre-emption", *Survival,* No. 44, Winter 2002-03, p. 54.
51. See, Waheguru Pal Singh, "India's Nuclear Use Doctrine", in Peter Lavoy, Scott *et al.*, eds., *Planning The Unthinkable,* Cornell University Press, New York, 2000, pp. 132-34. Perkovich also observes that in December 1982 US intelligence sources leaked reports that India's military leaders had prepared a contingency plan for launching air strikes against Pakistan's uranium enrichment plant at Kathua and the small reprocessing facility at PINSTECH in Rawalpindi. A front page 'Washington Post' story alleged that military advisors had proposed such a preventive attack to the then Prime Minister Mrs. Indira Gandhi nine months ago in march 1982 but Mrs. Gandhi had rejected it. Although Indian officials called the report 'absolute rubbish.' They countered that India and Pakistan were engaged in a very serious exercise for bringing about a rapprochement between the two countries, implying that this overrode any interest in a military strike. However, situation logic suggested that Indian military (or

other agencies) at least would prepare contingency plans for destroying or weakning Pakistan's nuclear capability before it could be used to threaten India. George Perkovich, *India's Nuclear Bomb : The Impact on Global Proliferation*, OUP, New Delhi, 2000, pp. 240-41.

52. Perkovich, Ibid. p. 289; and Raj Chengappa, *Weapons of Peace : The Secret Story of India's Quest to be a Nuclear Power*, Harper Collins, New Delhi, 2000, pp. 322-23. In 1986-87, India mobilized a quarter of a million troops just 20 miles from the Indo-Pak border opposite the Pakistani province *Sindh* in a military exercise code named "Brasstacks." The scale of military mobilization by India was unprecedented during peace-time. Indian troops carried live immunition, worsening the fear in Pakistan that India was likely to attack Pakistan along its Southern borders. At the time Pakistani experts thought that India might be preparing to relieve pressure in its Punjab province by attacking Pakistan. Indian scholars believed that the exercise was intended to stop Pakistan from allegedly interfering in the sikh insurgency in Punjab by threatening to retaliate against Pakistan's domestic 'trouble spot' in *Sindh*. More recent disclosures, however, suggest that brasstacks was staged by India as a deliberate policy of provoking Pakistan for war, so that India would have a pretext to attack and undermine Pakistan's self confidence and perhaps its territorial integrity. This threat was blocked by Pakistan's counter deployment of its armed forces and issuance of veiled nuclear threat. For a detailed account of brasstacks crises see, "Brasstacks and Beyond : Perception and Management of crises in South Asia", *Acid Research Report*, Programmes in Arms Control, Disarmament and International Security, University of Illinois at Urbana-Champaign, Urbana, 1995.

53. This would have included automatically an attack on Pakistan's nuclear facilities to remove the potential for a Pakistani nuclear riposte to India's attack. Relevant government agencies were not asked to contribute analysis or views to the discussion. Sunderji argued that India's cities could be protected from a Pakistani counterattack (perhaps a nuclear one), but, upon being probed, could not say how. One important advisor from the ministry of defense argued eloquently that India and Pakistan have already fought their last war, and there is too much to lose in contemplating another one. This view ultimately prevailed. Perkovich, n. 51, p. 280. 2

54. Athough Pakistan never declared its nuclear doctrine officially and authoritatively but some responsible persons in Pakistan have declared informally and unofficially some 'red-lines.' According to Pakistani General, Khalid Kidwai, Pakistan would resort to nuclear weapons' use in the event if: (i) India attacks Pakistan and conquers a large part of its territory, (ii) India destroys a large part either of its land or air force, (iii) India proceeds to the economic strangling of Pakistan, and (iv) India pushes Pakistan into political destabilization or creates a large scale international subversion. Polo Cotta-Ramnusino and Maurizio Martellini, Nuclear Safety, Nuclear Stability and Nuclear Strategy in Pakistan, Landau Network, Como, January 2002, p. 5.

Another Pakistani authority, Tariq Mahmud Ashraf, a retired Pakistani Air Force officer defined Pakistan's 'red-lines' as under:

(i) Penetration of Indian forces beyond a certain defined line or crossing of a river.
(ii) Imminent capture of an important Pakistani city like Lahore or Sialkot.
(iii) Destruction of Pakistan's conventional armed forces or other assets beyond an unacceptable level.
(iv) Attack on any of Pakistan's strategic targets such as dams or nuclear installations like Tarbela, Mangla, Kathua, Chashma etc.
(v) Imposition of blocked on Pakistan to an extent that it strangulates the continued transportation of vital supplies and adversely affects the war waging stamina of the country.
(vi) Indian crossing of the line of control (LOC) to a level that it threatens Pakistan's control over Azad Kashmir. Tariq Mahmud Ashraf, Aerospace Power : The Emerging Strategic Dimension, PAF Book Club, Peshawar, 2003, p. 148. Although these red lines have never been officially declared by any governmental authority of Pakistan but reflect obvious Pakistani sensitivities. How Indian authorities might translate these markers into war fighting guidelines, however, is anything but obvious.

55. This kind of threat of Indian airborne pre-emption strike against nuclear assets in Pakistan for the first time surfaced in 1980s as an attack on the uranium enrichment facility at Kathua and has been underlying theme in press and think tank commentary. Even Pakistani President Parvez Mushraf's address to the nation on 18 September 2001 touched on this threat as justification for Pakistan's decision to join the US led "Global War on Terrorism" without delay. Of the several reasons he set forth, the most graphic was India's unprecedented offer of the use of its air bases for US and coalition co-operations against the Taliban regime in Afghanistan. This would have meant foreign military over-flights on Pakistan's territory to Afghanistan, but could also have masked Indian surprise air attacks on Northern Pakistan. But allowing USA to use Pakistani air bases closer to Afghanistan obviated the Indian offer. See "Highlights of President Musharraf's Address to the Nation", *DAWN*, on-line edition, 19 September 2001.
56. A nuclear decapitation scenario in this context would mean attacking the other side's National Capital and targeting its leadership nods with nuclear weapons to shut down its central decision-making system, either to halt its offensive campaign abruptly or failing that to pre-empt coherent nuclear retaliation or limit its scale and effectiveness. Raj Chengappa, a senior Indian journalist, reports that former Indian Prime Minister Rajiv Gandhi took the first step to protect India's national leadership against a nuclear decapitation attack from Pakistan. He writes that after Rajiv's order in 1986, the then defence R and D chief, Arunachalam launched a cautious drive to enhance India's state of nuclear preparedness. Rajiv wanted a

command and control center set up which could not only withstand a nuclear attack but have sophisticated communication systems from which the Prime Minister could direct the country's armed forces during a war. Arun Singh, then minister of state for defense, was told to set a national command post at a secure location near the capital. See Chengappa, n. 52, p: 304. But another defense analyst Sumit Ganguly argues that neither side has the requisite capability to pursue a decapitating first strike against the other. See, Sumit Ganguly, Conflict Unending : Indo-Pakistan Tensions Since 1947, Columbia University Press, New York, 2001, p. 108. Deterrent optimist presume that India's nuclear arsenal is secure from attack, given its large landmass. It is necessary, but insufficient, for New Delhi's nuclear assets to be secure from attack, if India's national command authority could be subject to decapitation. India appears not to have attached a high priority to address this vulnerability. The Indian nuclear command authority decided to build only two bunkers to protect top officials from a potential nuclear strike, the first in New Delhi and the second within 250 miles of the city, in September 2003, five years after India became an overt nuclear power. For details see, Sumit Ganguly, "India to Build Nuclear-Proof Bunkers for Leadership", *Global Security Newswire,* 22 September, 2003.

57. Address by Indian defence Minister George Fernandes to 2nd International conference on *Asian Security in the 21st Century,* at Institute of Defense Studies and Analysis, New Delhi, 24-25 January, 2000. Also See, statement made by General V.P. Malik, "Limited War can Erupt Anytime", *Times of India,* New Delhi, 6 January 2000; and V.R. Raghavan, "Limited War and Nuclear Escalation In South Asia", *Non-proliferation Review,* No. 8, Fall-Winter 2001.
58. Address of Pakistani foreign minister to the *Carnegie International Non-proliferation Conference,* Washington D.C., 15 June 2001. http:// www.ceip.org/ files/nonprolif/prolif/2001/index .htm.
59. For details see, for detail Raghvan, n. 57.
60. Major General Ashok Krishna, *Deployment of India's Armed Forces Along the International Border (IB), The Line of Control (LOC) and At Sea,* 8 July 2002 at http://www.ipcs.org/ issues/700/788-mikrishna.htm
61. For details see, V.K. Sood and Pravin Sawhney, *Operation Prakram: The War Unfinished,* Sage, New Delhi, 2003.
62. In 2001-02, India was prepared to take the risk of coercing and even attacking Pakistan despite full knowledge of Pakistan's nuclear capability. A section of the Indian leadership was convinced that Pakistan will have a hard time operationalizing its nuclear first use doctrine in a limited conventional war. They believe, however, that the same is not true about conventional force retaliation. According to this logic, Pakistan would find its nuclear deterrence useless in this limited war scenario. However, Indian confidence regarding the possibility of escalation control, the predictable outcome of a war, and the faith of Indian leaders in the safety of nuclear weapons on full or near full alert status raises the question of whether India fully realizes the possible repercussions of its mobilization. It seems clear that the international political climate worked against any escalation

or war in South Asia. Reciprocal conventional force deployment by Pakistan led to a standoff that made it strategically difficult to fight a limited war, unless the war was expended, and that was not feasible. Feroz Hasan Khan, "Challenges to Nuclear Stability in South Asia", *Nonproliferation Review*, Vol. 10, No. 1, Spring 2003, p. 66.

63. For detail see, Raghvan, n. 57.
64. Banerjee, n. 13, p. 211.
65. Several years ago, a young German student piloted a simple aircraft, hoodwinked Soviet radar, and landed in the city of Moscow to prove precisely that even a superpower defence can be beaten by an amateur. Even in India, the air force radars failed to pick-up in time the aircraft which dropped illicit arms over Purulia in West Bengal. *Ibid.*, p. 212.
66. Shishir Gupta, "No Eyeball to Eyeball Any More in New War Doctrine", *Indian Express*, 6 March 2004. "Cold Start to New War Doctrine", *Times New Network*, 14 April 2004. http://times of India.indiatimes.com/articleshow/616847.cms
67. When a state attacks intended to destroy, largely or entirely, on a state's nuclear weapons before they can be used is called a "first-strike". Weapons that can take first strike and still strike back give a state "second-strike capability". Joshna S. Goldstein, *International Relations*, Pearson Education, New Delhi, 2003, p. 253.
68. Kapil Kak also present the similar views, "as vulnerability and costs rule out having the missiles in silos, a much larger number of missiles and launchers of the widest dispersion may be the only alternatives". Kapil Kak, "Command and Control of Small Nuclear Arsenals", in Jasjit Singh, ed., *Nuclear India*, Knowledge World, New Delhi, 1998, p. 280.
69. For a detailed study of India's and Pakistan's nuclear capabilities, postures and policies, see Rodney W. Jones, *"Minimum Nuclear Deterrence Postures in South Asia—An Overview"*, Final Report by Policy Architects International for DTRA/ASCO, October 2001, available at http://www.dtra. mil/about/organisation/south_asia.pdf. Also see, Robert S Norris and William M. Arkin, "Tables of Nuclear Forces", in Armament, Disarmament and International Security: *SIPRI Year Book*, OUP, Oxford, 1999., and Hans M. Kristensen and Joshua Handler, "World Nuclear Forces", in Armament, Disarmament and International Security: *SIPRI Year Book*, OUP, Oxford, 2002.
70. Washington based Institute for Science and International Security (ISIS) report put India's nuclear weapons inventory at between 60 to 105, with a median estimate of 80, and Pakistan 55 to 90, with a median estimate of 70. The ISIS president David Albright cautioned that these were merely estimates, there was reason to believe that, at least, in the case of Pakistan, number may be greater. Pakistan's nuclear weapons programme is mostly uranium based instead mostly of plutonium based in case of India, and Pakistan is believed to have estimated 1.1 tons of highly enriched uranium. Albright placed Russia, Pakistan, India and China among the list of vulnerable countries in terms of nuclear safety. *Times of India*, 9 September 2005.

The report is available at ISIS-online.crg/publications/southasia/ch-indpak.html

71. Robert, S. Norris, *et. al.*, "India's Nuclear Forces 2002", *Bulletin of The Atomic Scientists*, Vol. 58, No. 02, March/April 2002. p. 2.
72. Srinjoy Chowdhury, "Sukhois Capable of Hitting Chinese Targets", *Statesman*, 28 September 2002.
73. Raj Chengappa's account suggests that India first attempted to mate externally carried nuclear weapons pods with the Jaguar and later shifted to the Mirage-2000 for this mission. Chengappa, n. 52, pp. 327 and 382-84.
74. For details of Pakistan's nuclear capable F-16, see Tariq Mahmood Ashraf, *Air Power Imbalance and Strategic Instability in South Asia*, National Postgraduate School, Monterey, CA, 2005.
75. Since the early 1990s India and Pakistan have been steadily moving their nuclear deterrence from aircraft based to ballistic missile based with potentially devastating results for the South Asian stability. The introduction of nuclear capable ballistic missiles on a significant scale adds to the negative variables that collectively raise the risk of an inadvertent nuclear war breaking out in a region that is unstable principally due to the Kashmir territorial dispute. Ben Sheppard, "Ballistic Missiles: Complicating the Nuclear Quagmire", in D.R. Sardesai and Raju G.C. Thomas, eds., *Nuclear India in the Twenty First Century*, Palgave-Macmillan, New York, 2002, p. 189.
76. The *Prithvi* class of missiles is a road mobile, single stage, liquid fuelled, short range missile that employs propulsion technology from the Soviet SA-2 surface to air (SAM) missile. The *prithvi* is otherwise Indian in design. The *prithvi* program began in 1983 and was test fired in 1988. Three basic types *prithvis* currently exit. The *Prithvi*-I has a range sufficient to strike any significant target if deployed anywhere along the Indian border. The Indian army has reportedly ordered 100 of these missiles, which entered into serial production in 1997 and reportedly can be equipped with 5 types of warheads. A longer range variant of *Prithvi*-I, the *Prithvi*-II (SS-250), an air force version has also been developed. Underdevelopment is a *Prithvi*-III (SS-350), which will be used for naval purposes. This third variant also known as Dhanush, may be solid fueled. It is believed to be derived from the Russian SA-2. Published reports in September 2000 indicated an Indian government decision to proceed with production of 300 Prithvi missiles. "India to Make 300 Prithvi Missiles", The Hindu, 8 September 2000.
77. Norris, n. 71, p. 3.
78. The *Agni* missiles have been developed, reportedly with distant China as well as nearby Pakistan in mind, and have been tested in three versions, with a forth, intended to be of longer range, underdevelopment. The first variant, *Agni*-I, was demonstrated in various tests to ranges between 900 and 1200 km, and the second variant, *Agni*-II, to ranges between 1200 and 2000 km, each with notional payloads of 1000 kg. A third variant referred as again *Agni*-I, is Pakistan specific with a range of 700 km. This Pakistan specific missile reportedly weighs twelve tons and evidently uses only solid

fuel propulsion. It presumably lighter in weight than the variants with the liquid fuel engines, and easier to mount on road-mobile transport-erector-launchers (TELs) or on the rail road launch cars, India reportedly has been developing. A forth variant, *Agni*-III intended for ranges closer to 3000 km (using three sold fuel stages) with a 1000 kg payload has been tested, and is underdevelopment. See The Military Balance, 2003-04, IISS, London, 2003, p. 131.

79. Brahmos missile is a product of an Indo-Russian joint venture. Brahmos is a cruise missile which cruises horizontally and travels only in the atmosphere. It is a two stage vehicle that has a solid propellant booster and liquid propellant ramjet system. The Brahmos is the first and the only supersonic cruise missile that uses liquid ramjet technology. It cruises in the atmosphere at the speed faster than sound. It has been rated at 290 km in range when surface launched using the supersonic boost state, it may be capable of longer ranges if used only in sub-sonic mode or when launched from aircraft. It has been configured to launch from ground including silos and ships, submarines and aircrafts. Besides, it can blast off from a mobile platform on land, that is, from a vehicle. One may assume it as a nuclear capable, if equipped with a small enough nuclear warhead. For details, see Rahul Datta, "India to Go in for Cruise Missiles", *The Pioneer*, 15 June 2001. "Brahmos Launch a Big Breakthrough", *The Hindu*, October 30, 2003, "Before You Can Say Brahmos", *Hindustan Times*, 30 October 2003, "Brahmos Flight Tested", *The Hindu*, 30 October 2003, "Anti-ship Version of Brahmos Proves it Mettle", *The Hindu*, 3 December 2003., and R. Prasanam, "India Enters The Cruise Missile Race; Hyplane Avatar Reaches Planning State", available at http://www.google.com

80. *Hatf*-I theoretically could be nuclear capable but there are no credible reports that it is a nuclear equipped missile. *Federation of American Scientists*, Washington D.C., 9 March 2000, available at http://www.fas.org/nuke/guide/pakistan/missile/hatf-I.htm.

81. *Hatf*-III and *Hatf*-IV resemble to the Chinese export type designated M-11 and M-9 respectively. The Chinese designation of M-9 is DF-15 and of M-11 is DF-11. Here is a point to be noted that some confusion exists in the various published sources regarding the Pakistani designations of its own missiles (e.g. on *Hatf* sequence numbers, and on the names *Shaheen*-II, *Shadoz, Abdali* and *Ghaznavi*). See the *Federation of American Scientists* Website for characteristics of Chinese missile systems and what is believed to have been exported to Pakistan. http://www.fas.org/nuke/guide/china/theater/df-11.htm.

82. The name *'Ghauri'* is highly symbolic and taken from a Muslim historical figure, Sultan Muhammed (Shahubiddin) *Ghauri* who defeated the Hindu ruler Prithvi Raj in the last decade of 12th century. *"Prithvi"* is the name India has assigned to its short range ballistic missile. Thus Pakistan is attempting to manipulate public perceptions and show that it has developed a credible response to Indian missile capabilities. http;//www.pakmilitary.com/army/missles/ghauri.html.

83. For numerical trend data in the India-Pakistan military balance, see Rodney, W. Jones, "Force Modernization Trends: India and Pakistan", *Conventional Arms Modernization in Asia and the Pacific,* Asia Pacific Centre for Security Studies, Honolulu. http: www.policyarchitects.org/pdf/ForceModern_indiapakistan2.pdf. Also see Rodney W. Jones, "Conventional Military Asymmetry and Stability Among Emerging Nuclear States:India and Pakistan", *Forth Nuclear Stability Roundtable Conference on Strategic Stability and Global Change,* 12-13 March 2002. http: www.policyarchitects.org/pdf/NucStability_indiapakistan.pdf. Also see Devin T. Hegerty, "South Asia's Nuclear Balance", Current History, Vol. 95, April 1996.
84. It is not officially declared by government of India whether *Prithvi* missile is a nuclear or conventional warhead delivery system. Most of the strategic experts who have followed *Prithvi's* development concluded that it is a nuclear capable system and intended to send that message. Pravin Sawney, "Standing Alone : India's Nuclear Imperative", *Jane's International Defense Review,* November 1996, p. 28. Also see, Chengappa, n. 52, pp. 319-20, 361, 418.
85. Chengappa, *Ibid,* pp. 374-75.
86. Neil Joeck, "Maintaining Nuclear Stability in South Asia", *Adelphi Paper No. 312,* International Institute for Strategic Studies, London, 1997, pp. 68-69.
87. A number of reports suggest that India is interested in purchasing the jointly developed US-Israeli Arrow missile defense system from Israel. Because the US has played a major financial and scientific role in developing the Arrow, any legal export of the system by Israel would likely require prior US approval. Both the Senate and House Armed Services Committee have expressed reservations about a possible sale to India or other countries and reportedly have the following concerns:

    (i) Although the Arrow is a defensive system, it could possibly be reengineered into an offensive system.
    (ii) Its sale could possibly trigger a regional offensive arms race.
    (iii) Israel has allegedly transferred or attempted to transfer critical military technologies to countries of concern such as China.
    (iv) Such a sale could violate the provisions of the MTCR, to which US is a party.
    (v) Israel would profit from the sale of a product largely paid for by the United States and might also constitute competition to Raytheon's US patriot missile system.

    Andrew Feickert and K. Alan Kronstadt, "Missile Proliferation and the Strategic Balance in South Asia", *CRS Report RL 32115,* 17 October 2003, pp. 15-16. Also see John Donnelly, "Congress Warns Bush, Israel on Arrow Exports", *Defense Week,* Vol. 24, No. 22, 2 June 2003, p. 1.
88. *Ibid.* p. 16.

89. Ramatanu Maitra, "An Arrow to Washington's Heart", *Asia Times Online*, 20 August 2002; http: www.atimes.com/atimes/South_Asia/DH20Df0d.htm
90. George Koblentz, "Viewpoint: Theater Missile Defense and South Asia: A Volatile Mix", *The Nonproliferation Review*, Spring-Summer 1997, p. 55.
91. Shishir Gupta, "India Hopes for Patriot Nod", *Indian Express*, Bombay, 23 May 2003.
92. Kolentz, n. 90, p. 56.
93. Both India and Pakistan are believed to have their nuclear warheads and bombs separated from their missile and delivery aircrafts, thus providing a degree of security from undetected first use or accidental launch.
94. Kolentz, n. 90, p. 56.
95. Figure for power and range of the Phalcon's phased array radars and emission detection and location sensors are not publicly advertised but those for the aircraft detection and tracking radar are given as "several hundred kilometers", even for low flying aircraft. See http://www.globalsecurity.org/military/world/israel/phalcon.htm.
96. Paul, J. Bracken, *The Command and Control of Nuclear Forces*, Yale University Press, New Haven, 1983, p. 13.
97. For details see, Ashton B. Carter, *et al.*, eds., *Managing Nuclear Operations*, The Brooking Institution, Washington DC, 1987.
98. "Draft Report of National Security Advisory Board on Indian Nuclear Doctrine",http://www.indianembassy.org/policy/CTBT/nucleardoctrine aug 17 1999.html_.
99. "India Acquires Sophisticated Radars from Israel", *Indian Express*, 28 June 2002.
100. One reason for the refusal is Israel's decision to stockpile Arrow missile interceptors. Barbará Opall-Rome, "Israel Boosts Arrow Arsenal as War Looms", *Defense News*, 25 November 1 to December 2002.
101. "TES could be India's First Eye in the Sky", *Hindustan Times*, 24 October 2001.
102. Agha Shahi, Zulfiqar Ali Khan and Abdul Sattar, "Securing Nuclear Peace", *The News*, 5 October 1999.
103. "Geo-stationary satellite by year-end: Ata", *The Dawn*, 23 January 2002. http://www.dawn.com/ 2002/01/23/nat1.htm_.
104. In the United States, North American Aerospace Defense Command (NORAD) manages the task of detecting and assessing ballistic missile launches. Though most of the details about its operation are secret, independent analysts have managed to construct a broadly consistent picture of the general procedures that are followed. One such reconstruction is offered by Bruce Blair based on interviews with former NORAD officers. This can be simplified and summarized as a sequence of events with their allotted duration:

    (i) Observation of missile launch by satellites in geosynchronous orbit and relay of signal to ground stations for processing (half a minute after launch).

(ii) Decision by the ground station staff whether to forward this information to NORAD and other command centers assessing missile warnings (about 15seconds).

(iii) Convening of Missile Event Conference at NORAD. Command director would assess the reliability of satellite data, based on telephone communications with ground station operators, who would reverify the initial detection and confirm that it was not due to equipment malfunction. Strategic warning analysts, who look at intelligence estimates of the international political and military situation, and force deployments, are also consulted. The command director would then forward the level of confidence in the warning to the war rooms at the Pentagon and Strategic Command (3 minutes).

(iv) About four minutes after a possible missile launch, if the NORAD officer judged there was medium or high confidence in a warning, the information would go up the chain of command, that included the Joint Chiefs of Staff Chairman, and Defense Secretary, ultimately leading up to the President, and a Missile Attack Conference would be initiated. By this time, there may or may not have been separate warning from ground-based radars (4–6 minutes).

(v) There would now be less than 20 minutes remaining from the initial 30-minute flight time (assuming a Soviet ICBM). This would leave about 10 minutes for discussion, before a decision would have to be made whether US missiles were to be launched, rather than to ride out an attack in which the US ICBMs and early warning would be possibly destroyed.

(vi) If the decision was made to fire US missiles, it would take two minutes to send launch orders, three minutes to fire the Minuteman ICBMs, and several more minutes for the missiles to travel to a safe distance from their bases. This timeline adds up to about 30 minutes, which is comparable to an ICBM flight time from Russia, and would enable the retaliatory missiles to take-off just before the silos are destroyed. However, all of this assumes that every procedural and physical element in the early warning system works perfectly.

There is less information about Soviet (and now Russian) early warning systems. One description, again by Bruce Blair, suggests the following expected sequence of events following detection by satellites or ground-based radars of a possible missile launch:

(i) Positive attack identification from satellites (about one minute after launch) or radar would lead to a warning report by the Center for the Analysis of Missile and Space Situation, the Russian counterpart of NORAD, to Defense headquarters, general staff, and strategic rocket forces.
(ii) This center would send a signal to the President, Defense Minister, and Chief of General Staff (through the nuclear suitcase).

(iii) within 4–6 minutes after a missile launch, political and military leadership along with chief of early warning center would confer on warning.

(iv) If the early warning system provides dual sensor (i.e., radar and satellite) warning of attack, then general staff would send preliminary command activating communications system to nuclear forces. This communication link is normally kept disconnected.

(v) According to Russian procedures, the national command authority (President and Defense Minister) is allotted three minutes to discuss and authorize (or withhold) permission to launch Russian missiles.

(vi) To institute and transmit the launch order, with the unlock codes, takes about 2–3 minutes. A total of 12–13 minutes would have elapsed since incoming missile liftoff.

(vii) Once the order has been received it takes as long as 8 minutes for the Russian missiles to emerge from their silos. A total of about 20 minutes would have elapsed between the time of launch of the enemy attack and the launch of the Russian missiles.

Russian procedures are thus designed to beat the expected arrival time of ICBMs from the continental United States by a margin of 10 minutes. Russian concerns that these procedures may not work as planned led them to install in addition a "dead hand" that would automatically transmit launch orders.

For details see, Bruce G. Blair, *Global Zero Alert for Nuclear Forces,* Brookings Institution, Washington DC 1995, pp. 46-50; Michael D. Wallace *et al.*, "Accidental Nuclear War: A Risk Assessment", *Journal of Peace Studies,* Vol. 23. No. 1, March 1986, pp. 9-27; Pavel Podvig, "The Operational Status of the Russian Space-Based Early Warning System", *Science and Global Security,* Vol. 4, No. 3, 1994, pp. 363-84; Pavel Podvig, "History and Current Status of the Russian Early Warning System", *Science and Global Security,* Vol. 10, No. 1 2002, pp. 21-60., and Pavel Podvig, ed., Russian Strategic Nuclear Forces Cambridge, MA: The MIT Press, 2001, p. 438.

105. Bruce Blair, *The Logic of Accidental Nuclear War,* Brookings Institution *Press,* Washington, DC, 1993, pp. 342-43. Also see H.L. Abrams, "Strategic Defense and Inadvertent Nuclear War", in H. Wiberg, *et al.*, eds , *Inadvertent Nuclear War: The Implications of the Changing Global Order,* Pergamon Press, Oxford, 1993, pp. 39-55.

106. Ballistic missiles have a basic elliptically shaped trajectory. They are usually launched vertically, then turn towards the target during the boost phase whilst the motors are burning. The maximum speed is reached at the end of the boost phase, and the missile then coasts towards the target. The highest point of the trajectory is the apogee, and the missile is flying at its slowest speed then. After apogee the

missile accelerates as it returns towards the earth, and reaches maximum speed again just before re-entry into the atmosphere. Re-entry begins when the missile begins to be slowed down by the atmosphere, usually considered to be from 120 km altitude. Following re-entry, the missile slows as it descends towards the target. There are three major types of trajectory. The longest range is achieved by a 'minimum energy' trajectory, which has an apogee around 20 per cent of the range. The missile trajectory can be 'lofted' to a higher apogee, but this shortens the range and increases the flight time. This can be used to fly over a defensive system, and results in a steeper re-entry trajectory with a greater maximum speed. Alternatively, the missile trajectory can be 'depressed' to a lower apogee, which shortens the range and reduces the flight time. This can be used to fly below a defensive system and reduce the warning time provided by ground-based radars. The depressed trajectory has a flatter re-entry angle, and the highest re-entry speed.

107. An example of what came close to being a common mode failure was the case of the January 1968 crash of a B-52 over the early warning radar installed at Thule, Greenland. There was concern that the breakdown of communication from the radar could have been mistaken as an attack on the radar, a likely precursor to a full scale nuclear attack. To minimize such a misunderstanding, a B-52 bomber was constantly on airborne patrol over the radar to provide confirmation that the radar had not been attacked. If the bomber which crashed had destroyed the radar in the process, that would have given a dual signal to NORAD that a Soviet attack was underway, leading to increased alerts and possibly a nuclear attack. Scott D. Sagan, *The Limits of Safety: Organizations, Accidents and Nuclear Weapons*, Princeton University Press, Princeton, 1993, pp. 156-203.
108. It has been argued that in complex systems accidents are inevitable. See Charles Perrow, *Normal Accidents: Living with High-Risk Technologies*, Basic Books, New York, 1984.
109. *Ibid.*
110. For an elaboration of this argument see, M.V. Ramana, "Risks of Launch on Warning Posture", *Economic and Political Weekly*, 1 March 2003, pp. 860–64.
111. Christopher Walker and Michael Evans, "Pakistan Feared Israeli Attack", *The Times*, 3 June 1998. It has also been reported that Pakistan alerted its own F-16s during the crisis, which at least raises the possibility that the Pakistani intelligence services were issuing warnings based on Pakistani aircraft, not Israeli, located by radars installations in Pakistan. See Hanif Khalid, "Pakistan Moves to Stop Indo-Israeli Attack", *Rawalpindi Jang*, 4 June 1998; and John, F. Burns, "Nuclear Anxiety: the Indian Response", *New York Times*, 30 May 1998, p. 8.
112. The cause of the Ojheri explosion appears to have been a fire caused by an accidental rocket explosion during loading at the depot. It has also been claimed, however, that the "accident" was actually a deliberate act of sabotage against the munitions dump. See

Muhammad Yousaf and Mark Adkin, *The Bear Trap: Afghanistan's Untold Story* at http://www.afghanbooks.com/beartrap/and Samina Ahmed and David C. Courtright, eds., *Pakistan and the Bomb: Public Opinion and Options*, University of Notre Dame Press, Notre Dame, 1998, p. 96.

113. For example, on January 4, 2001, Indian Defence Secretary, Yogender Narain, led a special inspection of the Milan missile production facility in Hyderabad. The Milan missile--a short-range (2 kilometer) missile normally armed with a large conventional warhead had failed in test launches and during the Kargil war and Narain was to discuss the matter with the plants' managers and technical personnel. For reasons that remain unclear, the electrical circuitry was not disconnected and the live conventional warhead was not capped on the missile displayed for the visiting dignitary from New Delhi when the plant manager accidentally touched the start button, the missile launched, flew through the body of one official, killing him instantly and then nose-dived into the ground, catching on fire and injuring five other workers. The defence secretary was shocked, but unharmed. The official killed was the quality control officer for the Milan missile program. For detail see, "Doubts over BDL Safety Norms", *The Hindu*, 9 January 2001; "One Killed as Missile Fires Accidentally", *The Hindu*, 5 January 2001; "One Killed as Missile Misfires During Demonstration", *The Times of India*, 5 January 2001; and Lalita Iyer, "In House Strike", *The Week*, 21 January 2001, at http://www.the-week.com/21jan21/events6.htm. Similar rocket explosions have occurred with other nuclear powers. For example, in 1960, the commander of erstwhile Soviet Union's Strategic Rocket Forces was killed, along with many others, when a space rocket exploded while being inspected prior to launch. See James E. Oberg, *Uncovering Soviet Disasters*, Random House, New York, 1988, pp. 177-83.
114. T.S. Subramanian, "Issues of Safety: Former AERB Chairman Speaks Out", *Frontline*, 23 August 1996, pp. 105-07; A. Gopalakrishnan, "Disturbing Lack of Safety", *Frontline*, 23 August 1996, pp. 107-10; A. Gopalakrishnan, "Issues of Nuclear Safety", *Frontline*, 26 March 1999, pp. 82-85; and A.S. Panneerselvan, "Nuclear Safety: Radioactivity", *Outlook*, 19 June 2000.
115. Agha Shahi, "Command and Control of Nuclear Weapons in South Asia", Strategic Issues, Special Issue: *The Nuclear Debate*, No. 3, March 2000, p. 60.
116. Gurmeet Kanwal, "Command and Control of Nuclear Weapons", *Strategic Analysis*, Vol. 23, No. 10 January 2000, p. 1728.
117. Herbert, L. Abrams, "Human Reliability and Safety in the Handling of Nuclear Weapons", *Science and Global Security*, Vol. 2, 1991, pp. 325-49.
118. Pakistani Foreign Minister Abdul Sattar announced in June 2001 that Pakistan was studying the possible adoption of a PRP system. See http://www.ceip.org/files/projects/npp/resources/Conference%202001/sattar.htm.
119. *"Ashcroft Statement On 'Dirty Bomb' Suspect"*, CNN.com, 10 June 2002. http://www.cnn.com/2002/US/06/10/ashcroft.announcement/

120. Steven, E. Koonin, *"Radiological Terrorism"*, Statement before the Senate Foreign Relations Committee, 6 March 2002; http://units.aps.org/units/fps/newsletters/2002/april/cap02.cfm
121. "The Radiological Accident in Goiania", *International Atomic Energy Agency*, Vienna, 1988, http://www-pub.iaea.org/MTCD/publications/PDF/Pub0815_web.pdf. In Goiania, Brazil in 1987, scavengers rummaging through the remains of an abandoned health facility acquired a Cesium-137 source encased in a lead canister. The canister, filled with a "luminous blue powder" (Cs-137), found its way into the hands of children, friends, and family of the scavengers. Lacking any knowledge of the potential dangers of the powder, many came into contact with the sources, and several ingested it. Contamination continued throughout the small city until it was reported to the Brazilian government officials a week after the canister was opened. This well-documented case can be used as a point of reference for public response to a radiological incident. The impacts of the radioactive contamination of Goiania were both short-term and long-term. The immediate impact was difficult but not unmanageable. Over 100,000 people were screened for radioactive contamination, over 100 people were contaminated, and four people died. The longer-term psychological and economic effects, however, devastated the city and its inhabitants. Due to public perceptions and misperceptions, tourism to the area was down forty percent and still has not fully recovered. Agricultural and textile prices decreased by fifty percent. Fear of contamination was high and most places in Brazil boycotted goods from Goiania. Alex Niefert, "Case Study: Accidental Leakage of Cesium-137 in Goiania, Brazil, in 1987", *NBC-MED* Online; http://www.nbcme.dorg/SiteContent/MedRef/OnlineRef/CaseStudies /csgoiania.html
122. See Charles Ferguson, Tahseen Kazi and Judith Perera, *Commercial Radioactive Sources: Surveying the Security Risks*, Monterey Institute of International Studies, January 2003; and Peter D. Zimmerman and Cheryl Loeb, "Dirty Bombs: The Threat Revisited", *Defense Horizons*, No. 38, January 2004.
123. Lyudmila Zaitseva and Kevin Hand, "Nuclear Smuggling Chains, Suppliers, Intermediaries, and End-Users", *American Behavioral Scientist*, No. 6, February 2003, pp. 822-44, newsservice.stanford.edu/news/march6/database-36.html
124. A. Kumar *et al.*, *Safety and Security of Radioactive Materials--the Indian Scenario*, Bhabha Atomic Research Center, Trambay, Mumbai, 1998.
125. "Radioactive Material Worth Rs. 1.5 Mn Stolen", *Times of India*, 17 August 2003.
126. Alpha radiation can be blocked simply with a piece of paper; beta radiation requires only a thin piece of metal or glass for effective shielding; and gamma radiation requires thick lead or concrete. While shielding can protect individuals from radioactivity in their environment, internal damage will result if radioactive particles are inhaled or ingested. Attributes of radioactive material that are particularly important with respect to RDDs are half-life and activity. The half-life of a material is defined as the length of time it will take

for half of it to radioactively decay. An effective dirty bomb has a half-life that is neither too short nor too long. Radioactive sources with very short half-lives (hours or minutes or less) do not last long enough to give terrorists sufficient time to produce radiological weapons with those substances; nor do they exist long enough to contaminate places for an appreciable time. In contrast, those sources with very long half-lives (millions of more years) release radiation at much slower rates and typically would not be ideal for radiological weapons devised to maximize the output of radiation during a relatively short time period—the human timescale. Here the two gamma radiation sources Cobalt-60 (Co-60) and Cesium-137 (Cs-137) will be important for the terrorist use of RDDs. "Commercial Radioactive Sources: Surveying the Security Risks", *Monterey Institute of International Studies,* January 2003, p. 3. The activity of a material corresponds to the number of radioactive disintegrations per second. A common unit of measure of activity is the Curie (Ci), which corresponds to 37 billion decays per second. Naturally occurring radioactivity in the food that we eat or the air that we breathe contains miniscule amounts of radioactive activity (on the order of 10-11 Curies). By contrast, radioactive sources with levels of radioactivity from tens of Curies to a few thousand Curies could cause massive contamination if used in an RDD. The specific activity of a material is the activity per unit mass, which can be expressed in units of Curies per gram (Ci/g). Very dangerous levels of radioactivity require only a small amount of the substance for materials with a large specific activity. For example, merely nine grams of Cobalt-60—or the equivalent of two paper clips worth of material—can be used to make a dirty bomb that could cause mass disruption.

127. The effects caused by exposure to radiation on human health are medically classified as either deterministic or stochastic. An example of a deterministic health effect is radiation sickness. Here the health effect can be directly related to the radiation exposure as cause and effect. An example of a stochastic health effect would be cancer. Exposure to low levels of radiation over time will increase that risk, but in most cases individual cancers cannot be identified as the result of radiation exposure. The unit of measure of human radiation exposure, Roentgen Equivalent Man(REM), is a unit of measurement of the effect of ionizing radiation on the human body. Human beings typically receive 0.3 REM/year from natural sources of radioactivity and an additional 0.06 REM/year due to the lingering after-effects of atmospheric nuclear weapons tests for a total exposure of 0.36 REM/year. "How Does Radiation Effect the Public", *Nuclear Regulatory Commission,* 23 June 2003, http://www.nrc.gov/what-we-do/radiation/affect.html.

128. The radiation dose calculations in terms of Total Effective Dose Equivalent (TEDE) includes doses from radioactive material deposited on the ground, suspended in the air, and inhaled over a period of four days. In the United States, the TEDE calculated for an accident scenario is often used to understand what protective

action for the public is required by federal guidelines. The US Environmental Protection Agency (EPA) considers health effects possible for TEDE of fifty or above. A TEDE of one is the EPA's Protective Action Guide (PAG) limit. A calculated TEDE of ten or above would require evacuation under all circumstances from the contaminated area, whereas for a TEDE of one, taking shelter is recommended under hazardous environmental conditions. According to the US National Radiological Protection Board, deterministic effects generally arise shortly after exposure to a radiation dose, but only if this dose exceeds some threshold value. "What Effects Can Radiation Have on Health?" *National Radiological Protection Board 2004.* http://www.nrpb.org/faq/epidemiology/epid2.htm.

129. *Ibid.*
130. For exposure times less than one day, very high levels of acute radiation would be necessary for such short-term health effects. Deterministic health effects can occur for acute doses above ten to fifty REM. above 150 REM, death from radiation sickness is possible, with about half of all exposed persons dying who receive a dose of 600 REM. According to the EPA, stochastic effects are associated with "long-term, low-level (chronic) exposure to radiation and increased levels of exposure make these health effects more likely to occur, but do not influence the type or severity of the effect." "Understanding Radiation: Health Effects", *US Environmental Protection Agency,* 3 December 2002; http://www.epa.gov/radiation/understand/health_effects.htm#est_health_effects.
131. The nuclear regulatory bodies have established certain guidelines, which are an important benchmark for understanding the level of contamination in a given area. Within the United States, there is considerable debate about the amount of permissible radiation. The NRC, the International Atomic Energy Agency (IAEA), as well as the Health Physics Society (a non-governmental body of radiation experts) have set a limit of 0.1 REM/yr, or an additional four cancer deaths for every 100,000 people exposed. "What Effects Can Radiation Have on Health?" *National Radiological Protection Board,* 2004; http://www.nrpb.org/faq/epidemiology/epid2.htm.
132. *Special Weapons Primer: Nuclear Weapon Blast Effects,* Federation of American Scientists, Washington D.C., 21 October 1998, http://www.fas.org/nuke/intro/nuke/blast.htm.
133. Samuel Glasstone and Philip Dolan, *The Effects of Nuclear Weapons,* US Department of Defense, 1977, p. 38.
134. There are two types of radiation: initial radiation, which is emitted within the first minute after a detonation, and residual radiation, which is emitted thereafter. Residual radiation leads to the "fallout" effect.
135. Steve Fetter, "The Effects of Nuclear Detonations and Nuclear War", in Graham T. Allison Jr. *et al.*, eds., *A Primer for the Nuclear Age,* Occasional Paper, No. 6, Center for Science and International Affairs, Harvard University, MA: Cambridge, 1990, pp. 23-30.
136. This EMP effect is not limited to a high-yield weapon only but at low yields, it can also be extremely intense, as this effect is only weekly

dependent on yield. Although there is a 100,000 percent increase in weapon yield from a one KT device to a ten-megaton device, the maximum EMP effect only increases by twenty-five percent.Although the blast would destroy an area of approximately one square kilometer, the EMP from the nuclear detonation would be twenty-five times as large. Most of the electronics and communications capacity in this region would be ruined. If a nuclear weapon detonated near the Gateway of India in Mumbai, the blast effects would not reach out to the Mumbai stock exchange, but the EMP effect would be devastating. The greatest EMP effects would occur within the twenty-five square kilometers surrounding the blast, but even out to almost 100 square kilometers, the EMP damage would be significant. Post-detonation complications would be severe. Electronics and communication systems may be inoperable. Power grids may be affected in an area even outside the city limits. If this were to occur, communication among and between leaders could be compromised, as would be their transportation. With planes and helicopters using advanced avionics and with air trafficking systems affected, it is unclear whether transportation would be feasible. It took the United States and former Soviet Union decades to harden military nodes against EMP, and they are still susceptible to considerable damage. Just as importantly, US civilian systems are fully unprotected against such an attack.

137. Lisa Trei, "Database Exposes Threat from 'Lost' Nuclear Material", *Stanford Report*, Vol. 17, No. 22, Standford, 6 March 2002.

138. Lyudmila Zaitseva and Kevin Hand, "Nuclear Smuggling Chains, Suppliers, Intermediaries, and End-Users", *American Behavioral Scientist*, Vol. 46, No. 6, February 2003, pp. 822-44.

139. Z. Mian, M.V. Ramana, and R. Rajaraman, "Risks and Consequences of Nuclear Weapons Accidents in South Asia", *PU/CEES Report*, No. 326, September 2000.

140. In Palamores, it cost over $100 million to cleanup and repair the damage that was done to the surrounding environment. Luckily for all involved, the area where the accident occurred was not populated and the health effects were minimal. In Thule, four nuclear bombs carried by a B-52 bomber were engulfed in flames after the aircraft crashed. The high explosives surrounding each nuclear core detonated, resulting in the dispersal of nuclear material. It should be noted that in the case cited above, the B-52 was on alert. Steve Fetter and Frank Von Hippel, "The Hazard from Plutonium Dispersal by Nuclear-warhead Accidents", *Science and Global Security*, Vol. 2, No. 1, 1990, pp. 21-41.

141. Sidney Drell and Bob Peurifoy, "Technical Issues of a Nuclear Test Ban", *Annual Reviews of Nuclear and Particle Science*, Vol. 44, 1994, pp. 285-327.

142. *United States Nuclear Tests, July 1945 through September 1992*, http://www.fas.org/nuke/ guide/usa/nuclear/nv209nar.pdf.

143. Available online at http://nuclearweaponarchive.org/Russia/ Sovtestsum.html.

144. *Narrative Summaries of Accidents Involving U.S. Nuclear Weapons, 1950-1980,* U.S. Department of Defense in Coordination with Department of Energy, (Interim), 1981.
145. Jaya Tiwari and Cleve J. Gray, *"U.S. Nuclear Weapons Accidents"*, http://www.cdi.org/Issues/Nuke Accidents/accidents.htm
146. *Narrative Summaries of Accidents Involving U.S. Nuclear Weapons, 1950-1980,* U.S. Department of Defense in Coordination with Department of Energy, (Interim), 1981.
147. In the case of Palomares, 2.26 km2 were contaminated with high plutonium ground concentrations, in excess of 11.8 kBq/m2. E. Iranzo, S. Salvador and C.E. Iranzo, "Air Concentrations of 239Pu and 240Pu and Potential Radiation Doses to Persons Living near Pu-contaminated Areas in Palomares, Spain", *Health Physics,* Vol. 52, No. 4, April 1987, pp. 453-61.
148. William Arkin and Joshua Handler, "Naval Accidents 1945-1988", *Neptune Paper,* No. 3, Greenpeace
149. Shaun Gregory, *The Hidden Cost of Deterrence: Nuclear Weapons Accidents,* Brassey's, London, 1990, pp. 184-90.
150. *Ibid.,* p. 188.
151. *"Toxic Cloud Moves Along Russian Far Eastern Coast After Missile Fuel Leak"*, British Broadcasting Corporation, 16 June 2000.
152. Government of India, *Report of the Comptroller and Auditor General of India on the Ministry of Defence,* 1997; http://www.cagindia.org/reports/defence/1998_book1/index.htm.
153. Ayaz Ahmad Khan, "Air Accidents in Spite of High Efficiency", *Defence Journal,* August 1998. http://www.defencejournal.com/aug98/airaccidents.htm.
154. The most common type of nitric acid used as an oxidizer is RFNA (red fuming nitric acid) which consists of concentrated nitric acid that contains 5 to 20% dissolved nitrogen dioxide. Since nitric acid has a high specific gravity (1.5 to 1.6), it allows for a smaller missile. Compared to concentrated nitric acid (also called *white fuming nitric acid*) RFNA is more energetic, stable in storage and less corrosive to many tank materials. In order to make this even less corrosive, a little Hydrogen Flouride is added, which causes a flouride layer to form on the wall of the container, thus inhibiting the action of the nitric acid. This combination is called IRFNA. IRFNA gives off red-brown fumes that are poisonous and droplets on the skin cause burns and sores that do not heal readily. George P. Sutton, *Rocket Propulsion Elements: An Introduction to the Engineering of Rockets,* John Wiley and Sons, New York, 1992, p. 251.
155. For example see, Hormuz Mama, "Improved Prithvi Missile Launched", *International Defense Review,* 1 August 1992, p. 784.
156. David Wright, "An Analysis of the Pakistani Ghauri Missile Test of April 6, 1998", *Science and Global Security,* Vol. 7, No. 2, 1998; Joseph S. Bermudez, "A History of Ballistic Missile Development in the DPRK", Occasional Paper, No. 2, Monterey Institute of International Studies, Center for Non-Proliferation Studies, 1999; However, it has also been suggested that Ghauri may use RP1 (Kerosene) as fuel.

S. Chandrashekar, "The Origins and Antecedents of the Ghauri Missile—An Assessment", *Current Science,* Vol. 76, No. 3, 10 February 1999, pp. 280-85.

157. David Wright and Timur Kadyshev, "An Analysis of the North Korean Nodong Missile", *Science and Global Security,* Vol. 4, No. 2, 1994, pp. 129-60.
158. Chengappa, n. 34, p. 362 .
159. Greg Gerardi, "India's 333rd Prithvi Missile Group", *Jane's Intelligence Review,* Vol. 7, No. 8, 1995, pp. 361-64.

3

India's Missile Programme

The acquisition of ballistic and cruise missile capabilities as the delivery systems of conventional or weapons of mass destruction (WMD) is now at the top of the security agenda for many countries of the world. These delivery systems are of particular concern to already distorted security environment in many regions of Asia, because when tipped with conventional high explosive warheads or nuclear/chemical/biological warheads, they present a combination of capabilities and features unmatched by any other weapon.[1]

In case of South Asia, ballistic missiles were introduced just about two decades ago. Missile development programmes in the 1980s proceeded in tandem with covert nuclear weapons development but in 1990s, these programmes raised the proliferation concerns particularly after the 1998 nuclear tests and open declaration of India and Pakistan as having the status of nuclear weapon states. That's why both India and Pakistan have given high importance to ballistic missiles because these are the most reliable vehicles for the delivery of nuclear weapons intended to inflict mass destruction. Ballistic missiles are symbols of military power, and their speed and accuracy make it virtually impossible to take effective defensive measures against them.

These characteristics of ballistic missiles enhance the credibility of a nuclear deterrent based on their assured delivery capacity. The inherent vulnerability to a ballistic missile attack also endows a missile-based offensive nuclear force with exceptional psychological influence.[2]

India is situated in such an environment, which is confronted with increasing missile threats and deep-rooted animosities. It is surrounded with short and long-range ballistic missiles from China and Pakistan in the North and Indian Ocean in the West where the foreign naval fleets make their presence with sophisticated missile systems. Israel, Saudi Arabia and Iran also have missiles, which have negative security implications for India. In this situation India needs a true nuclear deterrent, a proven warhead with a proven delivery system. The land, sea and air delivery systems are the most necessary for the deterrence to be established. These delivery systems must be tested and deployed before a deterrent force is complete. Until the 1998 nuclear explosions, it was widely assumed that although India had proven credible designs for nuclear weapons but it had not perfected the missile-based delivery systems. Prior to 1998 nuclear tests, India's covert nuclear capability was deliverable by means of transport and fighter aircrafts alone. The impetus to missile delivery and the ballistic and cruise missile development programme is a post-*Pokhran*-II development. Additional inputs to the missile programme have come from the border conflict at *Kargil* in 1999 and the operation *Parakram* in 2002.[3]

Among all the developing states with aspirations for WMDs and long-range power projection capabilities, India alone has achieved a unique degree of success. Outside the group of the five legally accepted nuclear weapon states and Israel, India perhaps harbors the most sophisticated ballistic and cruise missile programmes in the world.[4] India's strategic missile programmes have matured to the extent that now it can deploy short and medium-range nuclear-tipped ballistic missiles in an operational mode against Pakistan and China.[5] Four decades of investments in a missile-related design, development, and manufacturing infrastructure have also made this sector less vulnerable to long-term disruption by technology denial regimes. More significantly, India's sophisticated civilian satellite launch capability makes it one of the few developing states theoretically capable of building an intercontinental ballistic missile (ICBM) within a decade.

Since May 1998 nuclear tests India has stepped up its missile programme developing not only land-based ballistic missiles but also sea launched missiles as India's minimum nuclear deterrent doctrine envisions a triadic nuclear defence. In addition to having acquired an extensive research and development infrastructure, India continues to acquire latest technologies from other states, particularly from Russia. The first phase of Indian missile programme, which is stretched from 1958 to 1970, starts with the establishment of the Defence Research and Development Organization (DRDO) in January 1958. The main aim of this organization was to make the country self-reliant in weapons and weapon systems and equipments. While negotiations were on for purchase of SA-2 surface-to-air missiles from the erstwhile Soviet Union, attempts were also made to build a missile system under a project based on collaboration with the Swiss, called 'Project Indigo.' The latter was given up in favour of former and the first SA-2s missiles were delivered in 1965-66.[6] During this phase, India's missile ambitions were confined to building a first-generation anti-tank guided missile (ATGM) and developing a three-ton thrust, liquid-fueled rocket engine most likely based on the Soviet SA-2 sustainer motor. The DRDO undertook both these projects with the objective of gaining scientific expertise and creating a technological infrastructure to build modern missiles indigenously in the long-term. There were no plans for the immediate serial production of missile systems. However, the DRDO's technical and organizational shortcomings, opposition from the armed services, and weak support from politicians and civilian bureaucrats in the government resulted in the failure and ultimately termination of both projects.[7]

The second phase of India's missile development programme seems to be affected from its civilian space programme. This phase spans the decade of the 1970s.[8] It was the time when the space programme was entering threshold capabilities.[9] The Indian missile programme effectively began in 1967 as a space programme and by 1972 had developed and test fired the *Rohini*-560 two stage, solid propulsion sounding rocket, which could reach an altitude of 334 km with a 100 kg payload.

A series of *Rohini* Rockets with varied ranges and payloads were subsequently produced and are in service. India first launched its small 17-tone Satellite Launch Vehicle SLV-3 space booster (300km/40kg) in 1979 and in 1980 successfully injected the 35 kg *Rohini*-1 satellite into near earth orbit.[10] During this period, the DRDO undertook two significant projects. The first, Project *Devil*, was an attempt to "reverse-engineering" of the Soviet SA-2 surface-to-air missile (SAM). The second, Project *Valiant*, was an ambitious attempt to develop a 1,500 km-range ballistic missile. Both projects emanated from encouragements given to the scientists in the DRDO by the Prime Minister and some influential bureaucratic advisors to Prime Minister. Design competence and political symbolism were the primary objectives of both projects. For these reasons and because of the peculiarities of India's civil-military relations, the armed services were kept at the margins of the decision-making process. But India lacked the scientific, engineering, and industrial base to build a long-range ballistic missile. Consequently, due to faltering progress, the Indian government terminated the *Valiant* programme in 1974. On the other hand, Project *Devil* proved to be a partial success. Although Indian engineers were unable to reverse-engineer the SA-2 missile system entirely, they apparently succeeded in developing two solid-fuel boosters and a three-ton, liquid-sustainer engine for the *Devil* missile.

The Indian government revived the missile program in 1980 by launching the Integrated Guided Missile Development Programme (IGMDP) under the aegis of DRDO in 1983 to develop a family of strategic and tactical guided missiles. The launch of IGMDP marks the third phase in Indian missile development programme, which spans up to mid-1990s. The aim of the programme was to design, develop and produce five missile systems and to demonstrate the re-entry technology through the *Agni* project. The original cost of the programme as sanctioned in July 1983 was Rs. 358.83 crore which was later revised to Rs. 784.06 crore. It also has foreign exchange provision of Rs. 291.17 crore. As many as 78 laboratories/academic institutions/public/private institutions were associated with the design and development of the project.[11] The motivations behind this decision were significant. The Indian government felt that the foreign arms suppliers were often reluctant to sell the kind of missiles demanded by the Indian armed forces. Moreover, the cost of imported missiles was often prohibitive and the missiles themselves were invariably not of the current generation. Even the then Soviet Union, the foremost arms supplier to India, had refused to sell some of its most advanced and latest missiles. Manufacturers of sophisticated missile systems were not willing to sell India because this country had successfully tested a nuclear device in 1974. Indian government thought that indigenous missiles would not only incorporate the very latest technologies but is also likely to reduce dependence on the imports of critical parts. The Indian government also wanted the design-production-deployment cycle to be drastically shortened.[12] The IGMDP involved the development of two strategic ballistic missile systems: two variants of a short-range ballistic missile (*Prithvi*), and a medium-range technology demonstrator (*Agni*). Under the programme, the DRDO also sought to develop medium and short-range SAMs (*Akash* and *Trishul*), and a third-generation ATGM (*Nag*). The years 1980-94, the third phase in India's missile programme, marked a turning point. During this period, India's forays into missile building were transformed from exercises in technology-gathering, reverse-engineering, and design competence into a full-fledged programme to build a series of operational missile systems. By 1996-97, the successful development of the *Prithvi*-1 (150 km-range) provided India with the technical option to deploy a limited nuclear strike capability against Pakistan. Similarly, two successful flight-tests of the 1,400 km-range *Agni* missile validated India's "re-entry vehicle" technology. The *Agni* programme thus served as a building block for the design and development of longer-range ballistic missile systems that would provide India with a nuclear strike capability against China in the future.

The fourth phase of India's strategic missile programme stretches from the mid-1990s until 2000. This phase was characterized by the partial success of IGMDP, and limited serial production of the *Prithvi* and *Agni* ballistic missiles. As a result, armed services acquired indigenous missile systems and DRDO has shifted its focus from technology demonstration to modifying missile systems to meet the field requirements of the user in terms of deployment and operation. Capitalizing on its successes with the *Prithvi* and *Agni,* the DRDO embarked on programmes to develop shorter and longer-range versions of the *Agni* (*Agni*-1 and *Agni*-III), a supersonic cruise missile (*BrahMos*) with Russian collaboration, and a naval variant of the *Prithvi* (*Dhanush*). The DRDO is also believed to be developing a sea-launched ballistic missile, the *Sagarika,* which is expected to become operational by 2010. In addition, India has sought the American, Russian and Israeli collaborations in the development of an anti-tactical ballistic missile (ATBM) system.

During the fifth phase, from 2001 until the present, DRDO has sought to improve the performance of the ballistic missiles developed during the late 1980s and early 1990s. Key initiatives in this phase include the incorporation of new features to improve the "hit to kill" capabilities of the missiles and the use of newer and lighter materials in the construction of the missile systems. Among other priorities are projects to build for Army and Air Force variants of the *BrahMos* supersonic cruise missile, air-to-air missiles, the development of 'smart' missiles that are smaller, lighter, agile, and can home in on targets with great accuracy; the development of hypersonic vehicles, nanotechnologies, homing guidance, very large systems integration, miniaturized electro-mechanical systems, system on chip, and newer materials such as ceramics and lightweight composites.

India was able to import a number of items for the programme before the MTCR came into existence in 1987.[13] A variety of Indian Research and Development Programmes exist for air-to-air, air-to-surface, anti-tank and air defence missiles, including unmanned air vehicles (UAVs) and cruise missiles. It is to be noted that India's acquisition of Russian airborne, naval and submarine missile systems and related military technologies include some dual capable ballistic and cruise missile systems such as the SS-NX-27 (P-900 Alfa), a hybrid cruise and ballistic missile.[14]

PRITHVI

Prithvi is a surface-to-surface missile. It is among the most modern short-ranged battlefield missiles in the world. It has the highest warhead-weight to overall-weight of any missile in its class. Developmental work on this single-stage, liquid-engine ballistic missile started in the early 1980s.[15] It was India's first indigenously developed ballistic missile which is part of IGMDP. It comes in three variants: SS-150/*Prithvi*-I, SS-250/*Prithvi*-II and SS-350/*Prithvi*-III. A related programme, known as Project K-15, is in developmental stage and will enable it to be launched from a submerged submarine[16] *Dhanush* (in Sanskrit/Hindi means bow) is a system consisting of a stabilization platform (bow) and the missile (arrow). The system can fire either the SS-250 or the SS-350 variants. There may likely be certain customizations in missile configuration to certify it for sea worthiness.

Prithvi-I is a battlefield support system for the army having the range of 150 km with 1000 kg payload. It is a single stage, dual engine, liquid fuel, road-mobile, short-range surface-to-surface missile, which is 8.56 meter, long and has a diameter of 1.1 meters. The rocket motor is approximately 6 meters long, and the warhead cone is about 2.5 meters long. Different kinds of warheads can be fitted on to the missile, and can be changed under battlefield conditions. The *Prithvi*-I and II variants are powered by two liquid propellant rocket engines designed and developed by the DRDO.[17] Flight-tests of the 150 km-range/1,000 kg payload, army-version of this missile began in 1987 and lasted until late 1993. Subsequent to user trials with the Indian Army in 1994, the missile entered serial production at *Bharat* Dynamics Limited (BDL), Hyderabad (Andhra Pradesh).[18] Missile has been inducted into the Indian army which has raised two missile groups, 333rd and 334th, both based in Secunderabad (Andhra Pradesh),[19] to handle all logistical and operational details related to the *Prithvi*. During peacetime, the missiles and their support equipments are reportedly stored in Secunderabad, Jalandhar (Punjab), and Jammu (Jammu and Kashmir).[20] Current numerical estimates of the Indian Army's *Prithvi* inventory range from 75-90 missiles[21] and reports published in 2003-2004 suggest that the army might acquire additional 30-50 missiles.[22]

SS-250/*Prithvi*-II is dedicated to the Indian Air Force having the range of 250 km with 500-750 kg payload. It is a single stage, dual engine, liquid fuel, road-mobile, short-range surface-to-surface missile which is 9 meter long and has the same diameter as *Prithvi*-I. In fact, it is a lighter and long range variant of *Prithvi*-I but roughly the same missile. DRDO has decided to increase the

TABLE 3.1
Prithvi-I Missile Specifications

Name	:	Prithvi-I/SS-150
Service	:	Indian Army
Length	:	9 meter
Maximum Diameter	:	1.1 meter
Number of Stages	:	One
Launch Weight	:	4400 kg. including payload
Propellant	:	Liquid (IRFNA and Xylidiene plus Triethylamine)
Number of Engines	:	Two (Gimbaled)
Case Material	:	Aluminum Alloy
Stage Fuel-Mass ratio	:	0.79
Payload	:	800-1000 kg.
Guidance	:	Strapped-Ins, optionally augmented by GPS Terminal Guidance Radar scene correlation?
Range	:	150 km.
Accuracy (CEP)	:	10-50 meters
Control System	:	Gimbaled engines plus aerodynamic control surfaces
Launch Platform	:	8×8 Tatra Transporter Erector Launche

Source : Government of India, Ministry of Defence, *Annual Report, 2006-07;* Shanon N. Kile, Vitaly Fedchenko and Hans M. Kristensen, "World Nuclear Forces", Armaments, Disarmament and International Security, *SIPRI Yearbook, 2006,* Oxford University Press, Oxford, 2006; and *The Military Balance, 2006-07,* International Institute for Strategic Studies, London, 2006.

payload capability of the SS-250/*Prithvi*-II variant to 1000 kg by using boosted liquid propellant to generate higher thrust-to-weight ratio. Flight-tests of the 250 km-range/500 kg-payload, Air Force-version of the *Prithvi* started in 1993.[23]

According to senior Indian defense officials, former Defense Minister George Fernandes and his successor Pranab Mukherjee, development trials of the *Prithvi*-250 have been completed; the missile is undergoing production and is in the process of being inducted into the Indian Air Force (IAF). The IAF's two missile squadrons, one of which may be called the 2203 Squadron, are

TABLE 3.2
Prithvi-II Missile Specifications

Name	:	Prithvi-II/SS-250
Service	:	Indian Air force
Length	:	8.56 meter
Maximum Diameter	:	1.1 meter
Number of Stages	:	One
Launch Weight	:	4600 kg. including payload
Propellant	:	Liquid (IRFNA and Xylidiene plus Triethylamine)
Number of Engines	:	Two (Gimbaled)
Case Material	:	Aluminum Alloy
Stage Fuel-Mass ratio	:	0.79
Payload	:	800-1000 kg.
Guidance	:	Strapped-Ins, optionally augmented by GPS Terminal Guidance Radar scene correlation?
Range	:	250 km.
Accuracy (CEP)	:	75 meters
Control System	:	Gimbaled engines plus Aerodynamic control surfaces
Launch Platform	:	8×8 Tatra Transporter Erector Launcher

Source : Government of India, Ministry of Defence, *Annual Report, 2006-07;* Shanon N. Kile, Vitaly Fedchenko and Hans M. Kristensen, "World Nuclear Forces", Armaments, Disarmament and International Security, *SIPRI Yearbook, 2006,* Oxford University Press, Oxford, 2006; and *The Military Balance, 2006-07,* International Institute for Strategic Studies, London, 2006.

being raised in Hyderabad (Andhra Pradesh).[24] However, the missiles will be moved closer to the border with Pakistan during a crisis or war. The IAF's *Prithvi* inventory is estimated at 25, although more recent reports suggest that the service might acquire an additional 50 missile systems.[25]

The missile has a range sufficient to strike any significant target in Pakistan if deployed anywhere along the Indian border. The regenerative cooled engines are gimbaled to operate independently, making it possible to steer the missile in all three axes using thrust vector control during flight. The single stage missile uses liquid fuel. The hypergolic liquid fuel employs inhibited red fuming nitric acid as an oxidizer and a 50:50 combination of xylidiene and triethlyamine as fuel.

The missile's volatile liquid fuel must be loaded immediately prior to launch, imposing certain delay before it is ready for launch. Once loaded, such missiles can stay in ready state for few months, however they can be loaded/unloaded only limited number of times.[26] The fuel tank is made of light aluminium alloy and completely sealed to facilitate easy cross-country transportation. The missile can be rapidly deployed from the vehicle and fired from a single launcher. Liquid fuel also

TABLE 3.3
Prithvi-III Missile Specifications

Name	:	Prithvi-III/SS-350/*Dhanush*
Service	:	Indian Navy
Length	:	8.56 meter
Maximum Diameter	:	1.0 meter
Number of Stages	:	2 (?)
Launch Weight	:	5600 kg. including payload
Propellant	:	Solid (HTPB/AP/AI)
Number of Engines	:	One
Case Material	:	Steel
Stage Fuel-Mass ratio	:	0.76
Payload	:	500-1000 kg.
Guidance	:	Strapped-Ins, optionally augmented by GPS Terminal Guidance Radar scene correlation?
Range	:	350-600 km.
Accuracy (CEP)	:	25 meters
Control System	:	Aerodynamic control surfaces
Launch Platform	:	8×8 Tatra Transporter Erector Launcher

Source : Government of India, Ministry of Defence, *Annual Report, 2006-07*; Shanon N. Kile, Vitaly Fedchenko and Hans M. Kristensen, "World Nuclear Forces", Armaments, Disarmament and International Security, *SIPRI Yearbook, 2006*, Oxford University Press, Oxford, 2006; and *The Military Balance, 2006-07*, International Institute for Strategic Studies, London, 2006.

allows greater in-flight maneuvering capability; the missile is capable of being maneuvered up to 15° in flight.

SS-350/*Prithvi*-III is a solid fuelled version with a 350 km range and a 1000 kg payload. It is a naval version of the *Prithvi (Dhanush*/SS-350).[27] This third variant, also known as *Dhanush*, is a two stage, solid fuel, road-mobile, short-range, surface-to-surface missile. Some sources say that *Sagarika* and *Prithvi*-III are two different acronyms for the same missile.[28] Its motor diameter is 1.0 meter, with a length of 6 meters. It uses a high-energy solid propellant (HTPB/AP/Al)[29] that allows greater range (350 to 600 km) and payload (500 to 1000 kg) capability. The missile has a distinctly new blunt nose cone/RV, characteristic of high-speed re-entry of longer-range missiles. Some reports indicate that *Prithvi*-III is a two-stage missile with a RV 6 integrated second stage that is likely to have a range of 1000 km with a 500 kg payload.[30] The missile is unlikely to have four clipped delta wings midsection of the missiles that is typical of *Prithvi*-I and II, and will rather have four small fins towards its rear to provide necessary maneuvering on re-entry using body lift. The case-bonded HTPB-based composite propellant and composite nozzle generate 16 tons of thrust for duration of 38 seconds.[31]

The first test of the *Dhanush* in April 2000 ended in failure.[32] However, after two subsequent successful ss-350 tests, the DRDO declared in September 2002 that *Dhanush* was "ready for induction after successful trials at sea."[33] In October 2004, DRDO conducted the first successful underwater launch of the *Dhanush* from an especially designed canister placed in an artificial body of water.[34] The DRDO also declared a subsequent offshore flight-test of the *Dhanush* in November 2004 from the INS *Subhadra* a success.[35] The missile and its sub-systems are also referred by the project name K-15 and have been placed on a fast track development path. In December 2004, Indian Defense Minister Pranab Mukherjee informed parliament that development flight-tests for the Dhanush had been completed.[36] Despite reports that the Indian Navy plans to purchase 25 missiles, it is uncertain whether the Indian Navy will deploy Dhanush in an operational role.

The solid fuelled *Prithvi* is self-contained, unlike the liquid fuelled *Prithvi* that require a large number of support vehicles. Also unlike its liquid engine counterpart, solid fuel is stable and does not require human handling. However liquid fuelled missiles are more accurate because the navigation and control systems can precisely control the impulse from the engine by controlling or limiting its thrust. Solid fuelled rockets cannot turn off thrust on demand and further due to manufacturing variances; actual impulse from a solid motor is not known in advance. These factors make control and aiming more challenging and thus missile accuracy suffers unless mitigated by other means. *Prithvi*-III retains the high accuracy of its liquid fuelled counterparts, by using aerodynamic control forces available all along its flight in higher and lower reaches of the atmosphere.

The *Prithvi* has four distinctive large clipped tip delta wings (2.6 meter span) located in the middle of the fuselage that gives significant manoeuvring capability to defeat ABM defences. Four smaller fins at the rear of the missile are used to control the missile's altitude and augment range using aerodynamic lift from the lifting body. Once fired, the missile is controlled by the gimbaled engine as well as the aerodynamic force from the wings and fins. *Prithvi*-II missile typically reaches a maximum altitude of approximately 80 km (Mach 4), thus spending most of the flight time in the upper reaches of the atmosphere. The large delta wings and body lift is used to generate additional lift during ascent and descent, allowing it to overcome the range restriction associated with pure ballistic flight. During descent, the large delta-wings in the mid-section generates lift allowing the missile to glide and fly (Mach 5) on a trajectory different from the predictable trajectory of a pure ballistic missile and ends in a steep descent at nearly 80° for superior CEP (Circular Error Probable).[37] *Prithvi*-I ascends to peak speed of 900 m/sec and when the thrust is cut-off and it rises to an altitude of 30 km before it glides to the target it. *Prithv*i-II does not limit the peak velocity and it also has larger fuel load.

The *Prithvi* can execute up to five waypoints en route to the target, thus maximizing the element of surprise. This makes it difficult for ABM defences to intercept the missile. The missile is coated with radar-absorbing paint to reduce its radar signature during flight, thus further reducing the probability of detection and interception. The missile's lifting configuration allows a shallower re-entry course, and steering along the way. This permits attacking targets not in line with the missile's launch azimuth and reduces turbulence and re-entry thermal stress. The shallow glide also allows better terminal guidance accuracy. The delta wing is placed at the center-of-mass of expended missile. Since the tail of liquid-fuelled engine is heavy as against the solid-fuelled stage, the delta wing on the *Prithvi*-I/II variants are backset and located approximately 3.2 meters (from tail) as against the Prithvi-III, where the fins are located a little forward (approximately 3.6 meters from tail).

The *Prithvi* uses a closed-loop, Strap-down Inertial Navigation System (SINS) for navigation and flight control. The SINS computer uses twin microprocessors and the missiles are guided to the target within a CEP equal to 0.01% of its range. During test, the missile reportedly achieved high accuracy rate. Unconfirmed reports suggest that some *Prithvi* missiles might have a radar scene correlation terminal guidance system.[38] India integrated indigenously developed Global Positioning System (GPS) receiver for augmentation of targeting accuracy to a few meters' CEP. India and Russia are working together on the development of a new generation of Global Navigation Satellite System (GLONESS) known as the Global' *Naya Navigatsionnaya Sputnikovaya Sistema* that will be operational by 2007.[39] Gloness-K satellites will be launched by Russian and Indian launchers and India will have access to military grade P code signal. The *Prithvi*-II reportedly has a terminal homing guidance and anti-radiation systems. A scheme to retrofit the *Prithvi*-I, with this capability, is planned. This capability is useful in attacking hard targets like armoured concentrations in their parking sites or radars. For field operations, the missile will be transported on an all-terrain; eight wheel Kolos Tatra 4×4 truck. The missile is deployed from the vehicle and fired from a simple launcher. Each battery of four *Prithvi* carrier vehicles will be accompanied by a missile re-supply and loading vehicle, a propellant tanker (only for the liquid-fuelled *Prithvi*-I and II variants) and also a command post to provide target data to the missile's guidance system before launch. It also has an integrated surveillance and mission support capability and other support vehicles and equipment. The *Prithvi*-III/SS-350 can be launched from the surface of the sea, as well as from under the sea.[40]

The *Prithvi* is a Pakistan-specific missile system and has reportedly been configured for nuclear delivery. In addition, the DRDO has designed a variety of conventional warheads for use in different battlefield support roles. The Indian government is believed to have upgraded the alert status of some nuclear-capable Prithvi missile units during the *Kargil* war with Pakistan,[41] and during the India-Pakistani military standoff that lasted from December 2001 until October 2002. According to more recent reports, however, the Indian government no longer plans to use the *Prithvi* as a nuclear delivery system. Instead the missiles will be armed with conventional warheads and be used as long-range artillery to attack Pakistan's strategic and theater reserves.[42] The *Prithvi* missiles are reportedly being equipped with GPS to improve accuracy. However, the DRDO has denied rumors that a solid-fuel version of the *Prithvi* is on the anvil.

Significantly, in December 1998 the Indian Army deployed the *Prithvi* SS-150 variant in a major military exercise for the first time since its induction. Code-named *Exercise Shiv Shakti* 98, the military exercise signified that the *Prithvi* had been further inducted into the military doctrine. If the missile were deployed in states like Kashmir, Punjab and Gujarat, which border Pakistan, it would place the cities of Islamabad, Lahore, Karachi, Hyderabad and many of Pakistan's strategic military installations within its range. An unspecified number of *Prithvi* missiles are based near Jalandhar in northern Punjab, for potential use as a tactical battlefield missile against Pakistan.

Although *Prithvi* is capable of carrying nuclear/strategic warheads, it is dedicated for battlefield use making use of conventional payloads such as pre-fragmented explosives, bomblets, incendiary, cluster munitions, sub-munitions, fuel-air and high explosives. *Prithvi* warheads are field interchangeable. The *Prithvi* was India's sole ballistic missile for many years before induction of the *Agni*-I/II intermediate range missiles. Thus even though the *Prithvi* missile groups had conventional warheads, it was assumed within the international strategic community that some were (or could be at short notice) configured with a strategic nuclear payload.[43] This created a problem for the Indian strategic community related to the concern that advanced deployment of the *Prithvi* during a build-up to war could blur the nuclear threshold and be destabilizing. This issue became a reality in

June 1999 at the height of the *Kargil* imbroglio. The concern was that advanced deployment of the *Prithvi* could be misinterpreted as lowering the nuclear threshold. Yet press reports after the crisis was resolved, indicated that four *Prithvis* and one *Agni* were activated.

Obviously the misinterpretation would not have happened if sufficient *Agni* missiles were around for the task or these were tasked for other targets.[44] Thus *Agni* missiles exclusively and distinctly serve the role of strategic missile, while the *Prithvi* Missile Groups are purely for conventional battlefield use. The fact that DRDO was forced to use available technologies and unable to secure support for engine redesign, to incorporate its own superior liquid fuel or the Indian Space Research Organization's more advanced solid fuel technology, testifies to the limited support for the *Prithvi*. After the *Agni*-I MRBM missile test in January 2002, K. Santhanam, former officer in RAW, DRDO technical advisor, nuclear scientist and former Director IDSA, stated that the *Prithvi* missile was never meant to carry nuclear warheads under normal circumstances. This indicates that the solid-fuelled *Agni* has completely taken over the 'nuclear' role from the liquid-fuelled *Prithvi*.

AGNI

The *Prithvi* SRBM, in all three versions, suffers from one fundamental weakness that it is extremely short-range. Even at maximum range (350 km) *Prithvi* family of missiles suffices only to target Pakistan, which is already well within Indian Air Force's strike coverage. So it does nothing to improve India's glaring weaknesses where target coverage *vis-a-vis* China is concerned. These short range limitations of the *Prithvi* family of missiles imply that even nuclear armed versions of the missile would not provide India with a delivery system capable of targeting important civilian and military assets within China.[45] Recognizing these limitations, India initiated the development of an intermediate-range missile system—the *Agni*. The missile comes in the following variants: *Agni*-TD/TTB (Technology Demonstrator/Technology Test Bed), *Agni*-II IRBM, *Agni*-I SRBM, *Agni*-IIAT IRBM, *Agni*-III IRBM and *Agni*-IV ICBM. Chronologically *Agni*-TD was first developed to quickly prove critical technologies, followed by the *Agni*-II IRBM, and then a short-range version missile called *Agni*-I. In defence literature/ publications this numbering system jumble, leading to the *Agni*-I name, often confuses readers. The development of the *Agni*-III and *Agni*-IV missiles with greater range and payload capability is under progress, albeit with great obfuscation to actual configuration and specification.

Agni-TD/TTB (Technology Demonstrator/Technology Test Bed)

The *Agni*-TD/TTB is a two-stage Intermediate Range Ballistic Missile (IRBM). In the early 1980s, it was conceived as a "technology demonstrator" (TD) to test propulsion, staging, and re-entry technologies for applications in medium and intermediate-range ballistic missile systems.[46] It became part of IGMDP in 1983, and was test fired for the first time in May 1989. It is a two-stage missile with the first stage using the solid-fuel booster motor of the SLV-3 satellite launch vehicle. This marked for the first time that India had used directly a component of its civilian space research programme for military purposes.[47] The second stage is possibly a shortened version of the *Prithvi*.[48] Work on the 1,200-1,500 km-range/1,000 kg-payload *Agni* TD most likely began in 1983. Between 1989 and 1994, the DRDO conducted three developmental flight-tests, of which two were successful. In 1994, the United States persuaded India to suspend testing of the *Agni* missile after three test flights. However, India referred the *Agni* as a "technology demonstrator project" to establish re-entry vehicle technologies rather than a weapon system.[49] As with the *Prithvi*, the USA has opposed the programme as another potential proliferation affront to the MTCR, which India has criticized as biased in favour of the major powers. Notwithstanding its justifications for the *Agni* development, India formally suspended the programme at the end of 1995.[50] India's turning point came when NDA government took office in March 1998 and conducted the nuclear explosion known as *Pokhran-II*. The then Prime Minister, Atal Bihari Vajpayee decided to expedite the development of *Agni* missile. The new government announced that a new version of the *Agni* with an extended range was under development.

Compared to the *Prithvi*, the *Agni* is a much larger system with a range of 2500 km and a payload of 1000 kg. The original *Agni* was an amalgam of the *Prithvi* and the SLV-3 booster. The *Agni*-TD/TTB was a cheap test vehicle to develop re-entry and guidance technology for use on a more advanced platform. The missile used a solid booster that was improved but similar to S-1 stage. Instead of developing a new solid motor for the second stage, which would have involved significant delays, it used a shortened version of the liquid fuelled *Prithvi* motor.

The first *Agni* launch on 22 May 1989 used a shortened *Prithvi* stage as the second stage. The second *Agni* test used a longer burn second stage that was ignited before separation thus obviating the need of six-ullage motors used in the earlier launch.[51] The RV used multi-directionally reinforced carbon-fiber preform (MRCP) technology. The last test of the basic '*Agni*-TD/

TABLE 3.4

Agni-TD/TTB Missile Specifications

Name	:	Agni-TD/TTB
Number of Stages	:	Two
Range	:	2500 km.
Mission	:	Technology Demonstration to develop re-entry and guidance technology
Propellant	:	Solid (HTBP) for first stage and Liquid (IRFNA and Xylidiene + Triethylamine) for second Stage
Case Material	:	Steel + Aluminium Alloy
Number of Engines	:	Two
Control System	:	Secondary Injection Thrust Vector Control System (SITVCS) with aerodynamic control Surfaces and for second stage Gimbaled Engines

Source : "Missile Proliferation in South Asia: India and Pakistan's Ballistic Missile Inventories", Factsheets, *Arms Control Today*, Arms Control Association, May 2002; Government of India, Ministry of Defence, *Annual Report, 2006-07;* Shanon N. Kile, Vitaly Fedchenko and Hans M. Kristensen, "World Nuclear Forces", Armaments, Disarmament and International Security, *SIPRI Yearbook, 2006,* Oxford University Press, Oxford, 2006; and *The Military Balance, 2006-07,* International Institute for Strategic Studies, London, 2006.

TTB' on 19 February 1994 was a major technical breakthrough for India. The system tested, included a manoeuvrable re-entry vehicle for increased accuracy with terminal guidance. This terminal guidance system reportedly consists of a scanning correlation optical system based on a scanning focal plane homing head in the infrared and millimeter wavelengths of the electromagnetic spectrum. Considerable un-informed comments exist regarding the fact that *Agni* was only tested to a range of 1450 km. No missile actually needs to be tested to a full range. It is possible to lift or depress the trajectory of the missile to simulate a longer range.

APJ Abdul Kalam stated that the missile could be fully deployed within two years. Kalam also asserted that the *Agni* was ready for serial production while some simultaneous development flights aimed at achieving a much greater performance are undertaken. Kalam claimed that no further test flights are necessary for the basic *Agni* system and that it is ready for production. In April 1995, the then Prime Minister PV Narasimha Rao denied allegations that under the pressure of USA and G7, India temporarily paused the *Agni* programme after completion of the TD phase and after three test flights.[52] In fact, during the time, Prime Minister Rao secretly sanctioned the development of an augmented version of the *Agni*[53] as well as to speed up efforts to build more advanced nuclear weapons[54] and set-up a nuclear command and control system for the safe custody, deployment, and employment of such weapons, distributed over the country to ensure survivability and safety totally under civilian control.[55] The *Agni*-TD programme ran its course with the development and proving of crucial technologies for full-fledged, multi-staged, long-range ballistic missiles, including re-entry and navigation avionics. This missile reached engineering status and it is believed that none were released to the military, although during the *Kargil* crisis few units were made ready as nuclear deterrence.[56] This model is not believed to exist anymore, having being superseded by the *Agni*-II that has been put on line production and operationalized.

Generally liquid fuelled missiles are more accurate because the navigation and control system can precisely control the impulse from the engine by controlling or limiting its thrust. Solid fuelled rockets can't turn-off thrust on demand and further due to subtle manufacturing variances and actual operating conditions the exact impulse from a solid motor isn't known before hand. All this makes control and aiming more challenging and the missile accuracy suffers unless mitigated by other means. The solid fuelled *Agni's* trajectory has a shallow re-entry angle and manoeuvring RV (MRV) use body lift aerodynamics to correct trajectory error, as well as reduce the thermal stress of re-entry. The *Agni's* RV has a velocity correction package to correct launch trajectory variances. Some *Agni* RV versions use a solid fuelled thruster cartridge of a known impulse, allowing the onboard guidance controller to trim velocity, using discrete combination of impulse quantum along desired spatial orientation.

The *Agni's* re-entry vehicle is designed to ensure that the temperature inside the vehicle does not exceed 60° Celsius, a condition necessary to protect the warhead and electronic systems placed inside. During tests, the re-entry vehicle technology was fully demonstrated when the nose-cone withstood temperatures of 3000° Celsius while the inside temperature was only 30° Celsius. The Agni RV-MRV Mk.1 nose tip is made of a multi-directionally woven, reinforced carbon-carbon fiber composite material.[57] The 0.8 meter diameter and 4 meter long, re-entry vehicle consists of five sections. Each of these sections is made up of a two-layer composite construction. The inner layer is made up of carbon/epoxy filament mould constructed on a CNC winding machine and is designed to bear structural loads. The outer layer is made up of carbon/phenolic filament wound construction and cured in an autoclave at 7 bar pressure.[58] The outer ablative layer ensures high thermal robustness for shock and temperature extremes.

The RV appears to house an integrated High Altitude Motor (HAM), instead of a separate Post Boost Vehicle and classic purely passive ballistic warhead seen in western missiles, that is liquid fuelled and is used to correct impulse variance of solid fuelled stages and subtle launch trajectory variance. The 1980-vintage RV was reportedly designed to be able to carry a BARC-developed, boosted nuclear weapon of 200 KT yield weighing 1000 kg., also of 1980 vintage design. After making room for new and lighter Indian thermonuclear weapon payload, of 1995 vintage design, the MRV has room for about 200 kg (estimated) liquid fuel in pressurized vessels. Although for velocity correction, approximately 50 to 80 kg. is estimated to be sufficient. There are indications that the MRV is intended to enter a gliding trajectory when it enters atmosphere at an altitude of 100 km.[59]

As far as propulsion of *Agni*-TD is concerned, in the first stage, the booster motor is one meter in diameter and ten meters in length. It has approximately 9 tons solid propellant and a mass fraction of 0.865 (estimated). The stage features three segments of propellant grain, with an internal star configuration for increased thrust during the initial boost phase. The motor case is made of a high-strength 15CDV6 steel and is fabricated by conventional rolling and welding techniques. The propellant used in Agni-TD consists of the AP-Al-PBAN composite propellant and later *Agni* variants use (HTPB) hydroxyl-terminated polybutadiene. The propellant is of star configuration with a loading density of 78%. It is case bonded with a liner system between propellant and insulation. The motor's nozzle is built from 15CDV6 steel; a carbon-phenolic thermal protection system is used for the convergent throat, high-density graphite is used for the throat, and carbon and silica-phenolic lining is used in the fore end and after end of the divergent [60]

Agni-TD used a reduced *Prithvi* stage as its second stage. The initial test flight used a shortened version of *Prithvi* with lesser fuel, later flights used full fuel configuration. The liquid fuelled second stage of *Agni*-TD required in addition, two types of 'Ullage and Retro Motors' to maintain positive G-forces during stage separation. Both the ullage and retro motors are made of HE-15 aluminium alloy and use a double-base propellant. The motors are lined inside with high silica glass-phenolic ablative liners. Defense Research and Development Laboratory (DRDL) has expertise in the design, production, inspection, qualification, static-testing, and flight-testing of propulsion systems.[61]

In 1999, the Indian government approved the development of a rail-road-mobile, single-stage, solid-motor, 700-800 km-range/1,000 kg-payload variant of the *Agni* missile. This variant, which was later dubbed as the *Agni*-I, was conceived as a bridge between the short-range *Prithvi* and the longer-range *Agni*-TD and *Agni*-II ballistic missiles. Between January 2002 and June 2004, the short-range variant of the *Agni* has been tested thrice successfully.[62] Senior Indian defence officials have suggested that although more user flight-tests are in the offing, the missile is ready for induction into the armed services.

The DRDO is also developing a 3,000-4,000 km-range variant of the *Agni*, often referred to as the *Agni*-III. The first developmental flight-test of the Agni III was initially slated for late-2003; the test was subsequently postponed to the first and second quarters of 2004.[63] Although Indian defense officials indicated in mid-2004 that DRDO had begun assembling a test-prototype, no development flight-tests of the *Agni*-III occurred during the year.[64]

The Indian Army is raising two missile groups: 444th and 555th:to induct and manage the *Agni*-I and II variants.[65] The DRDO is also reportedly training the Army in missile launch techniques, mounting warheads, and other technical parameters concerning the missile. According to the then DRDO Director V.K. Aatre, a "certain number of *Agni*-I and II ballistic missiles have been delivered to the Army."[66] Aatre's announcement was indirectly confirmed by Indian Defence Minister Pranab Mukherjee in December 2004 when he informed parliament that the *Agni*-I and II were in the process of induction.[67]

The *Agni* missiles have been designed and developed for delivering nuclear munitions. Despite earlier suggestions of the *Agni's* potential conventional role, this is now unlikely for reasons of cost-effectiveness and accuracy.[68] The *Agni*-I will most probably replace the Prithvi for nuclear-targeting missions against Pakistan. Although the longer-range variants of the Agni will inherently be capable of targeting Pakistan as well, they are primarily being developed to give India a nuclear strike capability against China.

AGNI-II

The continuous Chinese and North Korean assistance to Pakistan in the field of nuclear and missile systems created the serious security challenges to India during 1990s. Moreover, China itself posed security threats to India by improving and increasing its nuclear delivery systems. The strategic red line was crossed in 1998 when Pakistan tested the North-Korean supplied nuclear capable *Ghauri* missile, that could threaten India's heartland. The international support for nuclear and missile proliferation to Pakistan, trading in black-market for North Korean No-Dong missiles, exposure of Pakistani nuclear and missile black-market run by Pakistani scientist A.Q. Khan and the Pakistani Military, and other international security developments also worked as contributory factors in India's decision to go nuclear, resulting in the *Pokhran*-II nuclear test series and its weaponization by developing the *Agni* family of ballistic missiles that could deliver a variety of payloads over long ranges.

After the successful test launch of *Agni*-TD, India was able to develop *Agni*-II as *Agni*-I project had provided proven critical technologies and designs required for long-range ballistic missiles. Thus when the decision was made to build the *Agni* weapon system, some quick optimization and ruggedization was done to the basic '1980 vintage' design, including a solid fuelled second stage. Further the solid fuel chemistry, RV and avionics were brought up to state-of-the-art levels. As the *Pokhran*-II nuclear test proved a family of more powerful and lighter nuclear weapons, the 200 KT thermonuclear weapon is far lighter compared to 1000 kg earlier budgeted for the 200 KT boosted nuclear weapon. Thus a high yield weapon configuration now assumes a payload of 500 kg, including weapon and R.V. However, in the interest of rapid development the basic design that was earlier developed continued to be used and keeping the future option open, for more optimized missile design and lighter payload. The *Agni*-II missile is likely to be used by 555th Missile Group of the Indian Army.

Although flight-tests were suspended between 1995 and 1998, research and development on an improved variant continued uninterrupted.[69] Testing was revived in 1999.[70] Although accuracy is reduced with increased range, the *Agni* is believed to be fairly accurate, employing a closed-loop inertial guidance system, said to have been developed with a great deal of West German assistance.[71] Between April 1999 and August 2004, the DRDO conducted three successful developmental flight tests of *Agni*-II. The IRBM *Agni*-II was tested successfully for the first time on 11 April 1999, exactly 11 months after the *Pokhran*-II. The missile was launched from the IC-4 pad at Wheeler Island, *Balasore* to a range of over 2000 km.[72]

TABLE 3.5
Agni-Missile Specifications

Name	:	Agni-II
Length	:	20 meters
Maximum Diameter	:	1 meter
Launch Weight	:	16000 kg. including payload
Propellant	:	Solid (HTPB/AP/AI)
Number of Stages	:	2.5
Payload	:	800-1000 kg.
Warhead	:	Strategic nuclear (15 KT to 200 KT), Conventional HE-unitary, penetration, sub-munitions, incendiary or fuel air explosives.
Guidance	:	Strap Down-INS, optionally augmented by GPS terminal guidance with possible radar scene correlation.
Range	:	2000-3300 km.

Source : "Missile Proliferation in South Asia: India and Pakistan's Ballistic Missile Inventories", Factsheets, *Arms Control Today*, Arms Control Association, May 2002; Government of India, Ministry of Defence, *Annual Report, 2006-07;* Shanon N. Kile, Vitaly Fedchenko and Hans M. Kristensen, "World Nuclear Forces", Armaments, Disarmament and International Security, *SIPRI Yearbook, 2006,* Oxford University Press, Oxford, 2006; and *The Military Balance, 2006-07,* International Institute for Strategic Studies, London, 2006.

The *Agni*-II is a rail/road-mobile, two-stage, solid propellant system, though a liquid fuelled configuration and an improved guidance system is also available, the incorporation of the Global Positioning System (GPS) has been alleged.[73] After the test on January 17, 2001, the missile was cleared for production and it is possible that a production capacity (under-utilised at present) exists for 12 *Agni*-II missiles per year. On the January 17th test, the missile was alleged to have covered a range of over 2100 km with a 700 kg warhead. As this test was described as being in operational configuration, it might be assumed that the *Agni*-II missile will be deployed with a 700 kg warhead.[74] The range differential between the first (11 April 1999) and second (17

January 2001) tests can be explained by the use of a different trajectory and flight profile.[75]

The *Agni*-II can be launched from a rail-mobile launcher as well as from a road mobile launcher.[76] So it lends flexibility and reduces vulnerability to strikes. The *Agni*-II will reportedly always be in a ready-to-fire mode and can be launched within 15 minutes as compared to almost half a day of preparation for the *Agni*-TD. In May 2001, and again in July 2001, the incumbent Defence Minister Jaswant Singh informed the Cabinet Committee on Security (CCS) that the *Agni*-II missile is operational, limited production had begun and induction being planned during 2001-02. On 14 March 2002, the then Defence Minister George Fernandes informed Indian Parliament that the *Agni*-II has entered the production phase and is under induction. *Agni*-II is made by BDL in Hyderabad, with a production capacity of 18 missiles/year and costs about Rs. 35 crore for each missile.[77]

The *Agni*-II's first stage is largely similar to that of *Agni*-TD's first stage. However the *Agni*-II booster is believed to employ more energetic fuel similar to that used on the PSLV's (Polar Satellite Launch Vehicle) booster stage-ISP of 269 (vacuum) and 237 (sea-level). It has a propellant mass of 9 tons and a mass fraction of 0.865 (estimated). Its second stage weighs 4200 kg and uses solid fuel propellant. Its case is presumably made of the same material, high-strength 15CDV6 steel, as the booster stage for ease of manufacturing. This solid propellant stage has flex nozzles for thrust vectoring, for precise trajectory control. Unlike the *Agni*-TD, the solid fuel second stage does not require retro motors for proper stage separation. Evidently it uses a vented inter-stage.

The 1980-vintage RV was reportedly designed to be able to carry a BARC-developed, boosted nuclear weapon of 200 KT yield weighing 1000 kg, also of 1980 vintage design. After making room for new and lighter Indian thermonuclear weapon payload[78] of 1995 vintage design, the MRV has room for about 200 kg (estimated) liquid fuel in pressurized vessels. Although for velocity correction, approximately 50 to 80 kg is estimated to be sufficient. At least one variant type uses a set of solid fuelled cartridges for velocity trimming.

APJ Kalam said that the complete re-entry hypersonic flow was simulated in Computational Fluid Dynamics, on a super-computer. The RV is reported to have an altitude control system and aerodynamic manoeuvre fins, presumably to make missile defence more difficult.[79] Unconfirmed reports suggest that an improved optical or radar terminal phase correlation system has been developed to provide accuracy of around 40 meters CEP, although later reports have suggested that the accuracy was around 100 to 200 meters CEP. The RV largely inherits the basic shape, design and technology of the earlier Mk.1 RV of the *Agni*-TD.[80] The *Agni*-RV Mk.2 is more advanced than the western RVs, because it embodies propulsion, navigation and control all the way to the target.[81] The RV re-enters at an altitude of 100 km, at a shallow angle, with a gliding trajectory.[82]

In case of avionics, navigation and control, the Agni family of missiles uses a strap-down INS system for flight control and navigation.[83] Necessary inertial sensors were indigenously developed for the purpose, including laser rate gyros.[84] The then Project Director of *Agni*, Avinash Chander, said the effort to operationalise the missile system was complex, as it involved reducing the host of computer's processing information, both inside the missile and ground control systems, to a single control system. To ensure greater reliability of the missile, they reduced the mass of over 600 different sets of communication channels, involving 24 km of cabling, to just 10 pairs requiring one-eighth of the original wiring.

The *Agni* introduced a new concept by adopting MIL-STD-1553 data bus for all on-board communication and control device interconnection mainly INS system, Flight Control Computer, actuators and sensors. It is the standard that is adopted in new civilian and military aircraft (circuit routing and device mounting) and all the software in the *Agni*-II has been designed around this bus. DRDO sources claim that this reduces the number of connections and also makes the missile more rugged. However, some missile analysts feel that a standard databus may not be the best path to follow. It is said that a customized databus is better because in a standard databus, one tends to use off-the-shelf electronic devices whose performance may not be optimal. However, most modern missiles are moving towards digital buses using commercial off-the-shelf technology and which enables affordable sub-system replacement.

In case of accuracy, the *Agni*-II's navigation and aiming uses an advanced ground-based beacon system using a Time Delay of

Arrival (TDOA) technique, similar to a GPS system that constantly provides missile flight position and velocity updates and has been proven in test flights.[85] The TDOA system reportedly improved the accuracy by three times. India has demonstrated a measure of mastery in navigation sensors and flight control through its space programme. The placement accuracy in GTO (involving powered flight of 1000 seconds much of it in sub-G or gravity free environment) is far more complicated and delicate than that of the sub-orbital trajectory of an IRBM. Thus the GSLV-D2 and F01 GTO Apogee accuracy of 1965 PPM[86] and 361 PPM[87] respectively compares with *Agni*-II's 40 meter CEP at IRBM ranges with 13 PPM accuracy.[88]

With the confusion over the maximum range of *Agni*-II, comes further perplexity whether the missile is actually fitted with any form of terminal guidance system. This is not an easy question to dismiss with a glib negative answer. The RV of the missile is fitted with some rather prominent manoeuvring fins which permits the warhead to perform porpoising manoeuvres to evade and confuse enemy defences, implying built-in navigation, IMU and control system.[89] The *Agni*-II is fitted with a basic strap-down inertial navigation system, rather than with a more advanced (but expensive and less robust) gimballed or platform INS. This is by no means a mean feat, and does not itself mean that the missile has poor accuracy. It would mean, however, that the need for some kind of terminal guidance system is necessary—especially true since DRDO claims that the CEP for *Agni*-II is three times lower than that of the earlier *Agni* variant with CEP figures as low as 40 metres being mentioned.

DRDO stated, especially after the first *Agni*-II test, that it had tested a terminal guidance system which dramatically enhanced accuracy. For adjustments to missile trajectory during flight, which allow for higher accuracy, the second stage booster has a flex nozzle that enables change in the thrust vector direction. The flex nozzle technology was validated in the third stage motor of India's Polar Satellite Launch Vehicle (PSLV). Furthermore, it was alleged that the re-entry vehicle employs a terminal guidance radar operating in the C and S bands. Finally, re-entry adjustments have been optimized through on board control software that allows re-entry velocity trimming.

There were also early reports that a terminal guidance system based on ISRO technology was to be employed. This terminal guidance system is reported to be comprised of a scanning correlation optical system based on a scanning focal plane homing head in the infrared and millimeter wavelengths of the electromagnetic spectrum. However, it is not known whether this advanced terminal guidance system has been fully developed. Allegations about the employment of GPS assisted terminal guidance were effectively denied by DRDO scientists, as the external control of the GPS network was thought to be a liability.

DRDO's terminal guidance claim is at times belittled by certain quarters—often anti-DRDO naysayers—who speak in terms of the superior Chinese and North Korean guidance systems and their use by Pakistan. Such comments, usually unsupported by any meaningful evidence cannot be given weight on merit, but it does put renewed emphasis on the need for DRDO to be more forthcoming about the guidance system of the *Agni*-II. DRDO has nothing to lose and everything to gain by explaining a bit more about the guidance technologies used for *Agni*-II.

The first point of confusion regarding *Agni*-II, is what is the missile's maximum range? Analysis, using public domain data and ballistic calculations, shows that the range is greatly influenced by use or non-use of thrusters on the RV (required for velocity trimming) for propulsion as a HAM (High Altitude Motor). There seems to be room in the RV for about 200 kg fuel (solid or liquid) after allowing for a long but lightweight TN weapon. This RV integrated HAM is referred to as the half stage after the two solid fuelled stages. This stage provides a disproportional increase in range for a lighter RV payload. Thus development of lightweight nuclear weapons is paramount to the missile's range.

When the *Agni*-II was first launched, the then Defence Minster George Fernandes indicated that the maximum range of the *Agni*-II was 3000 km. Since then, ranges from 2000 km to 2500 km have been bandied about while APJ Abdul Kalam, at Aero India '98, stated that *Agni*-II had a maximum range of 3,700 km. The range of 2000 km can be excluded, as the system has been tested to greater range in both 1999 and 2001. Given the test to 2300 km in 1999 and 2100 km in 2001, with an apparently lighter payload, would indicate that a variation in trajectory was used and it may be possible to extrapolate some more accurate estimates of *Agni*-II's maximum range.

It would appear that *Agni*-II has a theoretical ability to hit a target 3000 km away with a 1000 kg overall payload—(a 250 kg RV's deadweight and a 750 kg warhead). It is suggested that a 200 kiloton 'boosted fission' warhead was earlier developed for the *Agni* system when it was on the drawing board in the late 80s, however after the *Pokhran*-II series of nuclear test in May 1998, the 200 KT boosted fission design has clearly given way to a 200-300 KT two stage thermonuclear design that is expected to be much lighter. Range changes can be made by either varying the payload or by altering the engine configuration.

Given the available data, it is therefore clear that *Agni*-II has a maximum range of somewhere in excess of 3000 km, and possibly as high as 3500 km with a 1000 kg payload. Greater range with a lighter payload however requires the RV to be qualified for higher re-entry velocity and corresponding Max-Q for thermal stress.[90] As the backbone of the Indian land-based nuclear deterrent, the real significance of the *Agni*-II is the fact that it is both road and rail mobile. This is an indication of India's desire not to put its missiles into vulnerable silos. The mobility of the *Agni*-II, combined with the sheer physical size of India renders the mobile IRBM a very secure and survivable delivery system. Furthermore, Raj Chengappa asserts that one of *Agni*-II missiles was tested with a nuclear weapon assembly, minus the plutonium core, mounted in the warhead assembly area to ensure that all systems, including safety locks, would work.[91]

AGNI-I

The *Agni*-I was undertaken as a crash project in October 1999 to cover the range between the *Prithvi*-II and *Agn*i-II. It is a Pakistan specific missile. The development of the *Agni*-I showed the reactive nature of the evolution of the IGMDP.[92] It is a single stage version of the *Agn*i-II missile. It stands at 15 metres, weighs 12 tons and serves as a medium range ballistic missile. The missile was rapidly developed after *Kargil* War when the need for an intermediate range missile was felt—addressing the range gap between the *Agni*-II and the *Prithvi*.[93] On the western front, the range of the Prithvi-I/II was found too short for strategic use and the *Agni*-II had too long range, requiring prolonged flight over Indian territory, and requiring lofted or depressed launch angle beyond usual limits, thus degrading accuracy. The *Agni*-I is effectively the *Agni*-II minus it's second stage. However, this configuration puts greater 'G force' stresses on the RV and avionics, when the stage completes (about 18G instead of Agni-II's maximum of 9G) its journey. The missile has been extensively flight tested.

According to Indian Government reports, the range is between 700-890 km with a 1000 kg payload.[94] With a special weapons load, *Agni*-I can reach 1200 km. The first test, from a road-mobile launcher, was conducted on 25 January 2002 to a range of 700 km and was termed an accurate and successful flight that met its mission objectives. A second test followed on 9 January 2003. The missile was then cleared for service in the Indian Army. *Agni*-I can carry a one-ton conventional or nuclear payload to most targets in Pakistan without having to be deployed at the borders. The core and triggers can be swiftly assembled by BARC and DRDO within India's avowed no-first-use paradigm.

Agni-I is designed to be launched from both a rail and road based mobile launchers.[95] A mobile missile system reduces vulnerability and allows for greater operational flexibility, while critics feel that the cost of these mobile systems could be higher and that they greatly increase the time for moving from one place to another.

The control over the 700-km-range *Agni*-I missile is expected to pass on to the 334th and 444th missile groups of the Indian Army. These groups along with the 335th missile group are likely to be entrusted with various *Agni* variants. No official confirmation is available about these two missile groups. It is unclear whether their control could pass on to the Strategic Force Command (SFC), created to handle the country's nuclear delivery assets.[96]

The propulsion of Agni-I is single stage rocket configuration and is similar to *Agni*-II's first stage. The avionics and maneuvering re-entry vehicle are also similar to *Agni*-II. DRDO's Chief Controller of R and D (Missiles), A.S. Pillai, stated that

TABLE 3.6
Agni-I Missile Specifications

Name	:	Agni-I
Length	:	15 meters
Maximum Diameter	:	1 meter
Launch Weight	:	12000 kg. including payload
Propellant	:	Solid (HTPB/AP/AI)
Number of Stages	:	1
Payload	:	800-1000 kg.
Warhead	:	Strategic nuclear (15 KT to 200 KT), Conventional HE-unitary, penetration, sub-munitions, incendiary or fuel air explosives.
Guidance	:	Strap Down-INS, optionally augmented by GPS terminal guidance with possible radar scene correlation.
Range	:	700-850 km

Source : "Missile Proliferation in South Asia: India and Pakistan's Ballistic Missile Inventories", Factsheets, *Arms Control Today*, Arms Control Association, May 2002; Government of India, Ministry of Defence, *Annual Report, 2006-07;* Shanon N. Kile, Vitaly Fedchenko and Hans M. Kristensen, "World Nuclear Forces", Armaments, Disarmament and International Security, *SIPRI Yearbook, 2006*, Oxford University Press, Oxford, 2006; and *The Military Balance, 2006-07*, International Institute for Strategic Studies, London, 2006.

Agni-I incorporates new guidance and control systems and there were also significant improvements in its re-entry technology and maneuverability. With only one stage, the weight is less but the thrust is the same, giving the missile more acceleration. An upgraded version of *Agni*-I was test-fired again on July 4, 2004 by improving its re-entry technology and maneuverability, and inducted into the army.[97] The 334 missile group of Army currently operates *Agni*-1 Missile while the *Prithvi* missile has been inducted into the 333 missile group. The missile again test fired for the forth time on 5 October 2007 from ITR Wheelers Island off the Orissa cost. This was the first training trial of the missile after the induction into the army. This first training trial will lead to full operationalisation to its complete induction process into the service. This is also of great strategic importance as this trial also helped determine the procedures and time required to launch the nuclear missile by the armed forces.

AGNI-IIAT

The *Agni*-IIAT is the result of a Continuous Improvement Program (CIP) with *Agni*-II. Different reports indicate India developing a more advanced version of *Agni*-II[98] putting into use, state-of-the-art technologies to significantly improve the *Agni*-II design as well as to adapt it to the newer and lighter nuclear payload, that was proven by the *Pokharan*-II series of nuclear tests.[99] The *Agni*-IIAT is likely to incorporate the following changes: (i) Stronger 250-Marging steel, resulting in a lighter

Table 3.7
Agni-IIAT Missile Specifications

Name	:	Agni-IIAT
Length	:	20 meters
Maximum Diameter	:	1 meter
Launch Weight	:	16000 kg including payload
Propellant	:	Solid (HTPB/AP/AI)
Number of Stages	:	2.5
Payload	:	300-1000 kg
Warhead	:	Strategic nuclear (15 KT to 200 KT), Conventional HE-unitary, penetration, sub-munitions, incendiary or fuel air explosives.
Guidance	:	Strap Down-INS, optionally augmented by GPS terminal guidance with possible radar scene correlation.
Range	:	3900 km

Source : "Missile Proliferation in South Asia: India and Pakistan's Ballistic Missile Inventories", Factsheets, *Arms Control Today*, Arms Control Association, May 2002; Government of India, Ministry of Defence, *Annual Report, 2006-07;* Shanon N. Kile, Vitaly Fedchenko and Hans M. Kristensen, "World Nuclear Forces", Armaments, Disarmament and International Security, *SIPRI Yearbook, 2006,* Oxford University Press, Oxford, 2006; and *The Military Balance, 2006-07,* International Institute for Strategic Studies, London, 2006.

booster stage case and greater fuel mass-fraction (estimated improvement from 0.86 to 0.88). (ii) Lightweight carbon composite motor casing[100] for the second stage, instead of steel casing, resulting in greater fuel mass-fraction (estimated improvement from 0.85 to 0.92). (iii) Lighter and tougher RV, with all carbon composite re-entry heat shield, multi-directional carbon re-entry nose tip and control surfaces. This postulated configuration is referred as *Agni*-IIAT that would be validated only when it is tested sometime in the future.[101]

DRDO has reported major success in newer, higher performance RVs, lighter composite material cases of the crucial second stage and booster case made of stronger Maraging steel. The form factor is almost same as the *Agni*-II, but the qualitative improvements in propulsion and warhead significantly improves its range and effectiveness.

Lighter and tougher RV, with all carbon composite re-entry heat shields with multi-directional carbon re-entry nose tip and control surfaces, the new lightweight composites can withstand temperatures of up to 6000° centigrade, thus capable of greater re-entry velocity.[102] The new RV is likely to be smaller in diameter, shorter in length and lighter compared to the MRV of the *Agni*-I/II. The new layout is also likely to result in a different HAM capability influencing missile range and accuracy.

The *Agni*-IIAT's first stage is largely same as that of the *Agni*-II. However use of Maraging steel increases the stage fuel mass fraction. The second stage case is reported to be filament wound composite material, with a vastly superior fuel mass fraction. Lightweight carbon composite motor casing[103] for Stage-II instead of steel casing, resulting in greater fuel mass-fraction (considering similar motors elsewhere estimated improvement from 0.85 to 0.92. The above changes have potential to greatly increase the missile's range to 5500 km (750 kg payload) and 7000 km (550 kg payload).

AGNI-III

India needs IRBMs with ranges from 1000 to 5000 km to build an effective and flexible missile deterrent force which can strike key strategic targets in China.[104] A missile is required to provide India with a flexible second-strike capability. The missile is expected to be dispersed far and wide in the Indian mainland; it's far-flung islands or its blue water naval assets dispersed across the world's oceans. The ability to reach all corners of a potential challenger, requires a range of between 5000 to 8000 km. India is reportedly developing a larger *Agni*-III missile, with a heavier payload and a longer range but in a compact configuration, i.e. thicker but shorter length. Apparently its development is driven by need for a more assured retaliation that can defeat emerging ABM defences and counter-measures. Such capability requires a compact missile that can also carry ABM counter-measure payloads along with weapons, in a configuration similar to multiple independently targetable re-entry vehicles (MIRV), albeit with state-of-the-art decoys.

This missile would also fulfil India's immediate requirements of deterrence against China. This missile was launched for the first time on July 9, 2006 from the ITR at Wheeler Island at 11.03 a.m. but the test failed and missile fell into the Bay of Bengal without hitting the target.[105] The test of this missile has been repeatedly delayed since November 2004 for a number of reasons. But finally on 12 April 2007, *Agni*-III was launched and it hit the target 3,000 km away in 13 minutes.[105] After Successful launch, India now has a nuclear capable missile that might be able to reach the central and south-western part of urban China from north-eastern Orissa.

Given all the obfuscation around actual names of Indian missiles under development (e.g. *Agni*-TD/TTB, *Agni*-I, *Dhanush, Sagarika, Surya*, etc.), it is possible that this missile eventually could emerge under the name of *Agni*-IV, the *Agni*-III name might be given to what has been described as the *Agni*-IIAT.

Agni-III is a short and stubby, two-stage, solid fuel missile that is compact and small enough for easy mobility and flexible deployment on multiple surface/sub-surface platforms. The missile is likely to support a wide range of weapons, with total payload weight ranging from 600 kg to 1,800 kg including decoys and other ABM counter-measures with a range of 3000 to 5500 km. Instead of conventional bus architecture, the RV is likely to be self-contained with high altitude thrusters, navigation and re-entry control systems. The Integrated Sensing and Processing (ISP) is expected to be similar to a large solid motor currently in use by ISRO. The second stage will likely incorporate flex nozzles, which are expected to provide necessary flight trajectory control.

TABLE 3.8
Agni-III Missile Specifications

Name	:	Agni-III
Length	:	13 meters
Maximum Diameter	:	1.8 meter
Launch Weight	:	34000 kg including payload (estimated)
Propellant	:	Solid (HTPB/AP/AI)
Number of Stages	:	2.5
Payload	:	600-1800 kg (three MIRV?)
Warhead	:	Strategic nuclear (15 KT to 200 KT), Conventional HE-unitary, penetration, sub-munitions, incendiary or fuel air explosives.
Guidance	:	Strap Down-INS, optionally augmented by GPS terminal guidance with possible radar scene correlation.
Range	:	5500 km

Source : "Missile Proliferation in South Asia: India and Pakistan's Ballistic Missile Inventories", Factsheets, *Arms Control Today*, Arms Control Association, May 2002; Government of India, Ministry of Defence, *Annual Report, 2006-07;* Shanon N. Kile, Vitaly Fedchenko and Hans M. Kristensen, "World Nuclear Forces", Armaments, Disarmament and International Security, *SIPRI Yearbook, 2006,* Oxford University Press, Oxford, 2006; and *The Military Balance, 2006-07,* International Institute for Strategic Studies, London, 2006.

AGNI-IV/SURYA

It is also reported that India is developing an ICBM called *Surya* or *Agni*-IV. The two stage *Agni*-III could eventually be converted into an *Agni*-IV ICBM with the addition of a third stage motor. The current geo-political situation does not see an urgent need for such capability, but given the highly uncertain international situation due to the global war on terrorism, the oncoming global oil/energy crisis and growing demands of Indian economic development the geopolitical situation can turn out to be very fluid. Thus national strategic demand may see India developing *Agni*-IV.

TABLE 3.9

Agni-IV/Surya Missile Specifications

Name	:	Agni-IV/Surya
Length	:	15 meters
Maximum Diameter	:	1.8 meter
Launch Weight	:	36000 kg including payload (estimated)
Propellant	:	Solid (HTPB/AP/AI)
Number of Stages	:	3
Payload	:	600-1800 kg (three MIRV?)
Warhead	:	Strategic nuclear (15 KT to 200 KT), Conventional HE-unitary, penetration, sub-munitions, incendiary or fuel air explosives.
Guidance	:	Strap Down-INS, optionally augmented by GPS terminal guidance with possible radar scene correlation.
Range	:	5000-6000 km

Source : "Missile Proliferation in South Asia: India and Pakistan's Ballistic Missile Inventories", Factsheets, *Arms Control Today*, Arms Control Association, May 2002; Government of India, Ministry of Defence, *Annual Report, 2006-07;* Shanon N. Kile, Vitaly Fedchenko and Hans M. Kristensen, "World Nuclear Forces", Armaments, Disarmament and International Security, *SIPRI Yearbook, 2006,* Oxford University Press, Oxford, 2006; and *The Military Balance, 2006-07,* International Institute for Strategic Studies, London, 2006.

The *Agni*-IV will essentially be an *Agni*-III missile with an additional third stage, making it a three-stage missile. Maneuvering Re-Entry Vehicle is essentially same as the *Agni*-III, but qualified for greater re-entry speed and stress. Information on *Surya* is limited and often contradictory. There are likely to be several *Surya* missile variants however reports over their ranges have varied. It seems clear that India intends to develop several versions of *Surya* missile. Reported ranges have varied from 5000 km to as much as 20000 km. Initially there could be two *Surya* missiles: *Surya*-I (5000-6000 km) and *Surya*-II (8000-12000 km), and possibly a *Surya*-III (20000 km). The *Surya*-I is sometimes referred to as the *Agni*-IV. Although it is not know exactly what range of the *Agni*-III and *Agni*-IV/*Surya* will be, India is technologically capable of developing missiles of at least up to 12000 km in a long-term. The *Suryas* are likely to be benefited from India's satellite launch-vehicle programme in the same way the previous *Agni's* programmes have.[106]

As far as *Agni* family of missiles is concerned, the production and deployment of these missiles leads to the confusion most of the time. Prior to the first test of the *Agni*-II, press reports emerged of facilities being created to produce between 10 and 12 *Agni*-II missiles per year, a figure sometimes reported as between 12 and 18 missiles per year. However, it is entirely unclear as to whether any such production facilities have been created. Both Jaswant Singh and George Fernandes during their tenures as Defense Ministers have claimed that the *Agni*-II is in production and is being inducted, apparently by the 335th Missile Group of the Regiment of Artillery. What is unclear is whether sufficient equipment and reloads exist to make 335 Missile Group operational. If production on the scale envisaged had commenced in 2001-02, some 12+ launchers and 24+ missiles should exist.

However, there has been no indication either from DRDO or BDL as to whether any production on that scale is in progress. India has opted to commence production of the *Agni*-II IRBM, entering service with 335th Missile Group, and to prepare for production of the *Agni*-I, which is to enter service with 334th Missile Group. Each *Agni* missile group will have some 8 launchers and at least as many missiles. Delivery of the *Agni*-II commenced in 2001-02 and the system should be fully operational with the Army by now. Even if production was ridiculously low, a figure of 18 to 24 *Agni*-II missiles should have been produced by now. However, the *Agni*-I entered service somewhat later and it would be surprising if more that 8 missiles were currently available for deployment. At present, it can be assumed that India's land-based missile deterrent depends heavily on *Agni*-II, *Agni*-I and *Prithvi*-II. It is estimated that there must be 18 to 36 *Agni*-II IRBM (3500 km range, 200 KT warhead) and 8 to 16 *Agni*-I MRBM (900 km range, 200 KT warhead) missiles in service[107] and 150 to 180 *Prithvi*-II SRBM (330 km range, 15 KT warhead) missile produced (12 nuclear armed).

In case of nuclear warhead, India's options are still relatively limited, though quite perfectly adequate. Since the first Peaceful Nuclear Explosion (PNE) in 1974 India adopted the recessed deterrence posture initially consisting of fission weapons (15 KT yield) followed by boosted fission weapons of 200 KT yield, suitable for the *Agni*-TD/TTB. The *Pokhran*-II 1998 '*Shakti*' series of nuclear tests were reportedly done to validate multiple weapon designs, of 1995 vintage. Interestingly the 200 KT boosted fission design of 1980 was not tested in *Pokhran*-II, ostensibly having long given way to a lighter and more efficient S-1 design. It is interesting to note that India has access to large quantities of Tritium, produced at an extremely low cost, which lends flexibility to Indian weapon design options that is not available or viable to prior nuclear weapon states.[108]

The primary warhead for the *Agni* family would be a 200 KT fusion weapon based on the *Shakti*-1 *Pokhran*-II test in 1998. The fusion weapon based on the S-1 design would have a mass of some 500 kg, based on the 450 kg mass of the 45 KT demonstration test, which used an inert mantle. It has also emerged that by 1982, the BARC/DRDO team had produced a design for a pure fission device that weighed between 170 and 200 kg for a yield of 15 KT—a huge change from the 1000 kg monster tested in 1974.[109] This would mean that a missile warhead based on this 1982 vintage design would weigh some 250-350 kg. Therefore, when considering the range and payload parameters of the *Agni* and *Prithvi* missiles, these figures must be borne in mind.

AKASH

The *Akash* is a mobile area defence medium-range, medium and high altitude surface-to-air missile with a range of 27 to 30 kilometers. It is a part of the IGMDP undertaken by the DRDO in 1983. The system has undergone a few tests earlier to gauge proposition parameters and predicted values. By 1998 five flight-trials had been conducted. It was successfully tested on February 27, 2001 and March 2, 2001 for operational and evaluation purposes and declared ready for serial production after user tests by Indian Air Force. *Akash* has a multi-target handling capability, and employs a command guidance system with provision for terminal guidance. It operates in conjunction with the Rajendra surveillance and engagement radar. This system will replace the SA-6/Straight Flush in Indian service and is also expected to be integrated with the S-300V (SA-10 Grumble) low-to-high altitude SAM in an integrated air defence system to counter SRBM/IRBM threats along the Pakistani and Chinese borders.

Table 3.10
Akash Missile Specifications

Name	:	Akash
Mission	:	Medium-range air-defense missile
Service	:	Indian Army/Air Force
Development Year	:	1983
Targets	:	aircrafts
Platform	:	warships, vehicles
Launcher	:	triple launch rail on tracked vehicle (lengthen BMP-2 armoured vehicle)
Contractor	:	Bharat Dynamics Ltd., Hyderabad, India
Length	:	5.80 m
Body Diameter	:	34 cm
Launch Weight	:	650 kg
Range	:	27 km
Speed	:	Mach 3.5
Altitude	:	15-22 km
Propulsion	:	ramjet with integrated rocket booster
Warhead	:	60 kg prefragmented HE
Guidance	:	command guidance, semi-active radar

Source : Government of India, Ministry of Defence, *Annual Report, 2006-07;* Shanon N. Kile, Vitaly Fedchenko and Hans M. Kristensen, "World Nuclear Forces", Armaments, Disarmament and International Security, *SIPRI Yearbook, 2006,* Oxford University Press, Oxford, 2006; *The Military Balance, 2006-07,* International Institute for Strategic Studies, London, 2006; and Andrew Feickert and K. Alan Kronstadt, "Missile Proliferation and the Strategic Balance in South Asia", *CRS Report for Congress,* RL32115, October 17, 2003.

The missile is based heavily on the SA-6 and is claimed that Rajendra is similar to the 30N6 Flap-Lid B engagement radar, used by the S-300 ATBM system. The *Akash's* first flight occurred in 1990, with development flights up to March 1997. Officials have said that the missile will also undergo user trials with the Army for integration with the S-300PMU-1 anti-tactical ballistic missile systems, of which the Army has purchased an unspecified number, as well as with AEW aircraft. Plans exist for a naval version in VLS mode.

The *Akash* uses an integral ramjet rocket propulsion system to give a low-volume, low-weight (700 kg launch weight) missile configuration, and has a low reaction time, from detection to missile launch, of 15 seconds. This allows the missile to carry a heavier warhead 60 kg. The solid-propellant booster accelerates the missile in 4.5 seconds to Mach 1.5, which is then jettisoned and the ramjet motor is then ignited for 30 seconds to Mach 2.8-3.5 at 20 g. *Akash* has a range of 27 km, with an effective ceiling of 15 km. It is capable of detecting and destroying aircraft flying at treetop height. Development is on to increase speed, maximum altitude and range to 60 km. A dual mode radar/infra-red seeker is also being developed, as is a longer-range version of the Rajendra radar, to give earlier warning and tracking of ballistic missile targets.

In appearance, *Akash* is very similar to the ZRK-SD Kub (SA-6), with four long tube ramjet inlet ducts mounted mid-body between wings. Four clipped triangular moving wings, mid-body, for pitch/yaw control. Forward of tail, four inline clipped delta fins with ailerons for roll control. Flight control surfaces operated by pneumatic actuators. The warhead has a lethal radius of 20 meters, weighs 60 kg and has Doppler radar proximity/contact fusing. The missile is believed to have tail G/H-Band beacon to assist tracking by engagement radar. Guidance system is inertial with mid-course command updates from Rajendra and semi-active radar seeker for terminal phase (final 3-4 seconds).

Rajendra is 3D phased-array surveillance/engagement radar developed by the Electronic Research and Development Establishment (ERDE). Also mounted on a modified BMP-1 chassis, like the *Akash,* the radar is capable of tracking 64 targets, engage 4 simultaneously and guide up to 12 missiles. The system is reportedly similar to the 30N6 (Flap-Lid B) engagement radar.

It has air surveillance, multiple target tracking and multiple missile guidance functions via multi-channel monopulse. It is featured by fully digital signal processing system with adaptive moving target indicator, coherent signal processing, FFTs, and variable pulse repetition frequency.

Mounted on a turntable, at the front of a raised platform behind the driver's station, the multi-element antenna arrangement folds flat, when the vehicle is in motion. Radar comprises surveillance antenna array with 4000 elements operating in the G/H-Band (4-8 GHz), engagement antenna array with 1000 elements operating in the I/J-Band (8-20 GHz), a 16-element IFF array and steering units. The surveillance radar range is 60 km against aircraft targets. A longer-range version is being developed. The Army intends to use the Rajendra radar in the artillery-locating role as well. An *Akash* battery consists of three missile launch vehicles (triple launcher on a modified BMP-1 chassis), a Rajendra fire control radar vehicle, a long-range surveillance radar vehicle and an armoured command vehicle. Series production of 25 missiles per year was expected to commence in 2000 at Bharat Dynamics Ltd. No reliable information has been received so far, as to whether *Akash* missile production has begun.

Powered by ram rocket propulsion and an air breathing engine, *Akash* can cut through electronic jamming with its electronic cuter-counter measure equipment. It has a capacity to carry 50 kg payload. The *Akash* self propelled launcher (ASPL) and Phased Array Radar have been developed, though it has yet to enter the production/induction phase. For training the men and officers in handling *Akash*, scientists have developed simulator of the missile's seeker head in look down role and battery level radar under clutter and jamming environment.

NAG

The *Nag* (Cobra) is a third generation, all weather, top-attack, fire-and-forget anti-tank guided missile. It is developed to counter contemporary advances in tank-armor especially the composite and reactive type. It is one of five missile systems developed by the DRDO under the IGMDP. Design work on the missile started in 1988 and the first tests were carried out in November 1990.[110]

The missile uses a tandem High Explosive Anti-Tank (HEAT) warhead to penetrate Explosive Reactive Armour (ERA) or composite (Chobham type) armour that is found in the latest tanks.[111] The system is expected to supercede Indian production of the Soviet origin 9K113 *Konkours* (NATO: AT-5 *Spandrel*) and Euromissile Milan M2 anti-tank missiles[112] As originally conceived, the *Nag* would have been available with three different types of guidance. These included a wire guided version, an infra-red version and a millimetric wave (mmW) version. The

Table 3.11
Nag Missile Specifications

Name	:	Nag
Mission	:	Tube-launched top attack anti-tank missile
Service	:	Indian Army
Development Year	:	late 1980s
Targets	:	Armoured vehicle (tank)
Platform	:	four-tube launcher mounted on a modified BMP-2 chassis, helicopter-launched on Cheetah
Contractor	:	Bharat Electronics Ltd, Bangalore, India
Length	:	1.25m (?)
Body Diameter	:	13cm (?)
Range	:	4-6 km
Propulsion	:	Solid propellant
Warhead	:	Tandem warhead
Guidance	:	Command guidance (radio-link) and hybrid mm-wave/passive infrared seeker

Source : Government of India, Ministry of Defence, *Annual Report, 2006-07;* Shanon N. Kile, Vitaly Fedchenko and Hans M. Kristensen, "World Nuclear Forces", Armaments, Disarmament and International Security, *SIPRI Yearbook, 2006,* Oxford University Press, Oxford, 2006; *The Military Balance, 2006-07,* International Institute for Strategic Studies, London, 2006; and Andrew Feickert and K. Alan Kronstadt, "Missile Proliferation and the Strategic Balance in South Asia", *CRS Report for Congress,* RL32115, October 17, 2003.

cumbersome nature of a wire guidance system had led to plans for this being dropped. Currently, guidance is based on an imaging infra-red (IIR) passive seeker that ensures a high-hit accuracy in both top- and front-attack modes.

The mmW seeker, on the other hand, is intended to operate as an optional system that can replace the IIR passive seeker as a module. Also incorporated into the guidance system, is a CCD camera. The missile has a weight of 42 kg and can engage targets at ranges up to 6 km. The *Nag* is claimed to be first anti-tank missile, which has a complete fiberglass structure.[113]

The *Nag* will be produced in two main versions. The land version has been tested from a tracked vehicle known as NAMICA (*Nag* Missile Carrier). The carrier is a stretched BMP-2 with an additional pair of road wheels and is manufactured by the Ordnance Factory, *Medak*. It carries four missiles in a ready-to-fire mode on the turret and more missiles can be reloaded without exposing the crew on the battlefield. With the IR version of the missile, targets are acquired using a thermal sight, and are then assigned to the nose-mounted IIR seeker.

Missile guidance is initially by area correlation around the target, then by centroid tracking. Terminal homing is by area correlation around the centroid.[114] *Nag* is also configured to be used on the Advanced Light Helicopter (ALH). Eight missiles are carried in two quadruple launchers. Launchers mounted on either side are linked to a nose-mounted stabilized thermal sight and a laser range-finder package.

Despite trials since 1990, problems with the guidance system held back successful trials for a long time. The first successful test firing of the missile using an IIR seeker was conducted on 9 September 1997.[115] Of the two existing types guidance systems, the IIR seeker is now fully developed.[116] The IIR version of the missile has undergone several rounds of successful flight trials since 1997. Flight testing of the helicopter-launched version was carried out from a specially rigged Mi-17 in March 1998.[117] This was followed by integration with ALH in mid-1999.[118] The Indian Army accepted the system for user trials in October 1999.[119] The development of the mmW seeker has been more problematic and it is unlikely that the seeker will enter service any time soon. The missile also employs sensor fusion technology for flight guidance.

During recent test flights, the missile's fire-and-forget capability has been established using the day version of the IIR passive seeker. On 20 January 2000, field tests of the *Nag's* Thermal Sight system saw the system identify and lock on to a T-55 tank at a range of 5 km. The tank was then engaged and destroyed at a range of over 4 km.[120] In its IIR form, the *Nag* has limited all weather capability. This has given added impetus to develop the mmW seeker. Efforts are on to provide special embedded on-board hunters that can hunt for targets using 'day seekers' and 'day-and-night seekers'. A special nitramine-based propellant has been developed for the Nag in order to meet its dual requirements of energy and smokelessness.[121]

Low rate serial production of the *Nag* began in February 2000. 25 missiles produced by BDL in 2000, will all be earmarked for user trials. The Indian Army has a requirement for 500 missiles and the Indian Air Force has a requirement for 100 missiles by 2004.[122]

ASTRA

Astra is a state-of-the-art beyond visual range air-to-air missile (BVRAAM) designed for a range of over 80 km in head-on mode and 20 km in tail-chase mode.[123] It can engage highly manoeuvring targets. The *Astra* missile programme is headed by the DRDO. The goal of this programme is to provide the Indian Air Force with an indigenously-designed BVRAAM to equip the IAF's Mirage 2000, MiG-29, Su-30MKI and the Light Combat Aircraft (LCA). A model of the *Astra* missile was first shown to the public at Aero India '98. On 25 July 2001 in Indian Parliament, the then-incumbent Defence Minister Jaswant Singh said that a feasibility study for the *Astra* has commenced, after the completion of which a project for development of the *Astra* is planned to be undertaken.

Development of this missile is likely to take about seven to eight years. The Indian government funded Rs. 1000-crore national project to develop a futuristic BVRAAM missile *Astra* in June 2004 for delivery by 2009. Led by the Hyderabad-based DRDL, this indigenously developed missile is estimated to cost Rs. 3 to 5 crore. The missile is expected to be at the high-end of tactical missiles, and propel India into the exclusive club of countries to possess such missiles.[124] The Mirage 2000H has been designated as the first potential platform for the *Astra* when the weapon enters service at the end of this decade. The *Astra* was first test fired on 9 May 2003.

TABLE 3.12
Astra Missile Specifications

Name	:	Astra
Mission	:	Medium-range air-to-air missile
Service	:	Indian Air Force
Platform	:	Mirage 2000, MIG-29, Sea Harrier, Su-30, and the Light Combat Aircraft [LCA]
Length	:	3.8m
Range	:	100 km+, 80 km head on, 20 km tail chase
Speed	:	Mach 4+
Launch Weight	:	154 kg
Air Launcher Weight	:	60 kg
Altitude	:	20 km
Propulsion	:	Solid
Burn Time	:	5.4 seconds.
Warhead	:	15 kg pre-fragmented, high explosive, directional warhead.
Guidance	:	Inertial midcourse with data-linked updates, active-radar terminal homing.
Fuse	:	Radar Proximity (laser proximity to follow).
Maximum turning	:	40 Gs (Yaw and Pitch) Acceleration

Source : Government of India, Ministry of Defence, *Annual Report, 2006-07;* Shanon N. Kile, Vitaly Fedchenko and Hans M. Kristensen, "World Nuclear Forces", Armaments, Disarmament and International Security, *SIPRI Yearbook, 2006,* Oxford University Press, Oxford, 2006; *The Military Balance, 2006-07,* International Institute for Strategic Studies, London, 2006; and Andrew Feickert and K. Alan Kronstadt, "Missile Proliferation and the Strategic Balance in South Asia", *CRS Report for Congress,* RL32115, October 17, 2003.

The missile is capable of operating in the altitude bracket from sea level to 20 km. It has a single stage smokeless solid fuel rocket with a burn time of 5.4 seconds. Its low drag low aspect ratio wings allows it to reach long range. It uses dual mode guidance, i.e. inertial navigation during midcourse and active radar homing in terminal phase. Secure data link allows midcourse re-tasking.[125] On board autopilot and guidance software uses Artificial Intelligence (AI) for accurate guidance and optimized trajectory. The on-board ECCM capability allows it to stay on course in spite of enemy ECM (deception or noise jamming) by target aircraft (self-protection jammer or dedicated EW aircraft). The 15 kg high explosive payload is pre-fragmented and proximity fuse armed. The guidance computer aims the shape charge to focus the explosive energy towards the target.

The *Astra* is intended to have performance characteristics similar to the R-77RVV-AE (AA-12), which currently forms part of the IAF's missile armoury. The missile is 3.8 metres long and is said to be configured like a longer version of the Super 530D, narrower in front of the wings. *Astra* uses a HTPB solid-fuel propellant and a 15 kg HE (high-explosive) warhead, activated by a proximity fuse. The missile has a maximum speed of Mach 4+ and a maximum altitude of 20 km. The missile is designed to pull a lateral acceleration of 40 g in both yaw and pitch planes using 4 fins at the rear as all moveable control surfaces. The missile can also be launched in close combat. Although designed to use a locally developed solid fuel propellant, DRDO is also looking at rocket/ramjet propulsion to provide greater range and enhanced kinematical performance.

The basic *Astra* design uses a metallic airframe with a long low aspect-ratio wing and a single-stage smokeless rocket motor. After launch, the missile will use a combination of inertial mid-course guidance and/or data-linked targeting updates before it enters its terminal acquisition phase. In a head-on engagement, the *Astra* will have a maximum range of 80 km. The missile's onboard radio-frequency seeker has been largely designed in India but incorporates a degree of outside assistance, according to DRDO sources. It will have an autonomous homing range of 15 km. The missile's warhead is a pre-fragmented directional unit, fitted with a proximity fuse. A radar fuse already exists for the *Astra*, but the DRDO is currently working on a new laser fuse.

TRISHUL

The *Trishul* (Trident) is a short range, quick reaction, all weather surface-to-air missile designed to counter a low-level attack. *Trishul* was launched for the first time in September 1985. It has been flight tested in the sea-skimming role and also against moving targets. It has a range of 9 km and is fitted with a 5.5 kg HE-fragmented warhead. Its detection of target to missile launch is around 6 seconds. The missile can engage targets like aircraft and helicopters, flying between 300 m/s and 500 m/s by using its radar command-to-line-of-sight guidance. It operates in the K-

TABLE 3.13
Trishul Missile Specifications

Name	:	Trishul
Mission	:	Short Range Surface-to-Air Missile
Service	:	Indian Army/Navy/Air Force
Development Year	:	1983
Targets	:	Aircrafts
Platform	:	Army: Twin launcher on a modified BMP-2 infantry vehicle Navy: Project 15 Dehli-class destroyers and Project 16 frigates Air Force: Czechoslovak Tatra kolos truck
Contractor	:	Bharat Dynamic Ltd., Hyderabad, India
Length	:	3.1 m(?)
Launch Weight	:	130 kg(?)
Range	:	500-9,000 m
Propulsion	:	Solid propellant
Warhead	:	5.5 kg HE fragmentation (Lethal radius: 20 m)
Guidance	:	Command-guided

Source : Government of India, Ministry of Defence, *Annual Report, 2006-07;* Shanon N. Kile, Vitaly Fedchenko and Hans M. Kristensen, "World Nuclear Forces", Armaments, Disarmament and International Security, *SIPRI Yearbook, 2006,* Oxford University Press, Oxford, 2006; *The Military Balance, 2006-07,* International Institute for Strategic Studies, London, 2006: and Andrew Feickert and K. Alan Kronstadt, "Missile Proliferation and the Strategic Balance in South Asia", *CRS Report for Congress,* RL32115, October 17, 2003.

band (20-40 GHz), which makes it difficult to jam. In the K-band three-beam system, the missile is initially injected into a wide beam, which then hands it over to a medium beam, which passes over to a narrow beam, guiding it to the target.

This missile has been developed for all the three services. Army and Air Force will use it against low flying aircrafts while the Navy will use it in a modified version against sea skimming missiles like the French Excocet and the American Harpoon. The *Trishul* has high manoeuvrability and is powered by a two-stage solid propellant system, with a highly powered HTBP-type propellant similar to the ones used in the Patriot. It is constructed of maraging steel to withstand the stress. Successful flight trials in a tube launched mode using folded fins against balloons and Pilot-less Target Aircraft (PTA) targets were carried out. One flight trial was guided throughout the trajectory using fixed line of sight and infra-red gathering guidance systems as per programmed flight. The army variant, *Trishul* Combat Vehicle (TCV), is based on a tracked BMP-1 infantry combat vehicle and houses all equipment including radars, command-guidance system and missiles.

Trishul is one of the longest-running DRDO missile development programs. The program began in 1984, and more than 40 test flights have been conducted. The then Defence Minister George Fernandes told Indian Parliament that while the *Trishul* had demonstrated a number of complex technologies, including an ability to defeat sea-skimming targets, it still had not been proved to be effective. By continuing the program as a technology demonstrator, India hopes that some of the technology from *Trishul* can be incorporated in other missile projects. The Indian Air Force, which had intended to adopt the *Trishul* for an airfield-defence role, recently turned against the project. The Army has also stated that the *Trishul* was unlikely to meet its requirements for a replacement for the Russian-designed OSA-AKM (SA-8b *Gecko*) self-propelled SAM system. The Indian Navy had designed recent warships to include the *Trishul* as their armament, so the decision not to make the system operational is likely to require selection of an alternative system and modification of the warships that were to use the *Trishul* missile. This leads to an expansion of the Indian procurement of the Israeli-built Barak SAM system, of which seven systems were already ordered and another 10 systems have been planned for.

BRAHMOS

The *BrahMos* missile is a product of joint venture of India and Russia. It is a supersonic cruise missile having a range of 280-300 km with a payload of 200-300 KG in joint partnership with the Russian entity, NPO Mashinostroyeniye.[126] The joint development work on the missile was started in 1998, while the joint company establishing the program was registered in 1995.[127]

TABLE 3.14
BrahMos Missile Specifications

Name	:	BrahMos
Mission	:	Supersonic anti-ship and land attack cruise missile
Development Year	:	1998
Platform	:	submarine, ship, aircraft and land-based Mobile Autonomous Launchers (MAL)
Launcher	:	Transport-Launch Canister (TLC)
Length	:	8.9 m (container)
Body Diameter	:	70 cm (container)
Wing/Fin span	:	1.4 m
Launch Weight	:	3,000 kg
Range	:	300 km
Speed	:	Mach 2-3
Altitude	:	14,000 m (max), 5-15 m (terminal phase)
Propulsion	:	Ramjet, solid propellant
Warhead	:	250 kg HE SAP, submunitions
Guidance	:	Inertial, active/passive radar

Source : Government of India, Ministry of Defence, *Annual Report, 2006-07;* Shanon N. Kile, Vitaly Fedchenko and Hans M. Kristensen, "World Nuclear Forces", Armaments, Disarmament and International Security, *SIPRI Yearbook, 2006,* Oxford University Press, Oxford, 2006; *The Military Balance, 2006-07,* International Institute for Strategic Studies, London, 2006; Andrew Feickert and K. Alan Kronstadt, "Missile Proliferation and the Strategic Balance in South Asia", *CRS Report for Congress,* RL32115, October 17, 2003 and Joseph Cirincione, John Wolsthal and Miriam Raj Kumar, *Deadly Arsenals: Nuclear Biological and Chemical Threats,* Carnegie Endowment for International Peace, Washington, D.C. 2005.

Derived from the Russian anti-ship missile called Yakhont, the *BrahMos* is a dual-mode cruise missile, with its primary mode as an anti-ship, with a backup capability to attack shore-based, radio-contrast targets. It is a Supersonic cruise missile that can be launched from submarine, ship, aircraft and land based Mobile Autonomous Launchers (MAL). The missile is launched from a Transport Launch Canister (TLC), which also acts as storage and transportation container. It cruises horizontally and travels only in the atmosphere.

Although *BrahMos* is an anti-ship missile but it has the capability to engage land-based targets also. The missile can be launched either in vertical or inclined position and will cover 360 degrees. The missile has identical configuration for land, sea and sub sea platforms. The air-launched version has a smaller booster and additional tail fins for stability during launch. The missile features a two-stage propulsion system employing a solid propellant booster with a liquid ramjet engine. Russia is believed to be primarily responsible for the propulsion system and systems integration, while India has responsibility for the on-board guidance system.[128] The first test of the missile in India was conducted in June 2001[129] at ITR, in Orissa. The missile was launched in vertical mode, where the missile was launched upward from the canister and directed towards the target point. This launch was the first in a series of flight-tests planned to demonstrate the capabilities of the system to the potential customers. The second flight test (D02) was conducted successfully, from ITR in Orissa, on 28 April 2002.[130] The missile was flown in a high-low-low trajectory to test the missile's sea skimming capabilities. In this flight, the missile was launched in an inclined configuration; as if it is onboard a ship. The mission objective was to establish the missile parameters and the performance of all the sub-systems, in the configuration. The post-flight analysis proved that all the set mission objectives had been achieved. Three developmental flight tests were conducted in 2003[131] followed by an additional three tests during 2004. During two tests conducted in November 2003 and 2004 respectively, the missile was successfully used to destroy a moving target from a warship at sea.[132]

Developmental flight tests of the naval variant of the *BrahMos* were reportedly completed in 2004 and the missile was expected to enter serial production very soon. In 2004, the Indian Navy (IN) placed a "letter of intent" with the joint Indo-Russian venture *BrahMos* Aersopace Ltd. to acquire an undisclosed number of the cruise missiles.[133] The first missile was expected to begin operational deployment by the end of 2005 and the navy proposes to arm both surface warships and submarines with the *BrahMos*.[134] The Indian Navy has ultimately begun the deployment of the missile on its warships. It has been installed on INS *Rajput* and the process of installing it on INS *Ranjit* is on.[135] BrahMos will be deployed on light warships and each ship will carry four missiles, two on their either side.

Beside the naval version, India is also developing Army and Air Force variants of the missile. Two tests of the Army variant were successfully conducted in June and December 2004.[135(a)] The CEO and Managing Director of *BrahMos* Aerospace Ltd. A. Sivathanu Pillai stated in December 2004 that development of the Air Force variant is expected to be completed within the next three to five years.[136] The Air Force version of the *BrahMos* will have reduced length and weight, employ a new booster and a cap nose. It will reportedly be deployed on board the SU-30MK1 that the IAF is acquiring from Russia.[137]

The *BrahMos* missile will be available for export to friendly countries when it will be ready for regular production. The foundation of the Joint Venture *BrahMos* is an example of integration and promotion of jointly developed high technology military products to the world market. India and Russia have announced plans to export the *BrahMos* to friendly third countries, with mutual consent. Production facilities for the *BrahMos* are being established in India and Russia; 20 Indian and 10 Russian companies are expected to participate in its manufacture.[138] In 2004, *BrahMos* Aerospace Ltd. signed an agreement with Russia's main arms export agency, Rosoboron export, to market the missile in the international market.[139] Some defence observers believe that the India will likely to use technologies acquired and developed under the *BrahMos* program to develop longer-range nuclear capable cruise missiles in the future.[140]

SAGARIKA

It is also being reported that India's Aeronautical Development Establishment is planning to develop a submarine-launched missile with significant engineering assistance, especially in underwater launch technology, from scientists associated with quasi-public research institutes in Russia.[141] There is considerable controversy over the *Sagarika*. Indian defence analysts have described it as a cruise missile program but the US Department of Defense has categorized the *Sagarika* as a submarine-launched ballistic missile.[142] The range, propulsion, payload, and other technical parameters of this missile remain unknown, except that it will probably arm India's nuclear submarine, the Advanced Technology Vessel (ATV).[143] Development work on the missile apparently began in 1992 and was expected to be completed by 2000. However, the program has met with considerable delays and the missile is not expected to become operational before 2010. The *Sagarika* program is believed to be driven by India's long-term goals to achieve a secure sea-based, second-strike nuclear capability.

India's efforts to achieve this status have mainly been indigenous and is supported by a diverse coalition of actors and institutions It succeeded, through its space programme, in achieving a relatively high-degree of autonomy in the development, engineering, and manufacture of first-generation ballistic missiles. Currently, the *Prithvi*-I and *Prithvi*-II are the only ballistic missiles in service with the Indian Army and Air Force respectively. The *Prithvi* missiles are inherently nuclear-capable, and an undisclosed number of *Prithvi*-I missiles have reportedly been modified to deliver nuclear warheads. However, the *Prithvi* suffers from several limitations such as its short-range, liquid-fueled engine, which add to the logistics burden, and fuel toxicity, which increases the difficulty of handling the weapon system in the field. Hence the *Prithvi* missiles will most likely be replaced by the *Agni* ballistic missiles for nuclear missions. The *Agni*-I, II and III ballistic missiles are likely to be the mainstay of India's land-based missile force in the future.

At present India does not maintain a constituted nuclear force on a heightened state of alert'. Although the nuclear-capable missiles and aircraft are under the control of individual armed services, India's consolidated nuclear force is administered by a tri-service Strategic Forces Command (SFC).[144] At the level of the civilian executive, India's Nuclear Command Authority (NCA) is responsible for the management of its nuclear forces and for making all decisions pertaining to the use of nuclear weapons. The NCA is a two-layered structure. It comprises a Political Council (PC) and an Executive Council (EC). The PC is chaired by the prime minister and is the sole body, which can authorize the use of nuclear weapons.

The success of Prithvi and Agni programmes has encouraged the Indian Government to pursue new missile programmes. These proposed programmes include both defensive and offensive missile systems. The list of defensive systems includes ATBMs designed to provide "point defence" for India's nuclear command and control centers and high-density population targets. Offensive weapon systems include an intermediate-range version of the Agni ballistic missile, the *BrahMos* cruise missile, and possibly the *Avatar* programme that would theoretically be capable of launching nuclear strikes from outer space.

However, these developments in the field of ballistic and cruise missiles capabilities undoubtedly enhanced the Indian strategic position in the South Asian region but simultaneously provoked Pakistan to accelerate its missile development programme which is already considered to be a response of IGMDP. Prior to the launch of Agni *missile* Pakistan's missile arsenal comprised primarily of *Hatf*-I and II missiles with ranges of 80 and 280 km. India's launch of *Agni* missile, in conjunction with the US denial of delivering F-16 aircrafts to Pakistan, is credited by many as central events that compelled Islamabad to pursue ballistic missiles as its primary means to deliver nuclear weapons. These and other related issues about Pakistan's missile development programme will form part of analysis of next chapter.

Notes and References

1. These missiles deliver their payloads faster than combat aircraft and largely assured of penetrating enemy airspace due to the lack of highly effective defences. They can travel at supersonic speeds, thus

reducing warning time, in some cases down to a few minutes. Moreover, they can cover enormous distances, from less than 100 km to over 10,000 km, thus potentially threatening the rear areas of a military theater or even the homeland of an opponent. In many cases missiles can strike a target with a high level of accuracy and with enormous force, often producing devastating damage before an opponent can react. Since they are unmanned, their use does not risk the loss of highly skilled military personnel, such as pilots. Furthermore, a missile will not defect or refuse to carry out orders. In addition, ballistic missiles are very difficult to defend against, especially if a potential opponent desires to intercept them before they can strike their intended targets. And unlike airfields or artillery bases, which are large, fixed, vulnerable targets prone to attack by a sophisticated military power, hidden or mobile missiles are hard to find and destroy. Finally, many types of missiles are relatively easy to deploy and operate, especially if compared to a trained air force with manned aircraft and a large infrastructure.

2. Feroz Hasan Khan, "Nuclear Signaling, Missiles and Escalation Control in South Asia", in Michel Krepon, *et. al.*, eds., *Escalation Control and Nuclear Option in South Asia,* The Henry L. Stmson Center, Washington D.C., November 2004, pp. 75-76.
3. Ashok, K. Mehta, "Missiles in South Asia : Search for an Operational Strategy", *South Asian Survey,* Vol. 11, No. 2, July-December 2004, p. 178.
4. The NPT recognized only those five countries as nuclear weapon states which had manufactured and exploded a nuclear weapon or other nuclear device prior to 1 January 1967.India refused to sign NPT because of its discriminatory character. NPT stops only the horizontal proliferation and not of vertical. India, therefore urges the nuclear powers that they ought to effect vertical non-proliferation, which in turn might induce others not to engage in nuclear proliferation. But, paradoxically, seeds of nuclear proliferation are inherent in the clause of NPT itself. For instance, under article iv of the treaty, signatories become automatically entitled to acquire nuclear capability under the guise of peaceful intent of nuclear energy. India, *Rajya Sabha Debates,* Vol. CLXXIII, No. 36, May 26, 1997, cols. 290-91 for NPT details, See Mahmed I. Shaker, *The Nuclear Non-Proliferation Treaty : Origin and Implementation,* 1959-79, 3 Vols., Oceana, New York, 1980.
5. A ballistic missile (BM) is a rocket powered during the boost phase of its flight, which then hurls by its own momentum in or above the atmosphere before it careens down on its target. Ballistic missiles travel several times faster than the speed of sound, making them extremely difficult to detect and shoot down. They are classified by a number of capabilities and characteristics, the first being range.

   The classifications of missiles by range is commonly broken down into five categories, Battlefield Short Range (BSRBM), Short Range (SRBM), Medium Range (MRBM), Intermediate Range (IRBM), and Intercontinental Range (ICBM). Another common classification is Theater Ballistic Missiles (TBMs), which denotes all SRBMs, MRBMs, and some IRBMs with a range under 3,500 km. This system of classification was devised for USA-USSR dialogue on ballistic missiles and thus refers to capabilities based on a conflict between those two powers (for example, an "intercontinental" ballistic missile can travel the distance between Russia and the United States). As a result of their situational categorization, current definitions vary between countries. A common classification of missile types and their ranges are as follows:

Ballistic Missile Classification Range
Battlefield short range (BSRBM) 0–150 km
Short range (SRBM) 151–1,000 km
Medium Range (MRBM) 1,001–3,000 km
Intermediate Range (IRBM) 3,001–5,500 km
Intercontinental Range (ICBM) +5,501 km

Missiles may be modified for longer ranges by lessening their payload, provided the modifications do not disrupt the balance and structure of the fuselage. This modification can include using a lighter warhead or lighter weight materials. Conversely, missiles can be equipped with heavier warheads by sacrificing range. This "range-payload tradeoff" complicates classifying missiles by range or payload capacity. The MTCR an international agreement where member nations agree not to sell ballistic missiles over 300 km, has been confounded in the past by countries cheating the regulations by manipulating the range payload tradeoff in order to make an exported missile legal by MTCR standards.

Countries with ballistic missile programs (such as Pakistan and North Korea) have also used the range-payload tradeoff as an easy way to gain greater versatility from their missiles, most notably to coax greater ranges out of old Russian Scud-Bs. Michael D. Swaine and Loren H. Runyon, "Ballistic Missile Development", *Strategic Asia 2001-02,* pp. 343-44.

6. Savita Pandey, "India's Missile Programme", *World Focus,* Vol. 18, No. 3, March 1997, p. 13.
7. Gaurav Kampani, "Stakeholders Analysis in the Indian Strategic Missile Program", *Non-proliferation Review,* Fall/Winter 2003, pp. 53-54. However, the seeds were sown for an indigenous plan, moves were made to set-up a missile establishment in the country. Experimental rockets (two-stage) were fired from Hyderabad in 1963, and work on development rocket propellant was also carried out at the DRDO's explosive laboratory. In 1965, the *ad hoc* electronics committee provided the impetus for sustaining these early developments. It concluded that since licensed production of the French Centaure rocket was established, work should proceed in developing propellants and guidance systems. Savita Pandey, n. 6.
8. In 1967, India began to develop sounding rockets, which became the basis for its satellite launch vehicle (SLV) programme in the 1970s. Ben Sheppard, "South Asia's Ballistic Missile Ambitions", in Raju

G.C. Thomas and Amit Gupta, eds., *India's Nuclear Security,* Vistaar Publications, New Delhi, 2000, p. 176. The dual use capability of SLVs makes it easy for proliferators to conceal their military intentions behind civilian appearances. Apart form Japan, no country has invested in the production of SLVs solely for non-military objectives.

9. Diffusion of technological capabilities in the industry that occurred through the space programme over the years appears to have helped India to run a separate missile programme. The Indian space programme and missile programme are organized separately, under the ISRO and DRDO respectively. A. Baskaran, "Export Control Regimes and India's Space and Missile Programme", *India Quaterly,* Vol. LVIII, No. 3 and 4, July-December 2002, pp. 222-23. For details about India's space programme, see various *Annual Reports, Department of Space,* Government of India; Dinshaw Mistry, "Technology for Defence and Development : India's Space Programme", in Raju, G.C. Thomas and Amit Gupta, eds., *Ibid.*; and Onkar Marwah, *India's Nuclear and Space Programme : Intent and Policy,* at http://www.space.com/Space Reporters Network Astronomy Discoveries/RaoIndiamoon 022502.htm.
10. By 1987, an augmented booster, the 35 ton Augmented Satellite Launch Vehicle ASLV (4000 km/150 km in low earth orbit), which is basically three SLV-3's strapped together, had began flight testing the much larger (275 ton) Polar Satellite Launch Vehicle PSLV (8000 km/1000 kg) is being developed to place in sun-synchronous polar orbit a one tone satellite. The PSLV could readily deliver a nuclear warhead over inter-continental distances, if re-engineered as a weapon system. India also developed a Geo-synchronous Satellite Launch Vehicle GSLV, employing both solid and cryogenically fueled stages. With an expected range of 14000 km and a payload of 2500 kg, the GSLV would have an even greater potential than the PSLV as an ICBM. For details see, Shikha Malhothra, Challenges to *India's Security : A Study of Its Perceptions and Nuclear Response,* unpublished, Ph.D. Thesis, Department of Political Science, University of Jammu, Jammu, 2004.
11. Savita Pandey, n. 6, p. 14.
12. Normally a missile system takes anything between 10-15 years to develop. To reduce this to a period of 8-10 years, it was decided that first missile to be developed would be a short range surface-to-air missile and a battlefield support missile, both of which did not require innovations in design and construction. It was also decided that DRDL should also go ahead with the design and development of an IRBM class launch vehicle. As a result, the battlefield support missile *Prithvi* was successfully test fired on 25 February 1988 barely five years after the IGMDP was okayed. This was a testimony to the remarkable success of its programme. A major reason why the IGMDP succeeded while other military R and D programmes failed is the organizational approach adopted for the missile programmes. The 'mission' of the development of a particular missile was made paramount, everything else (organizations, procedures, personnel,

finances etc.) was made sub-servient. Obvious as this approach might seem, in practice it was nothing short of revolutionary. Bureaucratic procedures for the first time took a back seat. Review teams for every missile met once in a month not only to review progress but also to take on the spot decisions without referring to any higher body. Financial clearances too were made at such meetings. The review teams composition ensured this. The teams included representatives from the ministries of defence, DRDL, finance and from other outside agencies involved in the IGMDP. For details see, Indranil Banerjie, "Integrated Guided Missile Development Programme", *Indian Defence Review,* July 1990; Also see, Mohammed Ayoob, "India and South Asia: The Quest for Regional Predominance", *World Policy Journal,* Vol. 7, No. 1, Winter 1989-90.

13. For example, India imported gyros from French and Swedish companies, hydraulic actuators from France, computers and motion simulators from the USA and the three axis measuring machines from West Germany. India also imported machinery and equipment required to develop carbon nose cones through its industry from Germany and the USA. Raj Chengappa, *Weapons of Peace : The Secret Story of India's Quest to Be a Nuclear Power,* Harper Collins, New Delhi, 2000, pp. 315-16, and 347. Also see, A.K. Sachdev, "India's Surface to Surface Missiles: The Doctrinal and Strategic Framework", *Strategic Analysis,* Vol. XXIV, No. 2, May 2000, pp. 268-69.
14. Rodney, W. Jones, "Minimum Nuclear Deterrence Postures in South Asia: An Overview", *Journal of South Asian and Middle Eastern Studies,* Villanova, Vol. XXV, No. 5, Summer 2002, p. 12. Also see, T.S. Gopi Rethinaraj, "Going Global : India Aims for a Credible Nuclear Doctrine", *Jane's Intelligence Review,* Vol. 13, No. 2, February 2001, p. 50.
15. N.C. Birla, ed., *Indian Defence Technology: Missile Systems,* Defense Research and Development Organization, Ministry of Defence, New Delhi, 1998, pp. ix-x; A.P.J. Abdul Kalam and Arun Tiwari, *Wings of Fire: An Autobiography,* Universities Press, Hyderabad, 1999, pp. 117-18.
16. "DRDO: Launching platforms for Project K-15", http://www.drdo.com/pub/techfocus/aug04/missile 13.htm: "India tests medium-range missile: BBC, 27 October 2004", http://news.bbc.co.uk/1/hi/world/ south_asia/3957587.stm "Prithvi-III test fired", *Times of India,* 27 October 2004. http:// times ofindia.indiatimes.com/articleshow/901642.cms.
17. Solid propellants are generally favored as they are safer to store and easier and quicker to put into action than liquid propellants. Countries that produce solid propellant missiles are generally considered to have a more technologically advanced missile programme than those of who produce liquid propellant missiles. Andrew Feickert and K. Alan Kronstadt, "Missile Proliferation and the Strategic Balance in South Asia", *CRS Report for Congress,* RL32115, 17 October 2003, p. 26.

18. For details see, 'India Missile Chronology' 1987-95; http://www.nti.org/e_research/profiles/India/Missile/1931_4696.html, (January 2005).
19. By October 1995, 20 pre-production *Prithvi* SS-150s were delivered to the Army to form the 333rd Missile Group based in Secunderabad. Two additional units have been formed since, the 444th Missile Group and 555th Missile Group. Typically, each group has 12 launchers, with possibly another three more in reserve. Reportedly 300 *Prithvis*, estimated to cost $ 200 million, would be manufactured at the state-owned Bharat Dynamics Limited (BDL) in Hyderabad at the rate of 36 missiles/year. Various technical tests of the SS-250 variant have been carried out. On 18 April 2001, in Parliament, the incumbent Defence Minister Jaswant Singh stated that the SS-250 was being inducted into the IAF, but apparently the IAF plans to use it only for familiarization/training. The *Prithvi* programme has continued to develop newer versions with improved range and accuracy. The tests on 23 January 2004 and 19 March 2004 were of the longer range, solid fuelled *Prithvi*-III variant meant for the IAF and were reportedly successfully tested for the 'runway denial' mission. Earlier tests in December 2001 proved an advanced homing facility.
20. Pravin Sawhney, "Army Organizes First Prithvi Missile Unit", *Asian Age*, New Delhi, 29 April 1995, p. 1; Rahul Bedi, "India pressured to halt Prithvi production", *Jane's Defence Weekly*, 15 April 1995, p. 5.
21. There are no authoritative estimates of the number of operational *Prithvi* ballistic missiles in India's inventory. For reported estimates see, 'India Missile Chronology,' for years 1998-2004, http://www.nti.org/e_research/profiles/India/Missile/1931_4696.html, (January 2005).
22. Bulbul Singh, "India to Build Missile Stocks While Seeking Missile Defense", *Aerospace Daily*, Vol. 207, No. 12, 17 July 2003, p. 2.
23. For developments concerning the Prithvi-II see, 'India Missile Chronology' for years 1993-2004", http://www.nti.org/e_research/profiles/India/Missile/1931_4696.html
24. Srinjoy Chowdhury, "IAF Increasing Prithvi Arsenal", *Statesman*, 9 September 2004.
25. Bulbul Singh, n. 22.
26. Fuel loading and draining is a very sensitive process, missile crews who operate them undergo intense training in three general phases; missile sub-system, handling and maintenance. An advanced simulator has been developed to train the missile crews in its operation.
27. "India to Test New Prithvi", *Aviation Week and Space Technology*, Vol. 148, No. 26, New York, 29 June 1998, p. 31.
28. *The Tribune*, 7 September 1998, www.tribuneindia.com/1998/98sep07/head6.htm; According to Defence Ministry sources *Sagarika* and *Prithvi*-III (naval *Prithvi*) were one and the same thing or two sides of the same coin. "These (*Sagarika* and *Prithvi*-III) are two different acronyms for the same missile for the Indian Navy which is under development.

29. For details See, "Large Size Solid Booster", *DRDO Technology Focus*, Vol. 9, No. 5, October 2001. http://www.drdo.com/pub/techfocus/oct2001/propulsion.htm
30. "Prithvi-III test-fired for first time", *The Hindu*, 28 October 2004, http://www.hindu.com/2004/10/28/stories/2004102807641300.htm.
31. "Large Size Solid Booster n. 29.
32. "Dhanush variant for land targets sought", *Hindustan Times*, New Delhi, 20 April 2000, http://www.hindustantimes.com/; Rahul Bedi, "Missile Test is 'Partial Success', says India", *Jane's Defence Weekly* 19 April 2000, p. 14.
33. Indian Missile Dhanush Ready for Navy", *Asia Pulse*, 30 September 2002.
34. "Prithvi-III test fired", *Press Trust of India*, 27 October 2004.
35. Dhanush test fired from Orissa coast", *Press Trust of India*, 7 November 2004; "Dhanush missile successfully test fired", *The Hindu*, 8 November 2004.
36. "Akash, Trishul, Nag missiles to user", *Press Trust of India*, 9 December 2004.
37. CEP is defined as the radius of a circle centered at the target within which 50 per cent of all missiles aimed at the target would be expected to impact and is the standard for measuring accuracy for missiles and bombs.
38. For details see, Prithvi /SS-150/-250/-350/(P-1/P-2/P-3/ and Dhanush: http://www.aeronautics. ru/archive/wmd/ballistic/
39. "Indo-Russian tie-up on Glonass satellite system". *Deccan Herald*, 20 December 2005.http://www. deccanherald.com/deccanherald/dec202005/state1861820051219.asp
40. "Naval Prithvi testing soon". *The Tribune*, 7 September 1998; www.tribuneindia.com/1998/98 Sep. 7/head6.htm
41. Chengappa, n. 13, p. 437.
42. "Indian Government to Hand Over Agni Missiles to Army", *Press Trust of India*, 2 September 2003.
43. The nuclear tests conducted in May 1998 proved that miniaturized nuclear warheads of various yields can also be fitted that and However, after the Agni-I MRBM test in January 2002, K. Santhanam, former RAW officer, DRDO technical advisor, nuclear scientist and former IDSA Director-stated that the *Prithvi* missile was never meant to carry nuclear warheads under normal circumstances. This indicates that the solid-fuelled Agni has completely taken over the 'nuclear' role from the liquid-fuelled Prithvi.
44. Clearly special weapons are complex systems and have deeper ramifications that have to be understood before weaponizing. Prithvi project was implemented as a morale booster for disheartened scientists in DRDL who had worked on the 'Devil' and 'Valiant' programmes that saw development of the 30 ton liquid fuelled engines. Kalam and Tiwari n. 15. Under Dr. Kalam the engineers evaluated the options to build on liquid fuel expertise built from Devil and Valient program versus solid fuelled motor technology developed by ISRO. To keep the morale of the DRDO engineers it was

decided to start the project using liquid propellant engine. And after the first few test flights the liquid fuelled Prithvi developed its own constituency. It reflected a sorry state of affairs when a weapons system implemented as a morale booster, ended up creating heartburn about lowering the nuclear threshold. D. Ramana, *Agni-I*, http://www.bharat-rakshak.com/

45. Ashley, J. Tellis, *India's Emerging Nuclear Posture*, RAND, Santa Monica, 2001, pp. 558-60.
46. The main objectives of this project were to test and validate—(a) Re-entry test vehicle to evaluate structure, guidance and control during re-entry into earth's atmosphere at hypersonic velocity. (b) The RV used multi-directionally reinforced carbon-fiber perform. (c) Rocket Staging (MRCP) technology. (d) Inertial Navigation System.
47. Gary Milhollin, "India's Missiles With a Little Help From Our Friends", *Bulletin of the Atomic Scientists*, November 1989, pp. 31-35.
48. *Jane's Defence Weekly*, 3 June 1989, p. 1052
49. "Indians Place Cloak over Missile Plans", *Defense News*, 11-17 Dec. 95, p. 5.
50. Whether the suspension is real and the result of diplomatic pressure, technical problems, or other factors, is not evident. India may have decided to put the *Agni* under wraps until it decides the larger related issue of whether to test nuclear (perhaps thermonuclear) warheads for its missiles in the face of US and other diplomatic pressures to sign the Comprehensive Test Ban Treaty. India indicates that it won't sign the Treaty unless the five major nuclear powers commit to a nuclear disarmament timetable. (Pakistan, understandably, won't sign the Treaty unless India does. In March 1997 the then Prime Minister H.D. Deve Gowda indicated that India would not give up the development of the *Agni* missile programme, a position echoed in July by Defense Minister Mulayam Singh Yadav, who denied that India had any immediate plans to further test fire the Agni missile. "India Puts Agni IRBM Program on Ice", *Jane's International Defense Review*, January 1996, p. 5; Also see, "Ballistic Missile Capabilities By Country", in *Tracking Nuclear Proliferation : A Guide in Maps and Charts, 1998*, Carnegie Endowment for International Peace, Washington D.C.,1998.
51. Chengappa, n. 13, pp. 371-72.
52. On April 28, 1995, the then Prime Minister Narasimha Rao refutes allegations that India has capped its missile programme under the pressure of USA. Replying to a debate in parliament, Rao asserts that India will not buckle under anybody's pressure, as far as it's defence preparedness is concerned. Pravin Sawhney, "Army Organizes First Prithvi Missile Unit", *Asian Age*, New Delhi, 29 April 1995, p. 1.
53. *"Annual Report"*, Ministry of Defence, Government of India, 1994-1995, p. 39; Raj Chengappa, "Nuclear Policy: Making Compromises", *India Today*, New Delhi, 30 April 1995, p. 36; Raj Chengappa, "Boom for Boom", *India Today*, New Delhi, 26 April 1999, http://www.india-today.com/.
54. On May 11, 1998, an Indian defence official reveals that contrary to popular perceptions that India had put its IGMDP on hold under US

pressure, the projects were never capped completely. The official stated, "How can we stop working on it? We cannot take a risk of reaching in a stage of technology-gap . . . capping the missile programme at this stage means creating a considerable technological gap, and India cannot afford to do that keeping in mind India's war-history." DRDO sources suggest that Pakistan's Ghauri has given the country [India] a golden opportunity to legitimize R and D on the sophisticated missile projects. "Agni project was never capped", *The Hindu*, Chennai, 11 May 1998, http://www.hinduonnet.com/.

55. On April 13, 1995 after a visit to DRDL in Hyderabad (Andhra Pradesh), Prime Minister Narasimha Rao sanctions approximately 6 billion rupees for the development of the *Agni* program. He also orders the DRDO to speed up efforts to build nuclear weapons and set up a nuclear command and control system for the safe custody, deployment and employment of such weapons. DRDO Chief, Dr Kalam sets up a special cell to ensure that nuclear cores at BARC in Trombay are scattered to several sites in the country to enhance their survivability; that the mechanism to ensure the mating of the core with the bomb assembly is achieved in the shortest time frame; that the command to trigger nuclear weapons remains under civilian control; and that it is a system that will win consent of at least three agencies to arm nuclear weapons. Chengappa, n. 13, p. 391.
56. Indian scientists allegedly ready four Prithvi and at least one Agni missile for possible nuclear counter-strikes against Pakistan during the Kargil border conflict. The missiles are activated to a state known as Readiness State-3. In this stage, warheads are kept ready to be mated with missiles at short notice. Indian scientists arm one Agni missile with a nuclear warhead during the Kargil conflict with Pakistan. The missile is allegedly deployed somewhere in Western India. Raj Chengappa, *Ibid.*, 437.
57. According to a DRDO report on Indian defence technology, "multi-directionally reinforced carbon-fiber preform structures form the potential backbones for high-performance advanced composites in polymeric, ceramic, and metal matrices. The technology can be used to control the thermal, mechanical, and physical properties of the composites by appropriate design parameters such as fiber orientation, fiber volume fraction, and fiber spacing. Such technology in different shapes such as blocks, cylinders, cones, and other near-net shapes exhibit superior structural integrity and produce highly engineered structural composites. They also exhibit a high-degree of damage tolerance and improved inter-laminar shear strength . . . these composites can continue to carry load even after noticeable fractures . . . the [MRCP] technology . . . has been successfully applied to missile re-entry nose-tips and rocket nozzles . . . the laboratory [DRDL] has developed the [MRCP] technology and developed the 3D and 4D performs for re-entry applications. It has also acquired expertise in design of weave configurations, the design and development of tooling and actual weaving process inspection and processing of multi-directionally reinforced performs. Matrix densification technology has been developed using a high-pressure

impregnation, carbonization and a high-temperature graphitization process. The multi-directional reinforced carbon fiber preforms have been successfully densified to withstand re-entry conditions. "Dr. N.C. Birla and B.S. Murthy, eds., "Airframe Structures and Composite Components", *Indian Defence Technology: Missile Systems*, DRDO, Ministry of Defence, December 1998, New Delhi, pp. 63-64.

58. Referring to India's 22 May 1989 Agni-I test, Kalam reveals that India's indigenously developed re-entry vehicle technology was fully demonstrated when the nose-cone withstood temperatures of 3,000 Celsius. The four-directional pre-form used in the nose cone of the Agni was made of carbon-carbon material. The temperature in the Agni payload was 30 Celsius. Kalam also states that the Prithvi will enter production in 1992. The Agni's re-entry vehicle is designed to ensure that the temperature inside the vehicle does not exceed 60° Celsius, a condition necessary to protect the warhead and electronic systems placed inside. The re-entry vehicle consists of five sections. Each of these sections is made up of a two-layer composite construction. The inner layer is made up of carbon/epoxy filament mould constructed on a CNC winding machine. The inner layer is designed to bear structural loads. The outer layer is made up of carbon/phenolic filament wound construction, and cured in an autoclave at 7 bar pressure. The outer layer is designed to bear thermal loads. "Our missile technology is most modern: Kalam", *The Hindu*, Chennai, 2 March 1991, p. 16; also see, Birla and Murthy, *Ibid.*, pp. 64-65.
59. "The heat generated during re-entry is not only dependent on atmospheric density, but is also inversely proportional to the square root of the radius of the RV's nose cone and proportional to the cube of its velocity. Hence, blunt nose RVs are heated less than slender ones; and lifting RV designs, which use the glider principle, produce less heat than ballistic hyperbolic descent designs because their velocity is typically lower. Thus, a full evaluation of thermal impacts during re-entry is dependent on both vehicle- and mission-specific criteria." http://www.globalsecurity.org/wmd/intro/bm-basics.htm
60. *NTI-Missile Chronology 1992:* http://www.nti.org/e_research/profiles/India/Missile/1931_2023. html
61. A. Subhananda Rao, "Development of Solid Propulsion Systems for Guided Missiles", in H.S. Mukunda and A.V. Krishnamurty, eds., *Recent Advances in Aerospace Sciences and Engineering,:* Interline Publishing, Bangalore, 1992, pp. 184-86.
62. Pratap Mohanty, "India Tests Nuclear Capable Missile", *Agence France Presse,* 4 July 2004; in Lexis-Nexis Academic Universe, 5 July 2004, http://web.lexis-nexis.com/; "India testfires upgraded Agni-I", *Times of India, 5 July 2004;* and Sandeep Dikshit, "Army's missile group to maintain Agni A-1", *The Hindu,* 5 July 2004.
63. "Agni III Missile to be Test-Fired 'When Required'—Indian Defense Minister", *BBC Monitoring International Reports,* 20 June 2004.
64. "3,000 km range *Agni*-III in final phase of integration: Aatre", *Press Trust of India,* 18 August 2004.

65. "India's *Agni*-I Missile Yet to be Handed Over to Army", *BBC Monitoring,* 13 January 2004.
66. "India deploying *Agni* missiles", *Press Trust of India,* 31 August 2004, Agni-III Launch Soon, Says Outgoing DRDO Chief", *Economic Times,* 1 September 2004.
67. "Akash, Trishul, Nag Missiles to User", *Press Trust of India,* 9 December 2004.
68. "Gandhi Hails Missile Test", *Delhi Domestic Service,* 22 May 1989; in FBIS-NES-89-097, 22 May 1989, p. 54; "Gandhi says Missile's Success Guards India's Independence", *St. Louis Post-Dispatch,* St. Louis, Missouri, 23 May 1989, p. 11A, and Dilip Bobb and Amarnath K. Menon, "*Agni*: Chariot of Fire", *India Today,* New Delhi, 1-15 June 1989, pp. 10-13.
69. Chengappa, n. 13, p. 391.
70. "Agni-II Missile Successfully Test Fired", *Indian Express,* 11 April, 1999; "Agni-II Joins Nation's Missile Showcase", *Hindustan Times,* New Delhi, 11 April 1999, and Raj Chengappa, "Boom for Boom", *India Today,* New Delhi, 26 April 1999 and <http://www.india-today.com/>.
71. Gary Milhollin, "India's Missiles With a Little Help From Our Friends", *Bulletin of the Atomic Scientists,* November 1989, pp. 31-35.
72. The Agni-II was test-fired from a converted rail carriage, with a carriage roof that slides open to allow the missile to be raised to the vertical for launch by two large hydraulic pistons. The launch process is controlled from a separate railcar. Splash down was 2000-2100 km. down range in the Bay of Bengal, on a trajectory designed to simulate a range of 2800-3000 km. The Agni-II missile can also be launched from a road TEL vehicle to a range of 2100 km. This missile has a theoretical maximum range of some 3000 km with a 1000 kg payload (conventional or strategic).
73. "India Takes Big Technological Leap With Agni-II test", *Deccan Herald,* 12 April 1999. The missile is fitted with fins on the re-entry vehicle to facilitate manoeuvres. see Also; M. Singh, "Agni-II Adds Firepower to Nuclear Deterrence", *Indian Express,* 12 April 1999. "The presence of GPS has been reported but is not confirmed."
74. "Technical Tune to Agni Test Before Talks", *The Telegraph,* 30 August 2004. "The sources said it was a contained test fire. This probably means that the Agni-II was not flown for the full range it was designed for and its trajectory was altered to simulate the distance. A series of telemetry stations on the ground and on a naval vessel at sea tracked its flight. Earlier tests were said to have checked the missile's re-entry control and guidance technology, the sources said. It takes the Agni about 12 minutes to travel its full range with a conventional payload." http://www.telegraphindia.com/1040830/asp/nation/story_3694401.asp
75. The range of the solid-propellant Agni-II intermediate range ballistic missile can be varied according to payload and trajectory. The objective of today's test would be to reduce the circular error of probability for the longer-range variant, meaning that the missile was probably carrying a reduced payload *ibid.*

76. A rail and/or road-based missile system reduces vulnerability and allows for greater operational flexibility, while critics feel that the cost of these mobile systems could be higher and that they greatly increase the time for moving from one place to another. Considering that except in some parts—for instance, India's north-eastern region—road infrastructure is available wherever rail tracks are available, the decision to become rail-mobile could mean, in strategic terms, that deployment in India's north-eastern region is to be considered a serious possibility.
77. "According to one estimate, it costs between Rs. 25 crore and Rs. 35 crore to produce the missile." "Technical Tune to Agni Test before Talks". n. 74; http://www.telegraphindia.com/1040830/asp/nation/story_3694401.asp
78. The then principal scientific advisor to the Indian government, Abdul Kalam, said that the Agni-II is designed to carry a nuclear warhead; he also stated that the May 1998 nuclear tests included a test of an Agni Class payload. Rahul Bedi, "Agni-II IRBM: Built to Carry Nuclear Warhead", *Jane's Defence Weekly*, Vol. 31, No. 17, 28 April 1999, p. 7.
79. "A lifting re-entry vehicle has many operational advantages over a non-lifting vehicle. Primarily, the re-entry loads can be minimized to almost any desired level, with flexibility in landing site selection. The vehicle has the ability to deviate its re-entry trajectory to reach selected landing sites cross range from the orbital track, and to fine tune de-orbit propulsion system errors. Spherical and ballistic vehicles can only de-orbit to selected sites which are on the orbital ground track. A disadvantage of the lifting shape over the non-lifting shape lies in the complexity and high cost associated with guidance and control of the lifting vehicle. A failure of the guidance or control system could render the vehicle uncontrollable and cause it to diverge a great distance off course." http://www.globalsecurity.org/ wmd/ intro/bm-basics.h
80. Agni is unlike long-range missiles developed by western missiles where the RV is a passive ballistic load, whose accuracy depends on the launching vehicle's exact insertion into the sub-orbital trajectory. A large inaccuracy associated with the first generation RV, involved spinning the RV for greater stability during re-entry. Second generation western missiles were mostly MIRV (Multiple Independently targetable Re-entry Vehicle) and the accuracy was greatly improved by the payload bus with HAM velocity correction package for more accurate sub-orbit insertion. It also allowed individual MIRV payloads to impart different velocities, so that each can be independently targeted to a different target, albeit in nearby vicinity of each other. As before the RV continued to be passive and purely ballistic.
81. The Agni-RV Mk.2 has some unique features such as:

    (i) the manoeuvring fins allow to:
        (a) Execute a non-ballistic trajectory to make interception more difficult.

(b) Overcome any perturbation due to high altitude atmospheric disturbance.
(c) Enable use of body lift at hypersonic velocity to glide the missile over longer ranges, thus reducing the thermal and physical stress at a modified Max-Q point.
(d) Trajectory error to be determined late into the fight and corrected using aerodynamic force during re-entry.
(e) Terminal manoeuvre dive for a more acute target interdiction angle improving CEP.
(f) Support a wider range of payload weight and configuration.

(ii) Integrated velocity correction package for greater precision; has a set of solid fuelled cartridge(s) that are used to correct impulse variances of solid fuelled stages and subtle launch trajectory perturbation.
(iii) Could also house an integrated High Altitude Motor (HAM) which is liquid fuelled.
(iv) Depending on the actual payload configuration, the HAM fuel load can be increased to trade range for a lighter and more compact weapon.
(v) The larger volume allows more sophisticated ABM (anti-ballistic missile) counter-measures

82. Chengappa, n. 13, p. 353.
83. For details see, Arun Vishwakarma and Sanjay Badri Maharaj, "Evaluating India's Land-Based Missile Deterrent", *Indian Defense Review,* Vol. 19, No. 4, Lancer Publishers.
84. DRDO reports that it may begin producing dry tuned gyros for missiles by the end of 1998. The dry tuned gyro after "detailed test evaluation, modeling, and S/W compensation" is expected to give "0.1 deg/hr, 200 ppm class performance." The design of a "fiber optic gyro...of open loop design is under progress", and a "close loop integrated optics version is likely to come to the laboratory model stage by the year 2000. A ring laser gyro of 0.1 deg/hr (1s) class is planned to be produced by 2000...with the participation of an academic institution where the first pre-production model has been developed and tested..." N.C. Birla and B.S. Murthy, eds., "Inertial Guidance and Sensors", *Indian Defence Technology: Missile Systems,* DRDO, Ministry of Defence, December 1998, pp. 157-58.
85. "The Agni-II incorporates a far more accurate terminal navigation and guidance system which constantly updates information about the missile flight path using Global Positioning System (GPS) information provided by ground-based beacons." The Indian Drive towards Weaponization, *Federation of American Scientists*. http://www.fas.org/nuke/guide/india/missile/agni-improvements.htm
86. "Second developmental flight of Geo-synchronous Satellite Launch Vehicle", Current Science, Volume 85, No. 5, 10 September 2003; "GSLV-F01 Launch Successful—Places EDUSAT in Orbit", ISRO.

http://isro.org/newsletters/spaceindia/julsep2004/GSLV%20FO1.htm
87. T.S. Subramanian, "EDUSAT Placed in Orbit", *The Hindu*, 21 September 2004.
88. It is worth noting that INS error differs for a ballistic missile versus an aircraft. Ballistic missile accuracy is only dependent on the INS accuracy up to the point when rocket fuel is expended (100 seconds for Agni-II) and it exits the atmosphere (> 90 km altitude), after that the trajectory is purely ballistic that is predetermined and easily computed. INS in a combat aircraft requires continuous operation of IMU and navigation computer throughout the flight during which the error keeps building as IMU sensors drift. A ballistic missile that can update its position and velocity from auxiliary means, can completely eliminate the built up error from INS and continue flight at a precise predetermined path, if necessary correcting the launch error by using: (i) Small velocity correction thruster package and/or (ii) Aerodynamic manoeuvring during re-entry (this requires active RV configuration with integrated INS and control system).
89. *Ibid.*
90. "Technical Tune to Agni Test before Talks."n. 74. *The Telegraph*, 30 August 2004. "The range of the solid-propellant Agni II intermediate range ballistic missile can be varied according to payload and trajectory. The objective of today's test would be to reduce the circular error of probability for the longer-range variant, meaning that the missile was probably carrying a reduced payload." http://www.telegraphindia.com/1040830/asp/nation/story_3694401.asp
91. Chengappa, n. 13, pp. 435-36.
92. Mehta, n. 3, p. 181.
93. In June 1999, India's external affairs and defence ministers, Jaswant Singh and George Fernandes, discussed the need for a ballistic missile to cover the gap between the short-range Prithvi and the longer-range variants of the Agni ballistic missile. K. Santhanam, "Agni-I: A short-range N-Missile India Urgently Needs", *Times of India*, Mumbai, 27 January 2002, http://www.timesofindia.com/
94. In October 1999, the Indian government approves the development of an 800-900 km range, road mobile, solid-propellant variant of the Agni ballistic missile. The development and first flight-test of the shorter-range variant of the Agni is expected within 15 months. *Times of India*, Mumbai, 27 January 2002, *ibid.*
95. One that can move on a standard broad-gauge rail system and also from a road-mobile launcher system. DRDO's Ahmednagar-based Vehicle Research and Development Establishment (VRDE) and the Pune-based Research and Development Engineers (R and DE) played important roles in validating the tractor-cum-transporter-*cum*-launcher.
96. *The Hindu*, 5 July 2004.
97. "Agni-I Test-Fired for Third Time, Now Ready for Induction", *Hindustan Times*, 5 July 2004. Also see other national dailies dated July 5, 2004.

98. "Long-range Agni missile gets go-ahead", *Times of India,* New Delhi, 1 June 2001. "India's Defence Minister Jaswant Singh informs the parliament's Consultative Committee on Defence, that the Agni ballistic missile is likely to be inducted into the armed forces in 2001-2002. Singh tells members of parliament that limited production of the operational missile system has commenced and the missile forms the bedrock of India's minimum deterrent. According to Singh, "No constraints in funds will be allowed to come in the way of the indigenous development of the integrated missile program" and the development of the Agni-II is proof of the country's determination to indigenize defence production. Indian defence sources claim that the government is also considering approving the development of missiles with a longer range than the Agni-II."
99. Pokharan-II test resulted in a lighter weapon payload, whereas the original RV was intended for a much heavier boosted fission weapon. In view of rapid developments however, the basic design earlier developed continued to be used and keeping the future option open, for more optimized and lighter payloads.
100. Advanced Systems Laboratory (ASL), Hyderabad: "The front-end technologies being developed include ultra high temperature composites, high performance composite rocket motor casings, radome for missiles and aircrafts, all-carbon re-entry vehicle structures, carbon composite canister technology, thrust vectoring through flex nozzles for large rocket motors, solid propulsion, control systems, system integration and explicit energy management guidance systems". http://www.ias.ac.in/currsci/feb 102004/372.pdf
101. "The range of the solid-propellant Agni-II intermediate range ballistic missile can be varied according to payload and trajectory. The objective of today's test would be to reduce the circular error of probability for the longer-range variant, meaning that the missile was probably carrying a reduced payload. Technical Tune to Agni Test Before Talks". n. 74;. http://www.telegraphindia.com/ 1040830/asp/nation/story_3694401.asp
102. "Defence Scientists Embark on Making 'Smart' Missiles." *The Hindu Businessline,* 02 October 2004.http://www.thehindubusinessline.com/2004/10/03/stories/2004100301340500.htm
103. "Composites: Use in Saucepan Handles, Artificial Limbs and the Agni Missile." *Current Science,* Vol. 86, No. 3, 10 February 2004. Advanced Systems Laboratory (ASL), Hyderabad. "The front-end technologies being developed include ultra high temperature composites, high performance composite rocket motor casings, radome for missiles and aircrafts, all-carbon re-entry vehicle structure, carbon composite canister technology, thrust vectoring through flex nozzles for large rocket motors, solid propulsion, control systems, system integration and explicit energy management guidance systems." http://www.ias.ac.in/currsci/feb102004/372.pdf
104. Brahma Challaney, "India's Trial by Fire", *Hindustan Times,* 21 October 1998.

105. *The Tribune,* 10 July, 2006.
105a. Raj Chengappa, "Building India's Missile Muscle", *India Today,* 30 April 2007. Also see *National Dailies* dated 13 April 2007.
106. Ben Sheppard, "Ballistic Missiles : Complicating the Nuclear Quagmire", in D.R. Sardesai and Raju G.C. Thomas, eds., *Nuclear India in the Twenty First Century,* Palgrave-Macmillan, New York, 2002, p. 194.
107. DRDO sources say that program to develop Surya is likely to cost $50 million and the missile will be ready for launch by mid-2001. An advanced version of the Surya will also be developed after the first missile is tested. In addition, twenty 2,000 km-range Agni ballistic missiles will be built at a cost of $ 150 million by the end of 2001. Vivek Raghuvanshi, "India to Develop Extensive Nuclear Missile Arsenal", *Defense News,* 24 May 1999, p. 14.
108. Tritium breakthrough brings India closer to an H-Bomb arsenal. "How tritium extracted from CANDU-type power reactors supports India's H-Bomb capability." *Jane's Intelligence Review,* January 1998. http://www.ccnr.org/india_tritium.html
109. George Perkovich, *India's Nuclear Bomb: The Impact on Global Proliferation,* OUP, New Delhi, 2000 , p. 242
110. Government of India *IGMDP Update.* New Delhi: Ministry of Defence 1996.
111. *Jane's Infantry Weapons* 1999/2000 Alexandria, VA: JIG 1999.
112. IGMDP update,n. 110.
113. 'Nag Update'. *Technology Focus,* DRDO January 1998.
114. *Jane's Armour and Artillery* 1999/2000 Alexandria, VA: JIG 1999.
115. "Nag test fired'. *Indian Express,* 11 September 1997.
116. 'India's Nag Ready for Production'. *Jane's Defence Weekly,* 06 January 1999.
117. *Indian Army Press Release,* 27 January 2000.
118. *Ibid.*
119. *Ibid.* See also 'Fire-and-Forget' System for Nag Tested'. *Times of India,* 22 January 2000.
120. *Indian Army Press Release,* 27 January 2000.
121. Indian Defence Yearbook 2000. Natraj Publishers, Dehra Dun, India 2000. n. 119.
122. *Indian Army Press Release,* 27 January 2000. See also 'BDL Launches Serial Production of Missiles'. *Deccan Herald,* 9 April 2000.
123. "Eventual Operational Range of Over 100 km." http://www.globalsecurity.org/military/world/ india/astra.htm
124. The US has a similar missile but heavier, while Israel also has a BVR missile, but the range is comparatively shorter. "DRDL to Develop Astra Missile". *Business Line,* 17 June 2004.
http://www.thehindubusinessline.com/2004/06/17/stories/2004061702730500.htm
125. "Astra missile to be tested this year", *Tribune News Service,* 9 February 2005. http://www.tribuneindia.com/2005/20050209/main5.htm
126. BrahMos Aerospace Private Limited was established in India as a Joint Venture through an Inter-Governmental Agreement between India and Russia signed in February 1998. The acronym BrahMos is

perceived as the confluence of two great nations represented by two great rivers, the Brahmaputra of India and the Moscow of Russia. DRDO from India and the Federal State Unitary Enterprise NPO Mashinostroyenia (NPOM) from Russia are the joint venture partners of the Company. The Company BrahMos endeavours to design, develop, manufacture and market the Supersonic Anti-Ship Cruise Missile Systems with the participation of multiple Indian and Russian institutions and industries

127. Debabrata Mohanty and Chandan Nandy, "Birth in Russia, Blast-Off in India", Telegraph, Calcutta, 12 June 2001, http://www.telegraphindia.com/; and Atul Aneja, "Indo-Russian Missile Tested", *The Hindu*, Chennai, 13 June 2001, <http://www.the-hindu.com/.
128. *Ibid.*
129. *Ibid.*
130. "BrahMos Test-Fired", *The Hindu*, Chennai, 29 April 2002.
131. "BrahMos Flight Tested", *Press Trust of India*, 12 February 2003; Brahmos Flight Tested", *Press Trust of India*, 29 October 2003 and "Anti-Ship Version of BrahMos Proves its Mettle", *The Hindu*, Chennai, 3 December 2003.
132. "Brahmos Test Fired Successful", *Press Trust of India*, 23 November 2003, Nationwide International News; in Lexis-Nexis Academic Universe, 1 December 2003, http://web.lexis-nexis.com/; Bulbul Singh, "BrahMos Cruise Missile Test-Fired from Destroyer", *Aerospace Daily*, 1 December 2003, Vol. 208, No. 42, News, p. 2; T.S. Subramanian, "Anti-Ship Version of BrahMos Proves its Mettle", *Hindu*, Chennai, 3 December 2003; "Brahmos successfully tested", *Press Trust of India*, 3 November 2004; in Lexis-Nexis Academic Universe, 3 November 2004, http://web.lexis-nexis.com/; "Brahmos anti-ship missile tested", *Business Line*, 4 November 2004.
133. "BrahMos supersonic cruise missile to be inducted in Navy next year", *Press Trust of India*, 26 August 2004; in Lexis-Nexis Academic Universe, 26 August 2004, http://web.lexis-nexis.com/.
134 "Naval version of Brahmos will be ready by 2005", *Business Insight*, 11 February 2004; T.S. Subramanian, "Anti-Ship Version of BrahMos Proves its Mettle", *Hindu*, Chennai, 3 December 2003.
135. *The Tribune*. 9 October 2007.
135a. "BrahMos test-fired successfully", *Business Insight*, 14 June 2004; T.S. Subramanian, "Kalam congratulates scientists", *Hindu*, 14 June 2004; T.S. Subramanian, "BrahMos launch successful", *Hindu*, 14 June 2004 and T.S. Subramanian, "BrahMos-II bang on target", *Hindu*, 22 December 2004, http://www.hinduonnet.com/.
136. "IAF variant of BrahMos likely in three years", *Times of India*, 13 December 2004.
137. *Ibid.*
138. *Ibid.*
139. Vladimir Radyuhin, "India, Russia to market BrahMos", *Hindu*, 8 April 2004.
140. Manoj Joshi, "Russia Gives Nuclear Edge to Indian Defence", *Times of India*, Mumbai, 19 January 2003.

141. Steven Lee Myers, "Russia is Helping India Extend Range of Missile, US Aides Say", *New York Times*, 27 April 1998, http://www.nytimes.com/
142. Rahul Roy Chaudhury, "Equipping the Navy for War on Land", *Times of India*, New Delhi, 13 July 1998, http://www.timesofindia.com/
143. Office of the Secretary of Defense, "Proliferation: Threat and Response", *US Department of Defense*, January 2001.
144. "India Establishes Strategic Forces Command", *Press Trust of India*, 4 January 2003, Nationwide International News; in Lexis-Nexis Academic Universe, 5 January 2003, http://web.lexis-nexis.com/; Edna Fernandes, "India Sets Up Nuclear Arsenal Command Structure", *Financial Times*, 6 January 2003, *World News*, p. 6; in Lexis-Nexis Academic Universe, 5 January 2003, http://web.lexis-nexis.com/.

4

Pakistan's Missile Programme

Pakistan's missile programme, like most other nations' missile programme, is inextricably linked to its nuclear and space programmes.[1] Pakistan Atomic Energy Commission (PAEC) was created in 1959 and was modeled after Atomic Energy Commission of the USA. Pakistan established its Space and Upper Atmosphere Research Commission (SUPARCO) at Karachi as part of the PAEC during the early 1960s and received early French rocket technology to produce sounding rockets.[2] SUPARCO started its work independently in 1964 and was brought under the control of the Ministry of Defence in 1969. When Pakistan decided to start indigenous missile development programme, SUPARCO became the core agency for this purpose; however, the attempts were not very successful.[3] The failure of SUPARCO to overcome the technical difficulties with the two indigenous types of missiles (*Hatf*-I and *Hatf*-II) and the success of Indian *Prithvi* missile programme pushed Pakistan towards off-the-shelf purchase of foreign missiles and related technology.

Pakistan began pursuing a ballistic missile programme seriously in the early 1980s as part of efforts to develop a deliverable nuclear strike capability against India. Although Pakistan's initial efforts appear experimental, the scale of

Islamabad's current programme clearly reflects a strategic requirement to build a diversified and survivable nuclear deterrent capable of targeting the bulk of the Indian landmass. However unlike India, whose development of missile-based power projection capabilities reflects both regional and extra-regional security concerns, Pakistan's ballistic missile effort is largely Indo-centric.

Islamabad's present nuclear dyad consists of nuclear capable combat aircraft and solid-motor and liquid-engine short-range ballistic missiles (SRBM). The F-16 combat aircrafts obtained from the United States during the 1980s were probably the earliest delivery systems in Pakistan's nuclear inventory.[4] Combat aircraft are operationally more reliable than ballistic missiles. In comparison to Pakistan's current inventory of SRBMs, they also offer other advantages such as greater payload and combat radius. However, despite these existing advantages, land-based ballistic missiles are emerging as the mainstay of Pakistan's nuclear strike force.

There are three main reasons for the growing dominance of the missile leg in the emerging Pakistani nuclear dyad. First, Pakistan has been unable to augment its fleet of modern combat aircrafts due to the past policies of military and economic sanctions by the USA designed to arrest and slow down Pakistan's nuclear weapons programme. Although Pakistan is now an ally of the USA in the global war on terrorism and no longer the target of proliferation sanctions, the latter has been hesitant to supply former with advanced combat aircrafts as it would invariably augment the Pakistan's nuclear strike capability. Second, the country's overall poor economic performance has prevented the Pakistani Air Force (PAF) from undertaking major fleet expansion and modernization efforts by making the switch from supplies by the USA to that of Europe and Russia. During the late 1990s, especially after India and Pakistan's May 1998 tests, American pressure combined with instability concerns in Pakistan prevented external suppliers from selling high-tech nuclear capable combat aircraft to Islamabad.[5] Finally, the unfolding and proposed advances in India's air combat, air-defence, and long-range reconnaissance capabilities are channeling Pakistani investments into a ballistic missile-based capability for which India has no defence at present.

Since the late 1980s and early 1990s, Pakistan has invested in both solid-motor and liquid-engine ballistic missile programmes with the assistance of both China and North Korea. Pakistan's reasons for investing in both solid and liquid propulsion technologies remain unclear. However, analysts speculate that the rival programmes could be the result of intra-institutional rivalry and one-upmanship between the Pakistani Atomic Energy Commission (PAEC) and Khan Research Laboratories (KRL), which have historically feuded over control and credits for Pakistan's nuclear weapons-related efforts.[6] This rivalry may have also carried over to the development of nuclear delivery systems. Furthermore, the diversification effort could also be viewed as a proactive attempt on the part of Pakistan's military to factor in possible bottlenecks or failure along one technological front, as well as an attempt to diversify suppliers in the face of efforts of the United State to restrict the international trade in weapons of mass destruction-capable ballistic and cruise missile technologies.

Although Pakistan's current fleet of missiles is restricted to SRBMs, the National Defence Complex (NDC) and KRL are actively pursuing programmes to develop medium-range ballistic missiles. Most analysts believe that the Pakistani military has achieved or is close to achieving the capability to mount nuclear warheads on its current ballistic missile fleet. Some reports even go so far as to suggest that Pakistan may be further along than India on the path of achieving nuclear operability.[7] The declared capabilities of Pakistan in this context can be analyzed by systematic evaluation of its delivery systems which is given below.

HATF-I

Pakistan is believed to have missile arsenal comprising primarily *Hatf*-I rockets[8] and *Hatf*-II missiles with ranges of 80 and 280 km even before 1989 but the existence of the missiles was publicly disclosed by Pakistan's Chief of Army Staff General Mirza Aslam Beg in February 1989.[9] Pakistan embarked on an indigenous ballistic missile effort with the launch of the *Hatf* program in the early or mid-1980s. The SUPARCO, Pakistan's primary civilian space agency, undertook the *Hatf* program.

The *Hatf*-I is a short-range ballistic missile. The missile's development began in the early 1980s, reportedly with China's aid, though Pakistan claims that it was produced without outside assistance. However, the *Hatf* missiles resemble the Chinese M-series missiles, so technical aid seems likely. Little is known about the missile or its role. It is likely that Pakistan's nuclear warheads are allocated to its longer-range missiles, the *Ghauris*, or *Haft*-V and *Haft*-VI, and the *Shaheen*-I and-II.

TABLE 4.1
Hatf-I Missile Specifications

Name	: Hatf-I
Mission	: Short-range-ballistic missile
Targets	: Cities and military sites in India
Platform	: Ground Mobile—TEL
Total Length	: 6.10 meter
Core Diameter	: 0.55 meters
Wing/Fin Span	: 82 cm
Total Mass	: 1500 kg
Propulsion	: One Stage Solid Rocket
Standard Warhead Mass	: 500 KG
Range	: 60-80 km
Guidance	: Unguided
CEP	: Unknown
Warhead	: Single
Yield	: Conventional, Chemical, or Nuclear possible
Contractor	: SUPARCO
First Test	: January 1989

Source : Shanon N. Kile, Vitaly Fedchenko and Hans M. Kristensen, "World Nuclear Forces", Armaments, Disarmament and International Security, *SIPRI Yearbook, 2006,* Oxford University Press, Oxford, 2006; and *The Military Balance, 2006-2007,* International Institute for Strategic Studies, London, 2006; and "Country Overview", Natural Resource Defense Council, Washington D.C.

The *Hatf*-I (name of the holy prophet's sword) is a single-stage, solid-propellant missile with a range of 60-80 km carrying a 500 kg payload, or 350 km range with a 100 kg payload.[10] In February 1989, Pakistan announced the successful firing of the *Hatf*-I which is believed to be based on French rocketry.[11] Although the *Haft*-I programme was believed to have been halted after three unsuccessful test flights, some of the technology associated with this missile was used in the development of the *Haft*-II programme.[12] A total of 17 tests were carried out before attempts to harness it as a weapon. *Hatf*-I was facing some serious problems such as the warheads were tended to break up during the flight, the guidance system was not satisfactory and accuracy was not up to the mark. Some reports claim that a few copies of the missile were produced and are armed with chemical warheads, though Pakistan does not appear to have a chemical weapons capability. The very short range Hatf-I does not have the range to reach beyond the Indian Desert, and would almost certainly be deployed with a conventional rather than nuclear warhead.[13] Although the possibility of operational use of the *Hatf*-I appears to be limited, there seems to be some development work being done on the missile, if the claim of *Hatf*-IA missile test is to be taken into consideration.

HATF-IA

Reports in 1992 indicate that an improved *Hatf*-I with a range of 100 km, known as *Hatf*-IA, was under development which was tested in February 2000 and is believed to have an extended range of 100 km.[14] This latest test was claimed to represent an improved version of the missile, with a larger payload and an improved range of up to 100 kilometers, rather than the 60-80 kilometers initially reported. It is a solid fuel missile, developed by PAEC.[15] It has a fairly modern guidance system and uses lighter material for its airframe and has a higher speed during flight. The carriage of a nuclear, biological or chemical warhead on such a missile can not be ruled out as an extension of options to counter India in limited conventional war.

HATF-II

Hatf-II is also believed to be a copy of French rocket like *Hatf*-I.[16] It is a two-stage solid-propellant missile with a range of 280 km carrying a 500 kg payload, or 450 km carrying a 300 kg payload. It is most likely a modified version of the *Hatf*-Icomposed of the second stage of the *Hatf*-I with a new boost motor added to the first stage.[17]

The *Hatf*-II missile was apparently developed in tandem with the *Hatf*-I in the early 1980s, possibly with Chinese aid. There was some confusion as to the name of the programme, it is sometimes also referred to as the *Shadoz* and *Abdali*,

TABLE 4.2
Hatf-II Missile Specifications

Name	:	Hatf-II
Mission	:	Short-range-ballistic missile
Targets	:	Cities and military cites in India
Platform	:	Ground Mobile—TEL
Length	:	9.75 meters
Diameter	:	0.82 meters
Wing/Fan Span	:	82 cm
Range	:	280-300 km
Weight	:	5500 kg
Payload	:	500 kg
Propulsion	:	Two Stage Solid Propellant
Guidance	:	Inertial
CEP	:	Unknown
Warhead	:	Single
Yield	:	Conventional, chemical, or nuclear possible (30-50 kt nuclear)
Primary Contractor	:	NDC

Source : Shanon N. Kile, Vitaly Fedchenko and Hans M. Kristensen, "World Nuclear Forces", Armaments, Disarmament and International Security, *SIPRI Yearbook, 2006*, Oxford University Press, Oxford, 2006; and *The Military Balance, 2006-2007*, International Institute for Strategic Studies, London, 2006; and "Country Overview", Natural Resource Defense Council, Washington D.C.

nomenclatures that cause considerable confusion.[18] The two *Hatf* missile variants were revealed in 1989. Little information is available on deployment. Both stages of the *Hatf*-II are believed to have solid propellant. It is reportedly a mobile system, but it is carried on converted World War-II era antiaircraft gun trailers instead of modern transporter erector vehicles. It is believed that the *Haft* II programme has been halted due to technical problems with its directional control system which remained unresolved even after the Chinese inertial navigation technology which was provided by China during 1991. The Pakistani allegedly shelved this system because of problems with guidance and control systems. Another consideration may have been the purchase from China of the M-11 missiles with similar capabilities.

The missile was demonstrated during the Pakistan day parade in 1992 and the *Hatf*-II nomenclature was probably transferred to the M-11 missile contracted from China as it is similar to that of the Chinese M-series missiles. In particular, the mastery of the more advanced solid-fuel technology, which the Chinese are now fielding after years of development, points to covert Chinese assistance.

Pakistan's SUPARCO developed a space launch vehicle to place its future satellite into low earth orbit. In January 1989, it was reported that Pakistan had a successful launch of an indigenous multistage rocket into deep space. The rocket was said to have reached an altitude of more than 640 km.[19] Two months later, Agence France Press reported that Pakistan had manufactured a rocket booster with a range of 640 km that was to be tested in Autumn of 1989; however, no such test is believed to have occurred.[20] According to a detailed report in a trade weekly publication, State Department officials said that the January 1989 test was the test of the *Hatf*-I and *Hatf*-II, which were announced in February 1989. The report said that the *Hatf*-II is the first stage of a planned multistage rocket to have a maximum range of 600 km.[21] In a possible reference to the same rockets, in May 1990, SUPARCO announced that the "test firing of two versions of scientific rockets had been successfully carried out."[22]

All versions of the *Hatf* are capable of delivering conventional high-explosive warheads. However, it is unclear if the missiles have been modified for nuclear delivery. Some analysts speculate that the *Hatf*-I, IA and II use an inertial guidance system. But U.S. government sources contend that the missiles are essentially inaccurate battlefield rockets.[23] Some analysts believe that the *Hatf*-I, IA and II are likely derivatives of the French Dauphin and Dragon sounding rockets. SUPARCO obtained the technology for building sounding rockets from the French company Aerospatiale (formerly Sud Aviation) in the early or mid-1980s. The French transfers most likely included technologies and equipment for solid-fuel casting, curing, and solid-rocket testing facilities.[24]

Although the *Hatf*-I was declared operational in 1992 and the *Hatf*-IA and II versions by the mid-1990s, but the missiles do not appear to have been manufactured in large numbers.[25] Neither do they appear to be in operational service with the Pakistani Army. The Pakistani Army flight-tested a *Hatf*-IA in February 2000; it also conducted two flight-tests of the *Hatf*-II version in May 2002 and March 2003. These tests suggest that the Army probably has a limited number of these systems in its inventory. However, the absence of large-scale manufacturing or an extended flight-test program indicates that the *Hatf*-I, I-A and II were interim contingency programmes, which are superseded by the *Ghaznavi*, *Shaheen*, and *Ghauri* ballistic missile programmes, with Chinese and North Korean assistance.

HATF-III/GHAZNAVI/M-11

Hatf-III or *Ghaznavi* is the missile which was formally adopted by the Strategic Forces Command on February 22, 2004. This appears to be an exact copy of the latest version of the DF-11 Mod 1. In 1992, Pakistan received from China between 30 and 80 M-11 (CSS-7/DF-11) unassembled missiles which are probably stored at Central Ordinance Depot at *Sargodha* Air Force Base.[26] Some reports reveal that more than 30 M-11s may be in storage at Pakistan's *Sargodha* air force base West of Lahore.[27] Other reports suggest that as many as 84 such missiles are deployed at the same Base.[28] At least 30 of the missiles are believed to be stored at the Pakistan Air Force base at *Sargodha* in Central Punjab. Satellite imagery of the base has revealed the existence of shelters for missile crates and their mobile launchers, missile maintenance areas, and missile crew quarters.[29] More missiles may be deployed at other undisclosed bases in Pakistan. But these reports are denied by Pakistan and China.[30] Pakistan's procurement of this weapon system was due in part to USA's refusal to deliver the F-16s in 1990, for which Pakistan had already made payment to the former.

During 1990-91, intelligence agency of the USA discovered the presence of an M-11 training missile in Pakistan with an accompanying TEL vehicle, which indicated that operational missile systems were likely to follow.[31] Beginning in 1992, these agencies tracked shipments of at least 30 M-11 ballistic missiles from China through the Pakistani port city of Karachi. Subsequently, China resorted to transferring components and sub-systems so that the missiles could be assembled in Pakistan.[32] Chinese missile technicians are also believed to have trained Pakistani Army personnel in the assembling and simulated launch of the missiles, which entered operational service in 1995 or 1996.[33] Around the mid-1990s, China also built a turnkey missile facility for the NDC at *Fatehjung* in Punjab. The *Fatehjung* missile facility is believed to be capable of building either complete missiles or most components and sub-systems of the M-11.

The M-11 missiles, which are capable of carrying a nuclear warhead to a range of 280 km, can probably be deployed in the field within a few days prior to its use.[34] Although China developed the export versions of the M-11 with high-explosive conventional warheads, yet the missiles in Pakistan's inventory are believed to be nuclear-capable.[35] In fact, separation of warhead is considered by many experts as a desirable characteristic for nuclear weapons delivery, but limited range precludes its use to strike New Delhi or large population centers lying beyond the Indian desert.[36] Like more recent versions of the Chinese missile, the *Ghaznavi*, another name given to the *Hatf*-III, employs an "aero spike" on the tip of the nose cone. This serves to push away air, creating less aerodynamic drag for the remainder of the missile, and is useful for extending the range of the missile if it employed a "depressed trajectory" or low altitude flight profile, where denser air would create more drag. It is also suspected of using a "depressed trajectory" to evade missile defences. A Pakistani video also notes that this missile uses a "post-separation attitude correction system" to ensure accuracy. It also features flat antenna arrays near the warhead stage. And, like the DF-11 Mod 1, the *Ghaznavi* very likely uses a range of warheads, including nuclear, high explosives, cluster munitions, thermo baric.

The DF-11/M-11/CSS-7 which goes by the dual nomenclatures *Hatf*-III and *Ghaznavi* in Pakistan, is a short-range, solid-propellant, road mobile, single-warhead ballistic missile. China began development work on the M-11 in the mid-1980s; the first flight-test of the missile is believed to have occurred in 1990, and it probably entered operational service in 1992. Analysts

Table 4.3
Hatf-III Missile Specifications

Name	:	Hatf-III/Ghaznavi
Mission	:	Short-range-ballistic missile
Targets	:	Cities and military sites in India
Platform	:	Ground Mobile—TEL
Length	:	10.0 meter
Body Diameter	:	1.0 meter (first stage), 56 cm (second stage)
Wing/Fin Span	:	82 cm
Range	:	290-300 km
Payload	:	500 kg
Guidance	:	Inertial
Status	:	Tested/Development
Launch Weight	:	6500 kg
Adopted by	:	Strategic Forces Command on February 22, 2004
Propulsion	:	Two Stage Solid
Warheads	:	Nuclear, High Explosive, Thrmobaric, Radio Frequency (30-50 Kt nuclear)
Contractor	:	NDC
Technical Source	:	China (M-11)

Source : Shanon N. Kile, Vitaly Fedchenko and Hans M. Kristensen, "World Nuclear Forces", Armaments, Disarmament and International Security, *SIPRI Yearbook, 2006,* Oxford University Press, Oxford, 2006; and *The Military Balance, 2006-07,* International Institute for Strategic Studies, London, 2006; and "Country Overview", Natural Resource Defense Council, Washington D.C.

believe that the M-11 has a throw-weight of 800kg over a maximum range of 280km. By trading payload weight for increased range, the M-11 could deliver a 500 kg payload over a range of 300 km. Control during the boost phase is probably exercised through vanes in the exhaust or small vernier motors with an inertial platform for guidance. It is also believed that the warhead assembly separates during flight and that there are four small fins mounted at the rear of the warhead section. However, it is not known if these four fins move, or are simply stabilizers. Some reports suggest that the missile has a terminal guidance system; the separating warhead section has a miniature propulsion system to correct the attitude before re-entry, as well as adjusting the terminal trajectory.[37]

In the early 1980s China is widely reported to have provided Pakistan with the blueprints for a 1966 design of a U-235 nuclear-implosion device, of the type used in the warhead that China flew on a DF-2A missile during its fourth nuclear test on 27 October 1966. This missile warhead was reported to weigh about 1,300 kilograms with a yield of about 12-25 kt. This warhead design would be too large to be carried on an M-11. Pakistan is believed to have a capability to deploy a nuclear warhead using plutonium and weighing around 500 kilograms. The missile has a separating warhead, making it desirable as a nuclear-weapons delivery system.

In 1991 the United States imposed economic sanctions, against both, China and Pakistan for China's transfer of M-11 missile-related equipments. The sanctions were lifted against China in 1992. On 25 August 1993 the United States imposed Category Two sanctions against certain Chinese and Pakistani entities that were involved in an M-11 missile-related transfer, which is prohibited under US law. Category Two sanctions are imposed on a nation if the transfer involves certain items in the MTCR Annex which contribute to missile development. The sanctions require denial of new export licenses for MTCR Annex items . . . and denial of US government contracts relating to MTCR Annex items with the sanctioned entities for two years. But the sanctions were lifted against China in 1994, when China reaffirmed its 1992 commitment to adhere to the Missile Technology Control Regime [MTCR] and made a number of new, related commitments. However, China remains Pakistan's principal supplier of missile-related technology. The sanctions against Pakistan were not lifted until they expired in 1995.

The Washington Post reported that intelligence officials of the USA were concerned that a partially completed factory in the suburbs of Rawalpindi would be ready in a year or two to produce precise duplicates of the M-11. The National Intelligence Estimate also stated that Pakistan may have developed nuclear warheads for the M-11.[38]

The public record does not disclose a consistent basis for application of the *Hatf*-III nomenclature to a specific missile system. On 3 July 1997 Pakistan conducted a missile test that unofficial press reports claimed with a range of 800-km range. However, the nomenclature associated with this test was never officially confirmed. The test followed an uproar in Pakistan over the alleged deployment of 250-kilometre range *Prithvi* missiles by India on Pakistan's border. While Indian sources asserted that the missile was a Chinese M-9. Analysts in the USA concluded that the missile was most likely an improved M-11. Very little additional information is available on this alleged launch.

The Pakistan Army conducted a launch of the *Hatf*-III/*Ghaznavi* in October 2003 to validate the missile's various design parameters.[39] Subsequent to this test, in February 2004, Pakistani President Pervez Musharraf formally announced the induction of the missiles into the Army's Strategic Forces Command.[40]

HATF-IV/SHAHEEN-I

The *Hatf*-IV or *Shaheen*-I is solid propellant, single warhead missile first revealed in 1999, also has no known Chinese equivalent, but its Chinese origins are more apparent than the *Shaheen*-II. It is reportedly developed by Samar Mubarak Mund's National Development Complex.[41] The nose section is very clearly a copy of that seen on the Chinese DF-11 Mod 1 missile first demonstrated in their October 1999 military parade. But the *Shaheen*-I is of 750km range. Its warhead stage has a post-separation atitude correction system, meaning that the *Shaheen*-I is capable of high accuracy and some degree of maneuvering to evade missile defences. In addition, both the *Shaheen*-I and *Ghaznavi*, employ stealthy warhead shaping to delay detection and complicate targeting.

TABLE 4.4
Shaheen-I/Hatf-IV Missile Specifications

Name	:	Shaheen-I
Other Designation	:	Hatf-IV
Mission	:	Short-range-ballistic missile
Service	:	Pakistani Army
Targets	:	Cities and Military sites in India
Platform	:	Modified MAZ 543 TEL (Scud's TEL)
Project Managed By	:	NDC (a subsidiary of PAEC)
Length	:	9.10 meters
Diameter	:	1 meter
Range	:	750 km
Total Mass	:	6200 kg
Warhead weight	:	850 kg
Propulsion	:	Single-stage solid propellant
Guidance	:	Inertial (Locally developed terminal guidance system)
CEP	:	Unknown
Warhead	:	Single
Yield	:	Conventional, Chemical or Nuclear
Location	:	Unknown
Technical Source	:	China

Source : Shanon N. Kile, Vitaly Fedchenko and Hans M. Kristensen, "World Nuclear Forces", Armaments, Disarmament and International Security, *SIPRI Yearbook, 2006*, Oxford University Press, Oxford, 2006; and *The Military Balance, 2006-2007*, International Institute for Strategic Studies, London, 2006; and "Country Overview", Natural Resource Defense Council, Washington, D.C.

The *Shaheen* missile programme was initiated in 1995 and assigned to the NDC.[42] The *Shaheen* project used the resources that were available within the various other institutions in Pakistan, supplemented with infrastructure created at the National Development Complex for capabilities which were not available elsewhere in Pakistan. The facilities of SUPARCO were utilized in the *Shaheen* project, along with the facilities of industry in Lahore, Karachi, Islamabad, Gujranwala, Sialkot, Gujarat and other cities. Missile components from these various facilities were brought to the NDC for final integration.

The Indian Test of the *Agni*-II IRBM was conducted on 11 April 1999. Pakistan responded on 14 April 1999 with a test firing of its *Ghauri*-II missile from the Jhelum region in northeast Pakistan. Samar Mubarik Mund, in charge of the *Shaheen* project, left for China and returned home on 14 April 1999. Then, on 15 April 1999, a successful test of *Shaheen* was conducted. Pakistan's Atomic Energy Commission said that it tested a single stage IRBM called the *Shaheen* for the first time with the range of 750 km. The missile was fired from Sonmiani, a coastal site near Karachi. It was claimed by the officials that missile can carry a one metric ton payload.

The test on 15 April 1999 marked the debut of the "*Shaheen*" (a royal white falcon) nomenclature in Pakistan's missile inventory, as well as the genesis of some confusion concerning its missile imports from China. The claimed 750 km range of the *Shaheen* is roughly double the standard range of the *Hatf*-III/M-11, and is consistent with the range of the much large Chinese M-9. Unconfirmed reports have suggested that China may have transferred a small number of M-9 missiles to Pakistan, in addition to the well-established transfer of M-11 missiles.[43] In any event, the still photos and video of *Shaheen*, released by Pakistan are clearly the M-9, not the M-11, and the *Shaheen* Transporter Erector Launcher TEL is clearly a modified version of the M-11 TEL. The two "*Shaheen*" missiles displayed in the military parade were apparently the improved longer-range CSS-7 Mod-II, rather than the original Mod-I exported to Pakistan in the early 1990s.

Pakistan is also developing a two-stage longer-range version of *Shaheen*, the *Shaheen*-II, which may also be called the *Haft*-VII. Its range is estimated to approach 2,500 kilometers and it was displayed at the Pakistan Day parade in March 2000. Both versions of the *Shaheen* are carried on mobile launchers. It is not clear whether the Shaheen-2 has been tested or equipped to carry nuclear weapons, but both developments are likely.

China started developing the M-9 in the mid-1980s. The first M-9 flight-test is reported to have occurred in June 1988, and the missile probably entered service in 1990. However, Pakistan first announced the test of an 800 km-range ballistic missile in July 1997.[44] This missile was subsequently designated *Hatf*-IV or

Shaheen-I and was publicly displayed for the first time during the National Day parade in March 1999. It was subsequently tested in April 1999, October 2002, and October 2003. The photographs of the missile displayed during the parade, and those of the tested version, along with its disclosed range and payload closely match the parameters of the Chinese M-9.

The DF-15/M-9 (NATO designation CSS-6) is a single-stage, solid-propellant, road mobile, short-range ballistic missile. It can reportedly deliver a 500 kg warhead over a range of 600 km; other reports suggest that with a smaller warhead, the missile could have a range of 800 km. Pakistani government statements suggest that the missiles in Pakistan's possession have a maximum range of 700-800 km, but the missile's payload capacity at that range remains unclear. Like the M-11 missiles, control during boost phase is exercised through exhaust vanes or small scale vernier motors. The M-9 has a reported 300 m CEP and is believed to employ some form of terminal guidance. Analysts suggest that the missile has a strapdown inertial guidance system with an onboard digital computer, which enables rapid targeting and eliminates need for wind corrections prior to launch. Unconfirmed reports suggest that the separating warhead section has a miniature propulsion system to correct the atitude before re-entry, as well as adjusting the terminal trajectory."[45]

Although China originally designed the export versions of the M-9 with a high-explosive conventional warhead, Pakistan is believed to have modified its missiles to make them nuclear capable.[46] The total number of M-9s in Pakistan's inventory remains unknown. The *Hatf*-IV / *Shaheen*-I was formally inducted into the Pakistan Army in March 2003.[47] However, the continuation of flight-tests even after the 2003 raises doubts whether all developmental concerns have been resolved.[48]

GHAURI-I/HATF-V/NO DONG

Pakistan carried out a successful flight-test of a medium range ballistic missile on April 6, 1998 from *Tilla Jogian* covering a distance of 1100 km towards *Nok Kundi* in the *Mekran mountains* of Bluchistan province in 9 minutes and 58 seconds. It climbed to a height of 350 kilometers before taking the direction to its target. This missile was first named *Hatf*-V[49] but the name was changed to *Ghauri* after the name of 12th century Afghan King *Mohammad Ghauri* who captured the western parts of India between 1176 and 1182, and then invaded the parts of northern India by defeating *Prithvi Raj* Chauhan in 1192. It has an optimum range of 1500 kilometers and can carry a payload of about 700 kg. The missile is in the research and development phase and is part of the Integrated Missile Research and

TABLE 4.5
Ghauri-I/Hatf-V Missile Specifications

Name	:	Ghauri-I
Other Designation	:	Hatf-V
Mission	:	Medium-range-ballistic missile
Service	:	Pakistan Army
Targets	:	Cities and military sites in India
Platform	:	Modified MAZ 543 TEL
Length	:	16.0 meter
Diameter	:	1.35 meter
Wing/Fin Span	:	2.4 meter
Launch Weight	:	16000 kg
Maximum Range	:	1500 km
Propulsion	:	Single-stage liquid
Payload	:	Single Warhead, 12000 kg
Warhead	:	30-40 Kt Nuclear, Chemical, High Explosive or sub munitions—800 kg
Accuracy	:	2500 meter
Guidance	:	Inertial with Terminal guidance
Primary Contractor	:	KRL

Source : "Missile Proliferation in South Asia: India and Pakistan's Ballistic Missile Inventories", Factsheets, *Arms Control Today,* Arms Control Association, May 2002; Shanon N. Kile, Vitaly Fedchenko and Hans M. Kristensen, "World Nuclear Forces", Armaments, Disarmament and International Security, *SIPRI Yearbook, 2006,* Oxford University Press, Oxford, 2006; and *The Military Balance, 2006-07,* International Institute for Strategic Studies, London, 2006; and "Country Overview", Natural Resource Defense Council, Washington, D.C.

Development Programme. The missile weight 16 tons and consists of 13 tons of fuel, a one ton warhead and the remaining weight is of the casing and equipment.

The Ghauri is a liquid-propellant, road-mobile ballistic missile. Press reports about the Ghauri flight test typically mention a maximum range of 1,500 kilometers for the missile, but the range of the test is usually given as 1,100 km with a flight time of 9 minutes and 58 seconds.[50] Although the Nationwide Association of Security Installation Company (NASIC) identifies the Ghauri as having a range of 1,300 km, David Wright concludes that range may be significantly shorter depending on the size of Pakistan's nuclear warheads and the precise configuration of the missile. The latter calculation turns on an assumption—that Pakistan's Ghauri is an "off the shelf" Nodong and gives the same range for both. Wright further observes that the Ghauri is slightly smaller—which suggests that it has made use of some indigenous Pakistani technology and hence its range may be shorter.

The *Ghauri* missile cannot be kept "on alert" as liquid-propellants are too corrosive to keep ballistic missiles constantly fueled. As a result, Pakistan is likely to adopt the Chinese model and keep its *Ghauri* missile inventory in storage with its warheads stored separately. Pakistan may feel that its nuclear weapons are too vulnerable in this mode. During the 1999 *Kargil* Crisis, the United States detected Pakistan moving its *Ghauri* missiles out of storage and concluded that the crisis was entering a particularly dangerous stage. Although Washington utilized strategic warning to intensify diplomacy, New Delhi might attempt to destroy Pakistan's missile forces before they were ready to fire.

Several reports have given the total mass of the *Ghauri* missile as 16 tones and the payload as 700 kg; are fuel masses of both 13 and 14 tones have been reported. However, a fuel mass of 14 tones would give a fuel fraction for the booster of 91.5%, which appears unrealistically high without access to very lightweight materials. On the other hand, a fuel mass of 13 tones would give a fuel fraction of 85%, which is a reasonable value assuming the missile body is made of aluminum, rather than steel (which Scuds are made of). Thus it is assumed that the missile has a total mass of 16 tones and a fuel mass of 13 tones.

If these figures for the *Ghauri* are correct, the missile appears to be somewhat smaller than the North Korean Nodong missile. The Nodong mass is estimated to be a couple of tones larger than these values (about 15 tones of fuel and 18.5 tones total mass if the body is made of aluminum). This is consistent with reports that the *Ghauri* was not a Nodong, although the design and technology are probably similar to that of the Nodong. Similarly, from the photos of the *Ghauri* launch that were released by Pakistani television, one can get a very rough estimate of the size of the missile. From this, the missile appears to be very roughly of the same size as, though possibly smaller than that of the Nodong, which is reported to be 15.2 meters long and 1.2 meters in diameter. The missile can reportedly be fired from a mobile launcher and is believed to be single stage. At least one report stated that the *Ghauri* is three-stage, but this appears to be a misinterpretation of Pakistani reports that the missile will formally be tested in three stages.

GHAURI-II

The *Ghauri*-II is believed to be an improvised version of *Ghauri*-I, possibly employing new propellants and a motor assembly. It was test fired on April 14, 1999, from Tilla Jogian and targeted to a point north of Jiwani town Bluchistan. In all probability, it was the second test of the same missile named *Ghauri*-I although some improvements may have been made in its design since the first launch in April 1998. It is a liquid fuel two stage missile with 18.0 meter diameter. Pakistan used the *Hatf*-V label for both the *Ghauri*-I and II.[51] Its range is believed to be 1150 km in comparison to the previous one launched in April 1998. Although it was claimed by a special bulletin on PTV that the range could be extended to 2300 km.[52] It could accommodate a 15 to 35 Kt nuclear warhead as well as the full range of warheads available for the *Ghauri*-I.[53] There are some anomalies in various sources and statements regarding the range of missile. According to the then Prime Minister Nawaz Sharif, the range of *Ghauri*-II is 2000 km and could carry a payload of 1000 kg. He claimed that the missile had flown to the distance of 1150 km while Abdul Quadir Khan claimed that it had flown to 1380 km. It is suspected that there may not be a *Ghauri*-II as a different missile but the same missile—the *Ghauri*-I—with some improvements. The logic behind this test of the missile as *Ghauri*-II seems to be an effort to manipulate the domestic public perceptions that Pakistan is keeping pace with the *Agni*-II of India.

Intelligence agencies of the USA have identified an assembly and storage facility for the *Ghauri* close to the KRL's Kahuta plant. Estimates of Pakistan's *Ghauri* inventory remain unknown, although information available in open sources suggests that Pakistan may have obtained between 12-25 missile systems from North Korea. Speculation also persists that North Korea may have transferred an entire production line for Nodong ballistic missiles to Pakistan.

KRL has also disclosed plans for longer-range versions of the *Ghauri*, *Ghauri*-II and possibly *Ghauri*-III. A more powerful engine for longer-range versions of the *Ghauri* is under development.[54] Some statements attributed to Pakistani nuclear scientists and government leaders suggest that the *Ghauri*-II will have a range of 1,700 km; other statements suggest that the *Ghauri*-III will have a strike-range of 2,000-3,500 km.[55] But details of the programmes remain unknown and unlike the proposed *Shaheen*-II, no mock ups have been displayed in public. However, analysts cite the presence of Pakistani missile scientists and engineers during North Korea's August 1998 Taepodong launch and speculate that the *Ghauri*-II and -III may either be a Taepodong or draw extensively on components and technologies from the latter program.

GHAURI-III

A *Ghauri*-III missile has also been reported to be in development with a possible range of 3000 km and motor tests for this missile were believed to have taken place in July and September 1999 at the KRL in Kathua.[56] Another source reveals that this North Korean Taepo Dong based missile was tested in August 2000.[57]

HATF-VI/SHAHEEN-II/M-18?

The NDC is reportedly also developing a 1700-2,500 km-range missile dubbed as the *Shaheen*-II, about which little is known.[58] Mock-ups of the missile displayed during the National

Day celebrations in March 2003 suggest that it is a two-stage, solid-motor, road mobile system, transported on a 12-wheel TEL vehicle. Analysts speculate that the *Shaheen*-II is possibly a two-stage version of the M-9, or more likely a copy of the M-18, which was publicly displayed at an exhibition in Beijing in either 1987 or 1988. The M-18 was originally advertised as a two-stage system with a payload capacity of 400-500 kg over a range of 1,000 km.[59] Intelligence sources of the USA suggest that Pakistan remains heavily reliant on external assistance for the *Shaheen*-II programme and that China is actively assisting Pakistan through the supply of missile components, specialty materials, dual-use items, and other miscellaneous forms of technical assistance.[60]

Like Shaheen-I, the Shaheen-II is also believed to be nuclear capable, and the largest and most capable ballistic missile of Pakistan. To date, this missile has no publicly identified counterpart in the Chinese missile arsenal, but one possibility might be the DF-25, a reported two-stage 1,700-2,500 km range solid-fuel missile. Development flight tests of the Shaheen-II began in March 2004 when a 26 ton missile was launched from Pakistan's Somiani Flight Test Range on the Arabian Sea on March 9, 2004.[61] According to the Chairman of Pakistan's National Engineering and Scientific Commission (NESCOM) Samar Mubarik mund, the missile covered a distance of 1,800 km during the test. Development flight-tests continued during 2005-2006.[62]

On the first test of the missile on March 9, 2004, the Pakistani military issued a statement saying, "Pakistan today successfully carried out the maiden test fire of the *Shaheen*-II surface-to-surface ballistic missile." In an interview with an English daily in Islamabad, the Director General of NDC and a member of PAEC, Samar Mubarik Mund said that the work is in progress on the long range *Shaheen*-II which can travel 2000 kilometers. He said the missile would be ready for testing by the end of 1998, though it was not launched until early 2004.

A pair of *Shaheen*-II ballistic missiles was displayed during the Pakistan Day parade in Islamabad on 23 March 2000. One of the missiles was carried on a 12-wheel TEL, while the other missile was carried on a Missile Transporter. These vehicles, based on a common chassis, are larger than the 8-wheel launcher used by the *Shaheen*, though they use a similar cab. During the parade, it was claimed that the *Shaheen*-II surface-to-surface missile had a range of 2,000 km.

Before the launch of the missile it had been displayed with two sets of guidance fins for each stage. But the missile tested in March 2004, and the one displayed at International Defence Exhibition and Seminar (IDEAS), had no fins at the second stage. Pakistani placards stated its range 2,000 km, but other sources note that this might be extended to 2,500 km with a lighter warhead.[63] While published sources give this missile accuracy measured in CEP of 350 m,[64] a Pakistani video claims that it is

Table 4.6
Shaheen-II Missile Specifications

Name	:	Shaheen-II
Service	:	Intermediate range ballistic missile
Targets	:	Cities and military sites in India
First Launch Date	:	March 9, 2004
Length	:	12.00 meter
Core Diameter	:	0.88 meter
Range	:	2000-2500 km
Weight	:	15000 kg
Re-entry vehicle weight	:	1000 kg
Propulsion	:	Two stage solid
Payload	:	750 kg
Warheads	:	Nuclear, High Explosive (15-35 Kt Nuclear)
CEP	:	350 meter
Contractor	:	NDC
Technical Source	:	China

Source : "Missile Proliferation in South Asia: India and Pakistan's Ballistic Missile Inventories", Factsheets, *Arms Control Today*, Arms Control Association, May 2002; Shanon N. Kile, Vitaly Fedchenko and Hans M. Kristensen, "World Nuclear Forces", Armaments, Disarmament and International Security, *SIPRI Yearbook, 2006*, Oxford University Press, Oxford, 2006; and *The Military Balance, 2006-07*, International Institute for Strategic Studies, London, 2006; and "Country Overview", Natural Resource Defense Council, Washington, D.C.

capable of "surgical precision". This may indicate that it incorporates a warhead post-separation correction system and/ or a satellite navigation update system, which may indicate a CEP of much less than 300 m.

The *Shaheen*-II is evidently a Pakistani version of the Chinese M-18, which was originally shown at the 1987 Beijing air show as a two-stage missile with 1000 km range carrying a 400-500 kilogram payload. This M-18 missile had the longest range of any of the current M-series missiles. The *Shaheen* series of missiles are evidently based on M-series imported from China by the PAEC's National Development Complex. The *Shaheen*-I, which was tested with considerable publicity on 15 April 1999, is evidently the Chinese M-11 which Pakistan purchased in the early 1990s. The *Shaheen*-II would appear to represent the Chinese M-18, although it is questionable whether Pakistan has actually obtained these missiles from China. There is no indication that China has transferred such missiles to Pakistan.

Pakistan has announced that development efforts are underway on a longer-range missile, designated the *Ghaznavi*, although no details of this system's proposed characteristics have been made public. Reports also indicate there may be a 4,000 km range *Shaheen*-III in development that would also serve as a space launch vehicle.[65]

HATF-VII/BABUR CRUISE MISSILE

Babur is Pakistan's indigenously made cruise missile. On August 12th, 2005 Pakistan publicly announced that it has successfully test fired nuclear-capable *Babur* cruise missile. Missile was launched from a land-based transporter erector launcher (TEL). With this test Pakistan has joined the elite club of twelve countries that posses cruise missile technology. *Babur* is part of Pakistan's *Haft*-VII missile series. *Babur* is described as a subsonic, low-level terrain-mapping, terrain-hugging missile that can avoid radar detection and strike with pinpoint accuracy with a range of 500 km.

Babur is designed to be extremely accurate. It is steered by an inertial navigation system (INS). INS measures every movement of the missile and every change of speed constantly calculating the missile's position. It is equipped with precision guidance system that allows the missile to hit small targets. It has been powered by cruise turbo-fan engine which enables the missile to reach at an approximate speed of 880 km/h. *Babur* design features can be compared with American BGM-109 Tomahawk cruise missile.

It can avoid radar detection to penetrate hostile defencive systems with pinpoint accuracy and could also be modified so it can be launched from ships, submarines and aircraft. Currently Pakistan is looking into modification that will enable the missile to be launched from its F-16s, Mirage and A-5 air platforms and naval platform such as Agosta 90B attack submarines and its Tariq Class frigates. In a statement issued by Inter Services Public Relations (ISPR) the spokesman said that Pakistan will be modifying the missile for air and sea launch configurations in coming months. He added that Pakistan is also working on a more advanced version of *Babur* (possibly named as *Babur*-II) with a range of 1,000 km with increased payload. Serial production of *Babur* has started in October 2005.

TABLE 4.7
Babur/Hatf-VII Missile Specifications

Name	:	Babur/Hatf-VII
Service	:	Medium range subsonic cruise missile
Targets	:	Cities and military sites in India
Length	:	7 meter
Wing Span	:	6.75 meter
Range	:	500 km
Speed	:	880 km/h
Warheads	:	Both conventional and nuclear
Status	:	Operational, undergoing serial production

Source : "Missile Proliferation in South Asia: India and Pakistan's Ballistic Missile Inventories", *Factsheets, Arms Control Today,* Arms Control Association, May 2002; Shanon N. Kile, Vitaly Fedchenko and Hans M. Kristensen, "World Nuclear Forces", Armaments, Disarmament and International Security, *SIPRI Yearbook, 2006,* Oxford University Press, Oxford, 2006; and *The Military Balance, 2006-07,* International Institute for Strategic Studies, London, 2006; and "Country Overview", Natural Resource Defense Council, Washington D.C.

Pakistan has a sizeable defence industrial complex to develop missile systems and related technology which include the Defence Science and Technology Organisation (DESTO), the Military Vehicle Research and Development Establishment (MVRDE), and the Armament Research and Development Establishment (ARDE). It established the Margalla Electronics and Institute of Optronics in the mid-1980s to manufacture radar and night vision devices. Pakistan could utilize these facilities, and the private industry to absorb the missile technology acquired from both China and North Korea and it could enhance the indigenous capability to execute its missile programme in the future.

Though the *Hatf*-I, IA, and II were declared operational in the early 1990s and the Pakistan Army tested the *Hatf* IA in February 2000, yet both programmes are likely to be discontinued. The *Hatf*-I, IA, and II are short-range systems and most major Indian urban and military targets lie beyond their range. Deployments close to the Indian borders during a crisis or war, coupled with improvements in real-time Indian reconnaissance capabilities, would leave them vulnerable to early detection and destruction. Although the *Hatf* missile series could conceivably serve as long-range artillery rockets but most observers suspect that they lack an accurate guidance system. Besides, some also argue that the early *Hatf* missiles lacked a guidance system altogether. Furthermore, most ballistic missiles are not as cost-effective as combat aircraft in conventional battlefield roles. Therefore, although the Pakistani Army may have acquired a limited number of *Hatf*-I, IA, and II in the early 1990s, yet these early missiles are unlikely to play any role in Pakistan's nuclear deterrent. Similarly, Pakistan's acquisitions of complete M-11 and possibly M-9 ballistic missiles, as well as a production line to build them from China, indirectly attest to the failure of the *Hatf*-II programme. Despite Pakistan's last conduct of a test of the *Hatf*-II in March 2003, the missile is unlikely to serve as part of an operational nuclear force. Hence, Ghauri will be the main missile in Pakistan's nuclear force. *Ghaznavi*/M-11 and *Shaheen*-I/(most likely M-9) ballistic missiles are also believed to be in operational service.

Unlike India, Pakistan's missile programme has largely been dependent on foreign assistance. After a brief and unsuccessful attempt in the 1980s to develop solid-fueled short-range ballistic missiles most likely derived from sounding rocket technology obtained from France, Pakistan turned to China and North Korea for assistance. Chinese assistance most likely encompassed equipment and technology transfers in the areas of solid-fuel propellants, manufacture of airframes, re-entry thermal protection materials, post-boost vehicles, guidance and control, missile computers, integration of warheads, and the manufacture of TELs for the missiles. Though China subsequently agreed to abide by MTCR guidelines under U.S. pressure, yet it has interpreted those guidelines narrowly. Similarly, Pakistan has relied extensively on North Korea for its liquid-engine ballistic missile programme. Pakistan's testing of its Ghauri (*Hatf-V*) 1,500 km medium range ballistic missile (IRBM) has raised regional security concerns. While the world has focused its attention on China as the silent partner behind Pakistan's developing missile capabilities but there is another significant sponsor—the North Korea.

The North Korea's involvement in the Pakistani missile programme, as well as its continued assistance to Egypt, Iran and Syria, illustrate that despite its worsening economic and political situation, it continues to expend time, money and precious resources upon its No-dong and Taep'o-dong missile programmes. In fact, these programmes along with the WMD, artillery and special operations forces are the few areas of expected growth within North Korea.[66] Former Pakistani Prime Minister Benazir Bhutto admitted in February 2004 that Pakistan obtained missile technology from North Korea in lieu of cash.[67] However, President Pervez Musharraf vehemently denies that Pakistan obtained ballistic missiles from North Korea, Musharraf only admitted that Pakistan purchased surface-to-air missiles from it.[68] In March 2003, the United States imposed sanctions on KRL and North Korea's Changgwang Sinyong Corporation for engaging in proliferation activities.[69] State Department of USA spokesperson explained that missile proliferation sanctions were imposed on North Korea for its involvement in the transfer of Category 1 items to a Category 1 missile programme in a non-MTCR country.[70]

However, Pakistan's current fleet of solid-fueled SRBMs suffers from range limitations. In order to strike targets in western

India, the missiles need to be deployed close to the Indo-Pakistani border, a condition that leaves them vulnerable to early detection and destruction. More significantly, the SRBMs lack the range to strike targets in eastern, central, and southern India. These shortcomings are expected to be addressed by the medium-range *Shaheen*-II and *Ghauri*-II programmes, which are under development at the NDC and KRL, respectively. Despite U.S. pressure, China is likely to stick to its commitment to help Pakistan in the development of the *Shaheen*-II medium-range ballistic missile programme. But unlike the past, when China transferred compete missile systems and assembly and production lines to Pakistan, the current pattern of Chinese assistance is apparently restricted to design advice, specialty materials, missile components, guidance systems, and related dual-use machine tools and technologies.

India's efforts to invest in theater ballistic missile defense through the acquisition of either the Israeli Arrow-2 or the PAC-3 systems of the USA could spur significant changes in Pakistan's missile programmes. An Indian theater missile defense would not create a leak-proof defence umbrella, a limited missile defence coupled with improvements in Indian long-range air and satellite-based reconnaissance capabilities could severely undercut the deterrence value of a Pakistani SRBM force. This latter trend, coupled with Chinese concerns over U.S. attempts to provide Taiwan with a theater missile defence capability, could lead to deepening cooperation between Beijing and Islamabad. In the future, China could conceivably help Pakistan develop intermediate-range ballistic missile systems, land and sea-launched cruise and ballistic missiles, and missiles with fast burning boosters using high-energy solid-propellants, multiple warheads, maneuverable re-entry vehicles, decoys, and other means to fool ballistic missile defences.

Notes and References

1. A.K. Sachdeva, *Pertinence of Pakistani Ballistic Missiles in the Indo-Pak Conflict,* Delhi, Papers-14, IDSA, New Delhi, 2000, pp. 6-7.
2. *Ibid.*
3. In the beginning, the SUPARCO was assigned to produce indigenous 122 mm multi-barrel rocket launcher system under an arrangement with North Korea. By 1981, it had become an autonomous

organization with a sizeable budget, and when in the mid 1980s, Pakistan decided on an indigenous missile programme, it was the natural choice for becoming the core agency for the purpose. It took two indigenous missile programmes—Hatf-I with a range of 80 km and Hatf-II with a range of 300 km—but the test launches of these two in 1989 were not very encouraging. There were some problems with separation of stages, heat shield for re-entry and advanced telemetry technology. *Ibid.*

4. "Pakistan", *Deadly Arsenals: Tracking Weapons of Mass Destruction,* Washington, DC: Carnegie Endowment for International Peace, 2002, pp. 207, 213-14.
5. However, the Pakistani Air Force is eagerly exploring options to upgrade its ageing fleet of combat aircraft. See, "Pakistan Air Force Weighing Various Aircraft As Procurement Options", The News, Islamabad, 15 May 2004.
6. The NDC, which had been working on strategic systems development under the PAEC laid claims to the development project. The other contender that surfaced was the Khan Research Laboratories (KRL) which under the stewardship of Dr. A.Q. Khan, had been entrusted with the development and manufacture of tactical weapon systems e.g. surface-to-air missiles and anti-tank guided missiles. After a keenly fought out turf battle, the PAEC emerged the victor and entrusted with the development of new strategic missile systems with active Chinese technical collaboration in March 1995. The project was placed under the charge of NDC head, Dr. Samar Mubarak Mand who was also the member (technical) of the PAEC. Experts were drawn from PAEC, SUPARCO, Defence Science and Technology Organization (DESTO) and Air Weapons Complex of the Pakistan Air Force (PAF). Since then the NDC has procured (from Chinese entities) all the required material and ingredients and acquired the technical know-how needed for the establishment of plants for indigenous manufacture of key ingredients of solid fuel propellants. A.K. Sachdeva, n. 1, pp. 7-8.
7. "Pakistan's Nukes Outstrip India's, Officials Say", MSNBC News, 6 June 2000, http://www. msnbc.news/.
8. Rockets are different from the missiles as they do not have guidance systems and are reliant on their launch trajectory in order to strike their intended target.
9. Ahmed Rashid, "Pakistan announces first successful test of its own missile", *Independent,* London, 6 February 1989;
10. "Hatf-1 Pakistan Missile Special Weapons Delivery Systems", Federation of American Scientists, November 2003, http://www.fas.org/nuke/guide/*pakistan/missile/hatf-1.htm.*
11. Zia Mian, *Pakistan's Atomic Bomb and the Search for Security,* Gautam Publishers, Lahore, 1995, p. 65. Also see Roger Frost, "Pakistan's New Defence Minister: on Missiles, Self-reliance and Afghanistan", *International Defence Review,* Surrey, UK, April 1989.
12. In January 1989, a successful launch of an "indigenous multistage rocket into deep space" was said to have reached an altitude of more than 640 km. This test of the Hatf-I and Hatf-II demonstrated

components of the longer-range Hatf-III, of which the Hatf-I is believed to be the second stage.

13. Some analysts speculate that the limited range and payload capacity of these rockets would preclude the use of a nuclear warhead and more likely payloads include high explosives, sub munitions and possibly chemical weapons.
14. On 7 February 2000, Pakistan conducted a test of the Hatf-I, which was characterized as a sequel to several previous tests. Amit Baruah, "Pak test fires Hatf-I missile", *The Hindu,* Chennai, 8 February 2000.
15. A.K. Sachdeva, n. 1, p. 10.
16. These missiles are believed to be product of French Eridan sounding rocket technology acquired by Pakistan and developed with Chinese assistance. Eridan was a two-stage rocket able to send a 250 kg payload to more than 300 km altitude, or a 130 kg payload to more than 425 km altitude. A total of 17 Eridan rockets were launched by France between 1968 and 1979. This sounding rocket had a liftoff mass of 2,127 kg, and was just 10 meters long.
17. S. Chandrashekar, "An Assessment of Pakistan's Missile Capability", *Missile Monitor,* Number 3, Spring 1993, pp. 7-8.
18. "Hatf-2/Shadoz-Pakistan Special Weapons Guide: Missiles", *Global Security.org,* http://www. globalsecurity.org/wmd/world/pakistan/ hatf-2.htm, November 2003; "Abdali" (Hatf-2) BRBM, *Pakistani Defence.com,*http://www.pakistanidefence.com/images/ AbdaliPictures.htm, January 2004.
19. http://www.fas.org/nuke/guide/pakistan/missile/hatf-2.htm# N_1_
20. *Ibid.*
21. *Ibid.*
22. *Ibid.*
23. "Pakistan derives its first "Hatf" missiles from foreign space rockets", *The Risk Report,* Volume 1, Number 8, October 1995, http:/ /www.wisconsinproject.org/countries/pakistan/hatf.html.
24. Chandrashekar, n. 17, pp. 5-6.
25. "Hatf Missiles 1/2/3", *Pak Directory,* November 2003, http:// www.pakdirectory.net/hatf missiles.asp.
26. For more etails of various reports and interpretations regarding this see, *CRS Report RL31555,* pp. 5-6. Also see, Douglas Jehl, "China Breaking Missile Pledge", U.S. Aides Say", *The New York Times International,* 6 May 93.
27. "Proliferation Missile Story Old Hat", *Intelligence Newsletter, No.* 268, 13 July 95.
28. Ranjit Kumar, "Yet Another Trial by Fire", *Navbharat Times,* 28 August 96, p. 6.
29. R. Jeffrey Smith and David B. Ottaway, "Spy Photos Suggest China Missile Trade; Pressure for Sanctions Builds Over Evidence that Pakistan has M-11s", *Washington Post,* 3 July 1995, p. A01.
30. "Pakistan Rejects Reports on Missiles", *Associated Press,* 3 July, 2000.
31. Bill Gertz, "Missile Deception", *Betrayal: How the Clinton Administration Undermined American Security,* , Regnery Publishing, Inc, Washington DC., 1999, p. 159.

32. R. Jeffrey Smith, "China said to sell arms to Pakistan; M-11 Missile Shipment may break vow to U.S.", *Washington Post,* 4 December 1992, p. and A10. Jim Mann, "China Said to Sell Pakistan Dangerous New Missiles", *Los Angeles Times,* 4 December 1992, p. 1.
33. Gertz, n,. 31, p. 268.
34. R Jeffery Smith, "Pakistan Has A-Weapons for Missiles, US Fears", *Herald Tribune,* 14 June, 1996.
35. "Pakistan", *Deadly Arsenals,* n. 4, pp. 213-14.
36. "Hatf-III/Shaheen-I/M-11-Pakistani Missile Special Weapons Delivery Systems", *Federation of American Scientists,* http://www.fas.org/nuke/guide/pakistan/missile/hatf-3.htm
37. "CSS-7 (DF-11/M-11)—People's Republic of China: Offensive Weapons", Duncan Lennox ed., *Jane's Strategic Weapon Systems,* Issue 25, Coulsdon, September 1997.
38. R. Jeffrey Smith, "China Linked to Pakistani Missile Plant", *The Washington Post,* 25 Aug 96, p. 1.
39. "Pakistan Test-Fires Nuclear-Capable Missile", *Agence France Presse,* 3 October 2003.
40. "President Says Pakistan Nuclear Programme "Here to Stay", *BBC Monitoring International Reports,* 21 February 2004; and B. Muralidhar Reddy, "We Will Never Roll Back N-Programme: Musharraf", *The Hindu,* Chennai, 22 February 2004.
41. "Missile Proliferation and the Strategic Balance in South Asia", *CRS Report for Congress 32115,* 17 October, 2003, p. 31.
42. It is believed that Shaheen was reversed-engineered from the Chinese M-9 missile, probably with Chinese technical assistance. It was test fired in April 1999 and February 2000 to a range of more than 600 kilometers. Pakistan's ballistic missile program supposedly follows two parallel tracks. The Khan Research Laboratories developed the Ghauri, while the Shaheen is the work of the Pakistan Atomic Energy Commission. The Shaheen project is directly managed by the National Defense Complex, a subsidiary of the Pakistan Atomic Energy Commission. To an extent, development of delivery vehicles may be driven by competition between the two institutions. Unlike the liquid-fueled Ghauri, the Shaheen uses solid fuel. Solid fuel can be left in the missile indefinitely, unlike liquid fuel, and therefore, dramatically decreases the time it takes to launch the missile, heightening deterrence.
43. Analysts speculate that Pakistan likely acquired an undisclosed number of M-9 ballistic missiles from China in the mid-1990s, although open source reports alleging M-9 transfers from China to Pakistan stretch back to the early 1990s. However, some analysts now believe that China probably also transferred an entire production line for M-9s to the Fatehjung missile facility that it built for Pakistan in the mid-1990s.
44. "Government Confirms Test-Firing of New Missile", *Agence France Presse,* 3 July 1997; in FBIS Document FTS19970703000413, 3 July 1997.
45. "CSS-6 (DF-15/M-9)—People's Republic of China: Offensive Weapons", Duncan Lennox, ed., *Jane's Strategic Weapon Systems.*

46. "Pakistan", *Deadly Arsenals,* n. 6, p. 214.
47. "Strategic Force gets Shaheen-1 Missile", *Japan Economic Newswire,* 6 March 2003, International News; in Lexis-Nexis Academic Universe, 7 March 2003, http://www.lexis-nexis.com/.
48. Rana Jawad, "Pakistan Test-fires Nuclear-Capable Missile", *Agence France Presse,* 8 October 2003, International News; in Lexis-Nexis Academic Universe, 9 October 2003, http://www.lexis-nexis.com/ and Bronwyn Curran, "Pakistan Test-fires Nuclear-Capable Missile", *Agence France Presse,* 14 October 2003, International News; in Lexis-Nexis Academic Universe, 15 October 2003, http://www.lexis-nexis.com/.
49. General Beg of Pakistan says that the name Hatf for the surface-to-surface missile was selected by the Research and Development (R and D) Committee of the General Headquarters (GHQ) of the Pakistan Army, as it was the name of the lance of the Holy Prophet which was used in many ghazva, and had the unique distinction of never missing its target. Similarly the name Anza, a lance of the Holy Prophet was selected for a similar consideration, for the shoulder-fired ground-to-air missile, which was also developed during the same period. Later the anti-tank Baktarshikan missile was also produced.
50. Many reports mention that the missile rose to an altitude of 350 km. This appears to refer to the apogee, or highest point of the trajectory, which occurs in the middle of the trajectory.
51. "Pakistan's Ballistic Response", *Frontline,* Vol. 16, No. 9, 24 April-7 May 1999.
52. A.K. Sachdeva, n. 1, p. 14.
53. "Missile Proliferation and the Strategic Balance in South Asia", CRS *Report for Congress 32115,* 17 October, 2003, p. 32.
54. "Pakistan to Test Latest Engine for Ghauri IV Missile—Daily", *BBC Monitoring International Reports,* 17 December 2003; in Lexis-Nexis Academic Universe, 17 December 2003, http://www.lexis-nexis.com/.
55. "Ghauri-III Engine Successfully Tested", Ausaf, Islamabad, 24 June 1999; in FBIS Document FTS19990624000013, 24 June 1999; "Pakistan Reportedly Begins Preparations For Testing Ghauri-3 Missile", *BBC Monitoring International Reports,* 21 April 2002; in Lexis-Nexis Academic Universe, 21 April 2002, http://www.lexis-nexis.com/.
56. *Hindustan Times,* 12 December, 1999.
57. Muralidhar Reddy, "UFOs were Ghauri-III fragments", *The Hindu,* 24 August, 2000.
58. "Pakistan's 'Multi-Stage' 2,500 km Range 'Shaheen-II' Missile Ready For Testing", *Dawn,* Karachi, 17 September 2000.
59. "Shaheen-II/Hatf-6/Ghaznavi: Pakistan Missile Special Weapons Delivery Systems", *Federation of American Scientists,* December 2003, http://www.fas.org/nuke/guide/pakistan/missile/shaheen-2.htm.
60. David E. Sanger and Eric Schmitt, "Reports Say China is Aiding Pakistan on Missile Project", *New York Times,* 2 July 2000, http://www.nytimes.com/; "Unclassified Report to Congress on the Acquisition of Technology Relating to Weapons of Mass Destruction

and Advanced Conventional Munitions", Central Intelligence Agency, 1 January-30 June 2001, http://www.cia.gov/cia/ publications/ bian/bian_jan-2002.htm.

61. "Pakistan Test Fires New Missile", *Deutsche Presse-Agentur,* 9 March 2004, Politics; in Lexis-Nexis Academic Universe, 9 March 2004, http://www.lexis-nexis.com/.
62. "Pakistan Scientist Says Missile Test Reassures Nation Over Nuclear Programme", *BBC Monitoring International Reports,* 10 March 2004.
63. Babar Ahmad, "Pakistan: Tests May Not Include Cruise Missile Tests", *Defencetalk,* September 8, 2004, http://www.defencetalk.com/ news/publish/article_001868.shtml
64. Duncan Lennox, "Hatf 6 (Shaheen 2)" *Jane's Strategic Weapon Systems,* June 15, 2004.
65. *Ibid.*
66. "Global Threats and Challenges: The Decades Ahead", Statement for the Senate Select Committee on Intelligence by Lieutenant General Patrick M. Hughes, USA Director, *Defense Intelligence Agency,* 28 January 1998.
67. Bhutto Says Pak Paid N Korea for Missile Tech", *The Economic Times,* Mumbai, 11 February 2004.
68. "Musharraf-N. Korea", *The Press Trust of India,* 26 June 2003, Nationwide International News; in Lexis-Nexis Academic Universe, 26 June 2003, http://www.lexis-nexis.com/.
69. "Imposition of Missile Proliferation Sanctions Against a North Korean Entity", *Federal Register,* 2 April 2003, Vol. 68, No. 63.
70. "State Department Regular Briefing", *Federal News Service,* 31 March 2003; in Lexis-Nexis Academic Universe, 2 April 2003, http:// www.lexis-nexis.com/.

5

Comparative Assessment

India and Pakistan have little transparency in their nuclear weapon and missile development programmes.[1] Hence it is very difficult to say authoritatively about their actual nuclear forces or operational policies. Both, India and Pakistan reportedly have refrained from deploying nuclear weapons operationally.[2] Neither has distributed weapons to operators ready for immediate use on aircrafts or ballistic missiles. In Indian case, custody of nuclear weapons apparently has not yet been transferred physically to the military from the control of the Atomic Energy Department and DRDO. Both countries effectively maintain a high level of secrecy not only about the physical and numerical properties of their nuclear weapons, delivery systems, command and control organization, operational plans for nuclear war, but even about their nuclear strategies and general force structure objectives, which makes the task of comparative assessment more difficult. While certain inferences can be made on the basis of both the countries' stated threat perceptions and technical capacities regarding their potential nuclear force structures, operational choices, and plausible doctrines. But one must be aware that there is scant evidence that either country has yet made longterm decisions about these issues. Even, if interim decisions on these matters have been made, they have not been disclosed. Much of the available literature is speculative and less reliable, and requires careful examination. Though the main focus of the present chapter is the comparative assessment of missile programmes of both the countries, yet it is pertinent to have a quick look on the nuclear programmes of both the countries from a comparative angle. While making the comparative assessment, in the first part, comparative assessment of nuclear programmes is made; in the second part missile programmes have been compared; and finally security implications of missile programmes have been evaluated.

COMPARISON OF NUCLEAR PROGRAMMES

There are basically two methods to make nuclear weapons. One is to obtain plutonium by processing U-238 which is the more complex method as compared to other technologies, and involves greater risks of failure and lapse of time. Its advantage lies in the scope for using exciting civilian nuclear reactors. The other method is to enrich U-235, which constitutes only 0.7 percent of natural uranium, to highly enriched uranium (HEU) with over 90 percent enrichment by elaborate isotope-enrichment processes, without the use of reactors and chemical separation.[3] India has gone for the first method while Pakistan for the second because of their divergent history of nuclear developments.

The Indian programme is mainly based on its two plants, Canadian Candu-type heavy water reactors at BARC, as wells as, a chemical reprocessing plant for plutonium separation in Trambay near Mumbai. The world Inventory of plutonium estimated that India had accumulated almost 300 kg weapons grade plutonium by the end of 1991.[4] Like most other nuclear ambitious states, India started on the nuclear weapons course via its civilian route through nuclear energy research which can be traced back to 1944.[5] In order not to depend overly on US supply of light water reactors, India took the Canadian aid for Candu reactors, with its large pool of trained scientists. India managed to move further from purely civilian nuclear base to nuclear weapons projects. The DAE and DRDO organized the

Pokhran-II tests. While DRDO develops advanced weapons, DAE operates the Atomic Energy Commission (AEC) and BARC, and takes care of designing as well. DRDO is responsible for producing high explosive components and weaponizing the nuclear devices. India took ten years to make an ambiguous response to china's maiden nuclear test in 1964. The explosion in May 1974 at *Pokharan* was officially called a PNE, though no one really believed it.[6] Ultimately the 1998 tests removed any doubts about Indian's ability to build a nuclear bomb.

On the other side, Pakistan adopted the clandestine route to make the nuclear bomb. It selected to steal and beg the nuclear technology from abroad to make the bomb.[7] In the mid-1970s the Pakistani scientist, Abdul Quadeer Khan stole gas-ultracentrifuge (GUC) secrets from Urenco, a German-British-Ducth consortium while working in Europe's civilian nuclear centers.[8] He took the blueprints from an enrichment plant at Almelo in Holland, and then in 1981 the A.Q. Khan Research Laboratory was set-up in Kathua in Pakistan.[9] Due to the tight non-proliferation measures after *Pokharan*-I, Pakistan set-up a circuitous network of hi-tech acquisition. It spread its clandestine tentacles in advanced countries.

There is a wealth of published information available about the evolution of Pakistan as a nuclear weapons power through clandestine means. It was helped in terms of materials, technology, maps and designs, and sophisticated equipments by France, UK, US, Holland, Germany, Italy and the Scandinavian countries indirectly, and above all, China.[10] Even through some of the clandestine deals were detected by the late 1980s. A.Q. Khan and Munir Khan, who headed the Pakastani Atomic energy commission, continued to maintain contact with European businessmen.[11] From the 1990s, Kathua started producing 45-100 kg of U-235 annually, which is enough to produce 3-7 bombs. In 1989, US pressure led the Bhutto government to stop HEU production, which was probably being produced over the past three years. But it was resumed in 1990, following Indo-Pak border skirmishes. Former Prime Minister Nawaz Sharif discontinued it again in 1991 while Pakistan continued to produce lightly enriched uranium. Pakistan is suspected to have broken the ban on uranium enrichment in the late 1990s. One estimate puts its weapons-grade uranium stockpile (excluding the materials used in its tests) at 335-400 kg till the end of May 1998. At 20 kg per weapon, Pakistan could make 16-20 weapons.[12]

Motivations

In case of rationale behind the nuclear programmes of India and Pakistan, there is a disagreement among the scholars. However one can not deny that deep-seated insecurity concerns might have been the dominant factors in their long-term nuclear weapon programmes.

While short-term domestic factors in India, such as the weak coalition government and a desire to appease the nuclear-scientific-technical cabal, may have forced New Delhi's hand in performing the 1998 tests, these explanations alone are insufficient to explain why India developed nuclear weapons in the first place.[13] While some argue that the country's nuclear programme served as the vehicle of national self expression and the goals of national identity construction, several long-term geopolitical factors were also at play. India has long held a genuine fear of the Chinese military threat, and Beijing's support to Islamabad's nuclear and missile programmes intensified this concern. Doubts concerning the extent of its superpower patron's security guarantee during the Soviet era, and later, collapse of Soviet union, exacerbated India's unease. Finally, the leaders in New Delhi were motivated by a desire for prestige and respect in the international community.[14] In case of Pakistan, its rationale appears to be simple in comparison to India's complex motivation. It was a cost-effective reaction to India's overwhelming military capabilities. Besides, the same long term realpolitik factors that drove India to nuclearization are also relevant in case of Pakistan.[15]

Pakistan feared its big neighbour and believed its superpower patron (USA) to be notoriously unreliable. Unlike India, Pakistan has also been tied to its continued linkage between its nuclear programme and the seemingly ineluctable Kashmir issue.[16] For Pakistan, its nuclear weapon programme is ostensibly a bargaining chip to be used to resolve the Kashmir issue, a tactic that is fraught with danger and miscalculation.

Ultimately, the roots of the nuclear programme of India and Pakistan run very deep. The factors motivated them to develop nuclear weapons are also pressuring them to expand and deploy the weapons. As a result, it will be difficult to force either side to destroy its nuclear arsenal. Even if the root causes for developing their nuclear weapons disappear, the weapon programme itself continues to generate powerful bureaucratic and public advocacy for its existence.[17] Thus South Asia is faced with nuclear weapons in both India and Pakistan for the foreseeable future, a situation that led former US President Bill Clinton to call this region as "the most dangerous place on earth."[18]

Weapons Capabilities

India has developed a massive indigenous civil and military nuclear infrastructure, while Pakistan lacks on extensive civil nuclear power infrastructure. Similarly latter's weapons programme is not as broad as that of India. India's programme has a significant civil nuclear energy component, whereas entire nuclear programme in Pakistan is focused on weapons applications. It is generally believed that Pakistan has been utilizing its nuclear programme primarily or solely to produce fissile material which could be used to make nuclear weapons. On the other side, a number of studies have concluded that India has not been employing the whole of its available capacity to produce weapon grade plutonium.[19]

Estimates on fissile material and nuclear weapons of both the countries vary according to the sources. In fact the estimation of the size of both the countries' inventory of separated weapon grade plutonium and highly enriched uranium (HEU) has become more difficult following their nuclear tests in May 1998. Both countries treat these numbers as highly classified, partly because such estimates provide a direct indication of the number of nuclear weapons they may possess.[20]

Though both the countries have not made any official statements about the size of their nuclear arsenal, The Natural Resource Development Council (NRDC) estimated that by 2002, India was having stockpile of approximately 30-35 nuclear warheads and Pakistan 24-48.[21] NRDC claimed that India is producing additional materials. It claims that Pakistani weapons are based on an implosion design that uses a solid core of highly enriched uranium, requiring an estimated 15-20 kg per warhead. Seismic measurements of the tests conducted on May 28-30, 1998, suggest that the yields were on the order of 9-12 kilotons and 4-6 kilotons respectively, lower than what Islamabad has announced. The same figure of nuclear arsenals for India and Pakistan has also been estimated as on 2002 by another prestigious magazine Bulletin of Atomic Scientists.[22] Carnegie endowment for International Peace, a well reputed organization, estimated in 2002 that India has produced enough weapons-grade plutonium for 50-90 nuclear weapons and a smaller but unknown quantity of weapons-grade uranium while Pakistan has produced 585-800 kg of highly enriched uranium, enough for 30-35 weapons. Pakistan has also produced a small but unknown quantity to weapons-grade plutonium, which is sufficient for estimated 3-5 nuclear weapons.[23] A report by US Department of Defense 2001, contends that India probably has a small stockpile of nuclear weapon components and could assemble and deploy a few nuclear weapons within a few days to a week. In case of Pakistan it says that its nuclear weapons are probably stored in component form and Pakistan probably could assemble the weapons fairly quickly.[24] Another study by Ashley J Tellis in 2001 asserts that India does not have or seek to deploy a ready nuclear arsenal, while in case of Pakistan it could not be said with certainty.[25] An article appeared in Jane's Intelligence Review in May 2002, reports that India's objective is to have a nuclear arsenal that is "strategically active but operationally dormant" which would allow India to maintain its retaliatory capability within a matter of hours to week, while simultaneously exhibiting restraint.[26] However, the study also maintains that in future, India may face increasing institutional pressure to shift its nuclear arsenal to a fully deployed status. On the other side, Pakistan's nuclear weapons are security driven and lack any doctrine. According to one more study, India is estimated to have 50-100 nuclear devices; its 100 megawatt Dhruva reactor has been operational since 1985, and has probably produced enough plutonium for 100 nuclear devices and continues to product sufficient plutonium for 5-7 nuclear devices annually. In case of Pakistan, the study estimates that Pakistan has enriched uranium sufficient for 40-

50 nuclear weapons, and is continuing to enrich uranium for perhaps 4-5 nuclear weapons annually. The Khan Research Laboratory is Pakistan's main uranium-enrichment facility. By the early 1990s, it was operating on an estimated 3000 centrifuges, and its capacity has presumably increased since then.[27] Rodney W. Jones, a noted scholar, assume that by the year 2000, each side has stockpile of at least 50-60 nuclear weapons (perhaps up to 100 in case of India) that can be prepared for use on short notice.[28] By projecting these numbers out to the coming years by the same methodology would suggest even higher figures than the conservative stockpiles. Nuclear Nonproliferation Review views 100-500 warheads equivalents for India, and 50-100 warheads equivalents for Pakistan.[29] Beside these estimations, some other organizations also have speculated about the nuclear arsenals of both the countries.[30] One of the major studies about nuclear weapons in South Asia was done by David Albright at the Institute for Science and International Security (ISIS) at Washington D.C. in USA in 2000.[31] This is the pioneering work which has been widely referred by a number of other authors. Albright calculated the size of India's stock of weapon-grade plutonium and Pakistan's inventory of separated weapon-grade uranium and weapon-grade plutonium.

India's Inventory is derived by estimating total production of weapons-grade plutonium in the *Cirus, Dhruva,* and power reactors and by subtracting draw downs from nuclear testing, processing losses, and civil uses of weapons-grade plutonium.[32] The median value, which is the value midway between the smallest and largest value, is about 310 kg of weapon-grade plutonium at the and of 1999 based on range of values between 5th and 95th percentiles, which are 240 kg to 395 kg.[33] In other words, it was 90 percent certain that the true value of India's inventory at the end of 1999 was between 240 and 395 kg, where the median value was about 310 kg (See Table 5.1)

Albright employed the measurement of 4.5 kg plutonium per nuclear weapon to calculate total number of nuclear weapons that India could have made using the available fissile material. Accordingly, the median estimate was about 65 weapons and the 5th and 95th percentiles were 45 and 95 weapons respectively. Albright estimated that Cirus and Dhruva

TABLE 5.1
Estimates of Nuclear Capabilities in India and Pakistan up to 1999

	Weapon-grade Plutonium		*Weapon-grade Uranium*		*Nuclear Weapon Equivalent*	
	Median (kg.)	*5th-95th percentiles (kg.)*	*Median (kg.)*	*5th-95th percentiles (kg.)*	*Median*	*5th-95th percentiles (kg.)*
(1)	*(2)*	*(3)*	*(4)*	*(5)*	*(6)*	*(7)*
India	310	240-395	Insignificant	Insignificant	65	45-95
Pakistan	5.5	1.7-13	690	585-800	39	30-52

Source : David Albright, "India's and Pakistan's Fissile Material and Nuclear Weapons Inventories end of 1999", Institute for Science and International Security, Washington D.C., 11 October 2000.

together produced 410 kg of weapons-grade plutonium, the power reactors produced about 25 kg and the draw down was about 125 kg.[34] In his calculation, Albright ignored any highly enriched uranium produced by India as insignificant.

In case of Pakistan, it is estimated that the inventory of weapons-grade uranium was done by taking into account factors such as enrichment capacity, the feed stock into the enrichment plant, and the amount of low enriched uranium produced during the 1990s. The estimated median value of Pakistan's inventory was 690 kg, and the 5th and 95th percentiles were 585 and 800 kg respectively. The number of nuclear weapons Pakistan could have made from its weapon grade uranium stock was estimated by employing a measure of 18 kg of weapon-grade uranium per weapon. Accordingly, the median value was 39 weapons, and the 5th and 95th percentiles were 30 and 52 weapons respectively. (See Table 5.1) Furthermore, Albright estimated that Pakistan could build a single nuclear weapon using the small amount of weapons-grade plutonium produced by one of its reactors.

By using the similar methods Albright has also estimated potential nuclear weapons capability of India and Pakistan, if they had decided to use reactor-grade civil plutonium. Using the measure of 8 kg of civil plutonium per weapon, he estimated that India could have produced 8300 kg of civil plutonium up to 1999 which is equivalent of 1040 weapons and Pakistan could have produced 600 kg of reactor-grade civil plutonium that is equivalent to 75 weapons. However, he acknowledged that civil plutonium is in spent fuel, and thus not suitable for use in nuclear weapons.[35]

Using the same methodology the potential nuclear arsenals in the future can be estimated, which depends upon the production of weapon-grade uranium and weapon-grade plutonium of both the countries. Since 1991 Pakistan is believed to have produced low enriched uranium. If Pakistan decided to resume its production of weapon-grade uranium, it would likely use its stock of LEU to produce weapon-grade uranium more quickly. If the enrichment output of Kathua plant remains fixed, Pakistan could produce about 300 Kg of weapon-grade uranium during the first year by utilizing its low enriched Uranium as feed for Kathua. In subsequent years, Pakistan is estimated to be able to produce about 110 Kg per year of weapon grade uranium, using naural uranium feed. In 2007, Pakistan is estimated to have enough weapon-grade uranium for over 74 nuclear weapons.

In addition, in April 1998 Pakistan commissioned an unsafe guarded reactor that is capable of producing about 10-15 Kg weapon-grade uranium per year enough for about 2-3 nuclear weapons annually. However his output is not considered in the analysis. Pakistan could also significantly increase Kathua's output, but this possible action is similarly not considered. There are some reports that Pakistan has started building a powerful new reactor for producing plutonium which will be a major expansion of its nuclear weapons capability. This new reactor will be capable to produce enough plutonium for 40-50 nuclear weapons per year, almost 20-fold increase from Pakistan's current capabilities.[36]

In case of India, it is estimated that as of early 1998, it was possessing seven times more nuclear weapons than Pakistan. Pakistan could reduce that margin to a factor of less than two over the next few years. If India wanted to maintain a significant lead over Pakistan, it would be forced to dramatically increase its fissile material production. Pakistan however is capable of matching such an increase (See Table 5.2).

In this way it is quiet likely that Pakistan went ahead to utilize its full capacity to produce 90 percent uranium since its nuclear tests in 1998. That means, while India has been following a restrained and limited approach towards building fissile material stockpile and nuclear weapons, Pakistan has been utilizing its entire capacity to build up not only fissile material stockpile but also building of nuclear weapons.

The US Department of Defense has identified various areas of nuclear technology which India and Pakistan were possessing up to 1996. The Department of Defense has employed a four-point scale—(i) limited capability, (ii) some capability, (iii) sufficient level of capability, and (iv) exceeding sufficient level of capability, to assess technological capabilities of different countries.[37] Sufficient level is defined as the capability required to produce entry-level weapons of mass destruction, delivery systems, or other hardware/software useful in WMD development, integration or use.

TABLE 5.2

India's and Pakistan's Cumulative Projected Fissile Material Stocks and Nuclear Arsenal Potential

Year	*India*		*Pakistan*	
	Weapon-grade Plutonium (Kg)	*No. of weapons*	*Weapon-grade Uranium (Kg)*	*No. of weapons*
1995	330	66	210	10
1996	350	70	210	10
1997	370	74	210	10
1998	390	78	500	25
1999	410	82	610	30
2000	430	86	720	36
2001	450	90	830	41
2002	470	94	940	47
2003	490	98	1052	52
2004	510	102	1160	58
2005	530	106	1270	63
2006	550	110	1380	69
2007	570	114	1490	74

Source : David Albright, *Factsheet: India and Pakistan-Current and Potential Nuclear Arsenal*, ISIS, Washington DC, 13 May, 1998.

The comparison has been made between the capabilities of India and Pakistan on the basis of analysis by US Department of defense by taking into account various developments since 1996 (See Table 5.3).

It is clear from the Table 5.3 that Pakistan is not for behind India's nuclear capability, particularly in areas such as fissile material production, design and development of nuclear weapons. Pakistan has developed sufficient capability or more than sufficient capability in enrichment feed-stock production, uranium enrichment processes, nuclear weapons design and development, safing, arming, fusing and firing and nuclear weapons development testing. While India appears to have superiority in heavy water production, tritium production and plutonium extraction, Pakistan has a clear superiority in uranium enrichment processes. India's advantage in plutonium and tritium production gives it an edge over Pakistan in developing high-yield weapons.

TABLE 5.3
Comparison of Nuclear Technological Capabilities between India and Pakistan

Technology/Weapon system	*India*	*Pakistan*
Enrichment feed-stocks production	XX	XXX
Uranium enrichment processes	Not known	XXX
Nuclear Fission Reactors	XXXX	XX
Plutonium Extraction (Preprocessing)	XXX	X
Lithium Production	Not known	Not known
Nuclear weapons—Design and Development	XXXX	XXXX
Safing, Arming, Fusing and Firing	XXX	XXX
Radiological weapons	XX	X
Manufacturing of Nuclear components	XXX	XXX
Nuclear Weapons Development Testing	XXX	XXX
Nuclear weapons Custody, Transport and Control	XXX	XXX
Heavy water production	XXXX	X
Tritium Production	XXXX	X

Note : X = Limited Capability, XX = Some Capability, XXX = Sufficient Level of Capability, XXXX-Exceeding Sufficient Level of Capability.

Source : *Nuclear Weapons Foreign Technology Assessments Summary*, US Department of Defense, Military Control Technologies List—Part-II: Weapons of Mass Destruction Technologies, 1996; Carnegie Endowment for International Peace, Washington D.C.; Institute for Science and International Security, Washington D.C.; and *SIPRI Year Books, 1996-2006*, Stockholm International Peace Research Institute, OUP, Oxford.

Pakistan has developed a comparable nuclear weapons capability over the years. Although India has developed strong capabilities by the early 1970s when Pakistan had almost no capability, the latter appears to have established very significant level of over all capability by the late 1990s. Although there is no clear evidence about the capability of Pakistan to produce tritium, it is likely that it has established a small facility for tritium purification by using the technology obtained clandestinely from Germany in 1987.

Doctrine

At doctrinal level, India has declared a nuclear "no-first-use" policy on 17 August 1999, and is in the process of developing a nuclear doctrine based on "credible minimum deterrence."[38] The contents of the "draft report" were partially revised and then embraced for the first time as government policy more than three years later in January 2003.[39] The National Security Advisory Board (NSAB), the main architect of draft, represented a cross section of India's military, political, intellectual and scientific community. Indian doctrine is based upon a retaliatory, no-first use policy with the goal of deterring nuclear attacks, although other reasons to use nuclear weapons may not have been ruled out completely. India may not have thought about other contingencies such as Pakistan using nuclear weapons on its own territory in response to an Indian invasion.[40] The main cornerstones of the doctrine include survivability, robust command and control, effective intelligence and early warning capabilities, planning and training, and finally the will to employ these weapons should deterrence fail.[41]

India's views on nuclear weapons are much different than that of Pakistan's, and may be designed for political utility, as well as for deterrence value. Targeting philosophy is not specifically spelled out in the draft nuclear doctrine, but there is a theme of punitive response and massive retaliation that would seem to imply a counter value strategy. Pakistan's major cities and industrial areas could be readily targeted and attacked with either aircraft or ballistic missiles.[42] Alternatively, India could target Pakistan's nuclear facilities in a counter force attack given the short ranges and knowledge of Pakistan's military capabilities.[43] The survivability of India's nuclear forces may be ensured through secrecy and dispersal, including separating weapons from delivery systems. India's nuclear doctrine may be in a state of transition, since it has mentioned of a nuclear triad and command and control functions that may not currently exist.[44]

On the other side, Pakistan has not publicly announced an official nuclear doctrine. However, there have been public statements by senior officials that may indicate in that direction. Major General Khalid Kidwai, Chief of Pakistan's Strategic Plan Division, provided a great deal of information on Pakistan's Doctrine in late 2000.[45] He claimed that four different scenarios could threaten Pakistan's existence as a state and cause the use of nuclear weapons. All four scenarios are in response to India's actions and include the loss of a large part of Pakistan's territory, destruction of a large part of Pakistan's military, economic strangulation, or other attempts to politically destabilize Pakistan. It could use nuclear weapons if faced with a major military defeat or the occupation or threatened occupation of vital areas.[46] These circumstances are in agreement with three general themes that may outline what Pakistan believes are the "red-lines" or point where it must use nuclear weapons. The first theme may be to deter a large-scale conventional war with India, particularly an Indian invasion with a goal of splitting Pakistan in half. The use of nuclear weapons in this scenario can be thought of as ensuring national survival. The second contingency could be to deter nuclear threats or nuclear coercion by India, and may include pre-emption of a nuclear attack by India. Finally Pakistan could resort to the use of its nuclear weapons to deter India from using its stockpile of chemical weapons as declared under the chemical weapons convention, although this does not resonate across other scenarios for the use of nuclear weapons.[47]

Pakistan may have a simple counter-value nuclear targeting doctrine to deter India by holding major population and economic centres at risk. Pakistan has developed longer-range ballistic missiles capable of reaching many of India's major cities. An alternative to targeting India's cities would be to target India's military forces, particular large mechanized formation that may be threatening Pakistan. Either missiles or aircrafts would be capable of attacking major military formations. Pakistan could use one or two nuclear weapons as a warning shot, by detonating the weapons on its own soil as a sign that further escalation would be severely punished.[48]

Pakistan's nuclear forces are an integral part of Pakistan's defensive strategy, and are viewed as the ultimate guarantee of national survival.[49] This doctrine does not include a "no-first-use" clause, leaving Pakistan with a *defacto* first use option to offset India's superiority, somewhat akin to NATO doctrine during the cold war. A "no-first-use" pledge could undermine the credibility of Pakistan's nuclear deterrence against a conventional attack by India.[50] In this way the overall asymmetry of means is reinforced by asymmetry of method, especially in nuclear doctrine.

Finally, the major aspects of nuclear programmes of India and Pakistan can be summarized as follow:

(i) Both the countries have not deployed their weapons operationally.

(ii) India's nuclear weapons programme is plutonium based while Pakistan has adopted uranium-based route. This is particularly because of different histories of their nuclear developments.

(iii) India's nuclear programme can be traced back to the 1940s while Pakistan is a latecomer to start in 1970s.

(iv) The major part of Indian nuclear weapons programme is indigenous but Pakistan took maximum help from China and North Korea. It has acquired the technology through clandestine methods.

(v) National self-expression, long-term geo-political factors, Chinese nuclear threat, desire to play the role in world politics have been the main factors to motivate India's programme. On the other side, Pakistan has a simple reason, e.g. cost-effective reaction to India's overwhelming military capabilities.

(vi) India's civil and military nuclear activities are extensive and much broader than Pakistan's.

(vii) India's nuclear weapons programme is limited and it does not utilize the entire capability available to produce weapons-grade material.

(viii) Pakistan's nuclear programme is "bomb centric" e.g., it makes weapons-grade material using almost the entire nuclear infrastructure and uses them to build nuclear weapons.

(ix) Pakistan is likely to possess sufficient number of nuclear weapons in short to medium term to match India's capabilities.

(x) Pakistan has received and is likely to receive in future significant technology assistance from China.

(xi) Both the countries have been able to achieve a high degree of self-reliance in producing weapon-grade materials and building nuclear weapons.

(xii) Although India appears to have a large stockpile of weapon-grade material and also has greater capability to produce more weapons-grade materials than Pakistan, this advantage or technological superiority is likely to disappear in the medium to long-term.

(xiii) India has a declared "no-first-use" nuclear doctrine while Pakistan lacks it. But unofficially it has declared some "red-lines", and crossing of these would compel Pakistan to think seriously for using nuclear weapons.

COMPARISON OF MISSILE PROGRAMMES

Though both the countries have missile systems capable of launching nuclear weapons, their missile programmes are yet to mature fully. Unlike the case of producing weapon-grade materials and nuclear weapons, the gap in missile programmes and capabilities between the two appears to be more clear and significant. Missile systems involve a large number of critical technologies, and the rate of technological change is relatively high, and therefore, catching up by a latecomer is likely to be more difficult without foreign assistance. Unlike the case of building nuclear weapons, where both India and Pakistan have already entered the production mode, their missile programmes still appear to be largely in the development phase. They are developing different types of missiles-based on solid and liquid propulsion system. Various areas have been selected to make a comparative assessment of missile programmes of both the countries.

Evolution and Motivations

The missile programmes of these countries differ both in terms of their scope and motivations. The Indian missile programme, like its nuclear programme, is a by-product as well as an extension of its civilian space programme which was started in 1967 and was sharply upgraded in 1970. At this stage, the space programme was entering threshold capabilities, and was greatly benefited from generous technological assistance from advanced industrialized countries.[51] It was claimed by the then Director of the Indian Space Commission in 1974 that India already possessed the ability to produce medium range ballistic missiles with locally produced solid fuels and guidance systems.[52] But it was in 1983 when India took it seriously by launching Integrated Guided Missile Development Programme (IGMDP) to develop a family of strategic and tactical guided missiles. The aim of the programme was to design, develop and produce four missile systems and to demonstrate the re-entry technology through the *Agni* project. The motivations behind this decision to launch IGMDP were significant. The Indian government felt that the foreign arms suppliers were often reluctant to sell the kind of missiles demanded by the Indian armed forces. Moreover, the cost of imported missiles was often prohibitive, and the missiles themselves were invariably not of the current generations. Even the former Soviet Union, the foremost arms suppliar to India has refused to sell some of its most advanced and latest missiles. Manufacturers of sophisticated missile systems were not willing to sell India because of its successful nuclear explosion in 1974. So, India has not only to develop indigenous missiles technologies itself but also has to reduce dependence on the imports of the critical parts.[53]

India also wanted the design-production-deployment cycle to be drastically shortened.[54] Apart form *Prithvi* and *Agni* series of ballistic missiles, India is also developing a super sonic cruise missile BrahMos with Russian collaboration, and simultaneously developing a sea-launched ballistic missile *Sagarika* which is expected to become operational by 2010. Though the desire to be a regional and global power, to be self-reliant in defence, and long-term power projections have been the reasons to embark on missile programme, yet security threat has been the main motivating factor behind India's missile programme. Since India is situated in an environment confronted with increasing missile threats and deep rooted animosities. It is surrounded with short and long-range ballistic missiles from China and Pakistan in the North, and Indian Ocean in the West where the foreign naval fleets make their presence with sophisticated missile systems. Israel, Saudi Arabia and Iran also have missiles, which have negative security implications for India. In this situation, India needs a true nuclear deterrent, a proven warhead with a proven delivery system. In fact, the impetus to missile programme is a post-*Pokhran* development. Additional inputs to the programme have come from the Kargil conflict in 1999 and the operation *Prakram* in 2002.[55]

On the other side, Pakistan has followed a route.... politically, technologically and militarily quite different from that of India's programme. Veiled secrecy and loud brandishing of missiles, launch failures and leapfrogging successes, evidence of massive foreign assistance and claims of totally indigenous production capability, denouncement of Indian missile tests and endeavours to more than match each Indian test, have all co-existed to make the Pakistani missile story a chequered one.[56] Like most other countries Pakistan's missile programme is also linked with its nuclear and space programme, however, peripherally. Pakistan established its Space and Upper Atmosphere Research Commission (SUPARCO) during early 1960s, and received early French rocket technology to produce sounding rockets.[57] But SUPRCO could not be successful to overcome the technical difficulties with its two indigeneous types of missiles (*Hatf*-I and II) and the failure forced Pakistan towards off-the-shelf purchase of foreign missile and related technology.[58]

Pakistan was first exposed to the menace of ballistic missiles in 1980s during the Afghanistan crises in which a large number of scuds were fired by erstwhile Soviet Union even across the line of control into Pakistani territory to strike the Afghan Mujahideen training camps sponsored by USA. Simultaneously, the similar missiles were being used by Iraq against Iran during the gulf war. These two incidents, however, raised the concerns of missile usage as attractive and effective delivery systems, and finally in 1988, India's first *Prithvi* test came as the final wake-up call for Pakistan, then in 1989, the

Indian test of long-range *Agni* ballistic missile forced Pakistan's military establishment on the need to develop the means of delivering nuclear strike with a high degree of certainty.[59] The same test also highlighted Pakistan's inferior missile capability.[60]

Unlike India, Pakistan does not seem ambitious to have the status of a regional or global power. Its missile programme is security-driven and totally India-centric. This can be clearly seen in the differences in target range capabilities of the missiles of the two countries. While all Pakistani missiles are only capable of reaching targets inside India but India needs only its *Prithvi* family of missiles to hit targets in Pakistan, all other Indian missiles' range capabilities go far beyond Pakistan. Even the names of the Pakistani missiles are the indications of India-centricity which were given after the Muslim raiders who attacked India like *Ghauri, Ghaznavi, Abdali, Babur,* etc. Hence it is clear that both the countries have different rationales for their missile programmes, however, the mutual security complex of the two remains main factor in their decisions.

Range and Capabilities

Conventional and nuclear capable missiles of both the countries with short and medium-ranges have sufficient reach to the targets in each other's territory.[61]

Pakistan's roadmap for ballistic and cruise missiles is based on a sound strategy to match India's production capacity of shorter range *Prithvis* and *BrahMos* as well as to acquire longer range ballistic missiles for greater reach to hit strategic targets in India.[62] Pakistan has an array of solid fuelled missiles in the 300-750 km range with payload from 500 to 1000 kg. These capabilities match the Indian *Prithvi* series and the *Agni*-I, in fact; they may have an edge over the Indian missiles. Pakistan has also tested liquid fuelled 1500-2500 km range missiles capable of carrying payloads from 500-1000 kg. India's *Agni*-II has a range of more than 2500 km and the *Agni*-III possibly up to 5500 km. Hence, the missiles of both the countries have an effective coverage of all relevant strategic targets in each other's territory.

TABLE 5.4
India's Missiles

Name	*Type*	*Range/Payload*	*Propellant*	*Status*	*Origin*
(1)	(2)	(3)	(4)	(5)	(6)
Prithvi-I	SSM	150 km./1000 kg.	Liquid	Operational	Indigenous
Prithvi-II	SSM	250 km./800-1000 kg.	Liquid	Operational	Indigenous
Prithvi-III/ Dhanush	SSM	350 km./500-1000 kg.	Solid	Development/Tested	Indigenous
Agni-I	SSM	700-850 km./800-1000 kg.	Solid	Development/Tested	Indigenous
Agni-II	SSM	2000-3300 km./800-1000 kg.	Solid	Serial Production	Indigenous
Agni-III	SSM	3000-5500 km./600-1800 kg.	Solid	Development/Tested	Indigenous
Agni-IV/Surya	SSM	5000-6000 km./600-1800 kg.	Solid	Underdevelopment	Indigenous
Akash	SAM	27km/60 kg. booster	Ramjet rocket	Underdevelopment/Tested	Indigenous
Nag	Anti-Tank	4-6 km.	Solid	Underdevelopment/Tested	Indigenous
Astra	AAM	100 km./15 kg.	Solid	Underdevelopment/Tested	Indigenous
Trishul	SAM	9 km./5.5 kg.	Solid	Underdevelopment/Tested	Indigenous
BrahMos	Cruise	300 km./250 kg.	Solid	Development/Tested	India/Russia
Sagarika	SLCM	350 km./500 kg. or 1000 km./500 kg.	Liquid	Underdevelopment	India/Russia

Source : *Federation of American Scientists*, Washington D.C.; *Nuclear Threat Initiative*, Washington D.C.; *Arms Control Association*, Washington D.C; and Government of India, Ministry of Defence, *Annual Report, 2006-07*, New Delhi.

Table 5.5
Pakistan's Missiles

Name	*Type*	*Range/Payload*	*Propellant*	*Status*	*Origin*
(1)	*(2)*	*(3)*	*(4)*	*(5)*	*(6)*
Name	Type	Range/Payload	Propellant	Status	Origin
Hatf-I	SSM	80-100 km./500 kg.	Solid	Operational	Indigenous
Hatf-II	SSM	280-300 km./500 kg.	Solid	Development/Tested	Indigenous/China
Hatf-III/Ghaznavi	SSM	290-300 km./500 kg.	Solid	Development/Tested	Indigenous/China
Hatf-IV/Shaheen-I	SSM	750 km./850 kg.	Solid	Development/Tested	Indigenous/China
Hatf-V/Ghauri-I	SSM	1500 km./800 kg.	Liquid	Development/Tested	Indigenous/North Korea
Ghauri-II	SSM	2300 km./800 kg.	Liquid	Underdelopment/Tested	Indigenous/North Korea
Ghauri-III	SSM	3000 km./?	?	Underdelopment/ Engine Tested	Indigenous/North Korea
Hatf-VI/Shaheen-II	SSM	2500 km./750 kg.	Solid	Underdelopment/Tested	Indigenous/China
Hatf-VII/Babur	Cruise	500 km./?	?	Tested/Serial Production	Indigenous

Source : *Federation of American Scientists*, Washington D.C., *Nuclear Threat Initiative*, Washington D.C.; *Arms Control Association*, Washington D.C; Government of Pakistan, Ministry of Defence, *Defence Year Book, 2003-04;* and *South Asian Survey*, Vol. 11, No. 2, July-December 2004.

FIG. 5.1
Estimated Ranges of Current and Potential Indian Ballistic Missiles

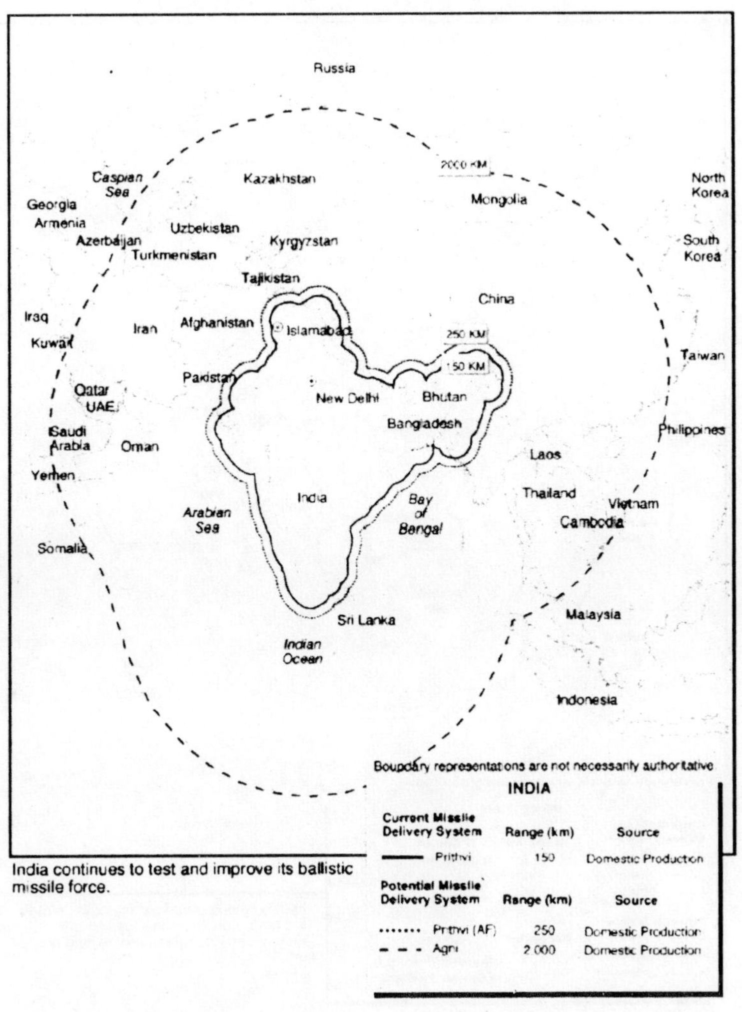

India continues to test and improve its ballistic missile force.

Source : Government of USA, Office of the Secretary of Defense, Department of Defense *Proliferation: Threat and Response,* Washington D.C., January 2001.

FIG. 5.2
Estimated Ranges of Current and Potential Pakistani Ballistic Missiles

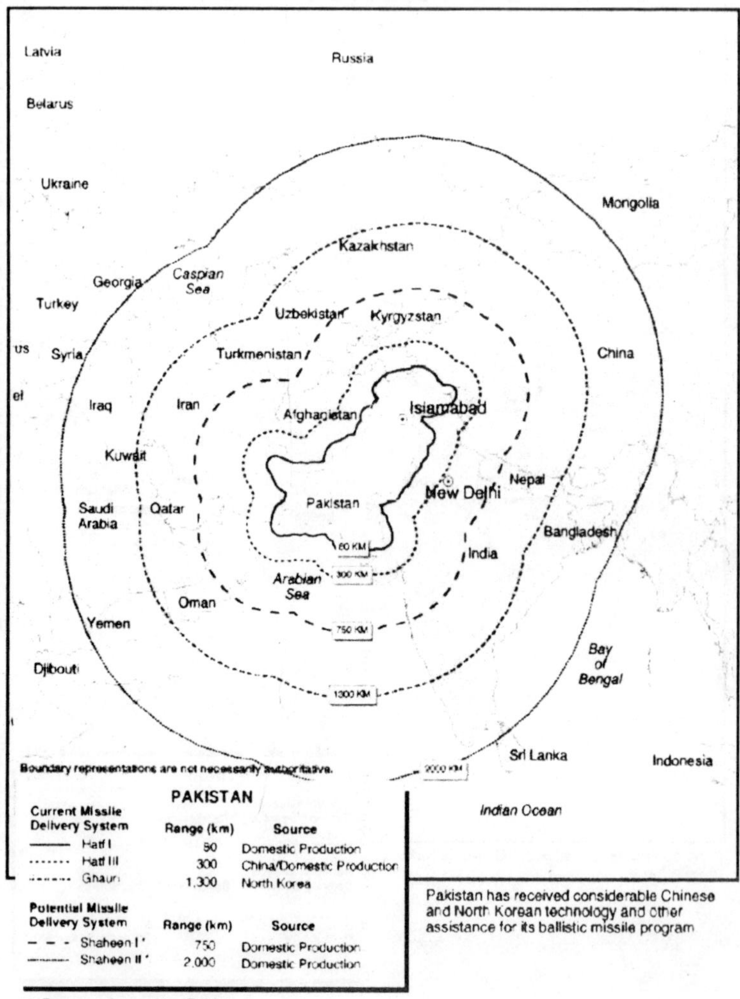

* Ranges claimed by Pakistan

Source : Government of USA, Office of the Secretary of Defense, Department of Defense *Proliferation: Threat and Response,* Washington D.C., January 2001.

State of Technology

In the area of missile related technologies, both the countries have demonstrated significant overall capabilities. Table 5.6 compares the technological capabilities, like airframe, propulsion, guidance and control, and weapons integration of Theater Ballistic Missile Systems (TBMs less than 3500 km range), Inter-Continental Ballistic Missiles (ICBMs), Cruise Missiles and Information Systems of both the countries.

TABLE 5.6
State of Missile-related Technological Capabilities of India and Pakistan

Sl. No.	*Technology/Weapon System*	*India*	*Pakistan*
(1)	*(2)*	*(3)*	*(4)*
	Whole Weapon Systems		
A.	Theatre Ballistic Missiles (TBMs)	XXXX	XXX
B.	ICBMs	XXX	XX
C.	Cruise Missiles	XXX	XX
A.	TBMs Sub-Systems		
1.	Airframe:		
(i)	Air Frame Extension to Liquid Fuelled Missiles	XXXX	XXX
(ii)	Post-Boost Vehicle	XXX	XX
2.	Propulsion:		
(i)	High-Energy Solid Fuelled Motors	XXXX	XXX
(ii)	Storable Liquid Propellant Engines	XXX	XXX
(iii)	Strap-on-Boosters	XXXX	XXX
3.	Guidance and Control:		
(i)	Floated Inertial Measurement Units	XXX	X
(ii)	Digital Navigation and Control	XXX	XX
(iii)	Post-Boost Position Realignment and Spin	XXX	X
4.	Weapons Integration:		
(i)	Bomblets or Submunitions	XXX	XX

(*Contd.*)

TABLE 5.6 (Contd.)

(1)	(2)	(3)	(4)
	(ii) Transporter/Erector Launchers Manufacturing	XXX	XX
	(iii) Separating Warheads	XXXX	XX
B.	ICBMs Sub-Systems		
	1. Airframe:		
	(i) Serial Staging	XXX	XX
	(ii) Parallel Staging	XXX	XX
	(iii) Strap-on-Boosters	XXX	XX
	2. Propulsion:		
	(i) High Energy Solid Propellants	XXXX	X
	(ii) Large Scale Cast Solid Grains	XXX	XX
	(iii) Large Turbo Pumps for Liquid Engines	XXX	XX
	3. Guidance and Control:		
	(i) GPS for Post-Boost Vehicles (PBV)	XXX	XX
	(ii) Small Guidance Computers to Fit on PBV	XXX	XX
	(iii) Terminally Guided Re-entry Vehicles	XX	XX
	4. Weapon Integration:		
	(i) Rentry Thermal Protection Materials	XXX	XX
	(ii) Post-Boost Vehicles	XXX	XX
	(iii) Bomblets	XX	XX
C.	Cruise Missile Sub-Systems		
	1. Airframe:		
	(i) Control Surface Actuators	XXX	XX
	(ii) High Wing Loading Aerodynamic Designs	XXX	XX
	2. Propulsion:		
	(i) High Thrust to Weight Jet Engines	XX	XX
	(ii) Small Turbine Engines	XXX	XX
	(iii) Advanced High Energy Fuels	XX	XX
	3. Guidance and Control:		
	(i) Radar Maps to Support Terrcom	X	X
	(ii) Digital Topographical Maps to Support GPS	XXXX	XXX

(Contd.)

TABLE 5.6 (*Contd.*)

(1)	*(2)*	*(3)*	*(4)*
	(iii) Dynamic Test Equipment	XXX	XX
	4. Weapons Integration		
	(i) Sprayers Adapted to Airstreams	XXX	XXX
	(ii) Small Nuclear Weapons	XXX	XX
D. Information Systems			
	(i) Information Communications	XXX	X
	(ii) Information Exchange	XX	X
	(iii) Information Processing	XXX	XX
	(iv) Information Security	XXX	XX
	(v) Information Systems Management and Control	XXX	XX
	(vi) Information Systems Facilities	XXX	XX

Note : X = Limited capability, XX = Some capability, XXX = Sufficient Level of Capability, XXXX-Exceeding Sufficient Level of Capability.

Source : *Nuclear Weapons Foreign Technology Assessments Summary,* US Department of Defense, Military Control Technologies List—Part-II: Weapons of Mass Destruction Technologies, 1996; Arms Control Association, Washington D.C; and *Bulletin of Atomic Scientists,* Chicago.

In case of short range ballistic missiles both the countries have developed sufficient or more than sufficient capabilities i.e., they have reached production stage. India is developing indigenously its *Prithvi* series of missiles and *Agni*-I while Pakistan is developing *Hatf* and *Shaheen* missiles. Both the countries have sufficient level of capabilities regarding short and medium-range ballistic missile technologies. Table number 5.6 shows that India has a clear superiority in case of ICBMs technology. It has an advantage in solid staging, parallel staging, strap on boosters, high energy solid propellants, large scale cast solid grains, turbo pumps, GPS system, guidance computers, re-entry thermal protection materials and post-boost vehicles while Pakistan is equally capable in case of re-entry vehicles and bomblets. India is also ahead in cruise missile technology. India has developed and tested its cruise missile *BrahMos* with Russian collaboration while Pakistan has developed and tested its *Babur* cruise missile with almost same range. However, India leads in control surface actuators, aerodynamic designs, small turbing engines, digital topographical maps, dynamic test equipment and small nuclear weapons, yet both have almost equal capabilities in high thrust weight jet engines, advanced high energy fuels and sprayers adapted to air stream. But in case of radar maps to support terrcom both have limited capability. As far as information system is concerned, India leads in information communication, processing, security, information systems management and control, and system facilities but in case of information exchange both lacks sufficient level of capability.

In fact, Pakistan is not far behind from India in various areas of missile technologies. If the whole weapon system is taken into consideration, it is found that both the countries have sufficient level of capability (however, exceeding sufficient level in case of India) in short and medium-range ballistic missiles. But in case of ICBMs and cruise missiles Pakistan has some capability while India has sufficient level of capability. However, this difference is likely to disappear in near future because of Chinese and North Korean assistance to Pakistan in these areas.

Organizational Infrastructure

Both the countries have a sizable organizational infrastructure but India dominates in this field. At the time of the launch of IGMDP in 1983, the industrial infrastructure in India was not so good. As a result the DRDO had to struggle to get support of industry even for small components. So a policy decision was taken to support the development of industrial infrastructure and production facilities for this purpose. Consequently, a lot of money was pumped in industries such as Walchandnagar, Godrej, HAL, and L&T which were the early companies to lent solid support to such ventures.

In the first successful flight of *Prithvi* in 1988, at least 35 industries were involved with a large number of other companies from the private sector based in Mumbai, Chennai and Hyderabad. Similar was the case with the next big success of *Agni* in 1989. Companies such as Kerala Hitech, Thiruvananthapuram, MTAR and SEC Industries in Hyderabad are the main examples. BDL also became the focal point for the production of the missiles. Nearly 40 industries made different components on outsourced terms, including critical systems like the missile launcher. Today parallel productions are going on and critical components are being made at multiple locations and industries. India has also introduced a system by which one industry is given up to a maximum 75 per cent of the contract for the fabrication of X component and the DRDO establishment will have the option of giving the rest to a second vendor.

Though, sanctions especially after the first successful launch of *Agni* in 1989, posed hurdles, but it has come as a boon for indigenization, which in a way has slightly delayed the development programmes, since India had to fabricate from the simplest to the most complicated system. In fact, India adopted a twin-fold approach to deal with such problem. First it took the development of all critical systems i.e., through the public sector in the DRDO and then gradually it spread them to the private sector as capabilities started rising. Dependence on foreign countries has come down drastically. On the other hand, the capabilities in avionics, aerospace, systems engineering and building of large systems that have been created proved to be a big plus for the country. Large system engineering projects such as the Light Combat Aircraft (LCA), Main Battle Tank and the Electronic Warfare projects have derived benefits from such expertise.

Till the 1990s the big challenge has been to meet the range and warhead carrying capacity for the missile. Hence, *Prithvi* today has been produced to reach 330 km, and *Agni's* newer versions will take it farther. But from 2002-2010 the focus is on accuracy to hit or hit to kill, this requires special technologies such as infrared and RF seekers embedded into the missiles with high precision homing devices. The Research Center Imarat (RCI) has developed these versions and is ready for tests. For example in *Nag*, the Focal Plain Array device and all weather day and night IR seeker have been developed by RCI and the Solid State Physics Laboratory (SSPL), New Delhi. The second big challenge is to upgrade the missile hit capability. Present versions are sub-munitions, which will be converted to include guidance system and multi-munitions, so that multiple targets can be hit. This requires high levels of miniaturization, for which the defence labs are gearing up.

In this way India's missile programme is supported by a diverse coalition of actors and institutions. This composite group is united by a common string of shared values; but members of the coalition also represent different, though often interrelated and overlapping, individual and institutional interests. Since the stakeholders' interests sometimes conflict, missile-related organizational and technical outcomes are determined by collective bargaining among them.

The above developments reveal that the diversification and growth of the missile coalition has partially transformed the underlying mandate of the missile programme. During the 1960s and 1970s, for example, the missile programmes were characterized by political symbolism and technological determinism. Both characteristics were the outcome of the domination of the DRDO and its political patrons in the coalition. However, technological symbolism and the DRDO's organizational interests are now giving way to strategically determined political objectives and the operational requirements of the armed services.

In the 1960s and 1970s, the DRDO and a handful of politicians and their civilian bureaucratic aides in the federal government, made up the primary stakeholders in the missile programme. Due to the peculiarity of India's civil-military relations, the armed services were largely excluded from defence planning related to strategic weapon systems. Furthermore, the armed forces doubted the DRDO's competence in producing major high-technology weapon systems. Due to the specificities of these institutional relationships, India's missile programmes were not based on actual user requirements. The goal was technology gathering and "reverse-engineering." Since there were no plans for the serial production and manufacture of actual weapon systems, the DRDO did not build sustainable alliances with government-owned public sector entities. Similarly, the secrecy surrounding the programmes effectively excluded private sector companies, quasi-governmental research institutes, and the growing body of civilian strategic analysts, who occupy influential positions in India's civil society, from participation.

Since then, however, the DRDO has succeeded in building a relatively robust alliance with the military. Limited production of the *Prithvi* and *Agni* ballistic missile systems has also given government-owned public sector companies a stake in the missile programme. The DRDO's adoption of a consortium approach by sub-contracting research, development, and manufacture to semi-autonomous institutions and private sector companies has also added to the list of the stakeholders in the missile programme. Furthermore, the programme has gained legitimacy due to support from vocal elements among India's lobby of civilian strategic analysts.

Strategic missile systems such as the *Prithvi* and *Agni* series have emerged as the center of the DRDO's efforts to develop major weapon systems. These weapon systems are not only important politically and strategically, but more so because they represent the DRDO's first success in developing a major weapon system that has gained acceptability from India's armed services. Even though the *Prithvi* and *Agni* represent vintage technologies from the 1950s and 1960s, in the Indian context, they are considered relatively state-of-the-art because of international curbs on the sale of long range missiles, and because India happens to be among the select few countries that has managed to develop them, despite technology denials from the United States and other developed countries. In India's case, the ballistic missile programmes have helped the DRDO partially transform its image from an institution that was synonymous with programme failures to an organization that symbolizes organizational and technological excellence. Equally significantly, the success of both programmes has provided political cover for the DRDO's inability to overcome developmental problems related to the *Akash* and *Trishul* SAMs, which were originally conceived as parts of the IGMDP in the 1980s.

Pakistan has a sizeable defence industrial complex which includes six weapons production and three R&D facilities—the Defence Science and Technology Organisation (DESTO), the Military Vehicle Research and Development Establishment (MVRDE), and the Armament Research and Development Establishment (ARDE). It established the Margalla Electronics and Institute of Optronics in the mid-1980s to manufacture radar and night vision devices. Pakistan could utilize these facilities, and the private industry to absorb the missile technology acquired from both China and North Korea and it could enhance the indigenous capability to execute its missile programme in the future. Already, Pakistan appears to have involved private industrial firms located in Lahore, Karachi, Islamabad, Gujranwala, Sialkot and in other cities for executing the *Shaheen* project. However, evidence suggests that Pakistan has been facing a number of difficulties in building defence technological capabilities in general and missile production in particular. Firstly, the inter-institutional linkages between various agencies such as public R&D laboratories, private industry and public sector industry in the country do not appear to be strong. The national level coordination in developing technological capabilities appears to be weak. Secondly, Pakistan does not produce basic strategic raw materials such as steel alloys and it entirely depends on foreign imports. Thirdly, the private industry in Pakistan appears to have almost no experience in manufacturing high-tech items and therefore it is unlikely to play a major role in missile projects before going through a long learning curve (between 10 to 15 years). And finally, there appears to be "an acute shortage of scientists and design engineers" due to the poor state of technical education in the country. Because of these problems, the success of Pakistan's missile development projects largely depends on foreign technological assistance, particularly the Chinese and the North Korean assistance. The history of Pakistan's missile programme suggests that it is highly unlikely that MTCR will prevent either China or North Korea from assisting Pakistan. Despite Pakistan's repeated statements about developing indigenous intermediate and long-range missiles, it does not appear to have the capability to develop such a missile on its own at present. It is highly unlikely to develop such a missile without active help from foreign countries, particularly either from China or North Korea.

Force Structure

India's "minimum nuclear deterrent" is based on a triad of land, air and sea-based nuclear forces in which ballistic and cruise missiles will be key components of the nuclear strike force. Currently, the *Prithvi*-I and *Prithvi*-II are the only ballistic missiles in service with the Indian Army and Air Force respectively. The *Prithvi* missiles are inherently nuclear-capable, and an undisclosed number of *Prithvi*-I missiles have reportedly been modified to deliver nuclear warheads. However, the *Prithvi* suffers from several limitations such as its short-range and liquid-fueled engine. These problems add to the logistics burden, fuel toxicity and handling the weapon system in the field. Hence the *Prithvi* missiles will most likely be replaced by the *Agni* ballistic missiles for nuclear missions. The existing and proposed inventory of missiles will most likely be reassigned to perform conventional battlefield support functions. The *Dhanush* is currently undergoing flight-trials. The underwater test of *Dhanush* suggests that India is developing submarine launched ballistic missile (SLBM) technology. However, the Indian Navy has not made a decision to deploy the *Dhanush* on board surface warships citing limitations of range and problems related to the missile's hypergolic and toxic liquid fuel. Besides, Indian Navy does not possess submarines capable of carrying and launching ballistic missiles. Despite these limitations, the Indian Navy might acquire a small number of these missiles and deploy them on board surface warships as part of the inter-services organizational battle to acquire a stake in the proposed "minimal deterrent."

The *Agni*-I, II and III ballistic missile are likely to be the mainstay of India's land-based missile force in the future. In comparison to the *Prithvi,* each of these variants of the *Agni* combines the advantages of longer-range, higher-payload, and solid-fueled motors. Although India is developing an intermediate-range ballistic missile and presumably has the technology to build intercontinental ballistic missiles (ICBM), it appears to have stopped well short of actually building an ICBM. In June 2004, the then Scientific Advisor to India's Defence Minister V. K. Aatre told reporters that "we have all the technologies...it (ICBM) needs a larger engine, longer burning time, improvement in the guidance system, among others... it's not a question of whether we can build an ICBM or not, but whether we want an ICBM, which I am not going to talk about."[63] New Delhi's restraint in this regard is probably the result of a conscious political choice to avoid threatening or challenging the legally recognized members of the nuclear club, with the exception of China, which India regards as a potential long-term threat to its security. Furthermore, as India moves in the direction of an operational nuclear force, Indian elites perhaps feel reduced pressure to rely on technological symbols to demonstrate political resolve.

As part of a programme to develop a secure, sea-based, second-strike capability, India is developing a submarine-launched missile: the *Sagarika*. The *Sagarika*, which is expected to arm India's ATV, is suffering from programme delays and is not expected to become operational before 2010. There is also controversy over the *Sagarika's* belonging to the cruise or ballistic class of missiles. In addition, the DRDO is also developing a supersonic anti-ship cruise missile, the *BrahMos*/PJ-10, in close collaboration with the Russia's NPO Mashinostroyeniye. Three versions of the missile are under development: a naval version for surface and sub-surface vessels; a land-attack Army version; and an aircraft-based version. Although the *BrahMos* is primarily an anti-ship cruise missile, many observers believe that the technologies acquired and developed under the programme will most likely to help India develop nuclear-capable long-range cruise missiles in the medium and long-term.

At present India does not maintain a constituted nuclear force on a heightened state of alert. The nuclear-capable missiles, non-nuclear warhead assemblies, and fissile cores are maintained in a de-alerted state by the individual armed services, the DRDO, and the Department of Atomic Energy (DAE), respectively, with plans to reconstitute them rapidly during an emergency or national crisis.[64] After much debate, deliberations and delay, the Indian government has entrusted operational control of India's nuclear missile force to the Indian Army. Although the Indian Air Force deploys an undisclosed number of nuclear-capable bombers and is actively planning to upgrade the air leg of the dyad, it has lost the inter-organizational battle with the Army for custody of India's nuclear missile force.[65]

Although the nuclear-capable missiles and aircrafts are under the control of individual armed services, India's consolidated nuclear force is administered by a tri-service Strategic Forces Command (SFC).[66] Chief of Defence Staff (CDS) ultimately heads a joint tri-service command, who reports to the

Chairman of the Chiefs of Staff Committee. Ultimately, however, the SFC will report to the CDS, who will act as the "single-point" military advisor to the Indian government and act as the interface between the civilian executive and the armed services.[67] At the level of the civilian executive, India's Nuclear Command Authority (NCA) is responsible for the management of its nuclear forces and for making all decisions pertaining to the use of nuclear weapons. The NCA is a two-layered structure. It comprises a Political Council (PC) and an Executive Council (EC). The PC is chaired by the Prime Minister and is the "sole body, which can authorize the use of nuclear weapons." The decisions of the PC are conveyed to the EC, headed by the Prime Minister's National Security Advisor, who then interfaces with the SFC to execute the political directives of the PC.

In case of Pakistan, the primary purpose of its ballistic missile force is to provide reliable delivery systems for nuclear (and perhaps chemical) warheads, in order to deter an Indian conventional or WMD attack, or to defeat India if deterrence fails. In addition, the transfer of ballistic missiles or missile-related technology could also serve in the future as an important source of foreign exchange or political influence, given Pakistan's serious economic problems, and especially if a fundamentalist Islamic government were to come to power in Islamabad. Some experts believe that conventionally-armed SRBM and MRBM systems are primarily designed to augment Pakistan's extremely limited offensive air capabilities against India (which holds a nearly three-to-one advantage in combat aircraft) and to field a more effective delivery system. However, the relatively small payload capacity, individual unit cost, and poor accuracy of Pakistan's existing and emerging SRBM and MRBM forces makes them a relatively inefficient and expensive means of delivering conventional explosives. Other than the possible exception of the *Hatf*-1, Pakistan's ballistic missile force is designed to deliver WMD warheads thereby compensating for the inferior and continually deteriorating state of the Pakistani conventional armed forces and hence will play an increasingly important role in Pakistan's deterrence strategy. As in the case of India, the specific size, configuration, disposition, and possible employment of Pakistan's ballistic missile force are not entirely known at present, since the force is still in the initial stages of development. Moreover, Pakistan is likely to strive to deploy a small, counter-value, minimum deterrence-oriented strategic missile force. Some experts argue that fear of a decapitating first strike by a larger and stronger India will eventually prompt Pakistan to deploy its future ballistic missile arsenal at a high state of readiness. However, a combination of pressure of USA, confidence in India's inability to locate Pakistan's missiles, and a desire to maintain firm central control over all nuclear weapons and delivery systems may prevent such a deployment. As with India, Pakistan's strategic missile arsenal will probably have the capacity to deliver chemical, biological, and nuclear warheads.

Confusion surrounds the operational status of Pakistan's ballistic missiles. At times, Pakistani government agencies and their spokespersons have deliberately resorted to using a plethora of nomenclatures to describe one or another missile programme; at other times, they have made unverifiable and contradictory statements concerning the range, payload, and operational status of different missile systems. Observers speculate that such attempts are probably a ruse to confuse and prevent external intelligence agencies and independent analysts from appraising the precise state of Pakistan's missile-related efforts. Nevertheless, tactics and deliberate ambiguity in an attempt to inflate capability should also be viewed as means to enhance nuclear deterrence, especially at a time when Pakistan's nuclear missile force is still in its developmental phase. However, intelligence agencies of the USA believe that the military's control over the missile programmes as well as the extent of Chinese and North Korean assistance make it likely that Pakistan is probably ahead than India in the path toward nuclear operability.

Though the *Hatf*-I, IA, & II were declared operational in the early 1990s and the Pakistan Army tested the *Hatf* IA in February 2000, yet both programmes are likely to be discontinued. The *Hatf*-I, IA, and II are short-range systems and most major Indian urban and military targets lie beyond their range. Deployments close to the Indian borders during a crisis or war, coupled with improvements in real-time Indian reconnaissance capabilities, would leave them vulnerable to early detection and destruction. Although the *Hatf* missile series could conceivably serve as long-range artillery rockets as most observers suspect that they lack an accurate guidance system. Besides, some also argue that the early *Hatf* missiles lacked a guidance system altogether. Furthermore, most ballistic missiles are not as cost-effective as combat aircraft in conventional battlefield roles. Therefore, although the Pakistan's Army may have acquired a limited number of *Hatf*-I, IA, & II in the early 1990s, yet these early missiles are unlikely to play any role in Pakistan's nuclear deterrent. Similarly, Pakistan's acquisitions of complete M-11 and possibly M-9 ballistic missiles, as well as a production line to build them from China, indirectly attest to the failure of the *Hatf*-II programme. Despite Pakistan's last conduct of a test of the *Hatf*-II in March 2003, the missile is unlikely to serve as part of an operational nuclear force.

However, the *Ghaznavi*/M-11 and *Shaheen*-I/(most likely M-9) ballistic missiles are believed to be in operational service. Pakistani missile crews have been observed conducting simulated launches. Other signs of operational capability include observations of procedures for dispersal during exercises and crises alerts, changes in alert status during crisis, missile tests to communicate political messages to India during crisis, as well as the construction of permanent launch sites along the India-Pakistan border.[68] Furthermore, China's alleged transfer of its fourth nuclear warhead design to Pakistan in the 1980s and latter's nuclear tests in May 1998 have led most observers to conclude that it has achieved or is close to achieving the capability to mount nuclear warheads on its SRBM force. In its report to US Congress on the acquisition of technology related to weapons of mass destruction, the CIA asserted that, "Chinese entities continued to work with Pakistan and Iran on ballistic missile-related projects during the second half of 2003. Chinese entity assistance has helped Pakistan move toward domestic serial production of solid-propellant SRBMs and has supported Pakistan's development of solid-propellant medium-range ballistic missiles (MRBMs). Chinese-entity ballistic missile-related assistance helped Iran move toward in its goal of becoming self-sufficient in the production of ballistic missiles."[69]

However, some Indian observers maintain that despite Chinese assistance, Pakistan's ballistic missile tests have not proceeded several technical and operational glitches need ironing out.[70] But such claims cannot be verified in the absence of independent evidence. Similarly, Pakistani leaders claim that the nuclear-capable *Ghauri*-I/Nodong has entered operational service with its Army, but the missile still appears to be undergoing developmental tests. Equally significant has been the success or state of Pakistan's efforts to mate nuclear warheads to this North Korean ballistic missile remains unknown.

Like India, Pakistan also does not keep its ballistic missile force on operational alert. During peacetime, the missile force and nuclear warheads are stored separately; the warheads themselves are believed to be stored in a disassembled form for security reasons. Plans exist to assemble nuclear warheads during a crisis or emergency, and arm the missiles with warheads at a subsequent stage. Integrated teams of military personnel and nuclear scientists/engineers probably undertake such a task, ensuring organizational checks and balances, as well as ensuring that no rogue commander or scientist could act independently of the national command authority. However, the precise make-up of such teams, as well as the operational procedures for warhead assembly, dispersal, arming of the missile force during a crisis, and delegation of authority for use during a conflict, remains tightly held secrets.

Indigenous/Foreign Assistance

In developing their missiles both the countries have adopted different approaches and routes. Pakistan has been dependent on foreign assistance mainly from North Korea and China while India to a great extent has adopted an indigenous base in this direction. Through its space programme, India succeeded in achieving a relatively high-degree of autonomy in the development, engineering, and manufacture of first-generation ballistic missiles. Though international "technology-denial" regimes delayed and added to the opportunity cost of India's ballistic missile programms but such regimes could not disrupt the process in the long-term.

With the help of West European and North American aerospace companies in the late 1960s and 1970s, the Indian government created an elaborate infrastructure for the development and manufacture of solid and liquid propellants, composites, structural materials, navigation, avionics, flight control, launch support equipments, computers, and software needed for civilian satellite launch vehicles. Simultaneously, government of India also began creating an infrastructure for designing, developing, testing, and building guided missiles. This included aerodynamic, structural, and environmental test facilities, liquid and solid propulsion test facilities, fabrication and engineering facilities, control, guidance, rubber, and computer facilities.

After the launch of the IGMDP in 1983, the DRDO further expanded and refurbished these facilities, and gained competence in the areas of solid propellants, composites, and advanced metallurgy. In 1987, India's Defence Research and Development Laboratory inaugurated a new state-of-the-art facility for designing and building modern missiles at Imarat Kancha near Hyderabad. The new facility was named Research Center Imarat (RCI). It includes an inertial instrumentation lab, full-scale environmental and electronic warfare test facilities, a composites production center, high enthalpy facility, and a missile integration and check out center.[71] In addition, India has built a dedicated test range on its east coast in Orissa (Chandipur-On-Sea) to test long-range missiles, air defence missiles, high 'G' maneuverable missiles, weapon systems delivered by aircraft, and multi-target weapon systems. Range tracking and acquisition radars, and some of the support equipment for this test range were imported from the United States and Russia in the 1980s and 1990s.[72]

Senior Indian defence officials have publicly claimed that India now has the capability to design, develop, and produce any type of missile.[73] They have claimed that the import contents of the *Agni* and *Prithvi* ballistic missiles have been reduced to about ten and five percent respectively.[74] However, the US Central Intelligence Agency believes that India still lacks engineering or production expertise in key missile technologies and continues to import missile-related and dual-use technologies and goods from entities in Russia and Western Europe.[75]

Despite its emergence as a potential "second-tier" supplier state, India is not a member of the Missile Technology Control

Regime (MTCR). It rejects participation in the MTCR on grounds that it is a victim of such technology-denial regimes, as such regimes are insensitive to its national security needs and interfere with the peaceful uses of space technology. In the past, senior Indian defence officials Sivathanu Pillai and Abdul Kalam have expressed the view that Indian missile programmes, both strategic and tactical, are not only aimed at providing the Indian military with weapon systems, but also to generate exports.[76] In 1994, the Indian defence ministry's Department of Defence Production and Supplies included the *Prithvi* in its catalogue of defence items available for export. Although no *Prithvi* exports have occurred to date, Indian defene officials have suggested that India may sell some of the missile's sub-systems in the international market.[77] Indian and Russian officials have publicly expressed their intent to export the *BrahMos/PJ-10* cruise missile to friendly 'third world countries' with mutual consent.[78]

But since the late 1990s, especially after the nuclear tests in May 1998 and the subsequent strategic dialogue with the United States, the Indian government has apparently resolved the internal debate on exports in favour of robust export controls on strategic nuclear, missile and related dual-use goods and technologies.[79] However, the recent indictment of the Indian company NEC Engineers Private Limited, for illegally exporting material and equipment that could be used in the manufacture of solid propellants for missiles to Iraq, has raised doubts about the efficacy with which Indian export control regulations and laws are practiced.[80]

Pakistan, on the other hand, at the time of launching of a programme to acquire ballistic missiles in the early 1980s, lacked the technological resources, industrial infrastructure, and human capital to undertake the development of such missiles indigenously. After a brief and unsuccessful attempt in the 1980s to develop solid-fueled short-range ballistic missiles most likely derived from sounding rocket technology obtained from France, Pakistan turned to China and North Korea for assistance.

In the early 1990s, the NDC, a subsidiary of the PAEC, acquired complete though unassembled M-11s and possibly an undisclosed number of M-9 SRBMs from China. Chinese assistance extended to training Pakistani missile crews in the assembling, maintenance, and simulated launches. During the mid-1990s, China apparently transferred an entire production line for M-11s and possibly M-9s to the NDC. Chinese assistance most likely encompassed equipment and technology transfers in the areas of solid-fuel propellants, manufacture of airframes, re-entry thermal protection materials, post-boost vehicles, guidance and control, missile computers, integration of warheads, and the manufacture of TELs for the missiles. Though China subsequently agreed to abide by MTCR guidelines under U.S. pressure, yet it has interpreted those guidelines narrowly. Beijing has apparently agreed not to supply category-I or complete ground-to-ground missiles, which would not cover air-launched cruise missiles. It also does not abide by the MTCR's key technological annex. Indeed, CIA has alleged that Chinese missile-related assistance to Pakistan increased in the wake of the latter's May 1998 nuclear tests, and that such assistance is critical for the success of Pakistan's medium-range, solid-fueled ballistic missile programme.

However, intelligence agencies of the USA are presently divided over whether Pakistan can produce short-range, solid-fueled ballistic missiles indigenously, or whether it remains dependent on support from Chinese entities. Some analysts believe that the NDC's Fatehjung missile plant, which was built with Chinese assistance in the mid-1990s, is a "soup-to-nuts" facility that can turn out replicas of the M-11s. However, other analysts believe that while the NDC plant can produce most parts and sub-systems of the Chinese SRBMs, Pakistan is still dependent on China for specialty materials, guidance systems, and other critical missile components.[81]

Similarly, Pakistan has relied extensively on North Korea for its liquid-engine ballistic missile programme. Pakistan's testing of its *Ghauri* (*Hatf-V*) 1,500 km medium range ballistic missile (IRBM) has raised regional security concerns. While the world has focused its attention on China as the silent partner behind Pakistan's developing missile capabilities there is another significant sponsor—the North Korea.

The North Korea's relationship with Pakistan dates back to the early 1970s. North Korea's own missile programme was started with the Scud-B missiles acquired from Egypt during the early 1970s.[82] During mid 1971, Pakistan approached North Korea in an effort to obtain critically needed weapons. As a result both the countries signed an agreement, and the first arms shipment from North Korea arrived in Karachi on 18 September 1971. The two countries also signed agreements for the mutual establishment of consulates, and the diplomatic relations were maintained, and North Korea continued its support to Pakistan providing artillery, multiple rocket launchers, ammunition, and a variety of spare parts through the late 1970s.[83] Even after the period of absence of military relations at time of General Zia's takeover in 1977, the foreign policies pursued by both countries during the 1980s witnessed their military advisors working concurrently in such countries as Libya and Iran.[84]

The testing of *Prithvi* and *Agni* during the late 1980s and early 1990s provoked the Pakistan to acquire missile capabilities.[85] It was however, the Iran-Iraq War which firmly established the basis for Pakistani-North Korea ballistic missile cooperation. During that conflict both the countries provided military and political assistance to Iran. The North Korea's assistance to Iran was critical within the field of ballistic missiles. It provided Iran with approximately 160 Scud Mod B (known as the Hwasong 5 in the North Korea) ballistic missiles as well as assisted it in establishing ballistic missile assembly, maintenance and production capabilities. It was during the Iran-Iraq war that the first known ballistic missile contacts between Pakistan and the North Korea occurred as engineers and advisors from both countries worked on Iranian missile programmes.[86] These contacts, aided by political developments during this period, resulted in the establishment of nuclear and ballistic missile-related cooperation between Pakistan and North Korea. Examples of this cooperation include: the North Korean sale of milling and drilling equipments to Pakistan, cooperative covert programmes to acquire nuclear and missile technologies from Germany, Pakistani provision of nuclear technology to the North Korea, etc.[87] It was also during this period that Pakistan first learned of the Iranian support for the North Korea's follow-on systems the 500 km Scud Mod C (known as the Hwasong 6 in the North Korea) and 1,300 km No-dong.

Pakistan's indigenous ballistic missile programme progressed slowly during the 1980s with the development of the *Hatf*-I and *Hatf*-II. Following India's February 1988 test of its *Prithvi* ballistic missile, China agreed to provide Pakistan with increased ballistic missile technology assistance and, more significantly, with both the 600 km M-9 (CSS-6/DF-15) and 280 km M-11 (CSS-7/DF-11) missiles. The first of these systems began arriving during late 1988. During early 1989 Pakistan announced that it had tested two 500 kg payload missiles one is having a range of 80 km and the other 300 km.[88] The consequent international uproar resulted in US suspension of billions of dollars in military and economic aid to Pakistan in October 1990 and a distinct chilling in China-US relations.[89]

Pakistani Prime Minister Benazir Bhutto also threw her full support for the acquisition of Chinese ballistic missiles and expanded Pakistan-North Korea missile and nuclear cooperation. An indication of this expanded cooperation was the visit by Pakistani officials to North Korea Sanum-dong missile development center to examine the No-dong missile system. This visit may have been related to the June 1992 failed or cancelled, No-dong test event.[90] Next month North Korean Deputy Premier Kim Yong-nam travelled to Pakistan and is said to have discussed the sale of Scud Mod C and No Dong missiles. North Korea's construction of a Scud Mod C factory in Syria is financed by Iran and China.[91] The Pakistani and Iranian specialists are believed to have been present for North Korea's 29-30 May 1993 test event in which one No-dong and three Scud Mod B/Cs were launched.[92] Benazir Bhutto traveled to China and North Korea in December 1993 just weeks after being re-elected as Prime Minister. Although she publicly denied it but subsequent events indicate that she was seeking, among other things, increased cooperation in the development of ballistic missiles, particularly, a system capable of striking strategic targets in India. Immediately after leaving Beijing, Bhutto traveled to North Korea on 30 December 1993 to request similar assistance.[93] That was the starting point of the *Ghauri* programme, the final agreement was signed in November 1995 during the visit of a high ranking delegation from North Korea to Pakistan.[94] Reportedly, this was brought to light when a shipment of ammonium per chlorate was seized in March 1996 on its way from Taiwan to SUPARCO in Pakistan. *Ghauri* is believed to be based on No Dong missile. India's interception in June 1999, of a ship carrying a large amount of missile technology from North Korea to Pakistan has raised the issue that North Korean missile technology may help Pakistan to achieve ranges up to 8000 km.[95]

China was aware of the problems it was encountering with its continued efforts in providing M-11 components and systems to Pakistan. It did not want to damage its relations with the US and other Asian countries by directly providing Pakistan with an IRBM. Yet it had a long standing and intimate defence relationship with Pakistan. So China developed a programme in which it would continue to finance the establishment and expansion of a ballistic missile infrastructure within Pakistan and provide the soft technology and engineering for a new Pakistani IRBM which would eventually be called the *Ghauri.* It became convenient for China to use North Korea as a conduit for assistance and provide hardware and components for its No-dong and Taep'o-dong programmes. China is also believed to have agreed to provide components in those areas which the North Korea was still struggling. In this way China was able to avoid the US pressure to stop the proliferation of missile technology. By 1997, China had become restrictive on missile sales to Pakistan, thereby pushing Pakistan further towards North Korea.

During April 1994, a delegation of the North Korean Foreign Ministry headed by Pak Chung-kuk, deputy to the Supreme People's Assembly, travelled to Iran and Pakistan.[96] In the September of same year, another delegation of North Korea, led by Choe Hui-chong, chairman of the State Commission of Science and Technology, travelled to Pakistan.[97] Then, during late November 1995, military delegation led by Choe Kwang (Vice-Chairman of the National Defence Commission, Minister of the People's Armed Forces, and Marshal of the Korean People's Army) travelled to Pakistan. It met Pakistani President Sardar Leghari, Defence Minister Aftab Shaban Mirani, Chairman of the Joint Chiefs of Staff, Chief of Naval Operations, Commander of the Air Force and various other military officials. Choe is also believed to have visited the missile-related production facilities in the Faisalabad, Lahore area and possibly even Jhelum (the area from which the *Ghauri* was subsequently launched).[98] Choe is believed to have finalized the agreement to provide Pakistan with either major components (possibly fuel tanks and rocket engines) from the No-dong or Taepo dong programmes or a modified No-dong missile. The agreed upon items were to be produced by the Fourth Machine Industry Bureau of the 2nd Economic Committee and a majority are believed to have been delivered to the Khan Research Laboratories in Spring of the following year by the Changgwang Sinyong Corporation (a.k.a., North Korea Mining Development Trading Corporation/Bureau).[99] On April 24, 1998 the State Department of USA imposed sanctions against both the Khan Research Laboratories and Changgwang Sinyong Corporation.[100] This was the second time that the State Department imposed sanctions against the Khan Research Laboratories. The first time it occurred during August 1993 in relation to Pakistan's acquisition of Chinese M-11 ballistic missiles. The Changgwang Sinyong Corporation was also responsible for supplying Iran with North Korean missile technologies, components and Hwasong 6 missiles during the mid-1990s. It, along with the Iranian Ministry of Defence Armed Forces Logistics and State Purchasing Office, were subsequently placed under U.S. State Department sanctions during June 1996.[101]

After the test of *Ghauri*, Pakistani scientist, Khan announced that Pakistan was in the process of developing a more capable ballistic missile—the *Ghaznavi*—with a range of 2,000 km.[102] This new system will likely to incorporate both technology and components from the Taepo-dong-I missile which was tested on August 31, 1998. In addition to missile related components and technologies the North Korea has provided Pakistan with the launcher utilized for the *Ghauri* test, and may be assisting in developing its own transporter-erector-launchers (TEL) or mobile erector launchers. The *Ghauri* launcher, like that for the No-dong, is an evolutionary development of the standard Russian MAZ-543TLM used for the R-17 Scud. The model provided to Pakistan is probably the same used for the No-dong.

This cooperation between North Korea and Pakistan was not limited to *Ghauri* programme only but it includes more missiles, nuclear and other defence related technology.[103] Some reports, in May 1989, reveals that the North Korea had offered to provide Pakistan with quantities of the high-explosive Hexagen.[104] During March 1996, the Korean cargo ship Chonsung was detained by Taiwanese authorities for improperly declaring 15 tonnes (200 barrels) of ammonia per chlorate (a key component in solid rocket fuels) which was being shipped to SUPARCO.[105] Pakistan has provided North Korea with access to western technology and systems which it could not easily obtain and has served as a conduit for covert acquisition programmes. It was Pakistan which provided North Korea with its first examples of the US manufactured Stinger SAM which had originally been supplied to the mujahidin during the Afghan war. It is likely that the No Dong and Taepo-dong programmes have also benefitted from access to various Chinese technologies that had previously been unavailable to it and from the data obtained from the *Ghauri* test launch (the *Ghauri* flew longer than any previously tested North Korean missile).[106]

The North Korea's involvement in the Pakistani missile programme, as well as its continued assistance to Egypt, Iran and Syria, illustrate that despite its worsening economic and political situation, it continues to expend time, money and precious resources upon its No-dong and Taep'o-dong missile programmes. In fact, these programmes along with the WMD, artillery and special operations forces are the few areas of expected growth within North Korea.[107] Former Pakistani Prime Minister Benazir Bhutto admitted in February 2004 that Pakistan obtained missile technology from North Korea in lieu of cash.[108] However, President Pervez Musharraf vehemently denies that Pakistan obtained ballistic missiles from North Korea, he only admitted that Pakistan purchased surface-to-air missiles from it.[109] In March 2003, the United States imposed sanctions on KRL and North Korea's Changgwang Sinyong Corporation for engaging in proliferation activities.[110] State Department spokesperson explained that missile proliferation sanctions were imposed on North Korea for its involvement in the transfer of Missile Technology Control Regime Category-1 items to a non-Missile Technology Control Regime country.[111]

North Korea is alleged to have supplied Pakistan with 12-25 operational Nodong ballistic missiles and their TEL vehicles.[112] North Korean assistance has also included technical support, including missile launch and telemetry crews. Analysts speculate that North Korea may have also transferred an entire production line of the Nodong ballistic missiles to KRL. After allegations surfaced in American newspapers that KRL had assisted North Korea with its centrifuge-based uranium enrichment programme in exchange for Nodong missiles, Pakistani President Pervez Musharraf stated that defence cooperation between the two countries had ended.[113] However, analysts believe that it will take Pakistan at least a decade or more to master and produce liquid engines indigenously. Until then, Pakistan will remain dependent on North Korea for importing complete liquid engines, or at least their major component parts, as well as the liquid propellants to fuel its missiles.[114]

Missile Defences

Missile defence in South Asia is relatively a recent development, which acquired attention during the late 1990s when there was news regarding the quest of India to get a shield against the threat of ballistic missiles. India, in its pursuit of ballistic missile defence, has taken two fundamental routes: one to acquire missile defence systems from abroad; and, second, to develop the system indigenously. India's missile defence acquisition efforts have revolved around variants of Russian S-300 Ballistic Missile Defence (BMD) system, the Israeli Arrow BMD and the American Patriot Advanced Capability-3 (PAC-3). India's indigenous efforts have centered on the domestically designed, *Akash*, a long range surface-to-air missile (SAM).

India's pursuit of missile defence dates back to the 1990s. As early as 1995, there were reports that India was negotiating to acquire air defence missile systems from Russia—the S-300 PMU-1, or later versions like S-300. The then Russian Deputy Defence Minister, Kokoshin, offered to sell S-300 missiles during his trip to India in 1995. Subsequently, in August 1995, the then Indian Defence Secretary, Nambiar, went to Russia to observe tests of the missiles near Moscow. Reportedly, in June 1996, the deal was finalised, and 27 S-300 missiles were delivered to

India. The $1 billion purchase was said to include six S-300 systems, with each combat system consisting of 48 missiles. These anti-missile batteries are reportedly already in operation.

According to other reports, Russia has already provided India with the Antey battalion module.[115] The Antey Corporation's S-300V, also known by its NATO designation, SA-12, is an advanced Russian surface-to-air missile system comprising two missile systems—the Gladiator for destroying ballistic missiles, and the Giant for use against aircraft and cruise missiles. In 1998, Antey unveiled a modification of the S-300V, nicknamed the "Antey-2500." The Antey-2500 module operating within an integrated air defence system can simultaneously engage up to eight IRBMs from a distance of 2500 km, or sixteen Tactical Ballistic Missiles (TBM) launched from a distance of 3000 km. In February 2006, it was reported in the Russian press that Russia has offered India to create a comprehensive air defence system using different air defences, including S-300 missile systems of various modifications. If the reports about Indian acquisition of Russian missile defence systems prove to be true, it would bring a qualitative improvement in the deterrence potential of India *vis-à-vis* China and Pakistan.

India has also shown interest in the Israeli Arrow ballistic missile defence system. Indo-Israeli relations improved considerably in the 1990s. Israel assumed the role of becoming the second biggest seller of weapons to India after Russia. India has acquired a number of weapons systems from Israel. The Arrow was jointly developed by Israel and the US. Arrow-2, an advanced version of Arrow, is designed to intercept short and medium-range ballistic missiles, and can detect and track up to 14 missiles simultaneously at distances as far a 500 km away. The Arrow system could potentially be used by India to counter Pakistan's nuclear-capable *Ghauri* and *Shaheen* missiles. Although Tel Aviv seems keen on selling Arrow system to New Delhi, the sale requires the approval of the US, since Arrow was a joint project and was partly funded by Washington. To date the US has not given approval for the sale of Arrow.

However, Israel has already sold India the Green Pine radar system, a component of the Arrow system, which tracks incoming missiles and transmits data to Arrow's management systems and interceptors. The radar can detect targets at ranges up to about 500 km. It can simultaneously track dozens of TBM, and can discriminate between TBMs, aircrafts and other missiles, as well as distinguish between real threats and decoys. Green Pine is transportable and is capable of predicting impact points of incoming tactical ballistic missiles. Out of the two Green Pine radars ordered by India, the first was delivered in 2001, and the system has been reportedly deployed.

The Green Pine radar's deployment along the Indian-Pakistani border potentially provides India with strategic advantage. Reportedly, the system covers all of Pakistan's military command centres and bases between Islamabad, the capital, and the Indian frontier and also provides India with surveillance of Pakistan's nuclear centres and missile sites. The Green Pine combined with the Russian S-300 or Antey ABM systems would provide India with missile defence cover to key parts of its territory against Pakistan and China's IRBMs.

In March 2004, Israel signed a $1.1 billion deal to sell three Phalcon Airborne Early Warning Command and Control Systems (AWACS) to India. The United States had given Israel the green light to sell the Phalcons to India which will be mounted on Russian Ilyushin aircraft.[116] The Phalcon system can pick up aircraft, including at low altitude, hundreds of kilometres away in any weather, day or night. Once deployed, the Phalcon system would provide India surveillance over much of Pakistan's territory. Combined with missile defence systems, Phalcon would enhance India's ability to counter a first strike by Pakistan.

Discussions have also been underway since 2002, for the sale of the US PAC-2/PAC-3 missile defence system to India. In February 2005, a US team, headed by Edward Ross from the Defence Security Cooperation Agency, had briefed New Delhi on technical details of PAC-2.[117] Moreover, India has attended several BMD workshops, conferences, and missile defence exercises over the past few years.[118] The Bush Administration has been giving signals that it is keen on selling the PAC system to New Delhi. In June 2005, the US cleared the sale of the (PAC-3) system to India on the eve of Defence Minister Pranab Mukherjee's visit to the US.[119] Again in September 2005, a high-level US defence team held detailed classified briefings of Indian officials on the PAC-3 system.[120]

PAC-3 is a surface-to-air guided missile defence system that provides advanced capability against cruise missiles, aircrafts, and short and medium-range ballistic missiles. The PAC-3 system has four main components—radar, command centre, launcher, and interceptor missiles. The system is capable of targeting and destroying multiple targets while evading countermeasures and decoys. The PAC-3, unlike previous models, relies on hit-to-kill technology to eliminate short and medium-range missiles. The PAC-3 interceptors are mounted on mobile launchers which can hold up to 16 interceptors each. The launchers are arranged to provide overlapping coverage, allowing PAC-3 to respond rapidly to attacks from all directions.

Other reports suggest that India has also been working on developing a missile defence system of its own. India's DRDO has reportedly been engaged in efforts since 1993 to modify its *Akash* surface-to-air missile into an interceptor capable of engaging ballistic missiles. *Akash's* range is approximately 27 km. According to India's DRDO, its range will be increased to 60 km and eventually to 120 km.[121] One of its important features is the Rajendra phased array radar which is capable of multi-target tracking and engagement.[122] It can reportedly track up to 64 targets at a range of 50 km. The stated goal of the eventual upgrade project is to intercept missiles with ranges up to 2000 km. This goal may be a little too ambitious and unrealistic given the difficulties the US has experienced developing the Theatre High Altitude Area Defence (THAAD) designed to intercept missiles with ranges up to 3500 km. Moreover, so far there have been no reports of *Akash* tests against ballistic missiles. However, it would be of great concern to both China and Pakistan if the US decides to transfer missile defence technologies to India since missile defences erode their nuclear deterrents *vis-à-vis* India.

In early 2005, there were reports that India was working on another missile defence system on the basis of *Prithvi* missile and the Israeli Green Pine radar. According to these reports, the DRDO intended to integrate this system into a missile defence system within a five-to-seven-year timeframe. The head of

DRDO's Integrated Guided Missile Development Programme, V.K. Saraswat, confirmed the ballistic missile defence programme, saying that the system was intended to provide a missile defence cover in a radius of over 200 km. Again, in July 2005, Indian Defence Minister Pranab Makherjee said that there was no question of accepting a missile shield from anyone and that India was developing its own.

Space satellites are integral components of missile defence systems. India also has some satellite potential to complement its missile defence efforts. These can be used for early warning to detect a ballistic missile from its launch, its approximate flight course, etc. The ISRO has been developing defence support programme satellites and their space-based infrared system. The Indian Remote Sensing (IRS) series of satellites are in orbit, which can be used for missile defence purposes.[123]

TABLE 5.7
India's Missile Defence Options

System	*Origin*	*Range (km)*	*Effective Against*
S-300V SA-12A Gladiator	Russia	6-75	Aircraft
S-300V SA-12B Giant	Russia	13-100	TBM, Cruise missile
Antey-2500	Russia	40-200	8 IRBMs with 2500 km range or 16 TBM with 3000 km range
Arrow 2	Israel	500	SRBM and MRBM
PAC-3	US	150	Cruise missiles, aircrafts, SRBM, MRBM
Akash	India	27	—
Prithvi	India	—	—

Source : Gregory Koblentz, "Theatre Missile Defence and South Asia: A Volatile Mix", *Nonproliferation Review,* Spring-Summer 1997; Andrew Feickert and K. Alan Kronstadt, *Missile Proliferation and the Strategic Balance in South Asia,* CRS Report for Congress, RL32115, October 17, 2003; and *Federation of American Scientists,* Washington D.C.

India's likely missile defence choices are, however, not clear so far. Although the DRDO and leading Indian defence technocrats have repeatedly asserted that the country has the capability to build missile defences, these claims need to be treated with care.[124] Many experts are sceptical of Indian claims to be able to build a truly indigenous BMD system, at least in the short to medium term.[125] In the past, many Indian initiatives termed as indigenous have faced critical snags or lagged far behind schedule. These include: the Light Combat Aircraft (LCA); the *Trishul* short-range SAM; and the *Nag* anti-tank guided missile. There are also recent, though unconfirmed, reports of possible abolition of the *Akash* missile programme, which would indicate that the project was not technically successful.[126] Even a technologically advanced state like the US has discovered that developing and integrating missile defence systems present unique challenges. India's capability to develop such complicated technologies is questionable in the short-term since these require a high degree of technological expertise, and decades of research and testing.[127]

Therefore, in the short to medium term, India's option could be to acquire the systems from abroad or go for a mix of imported systems and indigenous ones. Given the size of the country, a national BMD system is unlikely. Since BMD systems cost billions of dollars, from an economic point of view India cannot afford a nation-wide missile defence. This would suggest a limited point defence system to protect targets such as Nuclear Command Authority and other nuclear and missile establishments.

The architecture of such a system is also unclear. One possibility is deployment of a layered system with imported systems such as S-300, Arrow or PAC-3 providing the first layer of defence architecture while modified *Akash* providing a second layer of defence. While a near foolproof BMD system would require several layers of defences, the exorbitant costs of BMD systems would make any complex missile defence deployments unviable. Moreover, it seems unlikely that the US would allow the sale of Arrow system to India. The sale of the US PAC-3 systems might materialise in the next few years and provide India with limited missile defence cover. However, at present, India's most likely option seems to be the deployment of a variant of Russian S-300 system. India also has the option to integrate the Green Pine radar with Russian ABMs or its own systems.

However, there are a lot of other related issues that confront India as far as deployment of missile defences is concerned. There is some opposition within India against going for missile defences. Even if India managed to deploy missile defences, there is a question mark about its effectiveness against a ballistic missile attack.[128] Moreover, the astronomical costs of BMD systems weighed against the dubious gains from such a system is another major concern of the opponents of missile defences.

Some analysts question India's decision to acquire missile defences in the light of the country's perspective on nuclear weapons and deterrence. India's nuclear doctrine emphasizes the political utility of nuclear weapons, i.e. the potential of nuclear weapons to deter a nuclear war rather than winning one. Rajesh Rajagopalan states that, "there could be no clearer indicator that BMDs do not fit well within Indian strategic thought than the fact that no Indian doctrinal statements—neither the Draft Indian Nuclear Doctrine of the NSAB nor the official statement about India's nuclear doctrine that the Prime Minister's Office (PMO) released in early January 2003—even hint at the need for BMDs. In fact, I would go further: a decision to acquire such an ABM system directly contradicts the basis of the Indian nuclear doctrine."[129] Moreover, the Indian government has yet to explain to public the decision to acquire missile defences. Whatever the shape and size of Indian missile defence system are, its purpose seems neutralisation of a first strike by the adversary and having an assured second strike capability.

In response to India's BMD system, Pakistan would be forced to act in order to ensure the integrity of its nuclear deterrent. Although it is difficult to gauge Pakistan's response, it would depend on the type, size and shape of an Indian BMD. There are a number of options that Pakistan could possibly pursue. Pakistan could either go for its own defence systems or build up its offensive forces to overwhelm India's defences.

Pakistan's ability to produce its own missile defence systems is extremely limited both from technological point of view as well as from an economic one. Its prospects for acquiring the systems are also not very bright. The US, while showing eagerness to provide India with PAC-3 systems, has not shown any such inclination towards Pakistan. Russia is unlikely to provide its ABM systems to Pakistan since Indo-Russia relations have been strong for the past several decades, and Russia's relations with Pakistan have been minimal. Since Pakistan does not recognize Israel nor has any diplomatic relations with it, acquisition of BMD systems from Israel is not an option for Pakistan. China is perhaps the only country that could provide Pakistan with such systems since the two countries have a history of defence cooperation, and former is believed to be working on its own ABM capability. However, high cost of such systems may prevent Pakistan from going for this option.

A less costly and more effective option for Pakistan could be a qualitative and quantitative improvement in its nuclear and missile forces and its strategy. The simplest solution for Pakistan would be to go for a larger number of nuclear warheads and delivery systems, especially ballistic missiles. This would entail an increase in the number of missiles both Multiple Independently Targetable Re-entry Vehicles (MIRV-ed) and single warheads. Pakistan would also have to increase its fissile material production in order to have more warheads. The purpose of the numbers approach would be to saturate Indian defences. This would mean, for example, if India has the capability to intercept twenty-five missiles, Pakistan should have thirty.

Pakistan can also go for development of cruise missiles which are harder to defeat by missile defence systems. Pakistan has already taken steps in this direction by developing its *Babar* cruise missile. *Babar* is capable of carrying either conventional or nuclear warhead and has a range of 700 km. It can reportedly hit its target with pinpoint accuracy and can be fired from warships, submarines and aircrafts.[130] Most important of all, it is designed to avoid radar detection and penetrate undetected through a defensive system. If all these claims prove to be true, *Babar* could be an invaluable asset against Indian missile defence systems.

Pakistan can opt for strategies like mobility, dispersion and concealment to enhance survivability of its nuclear force in case of pre-emptive strike. This can be done through mobile launchers, using different systems, and by introducing simultaneous launches under combat conditions from dispersed sites. Pakistan could disperse and store its missiles in hardened silos, could build dummy missile silos, and deploy dummy missiles as well.

Another option for Pakistan could be deployment. This could entail maintaining assembled form of missiles to reduce the reaction time. This could be taken a step further to the level of actually deploying the assembled missiles tipped with nuclear warheads. However, this approach has many inherent dangers and should be a last resort option. India may also go for deployment of nuclear-tipped missiles in response, which would increase the risk of nuclear war. Maintaining missiles on hair-trigger alert would also increase the chances of accidental war. An extremely short missile flight time of 3-11 minutes between India and Pakistan combined with conflict-prone history of South Asia could give rise to an extremely dangerous and unstable situation. This option would, therefore, be counter-productive and should only be adopted as a last resort.

Pakistan can also go for a triad of nuclear forces. At present, Pakistan has land and air-based nuclear forces but no sea-based one. Although this approach would diversify Pakistan's nuclear forces and may ensure survivability of nuclear capability, it would be too costly for Pakistan and not viable in the short-term.

The drawback of the quantitative approach is that it would be costly and would engage Pakistan in an arms race with India. Pakistan can also pursue a qualitative approach to increase deterrence stability. This would include technological improvements in its offensive and defensive capabilities. These options could include improvements in the technical base of the delivery systems and associated technologies. Certain technologies can be developed to fog the enemy ABM systems and also to improve the penetration capacity of Pakistan's delivery systems. Some of these technologies can be improvement in electronic warfare capacity to confuse and defeat Indian radar ability to home-in on incoming targets; manoeuvrings warheads to create problems for the interceptors; and adding decoys to the delivery systems.[131]

In the short-term, a mix of qualitative and quantitative improvements in Pakistan's offensive capabilities might be a more viable solution for Pakistan. In the long-term, Pakistan needs to acquire advance technologies, like perfecting cruise missile technology, reducing the conventional asymmetry between India and Pakistan, to neutralise the effects of Indian missile defence systems.

Moreover, Pakistan can also pursue a diplomatic course by suggesting an ABM treaty between India and Pakistan, or by negotiating a zero missile regime between the two countries. However, these kinds of proposal like zero missile regime and many other nuclear restraint proposals have been rejected either by India or Pakistan in the past. Still the diplomatic option needs to be simultaneously pursued. The success of this option would depend on the willingness of both the states to cooperate.

As far as China is concerned, in the short to medium-term, it might respond to Indian missile defences by changing its deployment strategy, by increasing the readiness of its missiles, and by producing more tactical nuclear weapons. China may respond by tripling or even quadrupling of its deployed missiles against India. China could enhance its targeting capability against India through the proposed multiple independently re-entry vehicle (MIRV) capability that it is developing. However, placing multiple warheads on China's ballistic missiles would probably require Beijing to design and test a new warhead, which is currently prohibited by China's signature on the CTBT. China would also go for countermeasure technologies to defeat an Indian missile defence.

In the long-term, China may even respond by increasing the number of nuclear warheads and by deploying missile defences of its own. In the past, China has shown interest in having missile defences of its own. In 1993, China was reported to have acquired over a hundred Russian S-300 and S-300V systems which included technology transfer as well. There were also reports of Chinese acquisition of Patriot missile technology from Israel in early 1990s.[132] China is also thought to have several defence research and development efforts underway.[133] This means that in future China could develop and field limited missile defences of its own.

Future Plans

The success of *Prithvi* and *Agni* programmes has

encouraged the Indian Government to pursue new missile programmes. These proposed programmes include both defensive and offensive missile systems. The list of defensive systems includes ATBMs designed to provide "point defence" for India's nuclear command and control centers and high-density population targets. Offensive weapon systems include an intermediate-range version of the *Agni* ballistic missile, the *BrahMos* cruise missile, and the *Avatar* programme that would theoretically be capable of launching nuclear strikes from outer space.

The Air Force, which has lost the battle against the Army for overall control of India's missile-based nuclear delivery systems, now, appears to be backing the ATBM project to safeguard its redefined organizational goals as an air and space force. The Air Force is also actively pushing the *BrahMos* cruise missile project. The DRDO hopes that the *BrahMos* cruise missile could ultimately be configured for launch from air, land and sea-based platforms. Thus in the future, the Air Force could be expected to make the case for an air-leg of the proposed "minimal deterrent," using long-range strike aircraft with a standoff cruise missile capability. In this regard, the Air Force is also likely to support the DRDO's futuristic *Avatar* reusable space launch vehicle. The *Avatar* could theoretically be used as a nuclear delivery system with a global strike capability; it could also serve as an asset to strike enemy space-based surveillance and communication targets, or for ferrying civilian and military payloads into space. To make this project successful, there must be a consolidation of interests between the DRDO, the ISRO, and the Indian Air Force with active support from India's political leadership.

The DRDO is also actively consolidating its alliance with the Indian Navy by developing sea-launched versions of the *Prithvi* ballistic missile and by planning to configure the *BrahMos* cruise missile for launch from submarines and ships. The current version of the *BrahMos* has an anti-ship capability, but future systems will incorporate a land attack capability. The current sea-based version of the *Prithvi* (*Dhanush*) is limited by its short-range (350 km) and liquid-fueled engine. The missile's short range and the dangers associated with liquid fuel on board submarines and surface ships make it unlikely that the

Navy will accept the *Dhanush* for active deployment. However, the development of the *Dhanush* will most likely enable the Navy to stake a claim in India's emerging nuclear deterrent. There is also positive evidence to suggest that India is developing an SLBM capability. India's draft nuclear doctrine, which should be read as a statement of ambitions and future intent, does envisage a sea-based nuclear capability for reasons of operational flexibility and survivability. If New Delhi does indeed succeed in acquiring nuclear submarines and cruise missile technology from Russia in the near term, an Indian sea-based nuclear capability could emerge by the end of this decade.

In case of future ICBM it is doubtful that such kind of programme will have support from India's political elite or its military leadership. Unlike the 1970s and 1980s when the political accent was on developing technological artifacts for demonstration and symbolism purposes, current Indian programmes have a greater national security component. Since Indian strategic and military elites only perceive potential nuclear threats from China and Pakistan, it is feasible that India might restrict its ballistic and cruise missile programmes to intermediate and medium-range systems as a conscious political choice to avoid ruffling sensibilities of the other nuclear weapon states. Such a decision could also partly be a function of the growing strategic partnership with the United States and Israel in developing a limited ballistic missile defence.

On the other side, though Pakistan has a small force of nuclear-capable combat aircrafts in its nuclear force inventory, yet its land-based ballistic missiles are likely to become the mainstay of its nuclear strike force in the near future. Apart from Pakistan's poor economic performance and its lack of financial resources to modernize its air force in a significant way, external suppliers such as the United States, Russia, and the European Union remain hesitant to supply Islamabad with sophisticated combat aircraft due to instability concerns in Pakistan. Furthermore, the continuing modernization of the Indian Air Force through the acquisition of high-performance combat aircraft as well as substantive improvements in the latter's long-range reconnaissance and air defence capabilities are likely to degrade the deterrence value of the air leg of any Pakistani nuclear force in the future. These factors are likely to encourage Pakistan's continued reliance on a land-based ballistic missile nuclear force, for which India has no defence at present.

Given its limited technological and economic resource base, Pakistan appears to have resorted to a strategy of importing complete ballistic missile systems of different range categories and types, standardizing and optimizing their production, and then attempting to manufacture them indigenously through backwards vertical integration with assistance from foreign entities. Analysts believe that the NDC can now probably produce solid-fueled *Ghaznavi* (M-11) and *Shaheen*-I (possibly M-9) ballistic missiles in small batches. Over time, Pakistani missile scientists and engineers could improve the performance characteristics of these missiles by making modifications in the solid-propellant motors, achieving weight reduction through the use of lighter materials, and increase their accuracy through the use of either improved inertial navigation or the use of global positioning systems.[134]

However, Pakistan's current fleet of solid-fueled SRBMs suffers from range limitations. In order to strike targets in western India, the missiles need to be deployed close to the India-Pakistan border, a condition that leaves them vulnerable to early detection and destruction. More significantly, the SRBMs lack the range to strike targets in eastern, central, and southern India. These shortcomings are expected to be addressed by the medium-range *Shaheen*-II and *Ghauri*-II programmes, which are under development at the NDC and KRL, respectively. Despite U.S. pressure, China is likely to stick to its commitment to help Pakistan in the development of the *Shaheen*-II medium-range ballistic missile programme. But unlike the past, when China transferred compete missile systems and assembly and production lines to Pakistan, the current pattern of Chinese assistance is apparently restricted to design advice, specialty materials, missile components, guidance systems, and related dual-use machine tools and technologies.

It is also unclear whether KRL has the ability to produce the *Ghauri*-I/Nodong indigenously. Although North Korea is alleged to have transferred 12-20 operational missiles to Pakistan, it is uncertain whether cooperation extended to the transfer of a production line for the missiles as well. After KRL's alleged assistance to North Korea's centrifuge enrichment efforts came to light, Pakistan insisted that it had ended its defence cooperation programme with North Korea. Though continued secret contacts between entities in both countries cannot be ruled out, yet Pyongyang might find itself less inclined to continue with its programme of missile cooperation in the event of any future grand bargain with the United States that is backed by economic and security guarantees from China, Japan, South Korea, and Russia. Since the development of longer-range versions of the *Ghauri* would probably require the development of a new liquid-fuel engine entirely, or multi-staging involving liquid engines and solid motors, termination of North Korean assistance could result in a serious set back for Pakistan's *Ghauri*-II and III ballistic missile development efforts.

Although Pakistan tested the *Shaheen*-II in 2004, the *Ghauri*-II does not appear to be ready for frequent flight-tests. Independent analysts speculate that Pakistan might be able to flight-test both missiles in the near-term and possibly produce a small number of prototypes for test-demonstration purposes. However, Islamabad is unlikely to be able to build and deploy them in large numbers. This is largely because Pakistan does not have a large and vertically integrated research, development, and manufacturing infrastructure to build long-range rockets. Furthermore, there is poor coordination and integration between government-controlled research and development labs, public sector firms, and private sector companies. Although there is some evidence of private sector participation in the production of the *Shaheen*-I SRBM, on the whole, Pakistani private sector firms do not have much experience in manufacturing high-technology products. In addition, Pakistan does not as yet produce basic strategic materials, such as aerospace-grade specialty steels, alloys, and composites, for which it is entirely dependent on imports. This deficiency also extends to missile guidance, control and navigation systems, and components such as gyroscopes, missile computers, and accelerometers. Finally, Pakistan lacks the requisite human capital, a large and dedicated pool of aerospace scientists and engineers from which to draw on for a large-scale ballistic or cruise missile programme. Thus, Pakistan will most likely remain dependent on external suppliers for its MRBM programme in the short- and medium-term.[135]

Though Pakistani leaders have suggested that Islamabad might deploy nuclear-capable missiles at sea in the future, yet its navy does not appear to be pursuing either sea-launched cruise or ballistic missile programmes. Neither has the Pakistani navy made the case for the acquisition or development of nuclear submarines. At this point in time, the status of Pakistani navy as a junior service in comparison to the Army and Air Force, together with resource constraints, both technological and economic, constitutes the principal stumbling blocks to any Pakistani sea-based nuclear capability. Furthermore, it is also unclear whether China, which is in the midst of a gradual course correction in its relations with India, and already under considerable U.S. pressure to terminate missile assistance to Pakistan, would aid Islamabad in any proposed efforts to acquire a sea-based nuclear missile capability.

However, India's efforts to invest in theater ballistic missile defence through the acquisition of either the Israeli Arrow-2 or the PAC-3 systems of the USA could spur significant changes in Pakistan's missile programmes. An Indian theater missile defence would not create a leak-proof defence umbrella, a limited missile defence coupled with improvements in Indian long-range air and satellite-based reconnaissance capabilities could severely undercut the deterrence value of a Pakistani SRBM force. This latter trend, coupled with Chinese concerns over U.S. attempts to provide Taiwan with a theater missile defence capability, could lead to deepening cooperation between Beijing and Islamabad. In the future, China could conceivably help Pakistan develop intermediate-range ballistic missile systems, land and sea-launched cruise and ballistic missiles, and missiles with fast burning boosters using high-energy solid-propellants, multiple warheads, maneuverable re-entry vehicles, decoys, and other means to fool ballistic missile defences.

Nonetheless, it is highly unlikely that Pakistan would seek to develop an ICBM capability in the short- and medium-term. The technological difficulties of developing such a capability apart, Pakistan's security concerns are primarily Indo-centric.

Since medium and intermediate-range missiles would suffice to hold most targets in India hostage to the threat of a nuclear strike, Pakistani leaders currently regard an ICBM capability as a strategic irrelevance.

Finally, the major aspects of missile programmes of India and Pakistan can be summarized as following:

(i) However, both the countries have entered into the production mode in case of short and medium range missiles, but overall missile programmes still appears to be largely in the development phase.

(ii) Both the countries have different motivations behind their missile programmes. India has an aspiration to be a global power and simultaneously has security threat from Pakistan and China while Pakistan's programme is mainly security-driven and India-centric.

(iii) Both the countries have speeded up their missile programmes particularly after the nuclear tests of 1998 to configure the nuclear warheads.

(iv) India's missile programme is deeply linked with its space programme while Pakistan's programme is linked with its space programme peripherally.

(v) Missiles of both the countries have sufficient range to cover all the important targets deep inside each other's territory.

(vi) In the area of missile-related technologies, both the countries have demonstrated significant overall capabilities. But in case of ICBMs and cruise missiles Pakistan has limited capability while India has sufficient level of capability. However, this difference is likely to disappear in near future because of Chinese and North Korean assistance to Pakistan in these areas.

(vii) As far as organizational infrastructure is concerned, India has a wide base and coalition of various indigenous organizations and actors involved in the task of development of various missile components while Pakistan has a limited base and mainly dependent on foreign assistance.

(viii) Nuclear force structure of both the countries consists short-range missiles in operational mode and in near future medium-range missiles are likely to take place in the force.

(ix) Over the years, India has created a wider and deeper base in all areas of missile technology, partly through its civil space programme. Consequently, India has established strong indigenous base. But Pakistan has been dependent on foreign assistance particularly from China and North Korea up to a large extent.

(x) India is pursuing seriously the option of ballistic missile defence with the help of USA, Israel and Russia, and simultaneously developing indigenous system. Pakistan's response in this direction depends upon the type, size and shape of an Indian BMD. It could go either for its own defence systems or build up its offensive forces to overwhelm India's defences. Since Pakistan's ability to produce its own missile defence systems is extremely limited both from technological and economic point of view, so it could go for qualitative and quantitative improvement in its nuclear and missile forces and its strategy.

(xi) The future plans of India is to develop a nuclear triad to have a second-strike capability for which it is working on intermediate and intercontinental *Agni* ballistic missiles, BrahMos cruise missile, *Avatar* and SLBM *Sagarika*. Pakistan is working seriously on *Shaheen*-I, *Ghauri*-II and *Ghazanvi* ballistic and *Babar* cruise missiles.

Notes and References

1. The secrecy of nuclear defence programme in South Aria is not unique, it was and remains a priority of the nuclear programmes of the traditional nuclear weapons states too, especially with respect to the characteristics of nuclear weapons. The relative transparency on strategic nuclear capacity and delivery systems that prevails in the West today, and to some extent in Russia, is of quite recent origin. It was not characteristic of the Cold War period before Gorbachev's ascendancy in the Soviet Union, when serious negotiations began on the INF and START Treaties. Thereafter it still depended on well developed national technical means of intelligence, mutual acceptance of strategic parity and

political imperatives of nuclear crisis stability. Successful negotiation of nuclear arms reduction agreements with provisions for on-site inspections depended fundamentally on declining tension due to evidence of new self-restraint in geostrategic competition, and lowered expectations of confrontation and war. Analogues to these conditions have not yet taken hold in China, and may not be easily achieved in South Asia. This is not to say that increased nuclear transparency in Asia would not be beneficial for stability. It is merely a caution to readers that it does not exist there today, despite prolific writing by regional experts.

2. V.R. Raghavan, "Limited war and nuclear erealation in South Asia", *Non-proliferation Review,* Fall-Winter 2001, p. 84. Some accounts differ such as that by Raj Chengappa, who claims that India upgraded the alter status of four Prithvi missiles and at least one Agni during the Kargil crises. See Raj Chengappa, *"Weapons of Peace: The Secret Story of India's Quest to Be a Nuclear Power"*, Harper Collins, New Delhi, 2000. Similarly, Bruce Riedal, former Deputy National Security Advisor in the Clinton administration, has asserted that President Clinton confronted the Pakistani Prime Minister during a Blair House meeting with the assertion that Pakistani missiles had been armed with nuclear warheads. *Times of India,* 21 June, 2005. Also see, Samina Ahmad and David cotright, *South Asia at a Nuclear Crossroad,* Forth Freedom Forum, Joan B. Kroach Institute for International Peace Studies, March 2001. *New York Times* reveals that a variety of circumstances seemingly forced Pakistan at least to show its hand regarding the operation status of its small nuclear arsenal. In June 2001, Lt. Gen. Beg, former head of Pakistan's military, stated that Pakistan's 30 or so nuclear weapons were normally dissembled at a site many miles away from the delivery systems. John F. Burns, "Pakistan's nuclear secrets," *New York Times,* 27 June, 2001, p. 49. The operations in Afghanistan forced Islamabad to reiterate this stand with most of its nuclear devices left in component parts, not as assembled warheads. Furthermore, in light of tensions within Pakistan itself, separately stored uranium and plutonium cores and their detonation assemblies were moved on 7 October 2001 to six new secret locations around the country. See, Mansoor Ijaz and R James Woolsley, "How Secure is Pakistan's Plutonium," *New York Times,* 28 November 2001, p. A25.
3. Scott D. Sagan and Kenneth M Waltz, *The Spread of Nuclear Weapons: A Debate, W.W. Norton,* New Delhi, 1995. Also see, Jyotirmoy Banerjee, *Nuclear World,* Manas, New Delhi, 2002, pp. 195-96.
4. David Albright, "A Proliferation Primer," *The Bulletin of the Atomic Scientists,* June 1993, p. 17. Albright's later estimate put that figure at about 370 kg by the end of 1997, generated by the Two BARC (Trambay) reactors. This was equivalent of 74 nukes. David Albright, "The shots heard Round the World," *The Bulletin of Atomic Scientists,* July-August 1998, p. 24. Only 6 kg of plutonium or 25 kg uranium are needed to run a civilian reactor. The two BARC reactors are the Canada supplied 40-megawatt cirus and the indigenously built 100-megawatt Dhruva. Of the early 1960s vintage cirus performance deteriorated and was shut down for renovation at the end of the 20 the century. The 1974 nuclear test used circus-generated plutonium.

5. For a detailed account of history of nuclear science in India see, Ashok Kapur, *Pokhoran and Beyond: India's Nuclear Behaviour,* OUP, New Delhi, 2001. Also see, R.S. Anderson, *Building Scientific Institutions in India: Saha and Bhabha,* Centre for Developing Area Studies, McGill University, Occasional Papers, Series No. 11, 1975.
6. Twenty-three years later, the PNE's key scientist Raja Ramanna admitted that the explosion had been made to test a bomb. Jyotirmoy Banerjee, "Pokharan-II Fallout and Implications," *World Affairs,* Vol. 3, No. 3, July September 1999, p. 120.
7. Pakistan is still relying largely on illicit sources and smuggling routes to maintain its nuclear weapons making capability. *The Tribune,* 7 May, 2007.
8. The GUC spinning at supersonic speed, separates weapons-grade U-235 from U-238.
9. Joseph A. Yaeger, ed. *Non-Proliferation and US Foreign Policy,* Brookings, Washington, 1980, p. 102.
10. J.N. Dixit, *India-Pakistan in War and Peace,* Books Today, New Delhi, 2002, p. 337. Chinese assistance to Pakistan's nuclear programme is known to have commenced in 1976. In the years that followed China supplied fissile material, nuclear weapons designs and ring magnets for Pakistan's nuclear programme. Gary Milholtin, director of the Wisconsin Project on Arms control has aptly commented: "If you subtract China's help from the Pakistani nuclear programme, there is no Pakistani nuclear programme." Even today China is actively involved in constructing unsafeguarded plutonium processing facilities for Pakistan in Khushab and Chasma. G. Parthasarathy, "Missile and N-Proliferation Axis", *The Tribune,* 28 August, 2003.
11. Jyotirmoy Banerjee, n. 6, pp. 120-21.
12. David Albright, "The Shots Heard Round the World", *The Bulletin of The Atomic Scientist,* July-August 1998, p. 25.
13. See, P.R. Chari, "India's Nuclear Doctrine: Confused Ambitions", *Non-Proliferation Review,* No. 7, Fall-winter 2000, p. 123; Tehmina Mahmood, "India and Pakistan's Nuclear Explosions: An Analysis", *Pakistan Horizon,* 52, January 1999, pp. 42-43; and Sumit Ganguly, "Explaining Indian Nuclear Policy," Book Review, *Current History,* 98, December 1999, p. 438."
14. Other commentaries on the motivations behind India's nuclear weapons programme include Jaswant Singh, "Against Nuclear Apartheid," *Foreign Affairs,* No. 77, September-October 1998; Sumit Ganguli, "India's Pathway to Pokharan II: The Prospects and sources of New Delhi's Nuclear Weapons Programme," *International Security,* No. 23, Spring 1999, p. 149; C. Raja Mohan, "India's Nuclear Weapons and the Asian Balance", *Indian Defence Review,* No. 13, July-September 1998, p. 19; and Rahul Bedi, "Interview with George Fernandes," *Jane's Defence Weekly,* No. 29, 1 July 1998, p. 32.
15. There are several analysis about Pakistan's nuclear motivations, to include Samina Ahmed, "Pakistan's Nuclear Weapons Programme: Turning Points and Nuclear Choices," *International Security,* No. 23, Spring 1999, pp. 178-79; and Abdul Shakoor Khakwani, "Nuclear Proliferation in South Asia: A Case for the Regional Consensus," *Pakistan Horizon,* No. 47, July 1994, pp. 88-90.

16. Robert Karniol, "Interview with Senator Sartaz Aziz", *Jane's Intelligence Review,* No. 30, 25 November, 1998, p. 32. Also see Farzana Shakoor, "Nuclearization of South Asia and the Kashmir Dispute," *Pakistan Horizon,* No. 51, October 1998, pp. 67, 73-74.
17. See George Perkovich, *India's Nuclear Bomb: The Impact on Global Proliferation,* OUP, New Delhi, 2000, p. 448.
18. Ramehs Chandran, "Clinton Finds Line of Control Most Dangerous Place in World," *Times of India,* 11 March, 2000, p. 1.
19. See, George Perkovich, n. 17.
20. David Albright, "India's and Pakistan's Fissile Material and Nuclear Weapons Inventories End of 1999," *Defence and Technology,* Vol. 1, No. 6, October, 2002, p. 10.
21. In case of India's nuclear arsenal see, "India's Nuclear forces-2002," *NRDC Nuclear Note Book, 2003.* In case of Pakistan see, Pakistan's Nuclear forces 2001, *NRDC Nuclear Note Book 2002,* For the data of nuclear yield from May 1998 tests see, Terry C. Wallace, *The May 1998 India and Pakistan's Nuclear Tests,* Southern Arizona Seismic Observatory (SASO), University of Arizona, July 1998.
22. "India's Nuclear Forces, 2002", *Bulletin of Atomic Scientists,* Vol. 58, March 2002, p. 1. Also see, "Missile Proliferation and the Strategic Balance in South Asia," *CRS Report for Congress,* RL 32115, 17 October, 2003.
23. Joseph Cirincione *et al., Deadly Arsenals,* Carnegie Endearment for International Piece, June 2002, pp. 191-206.
24. "Proliferation: Threat and Response", *Report of US Defense Department,* January 2001.
25. Ashley J. Tellis, *India's Emerging Nuclear Posture,* RAND, Santa Monica, 2001. This study discusses India's pursuit of a "force in being" nuclear posture, which falls somewhere between a ready arsenal and a recessed deterrent—a collection of unassembled nuclear warheads, all kept under strict civilian control and separate from delivery systems.
26. T.S. Gopi Rethinaraj, "Nuclear Diplomacy Returns to South Asian Security Agenda," *Jane's Intelligence Review,* May, 2002, pp. 40-43.
27. Dinshaw Mistry, "Nuclear Asia's Challenges," *Current History,* April 2005, p. 178.
28. Rodney W. Jones, *Minimum Nuclear Deterrence Postures in South Asia: An Overview,* Final Report by Policy Architects International for DTRA/ ASCO, October 2001; http//www.dtra. mil/abut/organiza tion/ souty_asia.
29. Arian L. Pregenzer, "Securing Nuclear Capabilities in India and Pakistan: Reducing the Terrorist and Proliferation Risks," *Non-proliferation Review,* Vol. 10, No. 1, Spring 2003, p. 125. Also see Duncan Lennox, "Comparing India and Pakistan's strategic Nuclear Weapon Capabilities", *Jane's Strategic Weapon Systems,* May 30, 2002; http//www.janes.com/security/ international_security/news/jsnes 020530_1_n.shtml.
30. Raju G.C. Thomas, "India's Nuclear and Missile Programme: Strategy, Intention and Capabilities", in Raju G.C. Thomas and Amit Gupta, eds., *India's Nuclear Security,* Vistaar, New Delhi, 2000, p. 110; G. Balachandran, "International Nuclear Control Regimes and India's Participation in Civilian Nuclear Trade: Key Issues," *Strategic Analysis,* Vol. 24, No. 4,

October-December 2005, p. 570; Davin T. Hagerty, "South Asia's Nuclear Balance," *Current History,* April 1996. Also See, Franoise Heisbourg, "The Prospects for Nuclear Stability Between India and Pakistan", *Survival,* Winter 1998-99; and Amit Gupta, "South Asia Nuclear Choices: What Type of Force Structures may Emerge?", *Armed Forces Journal International,* September 1998.

31. David Albright, *India's and Pakistan's Fissile Material and Nuclear Weapons Inventories, end of 1999,* Institute for Science and International Security, Washington D.C., 11 October 2000.
32. US officials have recommended strongly that India's Cirus and Dhruva plutonium production reactors have a lifetime capacity, factor of about 40 percent while Indian officials have stated that the average capacity factor is significantly greater, as large as 60 percent. In this estimate, the most likely choice is selected as 40 percent with values up to 60 percent having a diminished probability of occurring. On the other end, a lifetime capacity factor less than 30 percent is viewed as highly unlikely. In the case of Pakistan, total enrichment capacity at the Kathua and the newer Gadwal facilities, a wide range of possible values is given equal probability of occurring. Albright, n. 20, p. 11.
33. The range in the values can be understood by considering the set of all values, which in this case vary between 180 kg. and 480 kg. Because values in the tails of the range carry a very low probability of being true, often only the values that fall between the 10th and 90th percentile are considered, which in this case are 250 kg. and 375 kg. respectively. To be more certain that the actual value lies in the range, the 5th and 95th percentiles can be selected, which are 240 kg. and 395 kg., respectively. One way to interpret the results is that in the latter case, there is 90 percent certainty that the true value lies between 240 and 395 kg. of weapons-grade plutonium, where the median value is about 310 kg. *Ibid.*
34. David Albright, n. 31. Also see, Raju G.C. Thomas, n. 30.
35. Albright, *Ibid.*
36. Satellite photos of Pakistan's Khushab nuclear site show what appears to be a partially completed heavy water reactor capable of producing enough plutonium for 40-50 nuclear weapons per year. According to the analysis by Institute for Science and International Security the dimensions of the new reactor suggest a capacity of 1000 megawatts or more. After comparing a sequence of satellite photos, the institute analysts estimated that new reactor was "a few years" from completion. Such reactor could produce over 200 kg of weapons-grade uranium per year, assuming it operates at full power a modest 220 days per year. Joby Warrick, "Bomb Factory, Pakistan building powerful new reactor," *The Tribune,* 25 July 2006.
37. *Nuclear Weapons Foreign Technology Assessment Summary,* US department of Defense, Government of USA, Washington D.C., 1996.
38. *India's Nuclear Doctrine,* Government of India, Text released to the press in New Delhi on 19 August 1999.
39. Also see, http://www.mea.India.nic.in
40. For example see, P.R. Chari, "India's Nuclear Doctrine: Confused Ambitions," *Non-proliferation Review,* Vol. 7, No. 3, Fall-Winter 2000,

pp. 123-35. Official doctrinal statements do not even mention critical issues such as missile defence and the relationship between nuclear and sub-nuclear levels of conflict.

41. For detail see, Waheguru Pal Singh, "India's Nuclear use Doctrine" in Peter R. Lavoy *et al.*, eds., *Planning the Unthinkable: How New Powers will use Nuclear, Biological and Chemical Weapons,* Cornell University Press, Ithaca, 2000; and Lt. Gen. Pran Pahwa, *Command and Control of Indian Nuclear Forces,* United Services Institution of India, New Delhi, 2002.
42. *India's Draft Nuclear Doctrine,* National Security Advisory Board on Nuclear Doctrine, 17 August, 1999.
43. Rodney W. Jones, *Minimum Nuclear Deterrence Postures in South Asia: An Overview,* Final Report by Policy Architects International for DTTRA/ASCO, October 2001, pp. 29-30.
44. Andrew C Winner and Toshi Yoshihara, *Nuclear Stability in South Asia,* The Institute for Foreign Policy Analysis, Spring 2002, p. 33.
45. Polo Cotta-Ramnusino and Maurizio Martellini, *Nuclear Safety, Nuclear Stability and Nuclear Strategy in Pakistan,* Landau Network, Como, January 2002, p. 5; Also see, Tariq Mahmud Ashraf , *Aerospace Power: The Emerging Strategic Dimension,* PAF Book club, Peshawar, 2003, p. 148.
46. Gaurav Kampani, *Placing the Indo-Pakistani Stand off in Perspective,* CNS Web Report, 8 April, 2002, p. 15. http://cns.miis.edu/pubs/reports/pdfs/indopak.pdf.
47. Zafar Iqbal Cheema, "Pakistan's Nuclear Use Doctrine and Command and Control", in Peter R. Lavoy *et al., Planning the Unthinkable: How New Powers Will Use Nuclear, Biological, and Chemical Weapons,* Cornell University Press, Ithaca, 2006, p. 176.
48. Rodney W. Jones, *Pakistan's Nuclear Porture: Quest for Assured Nuclear Deterrence: A Conjecture,* Vol. 19, Institute of Regional Studies, Islamabad, January 2002, p. 20; and Andrew C. Winner and Toshi Yoshihara, *Nuclear Statility in South Asia,* The Institute of Foreign Policy Analysis, Spring 2002, p. 39.
49. Andrew Koch, "India, Pakistan: Nuclear Arms Race off to a Slow Start," *Jane's Intelligence Review,* 1 January 2001, pp. 2-4; and Clay P. Bowen and Daniel Wolven, "Command and Control Challenges in South Asia," *The Non-proliferation Review,* Spring-Summar 1996, p. 26.
50. Zafar Iqbal Cheema, "Pakistan's Nuclear Use Doctrine and Command and Control," in Peter R. Lavoy *et. al., Planning the Unthinkable: How New Powers Will Use Nuclear, Biological, and Chemical Weapons,* Cornell University Press, Ithaca, 2006, p. 177.
51. Naeem Ahmad Salik, "Missile Issues in South Asia," *Non-Proliferation Review,* Vol. 9, No. 2, Summer 2002, p. 48.
52. *Ibid.*
53. The best indicator of this has been the fact though India acquired surface-to-air missiles and the BM-21 multi-barrel rockets from the erstwhile Soviet Union, it never went in for longer range SSM like the Frog, the SS-1 scuds or the SS-21 Tocha which were liberally supplied to all those who asked for them. See Manoj Joshi, "Dousing the Fire? Indian Missile Programme and the United States' Non-Proliferation Policy, *Strategic Analysis,* Vol. XVII, No. 5, August 1994, p. 557.

54. Normally a missile system takes anything between 10-15 years to develop. To reduce this to a period of 8-10 years, it was decided that first missile to be developed would be a short range surface-to-air missile (SAM) and a battlefield support missile, both of which did not require innovations in design and construction. It was also decided that DRDL should also go ahead with the design and development of an IRBM class launch vehicle. As a result, the battlefield support missile *Prithvi* was successfully test fired on 25 February 1998 barely five years after the IGMDP was okayed. This was a testimony to the remarkable success of its programme. A major reason why the IGMDP succeeded while other military R & D programmes failed, is the organizational approach adopted for the missile programmes. The 'mission' of the development of a particular missile was made paramount, everything else (organizations, procedures, personnel, finances, etc.) was made subservient. Obvious as this approach might seem, in practice it was nothing short of revolutionary. Bureaucratic procedures for the first time took a back seat. Review teams for every missile met once in a month not only to review progress but also to take on the spot decisions without referring to any higher body. Financial clearances too were made at such meetings. The review teams composition ensured this. The teams included representatives from the ministries of defence, DRDL, finance and from other outside agencies involved in the IGMDP. For details see, Indranil Banerjie, "Integrated guided Missile Development Programme," *Indian Defence Review,* July 1990. Also see, Mohammed Ayoob, "India and South Asia: The Quest for Regional Predominance," *World Policy Journal,* Vol. 7, No. 1, Winter 1989-90.
55. Ashok K. Mehta, Missiles in South Asia: Search for an Operational Strategy," *South Asian Survey,* Vol. 11, No. 2, July-December 2004, p. 178.
56. A.K. Sachdeva, *Pertinence of Pakistani Ballistic Missiles in Indo-Pak Conflict,* Delhi Papers-14, IDSA, New Delhi, 2000, pp. 3-4.
57. *Ibid,* pp. 6-7.
58. In the beginning, the SUPARCO was assigned to produce indigenous 122 mm multi-barrel rocket launcher system under an arrangement with North Korea. By 1981, it had become an autonomous organization with a sizeable budget, and when in the mid-1980s, Pakistan decided on an indigenous missile programme, it was the natural choice for becoming the core agency for the purpose. It took two indigenous missile programmes—Hatf-I with a range of 80 km and Hatf-II with a range of 300 km—but the test launches of these two in 1989 were not very encouraging. There were some problems with separation of stages, heat shield for reentry and advanced telemetry technology. *Ibid.*
59. Kathleen Barley, *Doomsday Weapons in the Hands of the Many,* University of Illionois Press, Urbana, 1991, p. 120.
60. At that time Pakistan was having only the Hatf-I with 80 km range and Hatf-II with 300 km range surface-to-surface missiles. These missiles, based on sounding rocket technology, were lacking guidance and control functions. See Cameron Binkley, "Pakistan's Ballistic Missile

Development: The Sword of Islam," in William Potter *et al.*, eds., *The International Missile Bazaar: The New Suppliers' Network,* Westview Press, Boulder, Colo, 1994, p. 85.

61. Ben Sheppard, "Ballistic Missiles: Complicating the Nuclear Quagmire," in D.R. Sardesai and Raju G.C. Thomas, eds., *Nuclear India in the Twenty-first Century,* Palgave-Macmillan, New York, 2002, p. 189.
62. Ashok K. Mehta, Missiles in South Asia: Search for an Operational Strategy," *South Asian Survey,* Vol. 11, No. 2, July-December 2004, p. 183.
63. "India Plans to Test 3,000 km Agni III Missile. This Year: Aatre," *Press Trust of India,* 4 June 2004; in Lexis-Nexis Academic Universe, 4 June 2004, http://web.lexis-nexis.com/.
64. Ashely J Tellis, *India's Emerging Nuclear Posture: Between Recessed Deterrent and Ready Arsenal,,* Rand, Santa Monica, 2001, pp. 251-723.
65. "Indian Govt. to Hand over Agni Missiles to Army," *Press Trust of India,* 2 September 2003, Nationwide International News; in Lexis-Nexis Academic Universe, 23 September 2003, http://web.lexis-nexis.com/.
66. "India Establishes Strategic Forces Command," *Press Trust of India,* 4 January 2003, Nationwide International News; in Lexis-Nexis Academic Universe, 5 January 2003, http://web.lexis-nexis.com/; Edna Fernandes, "India Sets-up Nuclear Arsenal Command Structure," *Financial Times,* 6 January 2003.
67. Rajat Pandit, "India All Set to Set-up Nuclear Forces Command," *Times of India,* Mumbai, 31 December 2002, http://timesofindia.indiatimes.com/.
68. Bruce Riedel, *American Diplomacy and the 1999 Kargil Summit at Blair House,* Center for the Advanced Study of India, Policy Paper Series 2002, http://www.sas.upenn.edu/casi/ reports/RiedelPaper051302.htm; and Bill Gertz, "Pakistan Builds Missile Sites Near Border With India; Bush Asks Nations to Ease Tensions," *Washington Times,* p. A1.
69. Unclassified Report to Congress, *Acquisition of Technology Relating to Weapons of Mass Destruction and Advanced Conventional Munitions,* 1 July Through 31 December 2003, Central Intelligence Agency, 1 July-31 December2003,http://www.cia.gov/cia/reports/721_reports/july_dec 2003.htm#15.
70. "Chinks in Pak's Missile Armoury," *Financial Express,* Mumbai, 31 May 2002.
71. Kalam and Tiwari, *Wings of Fire: An Autobiography,* Universities Press India Ltd., Hyderabad, pp. 125, 133-34.
72. "Nuclear Forces Guide," *Federation of American Scientists,* http://www.fas.org/; "Interim Test Range to be Upgraded," *Indian Express,* 17 August 1998, http://www.expressindia.com/.
73. V.K. Saraswat, Director, Research Center Imarat, "India's Missile Program is Spurring Industries," *Business Line,* 6 February 2004.
74. A.P.J. Abdul Kalam, *India Today,* New Delhi, 26 April 1999, <http://www.india-today.com/>; Kalam and Tiwari, n. 71, p. 153; Harbir K. Mannshaiya, "India's Prithvi," *International Defense Review,* August 1995, p. 24.
75. "Foreign Missile Developments and the Ballistic Missile Threat Through 2015," *Central Intelligence Agency,* December 2001, http://www.cia.gov/.

76. "India-Russia to develop air-launched version BrahMos," *The Hindu,* 6 December 2004.
77. Rajat Pandit, "New Delhi Planning to Sell Missiles to Friends," *Times of India,* Mumbai, 2 May 2003; "India to Export Missiles to Friendly Countries: Reports," *Agence France Presse,* 2 May 2003, International News; in Lexis-Nexis Academic Universe, 1 May 2003, http://web.lexis-nexis.com/.
78. Yuri Sidorov, "India Equipping Armed Forces With BrahMos Missile," *ITAR-TASS,* 21 July 2004; in Lexis-Nexis Academic Universe, 22 July 2004, http://web.lexis-nexis.com/; "Navy starts inducting BrahMos," *Business Insight,* 23 July 2004; Rajat Pandit, "Navy begins to induct BrahMos," *Times of India,* 24 July 2004.
79. For details see, Anupam Srivastava and Seema Gahlaut, "Curbing Proliferation from Emerging Suppliers: Export Controls in India and Pakistan," *Arms Control Today,* September 2003, http://www.armscontrol.org/,
80. Shishir Gupta, "The Indian Connection," *India Today,* 14 October 2002, http://www.india-today.com/.
81. R. Jeffrey Smith, 'China Linked To Pakistani Missile Plant; Secret Project Could Renew Sanctions issue," *Washington Post,* 25 August 1996, Section-A, p. A01; Tim Weiner, "U.S. Says It Suspects China is Helping Pakistan With Missiles," *New York Times,* 26 August 1996, p. 6; "Pakistan's Missiles," *Pittsburg Post-Gazette,* Pittsburg, Pennsylvania, 27 August 1997, p. A-4; in Lexis-Nexis Academic Universe, 26 August 1996, *http://www.lexis-nexis.com/*; Steven Erlanger, "U.S. Wary of Punishing China For Missile Help To Pakistan," *New York Times,* 27 August 1997, p. 6; and Douglas Waller, "The Secret Missile Deal," *Time,* 30 June 1997; *http://www.cnn.com/ALL POLITICS/1997/06/23/time/missiles.html.*
82. Although it had some rocket manufacturing experience with Soviet and Chinese designs before that. It acquired the doctrinal background for the development of Scud based missile systems through reverse engineering while progressing on the parallel path of nuclear weaponization. The nuclear ambition was more or less capped through the agreed framework arrived at between the US and North Korea in October 1994 while the missile programme continued even beyond that date. Sometime in 1989, North Korea had decided to graduate beyond the Scud variants it had been developing and producing to a much more ambitious design—the No Dong-1. Sachdeva, n. 56, p. 38.
83. "Pakistan, 'Strengthening Friendly Ties', Recognizes North Korea," *The New York Times,* 10 November 1972; Benjamin Welles, "Pakistan Said to Have Received North Korean Arms," *The New York Times,* 15 October 1971.
84. For example see: "Libya at a Glance," *The Washington Post,* March 25, 1986, p. 14; and "Iran Quietly Trying to Regain Friends Abroad," *The Associated Press,* October 21, 1985.
85. McCarthy, Timothy V., "India: Emerging Missile Power," in eds., William C. Potter and Harlen Jencks, *The International Missile Bazaar: The New Suppliers Network,* Westview Press, Boulder, Colorado, 1993, pp. 201-34;

and Indranil Banerjie, "The Integrated Guided Missile Development Program," *Indian Defense Review*, July 1990, p. 99.

86. For example see: "Missiles-Context-Iran," *United Press International*, August 1, 1985; and Anderson, Jack; and Van Atta, Dale. "North Korea Aids Iran's War of Terror", *The Washington Post*, February 3, 1986, p. B1.
87. Gordon, Marcy, "Iraq-Nuclear-Probe," *The Associated Press*, 21 October 1992; Smith, R. Jeffrey, "Dozens of U.S. Exports Went to Iraqi Arms Projects," *The Washington Post*, 22 July 1992; "DPRK Drive for Science, Technology Analyzed," *Sin Tong-a*, No. 12, December 1990, pp. 212-28, as cited in FBIS-EAS-91-017, 25 January 1991, pp. 32-41; and Milhollin, Gary. "Asia's Nuclear Nightmare: The German Connection," *The Washington Post*, 10 June 1990.
88. "Pakistan in Missile Build Claim," *Jane's Defense Weekly*, 18 February 1989, p. 267.
89. Gedda, George, "US-Chine," *The Associated Press*, 30 January 1992.
90. Interview data; Bermudez Jr., Joseph S., and Gerardi, Greg, "An Analysis of North Korean Ballistic Missile Testing," *Jane's Intelligence Review*, Vol. 7, No. 4, April 1995, pp. 184-91; and Gertz, Bill. "Iran-Bound Mystery Freighter Carried Parts for Missiles," *The Washington Times*, 16 July 1992, p. A3.
91. "North Korea Strengthens Ties With Syria, Iran and Pakistan Foreign Minister Makes Official Tours," *North Korea News*, No. 645, 24 August 1992, pp. 5-6; "Foreign Minister Kim Yong-nam Visits Syria, Iran and Pakistan," *North Korea News*, No. 641, 10 August 1992, p. 5; "Kim Yong-nam Leaves for Syria, Iran, Pakistan," *Pyongyang KCNA*, 27 July 1992, as cited in FBIS-EAS-92-145, 28 July 1992, p. 15; and Weymouth, Lally. "In Israel, a New View of Syria," *The Washington Post*, 6 July 1992.
92. Bermudez Jr., Joseph S., and Gerardi, Greg, "An Analysis of North Korean Ballistic Missile Testing," *Jane's Intelligence Review*, Vol. 7, No. 4, April 1995, pp. 184-91; and Gertz, Bill. "Iran-Bound Mystery Freighter Carried Parts for Missiles," *The Washington Times*, 16 July 1992, p. A3.
93. "Bhutto Holds News Conference, Departs for DPRK," *Radio Pakistan Network*, 29 December 1993, as cited in FBIS-CHI-93-248, 29 December 1993; "Bhutto Holds News Conference, Departs for DPRK," *Xinhua*, 29 December 1993, as cited in FBIS-CHI-93-248, 29 Dec. 1993; "Denies Possible Talks on Missiles," *Radio Pakistan Network*, 26 December 1993, as cited in FBIS-NES-93-246, 27 December 1993
94. A.K. Sachdeva, n. 56, p. 39.
95. "Missile Proliferation and the Strategic Balance in South Asia" *CRS Report for Congress 32115*, 17 October, 2003, p. 32.
96. "Foreign Ministry Group Leaves for Iran, Pakistan," *KCNA*, 31 March 1994, as cited in FBIS-EAS-94-063, 1 April 1994, p. 13.
97. "Science Delegation Leaves for Pakistan 26 September," *KCNA*, 26 September 1994, as cited in FBIS-EAS-94-187, 26 September 1994.
98. "Delegation Visiting Pakistan Attends Banquet," *Pyongyang Korean Central Broadcasting Network*, 24 November 1995, as cited in FBIS-EAS-95-227; "Choe Kwang Delegation Meets Pakistani President," *Pyongyang Korean Central Broadcasting Network*, 22 November 1995, as cited in FBIS-EAS-95-226; "Choe Kwang-Led Delegation Arrives in Pakistan,"

Pyongyang Korean Central Broadcasting Network, 20 November 1995, as cited in FBIS-EAS-95-224; and "Military Delegation Leaves for Pakistan," *Pyongyang Korean Central Television Network,* 19 November 1995, as cited in FBIS-EAS-95-223.

99. "Imposition of Missile Proliferation Sanctions Against Entities in North Korea and Pakistan," *Federal Register,* Government of USA, Volume 63, Number 85, Washington D.C., 4 May 1998.
100. *Ibid.*
101. "Imposition of Missile Proliferation Sanctions Against Entities in Iran and North Korea," *Federal Register,* Department of State, Government of USA, Volume 61, Number 114, Washington D.C., June 12, 1996.
102. Sachdeva, n. 56, p. 39.
103. Koch, Andrew "Pakistan Persists with Nuclear Procurement," *Jane's Intelligence Review,* March 1997, Volume 9, Number 3, p. 131.
104. "DPRK Offers 'Explosive Chemical' to Pakistan", *Delhi Domestic Service,* 29 May 1989, as cited in FBIS-NES-89-102, 30 May 1989, p. 60.
105. DPRK Chemicals Bound for Pakistan Reportedly Seized," *Hitel Database,* 13 March 1996, as cited in FBIS-EAS-96-062-A; and "Taiwan Reportedly Finds `Nuclear Material' on DPRK Ship," *KBS-1,* 10 March 1996, as cited in FBIS-EAS-96-048.
106. "N. Korea Set for More Ballistic Missile Tests," *Jane's Defense Weekly,* 23 October 1996, Vol. 26, No. 17, p. 5; and Bermudez, Jr., Joseph, S., and Gerardi, Greg, "An Analysis of North Korean Ballistic Missile Testing," *Jane's Intelligence Review,* Vol. 7, No. 4, April 1995, pp. 184- 91.
107. *Global Threats and Challenges: The Decades Ahead,* Statement for the Senate Select Committee on Intelligence by Lieutenant General Patrick M. Hughes, USA, Director, Defense Intelligence Agency, 28 January 1998.
108. "Bhutto Says Pak Paid N. Korea for Missile Tech," *The Economic Times,* Mumbai, 11 February 2004.
109. "Musharraf—N. Korea," *The Press Trust of India,* 26 June 2003.
110. "Imposition of Missile Proliferation Sanctions Against a North Korean Entity," *Federal Register,* Government of USA, Vol. 68, No. 63, Washington D.C., 2 April 2003.
111. "State Department Regular Briefing," *Federal News Service,* 31 March 2003; in Lexis-Nexis Academic Universe, 2 April 2003, *http://www.lexis-nexis.com/.*
112. Joseph S. Bermudez, *A History of Ballistic Missile Development in the DPRK,* Occasional Paper No. 2, Center for Non-proliferation Studies, Monterey: 1999, http://www.cns/pubs/opapers /op2/index.htm.
113. "Pakistan denies aiding N. Korea: Pyongyang's Nuke Plans," *Dawn,* Karachi, 7 November 2003, *http://www.dawn.com/.*
114. A. Baskaran, *An Assessment of Nuclear and Missile Developments in South Asia,* Paper Presented at Seventh Annual Conference on Economics and Security, Burwalls Hall, Bristol University, 26-28 June 2003, p. 22; http://carecon.org.uk/Conferences/Conf2003/papers/paper%20Baskaran.pdf
115. Maria Sultan, "Emerging NMD Technologies and the South Asian Context," *Caspian Brief,* No. 26, August 2002, pp. 4-5.

116. "Israel and India Seal Radar Deal," *BBC News,* 5 March, 2004.
117. Qudssia Akhlaque, "Patriot Sale to India will Fuel Arms Race: FO – Concern Conveyed to US," *Dawn,* 24 February 2005.
118. India was invited to a missile defence conference in Dallas in June 2002. India also participated in the Multinational Ballistic Missile Defence Conference in Kyoto, Japan in June 2003, and in Berlin in July 2004. India observed the Roving Sands missile defence exercise in June 2003 as well as in 2005. An India-US bilateral meeting on the subject of missile defence was held on 3-4 March 2005 in Hyderabad, India.
119. *Indian Express,* 14 June 2005.
120. "India Briefed on Patriot Missile," *BBC News,* 9 September 2005.
121. Zafar Nawaz Jaspal, "India's Anti-Ballistic Missile Programme: Impact on Pakistan's Security," *IPRI Journal,* Vol. II, No. 2, Summer 2002, p. 64.
122. A phased array radar uses multiple beams and frequencies, controlled electronically, that allow it to scan the atmosphere to quickly provide a full three-dimensional picture of the atmosphere and incoming missiles.
123. Zafar Nawaz Jaspal, "India's Anti-Ballistic Missile Programme: Impact on Pakistan's Security," *IPRI Journal,* Vol. II, No. 2, Summer 2002, p. 63.
124. Rajesh Rajagopalan, "Missile Defences in South Asia: Much Ado About Nothing," *South Asian Survey,* Vol. 11, No. 2, 2004, p. 213.
125. See Naeem Ahmed Salik, "Missile Issues in South Asia," *The Non-proliferation Review,* Summer 2002, pp. 49-50.
126. Khalid Banuri, "Missile Defences in South Asia: The Next Challenge," *South Asian Survey,* Vol. 11, No. 2, 2004, p. 195.
127. To be reliable, BMD has to accomplish four distinct missions: to detect attacking missiles; to track missiles and, where relevant, re-entry vehicles/warheads; to discriminate between warheads and decoys; to destroy attacking missiles and/or warheads. Each of these mission requirements presents particular technological and military challenges. Rebecca Johnson, *Issues on Missile Defence and Alternatives,* Submission to Standing Committee on National Defence and Veteran Affairs, Simons Centre of Peace and Disarmament Studies, May 2003, p.11; http://ligi.cfhosting.ca/admin/Information/72/030604issues_missile_defense.pdf
128. Patriot anti-missile systems were deployed in 1991Gulf War by the US. Initially the Army claimed a success rate of 96% against Iraqi Scud missiles but after a congressional investigation, the Army revised its claims down to 52% of hitting the missiles, and only 25% success in destroying the missiles. http://www.ceip.org/programs/npp/brief27.htm. PAC-3 was deployed during Operation Iraqi Freedom in March 2003. Its success rate was less than 50%, and it shot down a British fighter, and targeted and almost shot down a US Air Force F-16 fighter. See Alex Stone "Patriot Games", *Daily Express,* 2 April 2003, http://www.tnr.com/doc.mhtml?i=express&s=stone040203. Moreover, the latest PAC-3 test in November 2005 was unsuccessful. The Israeli Arrow system has a better success rate which has been estimated at 75-95%. The S-300V tests against 600 km TBMs have demonstrated a single shot

probability of 40-70%. For details see, Gregory Koblentz, "Theatre Missile Defence and South Asia: A Volatile Mix," *Nonproliferation Review*, Spring-Summer 1997, p. 55.

129. Rajagopalan, n. 124, p. 214.
130. "Pakistan Test-Fires Babar Missile," *The Tribune*, July 27, 2007.
131. Maria Sultan, "Emerging NMD Technologies and the South Asian Context," *Caspian Brief*, No. 26, August 2002, p. 10.
132. Rajagopalan, n. 124, p. 210.
133. Mark Stokes, *China's Strategic Modernisation: Implications for the United States*, Carlisle, PA: Strategic Studies Institute, US Army War College, September 1999, pp. 114-5. Also see "PLA Tests State-of the Art Laser Weapons, Developing TMD," *China Reform Monitor*, No. 261, 30 November 1999.
134. A. Baskaran, *An Assessment of Nuclear and Missile Developments in South Asia*, Paper Presented at Seventh Annual Conference on Economics and Security, Burwalls Hall, Bristol University, Bristol, 26-28 June 2003, 16-26; http://carecon.org.uk/Conferences/Conf2003/papers/paper%20Baskaran.pdf
135. *Ibid.*

6

Security Implications

Missile developments in South Asia have serious security implications on regional as well as global level. At regional level, the inventory and types of missiles increase an escalation of tension between the relations of India and Pakistan on the one hand, and between India and China on the other. At global level, the developments in the South Asia have serious rather negative implications on the non-proliferation regime, and encouraging the other states to pursue nuclear and missile programmes.

Mobility of Missiles during the period of crisis in South Asia faces various potential operational problems which may prompt escalation. The command system requires timely and accurate information. At present, the capacity to collect this information is limited. India and Pakistan rely on remotely piloted vehicles (RPVs), human and electronic intelligence. In the absence of comprehensive and accurate intelligence, there is a significant chance that an adversary will misread passive dispersal and initiate its own deployment as a result. During a crisis, India and Pakistan could enter into a spiral of escalation. One side could interpret the defensive moves by the other as threatening. Steps taken to counter the perceived threat would be matched in turn by the other, resulting in further escalation. During a condition of heightened tensions, the intelligence organizations in both countries will likely have a tendency to report the first indications of activity even if not confirmed.

Though wide and flexible dispersal is within the capability of both countries, but if exercised, it will underscore the problem of control. Dispersal of missiles during a crisis is understandable within the context of preserving survivability. The foremost dilemma facing the command authority will be retaining centralized control. Assertive negative control is desirable for stability but will undermine the effectiveness of the missile system to rapidly respond if required. Pre-delegation, on the other hand, will increase the risk of inadvertence. The command system will thus be under extreme stress if dispersal or deployment ever takes place. The principal decision-making problem is how to make an optimum trade-off between battle effectiveness and safety. The evolving national command systems will have to find an answer to this problem, which was not easily solved in the Cold war.

However, both countries have sufficient territorial space and variety of terrain for dispersal and concealment but the road network is not well developed in both countries. Conditions for mobility are harsh and compounded by generally hostile weather. Physical security of the weapons is not up to the mark. There are multiple modes for missile deployment each having its own unique problems of safety in movement. The variety of missiles available may further compound the safety issues of mating them with the warhead—both conventional and nuclear.

Greater instability results when the potential operational problems of missiles just described are linked with the deployment of nuclear weapons. At least four major considerations will play into decisions by India and Pakistan to undertake nuclear deployment. *Firstly,* there is problem regarding political and technical control. The imperative for political control is critical and deployment will pose a major control challenge. To ensure survivability, there will be a tendency to deploy a large rather than a small proportion of the national nuclear arsenal. The command and control requirements are fundamentally the same for any number of deployed nuclear weapons. Dispersal may involve different configurations ranging from prepared nuclear weapons integrated with their delivery means to separated nuclear weapon components moving independently from delivery systems. Pressure on the command system to pre-delegate authority will rise as a crisis spirals. The political release to fire nuclear weapons could be technically controlled by incorporating permissive action links (PALs) in weapons. A PAL is a coded switch that controls the arming of the weapon. PALs require the entry of a code in order to open circuits that arm the weapon. Even if PALs are used, the decision to delegate authority and release warheads to military units in the field will be excruciatingly difficult for both India and Pakistan.

Secondly, there is problem regarding communication. The essence of command and control is to have several layers of redundant communication to ensure effective assertive control. The absence of assured redundancy and secure communication will remain a prime concern. Overcoming electronic jamming in a conventional war, and electromagnetic pulse (EMP) effects in the event of outbreak of a nuclear war, will be other critical needs.

Thirdly, there is a Need for Physical Security of nuclear weapons. The possibility of nuclear weapons being stolen is remote, as multiple tiers of security will always be present, but concerns about safety and security will certainly grow during deployment. Deployment will increase the importance of physical control by the command system even if use control systems such as PALs are incorporated.

Fourthly, India and Pakistan will face international opprobrium if they opt to deploy nuclear weapons. Although the international community may have reluctantly accepted their possession of nuclear weapons, the transition to operational deployments will likely lead to sanctions and isolation. This factor is unique to South Asia and constrains the implementation of deterrence strategies by Pakistan and India. For example, during the *Kargil* conflict, reports that both countries had activated and deployed their nuclear missile forces triggered intense international pressure on both countries. National actions, such as signaling, that play a role in deterrence strategy may thus be constrained by international pressure. In contrast, offensive conventional force deployments do not seem to engender the same level of concern in the international community.

Beside these operational problems in South Asia, missiles themselves pose serious security problems due to their peculiar characteristics. Ballistic missiles represent the fastest means for delivery of weapons of mass destruction from one country to another. In a matter of few minutes, a missile can cover a distance of hundreds of kilometers. Hence, these delivery systems themselves could become a source of tension and could by their nature and disposition increase the incentive to attack first in a crisis.[1]

TABLE 6.1
Estimated Time Duration of Some Possible Missile Flights in South Asia

Launch Point	*Target*	*Distance (km.)*	*Estimated Total Flight times (minutes)*
Airbase Near Karachi	Thiruvananthapuram	2000	13
Sargodha Airbase	Mumbai	1470	11
Agra Airbase	Karachi	1128	10
Agra Airbase	Lahore	608	8
Sargodha Airbase	New Delhi	581	8
Depressed Trajectory Flight		600	5

Source : Zia Mian, R. Rajaraman and M.V. Ramana, "Early Warning in South Asia : Constraints and Implications", *Science and Global Security,* Vol. 11, 2003, pp. 109-50.

In case of South Asia, short range missiles can attack on national capitals of adversaries even less than five minutes leaving little time for warning and protective measures due to the close geographical proximity. Since geography is fixed, flight times only change as the targets and launch points change. There is some potential for relatively long-range missiles to be used against short-range targets by flying in a depressed trajectory mode and decreases the typical time of flight by 2 or 3 minutes.[2] The countries, India and Pakistan, share a nearly

3000 km land boundary, and cities such as Lahore and Amritsar are only tens of kilometers from the border. Islamabad is less than 100 km from the border and New Delhi is also less than 400 km from the border. Missile flight time is short even reduced less than five minutes to reach the destinations. Warning times are even less due to the time required for sensors to detect the missile during flight. Response times are further reduced because of delays in communicating to decision-makers, assessing information, making decisions, and finally giving orders on how to respond. It is likely that this process might not be completed before a threatening missile has reached its target. It also may result in a launch-on-warning posture in which countries respond prematurely before having time to fully asses the warning information received. Though India has declared a no-first-use policy for nuclear weapons but Pakistan has not adopted such a policy due to perceived conventional military asymmetries. While there is an asymmetry in strategic depth between India and Pakistan, the fact that each country has critical assets near the border means that they both face potentially short response times in the case of missile attacks which may prompt any side to take a quick but wrong decision which may escalate the war.

Autonomy after launch of a missile is another problem which has a negative impact on stability factor in the region. Once launched missiles are fully autonomous and can not be recalled or diverted. The lack of control once a missile is launched means that the reliability of command and control system is crucial. In contrast, there are cases of manned aircraft being recalled or diverted to other targets during flight. During period of tension, an authorized or accidental launch might precipitate a conflict and hence has a negative effect on the stability of the region.

Ambiguity regarding type of warhead mounted on a missile launched also creates the confusion among decision makers because government statements frequently describe a missile system as nuclear capable. This has resulted in the perception that ballistic missiles in the inventories of India and Pakistan have both conventional and nuclear warheads. Even if this is not the reality, the assumption on the receiving end will likely be that any missile launched against it must be carrying a nuclear warhead.[3] Aircrafts have been used in a conventional role in South Asia during wars historically while ballistic missiles have never been used in any role. Thus aircraft, even if capable of carrying a nuclear warhead do not carry the same danger of misperception once detected. Ambiguity regarding the nature of the warhead is exacerbated by the operational requirement for opaqueness regarding the number and location of missiles. Short-range, conventionally armed, ballistic missiles could quite conceivably be used within the context of limited war. A dual nuclear-conventional capable system is therefore quite destabilizing because the opposing command systems will likely have little reliable information about its mission or nature of its warhead. Therefore, ambiguity about the type of a missile warhead strongly decreases the stability.

Due to the lack of sophisticated and up-to-date early warning systems the missile launch data can be misinterpreted and may result in nuclear escalation accidentally. Concerns over misinterpretation of missile launch data are real. During the cold war there were a number of incidents involving accidents and misinterpretations related to nuclear weapons and delivery systems.[4] While there was a sufficient time in the context of longer range ICBM missiles threats of USA and former USSR but such time would not be available with the short flight times associated with the Indian and Pakistani missiles. Moreover, there is evidence that neither India nor Pakistan has focused sufficiently on the danger that a missile test launch during a crisis could be misperceived as the start of a nuclear attack. Though, there is an agreement as part of the Lahore accords in January 1999, to provide missile test launch advance notification, but even such an agreement is not a fool-proof solution. Moreover, both Pakistanis and Indians appear to be planning to use their missile test facilities for actual nuclear weapons launches during war which further increases the confusion regarding the missile test perceived as real attack.

Apart from these technical issues, introduction of ballistic missile defence (BMD) in the region will pose certain other negative implications for the region. An Indian BMD system, whatever its shape and size, whatever its operational shortcomings, will have a major political and psychological impact on both Pakistan and China. Both Pakistan and China would respond to an Indian BMD by bringing quantitative and qualitative changes in their nuclear forces, deployment postures, and perhaps go for missile defences of their own. India would in turn be affected by a buildup of offensive weapons and technologies by Pakistan and China, and would have to enhance its own capabilities in response. This action-reaction spiral is likely to give rise to a regional arms race.

China, India and Pakistan are enmeshed in a complex three-cornered interaction with great potential for instability. China and India fought over their disputed boundaries in 1962, and India and Pakistan have gone to war three times, in 1948, 1965 and 1971 and a limited war in 1999. All three states share "lines of actual control" apart from the international borders. In this scenario, the introduction of missile defences will play a destabilising role, disturbing existing patterns of deterrence. Although all three states pledge to minimum deterrence, leaders in all three capitals have also said that deterrence is not a static concept; the requirements of each state would, therefore, depend on what the others are doing or might seek to do.[5]

The pursuit of missile defences by India would increase the chances of conflict between India and Pakistan. The deployment of missile defences, irrespective of whether they are effective or not, could create a false sense of security among political and military leadership of India and invite military adventurism or even a pre-emptive strike against Pakistan particularly. India and Pakistan have already fought over the issue of Kashmir. In a region where incidents like a terrorist attack on the Indian parliament in 2001 can become the reason for a massive buildup on Pakistani borders, introduction of missile defences would increase India's inclination towards a more aggressive posture with possible disastrous consequences for the security and stability of the region. Missile defence would also put Pakistan at a disadvantage in a conventional conflict, while surveillance and radar components of missile defence systems would put India at an advantage. Thus, missile defences would also accentuate the conventional imbalance between India and Pakistan.

Moreover, possible changes in the deployment posture of China and an actual deployment of Pakistani nuclear arsenal would decrease the nuclear threshold between the three nuclear powers in the region. With less escalation ladders and even less decision-making time, the chances of miscalculation and accidental nuclear war would increase. The chances of a calculated nuclear exchange would also increase.

Missile defences will also have a negative impact on arms control efforts. Transfer of BMD technologies from Washington to New Delhi or from Tel Aviv to New Delhi would violate Missile Technology Control Regime (MTCR).[6] Missile defence would undermine regional and global nuclear arms control initiatives and reverse the process of reducing the number of MIRV warheads in nuclear stockpiles. It would generally weaken China's support for the CTBT, the MTCR, and the Fissile Material Cut-off Treaty (FMCT) negotiations. India and Pakistan would also reconsider their support for FMCT in their pursuit of increased number of nuclear weapons. Improvement of warhead designs by Pakistan might necessitate nuclear testing, disturbing the nuclear test ban between India and Pakistan, and would also lessen the chances of either India or Pakistan supporting the CTBT.[7] China's efforts to develop MIRV warheads would also require testing. The net effect would weaken support for non-proliferation efforts in the region.

The effect of these developments would be to fuel an arms race between the three nuclear powers in the region. Perhaps not an arms race in the real sense of the word, but it would mean having definitely more offensive arms and technologies in the region. Moreover, New Delhi's deployment of missile defences is likely to jeopardise improved relations between India and China. It would have a negative impact on the peace process between India and Pakistan. India's move to counter Pakistan's nuclear deterrent could also make the resolution of the Kashmir dispute more remote and greatly increase the chances of conflict over the issue.

The social and economic development of the region would also be affected. A region that has high rate of poverty and is underdeveloped, increased spending on offensive and defensive weapons would further retard development and increase poverty. In addition, India's social and economic development might be adversely affected if funding for missile defences is added to military expenditures. Pakistan would also have to increase its defence expenditure to compensate for qualitative and quantitative changes in its nuclear arsenal and forces. This would amount to unnecessary burden on economies of both the countries, and diversion of resources from much-needed development. Hence, it can be said finally that missile progammes in South Asia have serious security implications both at regional and global level.

Notes and References

1. Strobe Talbott, U.S. Diplomacy in South Asia: A Progress Report, U.S. Department of State Dispatch, 16 December, 1998.
2. M.V. Ramana, *et. al.*, "Nuclear Early Warning Issues in South Asia: Problems and Issues", *Economic and Political Weekly*, 17 January 2004.
3. Naéem Ahmad Salik, "Missile Issue in South Asia", *The Non-proliferation Review*, Summer 2002, Vol. 9, No. 2, pp. 47-48.
4. For details see, Scott D. Sagan, The Limits of Safety: Organizations, Accidents and Nuclear Weapons, Princeton University Press, Princeton, 1993.
5. Michael Krepon, Missile Defence and Asian Security, Report 45, presented to the Stimson/CAN NMD-China Project on February 20, 2002.
6. Michael Quinlan, South Asia Nuclear Briefs, at http://www.iiss.org/newsite/showpage.php? pageID=78
7. Both India and Pakistan declared unilateral nuclear test moratoria in the aftermath of the May 1998 nuclear tests. This was formally recognized in the February 1999 Lahore declaration, and both parties agreed to continue the moratorium.

7

Conclusion

After the nuclearization of India and Pakistan the security scenario in South Asia became more uncertain, tension-ridden and unstable than before. Both the countries are spending enormous sums on the production, deployment, targeting, defence, supervision, and control of their nuclear weapons and delivery systems, as well as, on building the infrastructure that would generate the fissile material, warheads, aircrafts, missiles, and command and control systems necessary for their nuclear programmes. These weapons of mass destruction tend to defy all rational calculations of security risks and ways of meeting them. The hostilities, distrust, suspicion and misperceptions between both the adversaries along with the very presence of nuclear weapons and missile systems put the region on a high risk of nuclear escalation.

To assume that South Asia's nuclearization is going to promote regional stability is false, as deterrence is not likely to work in the region. Rather vertical and horizontal proliferations have increased the possibility of nuclear war if not by design then by accident/miscalculation. Success of nuclear deterrence depends upon: (i) prevention of conventional war; (ii) second-strike capability; (iii) avoidance of accidental nuclear wars and

(iv) safety of nuclear weapons. These four prerequisites seem to be missing in the context of South Asia. *First,* the prevailing India-Pakistan hostilities and suspicion are sufficient reasons for the beginning of conventional war between them. As long as such possibilities exist, the chances of nuclear exchange can not be ruled out. *Second,* the lack of second-strike capability between them also creates the fear of pre-emptive attack. This fear can be overcome through defence measures like hardening, mobility, dispersal and concealment of nuclear weapons. But in this manner India and Pakistan will increase the susceptibility of their forces due to failure of connectivity. As a result, development of nuclear triad in the form of long range bombers, land-based and submarine based missiles will be required. But India and Pakistan lack this nuclear triad. Third, command and control of the strategic forces, known as command, control, communication, computers and intelligence (C^4I), is an extremely crucial factor in the use of such weapons. It provides a link between the national command authority and the personnel who have physical control of the weapons. In case of Indian and Pakistani lack of requisite nuclear command and control system, nuclear safety and related technical issues enhance the possibility of accidental nuclear war. Besides, inadequate warning systems, short flight times, false alarms and non-institution of Personnel Reliability Programmes (PRPs) by both of them may increase the chances of such warfare. Missile test launch during a crisis could also be misperceived as the start of a nuclear attack. *Finally,* the political and social turmoil in the region increases the threat from both insiders and outsiders to nuclear facilities, material and weapons, and fear that nuclear weapons and facilities could fall into the hands of terrorists. Presence and threats from terrorist outfits like Al Qaeda in this region further escalate such threat scenarios. Delegation of authority to field operations may further complicate the problem of providing security.

Mere possession of nuclear weapons without an appropriate delivery system will not be adequate and will fail to provide a credible capability. Hence, deterrence requires credible delivery systems, and missiles are ideally suited, and one of the most credible means for the delivery of nuclear weapons. Many of the military advantages of missile systems, such as mobility, speed and long range make them weapons of choice. They deliver their payloads faster than combat aircrafts, and provide assurance of penetrating enemy's airspace due to the lack of availability of effective defence mechanisms against them. They can travel at supersonic speeds, reducing warning time, in some cases down to a few minutes. Moreover, they can cover enormous distances, from less than 100 km to over 10,000 km, thus potentially threatening the rear areas of a military theater or even the homeland of an opponent. In many cases missiles can strike a target with a high level of accuracy and with enormous force, often producing devastating damage before an opponent can react. Since they are unmanned, their use does not risk the loss of highly skilled military personnel, such as pilots. Furthermore, a missile will not refuse to carry out orders. In addition, missiles are very difficult to defend against, especially if a potential opponent desires to intercept them before they can strike their intended targets. Unlike airfields or artillery bases, which are large, fixed, vulnerable targets prone to attack by a sophisticated military power, hidden or mobile missiles are hard to find and destroy. Many types of missiles are relatively easy to deploy and operate, especially as compared to a trained air force with manned aircraft and a large infrastructure. Missiles are also less hampered by poor weather and darkness than pilots and aircrafts, and in many respects are less technologically demanding to maintain and support than modern combat aircrafts. That's why both the countries in South Asia are configuring their nuclear weapons according to the missile systems rather than aircrafts. Simultaneously, they are developing more sophisticated and less vulnerable ballistic and cruise missiles capable of launching from land, air and sea.

Missile development in India has been able to achieve a unique degree of success. Beginning with the establishment of DRDO in 1958, its missile programme has attained maturity to the extent that now it can deploy short and medium-range nuclear-tipped ballistic missiles in an operational mode capable of using against Pakistan and China. The launch of IGMDP in 1983 has been a landmark in the development of ballistic missiles which was aimed to design, develop and produce five missile systems: *Prithvi, Akash, Trishul, Nag* and *Agni.* It has successfully demonstrated the re-entry technology through the

Agni project. But it was only after the nuclear tests of May 1998 India speed up its missile programme from land-based ballistic missiles to that of sea launched missiles as its minimum nuclear deterrent doctrine envisions a triadic nuclear defence.

Currently India has not only developed short and medium range *Prithvi* and *Agni* series of ballistic missiles, but also working towards the development of longer range versions of *Agni*, supersonic cruise missile *BrahMos* (with Russian collaboration), a naval variant of the *Prithvi* (*Dhanus*h) and ICBM *Surya*. The DRDO is also believed to be developing a sea-launched ballistic missile, the *Sagarika,* which is expected to become operational by 2010. In addition, India is also engaged in collaboration with America, Russia and Israel to develop an anti-tactical ballistic missile (ATBM) system. DRDO is also busy to improve the performance of the ballistic missiles developed during the late 1980s and early 1990s. Key initiatives in this direction include the incorporation of new features to improve the "hit to kill" capabilities of the missiles and the use of newer and lighter materials in the manufacturing of the missile systems. Among other priorities it is developing Army and Air Force variants of the *BrahMos* supersonic cruise missile, air-to-air missiles, smart missiles (that are smaller, lighter, agile, and can home in on targets with great accuracy), hypersonic vehicles, nanotechnologies, homing guidance, large systems integration, miniaturized electro-mechanical systems, system on chip and newer materials (such as ceramics and lightweight composites).

Pakistan has also been engaged in the development of its missiles since early 1960s. Its process started with the establishment of Space and Upper Atmosphere Research Commission (SUPARCO) at Karachi as part of its Atomic Energy Commission. It started with the technological support received from France to produce sounding rockets. SUPARCO started its indigenous missile development programme but it has not been very successful, as two indigenous systems *Hatf*-I and II developed by it failed miserably. To overcome the failures of SUPARCO and simultaneous success of India's *Prithvi* missile programme might have pushed Pakistan towards off-the-shelf purchase of foreign missiles and related technologies. However, in the early 1980s, to deliver its nuclear strike capability it again started its missile programme seriously. However, undoubtedly Pakistan's missile efforts were largely remained India-centric as is evident from its target range, capabilities and nomenclature of missiles. Besides, Pakistan's programme was not linked with its space or civilian rockets development programmes, as is evident from its very limited scientific and industrial base. That might have been the reason that most of its programme was developed with components and technical assistance obtained from France, Germany, and United States. However, in this process, much important role has been played by China and North Korea. As a result, Pakistan has been able to possess *Hatf*-I, *Hatf*-II, and *Ghauri*-I in operational mode and working on the improvised versions of *Ghauri, Ghaznavi, Shaheen,* and *Babar* cruise missile.

While comparing the nuclear programmes of both the countries it has been found that India has started its programmes as early as in the1940s, while Pakistan has been a late entrant as it starts its programmes as late as in 1970s. Consequently, the latter had to be dependent on foreign assistance particularly from China and North Korea to catch up the former. However, both the countries are now declared nuclear weapon states but they have not yet deployed their weapons operationally. Though India's civil and military nuclear activities are extensive and much broader than that of Pakistan but it never utilized its entire weapons-grade material production capabilities. While Pakistan always thought for acquisition of such technologies in terms of its utilization for warfare. As a result, India's weapon programme is limited, whereas Pakistan's nuclear programme is bomb-centric, and it uses almost its entire nuclear infrastructure to build nuclear weapons. Consequently, Pakistan is likely to possess sufficient number of nuclear weapons in short to medium term to match India's capabilities. In case of doctrine and strategy, India has declared 'no-first-use' principle while Pakistan lacks it but unofficially declared some red-lines, crossing of which would compel it to think seriously to use the nuclear weapons.

Comparative assessment of their missile programmes reveals that though both the countries have started their missile programmes much earlier but their programmes got momentum only after the nuclear tests in May 1998. And now both the countries possess sufficient quantity and quality of missiles to cover all the important targets deep inside each other's territory. Nuclear forces of both the countries at present consist short-range missiles in operational mode and likely to be replaced by medium-range missiles in near future. Technologically, both the countries have demonstrated significant overall capabilities. But in case of ICBMs and cruise missiles India has attained the mastery, whereas in case of Pakistan it seems to reach the stage of limited capability. Consequently, the latter is busy in acquiring such technologies from China and North Korea. Infrastructure wise India has wider base than that of Pakistan, because its programme is linked with numerous indigenous organizations and departments engaged in related technologies. Pakistan's base seems to be limited in this direction due to its dependent on foreign assistance rather than indigenous know-how.

Despite India's collaboration with the USA, Israel and Russia for the pursuit of ballistic missile defence option, due attention has been paid by it towards the development of its indigenous base. Pakistan's ability to produce its own missile defence is weak both because of its technological and economic constraints, as well as, its reactive policy in response to India's developments. Given the infrastructure and policy postures India seems to have been busy in developing a nuclear triad required for second-strike capability. It is evident from its efforts towards the development of intermediate and intercontinental *Agni* ballistic missiles, naval versions of *Prithvi* and *BrahMos* cruise missile, and SLBM *Sagarika*. Consequently, Pakistan also seems to be working seriously on *Shaheen*-I, *Ghauri*-II and *Ghazanvi* ballistic and *Babar* cruise missile options.

Above Missile development programmes have serious security implications at regional and global level. Potential operational problems regarding the mobility of missiles during the period of crisis may lead to escalation between the two countries. Besides, due to the lack of comprehensive and accurate intelligence one side may misread passive dispersal of weapons, and can interpret the defensive moves of other as threatening, and initiate a chain reaction regarding deployment of such missiles. Consequently, India and Pakistan could enter into a spiral of escalation.

Moreover, these delivery systems themselves could become a source of tension and could by their nature and disposition increase the incentive to attack first in a crisis. In South Asia, short range missiles can easily attack on national capitals of adversaries within a span of less than five minutes leaving little time for warning and protective measures due to the close geographical proximity. An accidental or even authorized test launch during period of tension may precipitate a conflict and hence affects the stability of the region in a serious way. Ambiguity regarding type of warhead mounted on a missile launched also creates the confusion among decision-makers because government statements frequently describe a missile system as nuclear capable. The assumption on the receiving end may likely to read any missile launched as a missile carrying a nuclear warhead.

Introduction of ballistic missile defence (BMD) has further complicated the already surcharged scenario in the region. Response to an Indian BMD may bring quantitative and qualitative change in Pakistan's nuclear force structure, deployment postures, and decisions to go for its own missile defence. This action-reaction spiral is likely to give boost to the phenomenon of arms race in South Asia which will increase the chances of conflict between India and Pakistan. Even these BMDs could create a false sense of security among political and military leadership and are likely to invite military adventurism or even a pre-emptive strike against adversary.

These missile development programmes may have negative fallouts on global arms control efforts. Transfer of BMD technologies from Washington or Tel Aviv to New Delhi would violate Missile Technology Control Regime (MTCR). It may reverse the process of reducing the number of warheads in nuclear stockpiles. It would also weaken the support for the CTBT, MTCR, and Fissile Material Cut-off Treaty (FMCT) negotiations. Improvement of warhead designs by Pakistan might necessitate nuclear testing, disturbing the nuclear test ban between India and Pakistan in the short-run, and likely to weaken their support for non-proliferation efforts in the region. Deployment of missile defences by India may also jeopardize the ongoing peace process with Pakistan and China. Moreover, increased spending on offensive and defensive weapons would further retard developmental activities in this poverty ridden region of South Asia. This process is tantamount to enhance the unnecessary burden on economies of both the countries and lead to the diversion of their resources from much-needed developmental tasks.

Hence, it can be discerned that South Asian region is facing a serious problem of counter-proliferation which is likely to make the deterrence inoperative. Both the countries are badly involved in a process of tit for tat nuclear and missile race. Though, Pakistan perceives India as a threat and, therefore, is engaged in increasing its weapons stockpiles, but India, in addition to Pakistan, views China also as a factor in its security planning. Consequently, both are obsessive for weapons of mass destruction, and undermining the risks of nuclear and missile proliferations. In developing these weapons, India's efforts have been mainly indigenous while Pakistan has been dependent on foreign assistance particularly from China and North Korea. As a result, Pakistan is not far behind in case of weapons inventories. India's efforts for BMD further compelling Pakistan to enhance its capability to counter the Indian moves for superiority. All these movements in the region are creating serious threats to non-proliferation regime and arms control measures at regional and global level. Social and economic development of the region is also hampered because of huge investments in the weapons programmes.

Now, when presence of nuclear weapons and missiles with devastating results is the hard reality in South Asia, both the countries, as responsible nuclear neighbours, need to carefully evaluate the overall security situation in the region. Nuclear and missile issues should be addressed through both short and long-term measures. Both the countries need to work towards a commitment that large-scale mobilization of their conventional forces should not take place in future. Simultaneously, they should avoid indulging in any kind of conventional conflict to avert nuclear escalation. However, in the absence of a formal regime based arrangement to prevent mobilization of their forces and conventional war fighting, a process of peace and security building, if initiated sincerely, could allow tensions to be reduced. This in turn could enable far-sighted leaders on both sides to build firebreaks against triggering events. To avoid the miscalculations leading to accidental war, both the countries could refrain from carrying out any missile flight test during period of crisis. Beyond providing prior notification, on which there is already a preliminary understanding between them, both sides could formally agree that missile flight tests would be suspended during crisis. However, it would be difficult to define exactly what would constitute a period of crisis, but efforts to agree on criteria would themselves be productive and possibly facilitate more detailed confidence-building measures regulating missile flight tests. Both the countries could also conclude an agreement not to mate delivery systems with warheads during peacetime, and not to pre-delegate authority to field commanders in normal times. To check the threat of nuclear terrorism, both the countries need to adopt strict security measures, and must continue to track the numerous groups and individuals engaged in overt and covert violent activities or terrorism in their respective territories. Enhanced levels of surveillance of land borders and coastlines are necessary to monitor the goods and people across their respective international borders. Both need to acquire modern technology and equipments to upgrade the physical security of nuclear weapons components, material and installations including radioactive waste storage and disposal facilities. Certain measures must be adopted by both the sides to provide buffers against command and control shortcomings, and to generate commitments on both sides to develop effective accident-response, risk reduction, and crisis management tools and procedures.

National leaders must maintain absolute control over the status of nuclear weapons and missiles in the region. The top political authorities and senior leaders must be fully informed by custodians of even passive moves of missiles or nuclear weapons. During crisis, missiles can only be moved after the explicit authorization of the National Command Authorities. National leaders need to inform allies, major powers, and the adversary about the nature of missile moves contemplated or underway. To the extent possible, greater clarity needs to be provided when missiles moves are of a defensive nature. Moreover, in addition to existing communication channels, Nuclear Risk Reduction Centers could be established in each capital and conveniently located for easy access by top leaders. Finally, some arms control agreements must be done to reduce the danger. Several conceptual options are available for arms control measures intended to reduce the destabilizing effects of strategic missiles. It would be wise to ban flight tests of ballistic missiles with ranges of 150 km or less. Geographic non-deployment zones for mobile missiles in border regions may be established. Missiles with ranges up to 150 km should be eliminated because they are perceived to have both conventional and nuclear missions. This ambiguity lowers the nuclear threshold. Both the countries could also designate certain types of missiles as having only conventional missions. Hence, all these measures could improve bilateral and regional security in South Asia while retaining the deterrent value of nuclear arsenals.

APPENDIX I[1]

INDIA'S NUCLEAR DOCTRINE

1. PREAMBLE

The use of nuclear weapons in particular as well as other weapons of mass destruction constitutes the gravest threat to humanity and to peace and stability in the international system. Unlike the other two categories of weapons of mass destruction, biological and chemical weapons which have been outlawed by international treaties, nuclear weapons remain instruments for national and collective security, the possession of which on a selective basis has been sought to be legitimised through permanent extension of the Nuclear. Non-proliferation Treaty (NPT) in May 1995. Nuclear weapon states have asserted that they will continue to rely on nuclear weapons with some of them adopting policies to use them even in a non-nuclear context. These developments amount to virtual abandonment of nuclear disarmament. This is a serious setback to the struggle of the international community to abolish weapons of mass destruction.

India's primary objective is to achieve economic, political, social, scientific and technological development within a peaceful and democratic framework. This requires an environment of durable peace and insurance against potential risks to peace and stability. It will be India's endeavour to proceed towards this overall objective in cooperation with the global democratic trends and to play a constructive role in advancing the international system toward a just, peaceful and equitable order.

Autonomy of decision-making in the developmental

process and in strategic matters is an inalienable democratic right of the Indian people. India will strenuously guard this right in a world where nuclear weapons for a select few are sought to be legitimised for an indefinite future, and where there is growing complexity and frequency in the use of force for political purposes.

India's security is an integral component of its development process. India continuously aims at promoting an ever-expanding area of peace and stability around it so that developmental priorities can be pursued without disruption.

However, the very existence of offensive doctrine pertaining to the first use of nuclear weapons and the insistence of some nuclear weapons states on the legitimacy of their use even against non-nuclear weapon countries constitute a threat to peace, stability and

This document outlines the broad principles for the development, deployment and employment of India's nuclear forces. Details of policy and strategy concerning force structures, deployment and employment of nuclear forces will flow from this framework and will be laid down separately and kept under constant review.

2. OBJECTIVES

In the absence of global nuclear disarmament India's strategic interests require effective, credible nuclear deterrence and adequate retaliatory capability should deterrence fail. This is consistent with the UN Charter, which sanctions the right of self-defence.

The requirements of deterrence should be carefully weighed in the design of Indian nuclear forces and in the strategy to provide for a level of capability consistent with maximum credibility, survivability, effectiveness, safety and security.

India shall pursue a doctrine of credible minimum nuclear deterrence. In this policy of "retaliation only", the survivability of our arsenal is critical. This is a dynamic concept related to the strategic environment, technological imperatives and the needs of national security. The actual size components, deployment and employment of nuclear forces will be decided in the light of these factors. India's peacetime posture aims at convincing any potential aggressor that:

(a) Any threat of use of nuclear weapons against India shall invoke measures to counter the threat; and
(b) Any nuclear attack on India and its forces shall result in punitive retaliation with nuclear weapons to inflict damage unacceptable to the aggressor.

The fundamental purpose of Indian nuclear weapons is to deter the use and threat of use of nuclear weapons by any State or entity against India and its forces. India will not be the first to initiate a nuclear strike, but will respond with punitive retaliation should deterrence fail.

India will not resort to the use or threat of use of nuclear weapons against States which do not possess nuclear weapons, or are not aligned with nuclear weapon powers.

Deterrence requires that India maintain:

(a) sufficient, survivable and operationally prepared nuclear forces,
(b) a robust command and control system,
(c) effective intelligence and early warning capabilities,
(d) comprehensive planning and training for operations in line with the strategy, and
(e) the will to employ nuclear forces and weapons.

Highly effective conventional military capabilities shall be maintained to raise the threshold of outbreak both of conventional military conflict as well as that of threat or use of nuclear weapons.

3. NUCLEAR FORCES

India's nuclear forces will be effective, enduring, diverse, flexible, and responsive to the requirements in accordance with the concept of credible minimum deterrence. These forces will be based on a triad of aircraft, mobile land-based missiles and sea-based assets in keeping with the objectives outlined above.

Survivability of the forces will be enhanced by a combination of multiple redundant systems, mobility, dispersion and deception.

The doctrine envisages assured capability to shift from peacetime deployment to fully employable forces in the shortest possible time, and the ability to retaliate effectively even in a case of significant degradation by hostile strikes.

4. CREDIBILITY AND SURVIVABILITY

The following principles are central to India's nuclear deterrent:

1. Credibility

Any adversary must know that India can and will retaliate with sufficient nuclear weapons to inflict destruction and punishment that the aggressor will find unacceptable if nuclear weapons are used against India and its forces.

2. Effectiveness

The efficacy of India's nuclear deterrent be maximised through synergy among all elements involving reliability, timeliness, accuracy and weight of the attack.

3. Survivability

(i) India's nuclear forces and their command and control shall be organised for very high survivability against surprise attacks and for rapid punitive response. They shall be designed and deployed to ensure survival against a first strike and to endure repetitive attrition attempts with adequate retaliatory capabilities for a punishing strike which would be unacceptable to the aggressor.

(ii) Procedures for the continuity of nuclear command and control shall ensure a continuing capability to effectively employ nuclear weapons.

5. COMMAND AND CONTROL

Nuclear weapons shall be tightly controlled and released for use at the highest political level. the authority to release nuclear weapons for use resides in the person of the Prime Minister of India, or the designated successor(s).

An effective and survivable command and control system with requisite flexibility and responsiveness shall be in place. An integrated operational plan, or a series of sequential plans, predicated on strategic objectives and a targetting policy shall form part of the system.

For effective employment the unity of command and control of nuclear forces including dual capable delivery systems shall be ensured.

The survivability of the nuclear arsenal and effective command, control, communications, computing, intelligence and information (C412) systems shall be assured.

The Indian defence forces shall be in a position to, execute operations in an NBC environment with minimal degradation;

Space based and other assets shall be created to provide early warning, communications, damage/detonation assessment.

6. SECURITY AND SAFETY

Security: Extraordinary precautions shall be taken to ensure that nuclear weapons, their manufacture, transportation and storage are fully guarded against possible theft, loss, sabotage, damage or unauthorised access or use.

Safety is an absolute requirement and tamper proof procedures and systems shall be instituted to ensure that unauthorised or inadvertent activation/use of nuclear weapons does not take place and risks of accident are avoided.

Disaster control: India shall develop an appropriate disaster control system capable of handling the unique requirements of potential incidents involving nuclear weapons and materials.

7. RESEARCH AND DEVELOPMENT

India should step up efforts in research and development to keep up with technological advances in this field.

While India is committed to maintain the deployment of a deterrent which is both minimum and credible, it will not accept any restraints on building its R&D capability.

8. DISARMAMENT AND ARMS CONTROL

Global, verifiable and non-discriminatory nuclear disarmament is a national security objective. India shall continue its efforts to achieve the goal of a nuclear weapon-free world at an early date.

Since no-first use of nuclear weapons is India's basic commitment, every effort shall be made to persuade other States possessing nuclear weapons to join an international treaty banning first use.

Having provided unqualified negative security assurances, India shall work for internationally binding unconditional negative security assurances by nuclear weapon states to non-nuclear weapon states.

Nuclear arms control measures shall be sought as part of national security policy to reduce potential threats and to protect our own capability and its effectiveness.

In view of the very high destructive potential of nuclear weapons, appropriate nuclear risk reduction and confidence building measures shall be sought, negotiated and instituted.

Note and Reference

1. Government of India, National Security Advisory Board, *Draft Report of Indian Nuclear Doctrine*, 17 August 1999; and *Draft Report of National Security Advisory Board on Indian Nuclear Doctrine*, Embassy of India, Wahington D.C., 17 August 1999; http://www.indianembassy. org/policy/CTBT/nuclear_doctrine_aug_17_1999.html

APPENDIX II[1]

3 August 2007

AGREEMENT FOR COOPERATION BETWEEN THE GOVERNMENT OF THE UNITED STATES OF AMERICA AND THE GOVERNMENT OF INDIA CONCERNING PEACEFUL USES OF NUCLEAR ENERGY (123RD AGREEMENT)

The Government of India and the Government of the United States of America, hereinafter referred to as the Parties,

RECOGNIZING the significance of civilian nuclear energy for meeting growing global energy demands in a cleaner and more efficient manner;

DESIRING to cooperate extensively in the full development and use of nuclear energy for peaceful purposes as a means of achieving energy security, on a stable, reliable and predictable basis;

WISHING to develop such cooperation on the basis of mutual respect for sovereignty, non-interference in each other's internal affairs, equality, mutual benefit, reciprocity and with due respect for each other's nuclear programmes;

DESIRING to establish the necessary legal framework and basis for cooperation concerning peaceful uses of nuclear energy;

AFFIRMING that cooperation under this Agreement is between two States possessing advanced nuclear technology, both Parties having the same benefits and advantages, both committed to preventing WMD proliferation;

NOTING the understandings expressed in the India-U.S. Joint Statement of July 18, 2005 to enable full civil nuclear energy cooperation with India covering aspects of the associated nuclear fuel cycle;

AFFIRMING their support for the objectives of the International Atomic Energy Agency (IAEA) and its safeguards system, as applicable to India and the United States of America, and its importance in ensuring that international cooperation in development and use of nuclear energy for peaceful purposes is carried out under arrangements that will not contribute to the proliferation of nuclear weapons or other nuclear explosive devices;

NOTING their respective commitments to safety and security of peaceful uses of nuclear energy, to adequate physical protection of nuclear material and effective national export controls;

MINDFUL that peaceful nuclear activities must be undertaken with a view to protecting the environment;

MINDFUL of their shared commitment to preventing the proliferation of weapons of mass destruction; and

DESIROUS of strengthening the strategic partnership between them;

Have agreed on the following:

ARTICLE 1—DEFINITIONS

For the purposes of this Agreement:

(A) "By-product material" means any radioactive material (except special fissionable material) yielded in or made radioactive by exposure to the radiation incident to the process of producing or utilizing special fissionable material. By-product material shall not be subject to safeguards or any other form of verification under this Agreement, unless it has been decided otherwise by prior mutual agreement in writing between the two Parties.

(B) "Component" means a component part of equipment, or other item so designated by agreement of the Parties.

(C) "Conversion" means any of the normal operations in the nuclear fuel cycle, preceding fuel fabrication and excluding enrichment, by which uranium is transformed from one chemical form to another—for example, from uranium hexafluoride (UF6) to uranium dioxide (UO2) or from uranium oxide to metal.

(D) "Decommissioning" means the actions taken at the end of a facility's useful life to retire the facility from service in the manner that provides adequate protection for the health and safety of the decommissioning workers and the general public, and for the environment. These actions can range from closing down the facility and a minimal removal of nuclear material coupled with continuing maintenance and surveillance, to a complete removal of residual radioactivity in excess of levels acceptable for unrestricted use of the facility and its site.

(E) "Dual-Use Item" means a nuclear related item which has a technical use in both nuclear and non-nuclear applications.

(F) "Equipment" means any equipment in nuclear operation including reactor, reactor pressure vessel, reactor fuel charging and discharging equipment, reactor control rods, reactor pressure tubes, reactor primary coolant pumps, zirconium tubing, equipment for fuel fabrication and any other item so designated by the Parties.

(G) "High enriched uranium" means uranium enriched to twenty percent or greater in the isotope 235.

(H) "Information" means any information that is not in the public domain and is transferred in any form pursuant to this Agreement and so designated and documented in hard copy or digital form by mutual agreement by the Parties that it shall be subject to this Agreement, but will cease to be information whenever the Party transferring the information or any third party legitimately releases it into the public domain.

(I) "Low enriched uranium" means uranium enriched to less than twenty percent in the isotope 235.

(J) "Major critical component" means any part or group of parts essential to the operation of a sensitive nuclear facility or heavy water production facility.

(K) "Non-nuclear material" means heavy water, or any other material suitable for use in a reactor to slow down high velocity neutrons and increase the likelihood of further fission, as may be jointly designated by the appropriate authorities of the Parties.

(L) "Nuclear material" means (1) source material, and (2) special fissionable material. "Source material" means uranium containing the mixture of isotopes occurring in nature; uranium depleted in the isotope 235; thorium; any of the foregoing in the form of metal, alloy, chemical compound, or concentrate; any other material containing one or more of the foregoing in such concentration as the Board of Governors of the IAEA shall from time to time determine; and such other materials as the Board of Governors of the IAEA may determine or as may be agreed by the appropriate authorities of both Parties. "Special fissionable material" means plutonium, uranium-233, uranium enriched in the isotope 233 or 235, any substance containing one or more of the foregoing, and such other substances as the Board of Governors of the IAEA may determine or as may be agreed by the appropriate authorities of both Parties. "Special fissionable material" does not include "source material". Any determination by the Board of Governors of the IAEA under Article XX of that Agency's Statute or otherwise that amends the list of materials considered to be "source material" or "special fissionable material" shall only have effect under this Agreement when both Parties to this Agreement have informed each other in writing that they accept such amendment.

(M) "Peaceful purposes" include the use of information, nuclear material, equipment or components in such fields as research, power generation, medicine, agriculture and industry, but do not include use in, research on, or development of any nuclear explosive device or any other military purpose. Provision of power for a military base drawn from any power network, production of radioisotopes to be used for medical purposes in military environment for diagnostics, therapy and sterility assurance, and other similar purposes as may be mutually agreed by the Parties shall not be regarded as military purpose.

(N) "Person" means any individual or any entity subject to the territorial jurisdiction of either Party but does not include the Parties.

(O) "Reactor" means any apparatus, other than a nuclear weapon or other nuclear explosive device, in which a self-sustaining fission chain reaction is maintained by utilizing uranium, plutonium, or thorium or any combination thereof.

(P) "Sensitive nuclear facility" means any facility designed or used primarily for uranium enrichment, reprocessing of nuclear fuel, or fabrication of nuclear fuel containing plutonium.

(Q) "Sensitive nuclear technology" means any information that is not in the public domain and that is important to the design, construction, fabrication, operation, or maintenance of any sensitive nuclear facility, or other such information that may be so designated by agreement of the Parties.

ARTICLE 2—SCOPE OF COOPERATION

1. The Parties shall cooperate in the use of nuclear energy for peaceful purposes in accordance with the provisions of this Agreement. Each Party shall implement this Agreement in accordance with its respective applicable treaties, national laws, regulations, and license requirements concerning the use of nuclear energy for peaceful purposes.
2. The purpose of the Agreement being to enable full civil nuclear energy cooperation between the Parties, the Parties may pursue cooperation in all relevant areas to include, but not limited to, the following:

a. Advanced nuclear energy research and development in such areas as may be agreed between the Parties;
b. Nuclear safety matters of mutual interest and competence, as set out in Article 3;
c. Facilitation of exchange of scientists for visits, meetings, symposia and collaborative research;
d. Full civil nuclear cooperation activities covering nuclear reactors and aspects of the associated nuclear fuel cycle including technology transfer on an industrial or commercial scale between the Parties or authorized persons;
e. Development of a strategic reserve of nuclear fuel to guard against any disruption of supply over the lifetime of India's reactors;
f. Advanced research and development in nuclear sciences including but not limited to biological research, medicine, agriculture and industry, environment and climate change;
g. Supply between the Parties, whether for use by or for the benefit of the Parties or third countries, of nuclear material;
h. Alteration in form or content of nuclear material as provided for in Article 6;
i. Supply between the Parties of equipment, whether for use by or for the benefit of the Parties or third countries;
j. Controlled thermonuclear fusion including in multilateral projects; and
k. Other areas of mutual interest as may be agreed by the Parties.

3. Transfer of nuclear material, non-nuclear material, equipment, components and information under this Agreement may be undertaken directly between the Parties or through authorized persons. Such transfers shall be subject to this Agreement and to such additional terms and conditions as may be agreed by the Parties. Nuclear material, non-nuclear material, equipment, components and information transferred from the territory of one Party to the territory of the

other Party, whether directly or through a third country, will be regarded as having been transferred pursuant to this Agreement only upon confirmation, by the appropriate authority of the recipient Party to the appropriate authority of the supplier Party that such items both will be subject to the Agreement and have been received by the recipient Party.

4. The Parties affirm that the purpose of this Agreement is to provide for peaceful nuclear cooperation and not to affect the unsafeguarded nuclear activities of either Party. Accordingly, nothing in this Agreement shall be interpreted as affecting the rights of the Parties to use for their own purposes nuclear material, non-nuclear material, equipment, components, information or technology produced, acquired or developed by them independent of any nuclear material, non-nuclear material, equipment, components, information or technology transferred to them pursuant to this Agreement. This Agreement shall be implemented in a manner so as not to hinder or otherwise interfere with any other activities involving the use of nuclear material, non-nuclear material, equipment, components, information or technology and military nuclear facilities produced, acquired or developed by them independent of this Agreement for their own purposes.

ARTICLE 3—TRANSFER OF INFORMATION

1. Information concerning the use of nuclear energy for peaceful purposes may be transferred between the Parties. Transfers of information may be accomplished through reports, data banks and computer programs and any other means mutually agreed to by the Parties. Fields that may be covered include, but shall not be limited to, the following:

   a. Research, development, design, construction, operation, maintenance and use of reactors, reactor experiments, and decommissioning;

b. The use of nuclear material in physical, chemical, radiological and biological research, medicine, agriculture and industry;
c. Fuel cycle activities to meet future world-wide civil nuclear energy needs, including multilateral approaches to which they are parties for ensuring nuclear fuel supply and appropriate techniques for management of nuclear wastes;
d. Advanced research and development in nuclear science and technology;
e. Health, safety, and environmental considerations related to the foregoing;
f. Assessments of the role nuclear power may play in national energy plans;
g. Codes, regulations and standards for the nuclear industry;
h. Research on controlled thermonuclear fusion including bilateral activities and contributions toward multilateral projects such as the International Thermonuclear Experimental Reactor (ITER); and
i. Any other field mutually agreed to by the Parties.

2. Cooperation pursuant to this Article may include, but is not limited to, training, exchange of personnel, meetings, exchange of samples, materials and instruments for experimental purposes and a balanced participation in joint studies and projects.
3. This Agreement does not require the transfer of any information regarding matters outside the scope of this Agreement, or information that the Parties are not permitted under their respective treaties, national laws, or regulations to transfer.
4. Restricted Data, as defined by each Party, shall not be transferred under this Agreement.

ARTICLE 4—NUCLEAR TRADE

1. The Parties shall facilitate nuclear trade between themselves in the mutual interests of their respective

industry, utilities and consumers and also, where appropriate, trade between third countries and either Party of items obligated to the other Party. The Parties recognize that reliability of supplies is essential to ensure smooth and uninterrupted operation of nuclear facilities and that industry in both the Parties needs continuing reassurance that deliveries can be made on time in order to plan for the efficient operation of nuclear installations.

2. Authorizations, including export and import licenses as well as authorizations or consents to third parties, relating to trade, industrial operations or nuclear material movement should be consistent with the sound and efficient administration of this Agreement and should not be used to restrict trade. It is further agreed that if the relevant authority of the concerned Party considers that an application cannot be processed within a two month period it shall immediately, upon request, provide reasoned information to the submitting Party. In the event of a refusal to authorize an application or a delay exceeding four months from the date of the first application the Party of the submitting persons or undertakings may call for urgent consultations under Article 13 of this Agreement, which shall take place at the earliest opportunity and in any case not later than 30 days after such a request.

ARTICLE 5—TRANSFER OF NUCLEAR MATERIAL, NON-NUCLEAR MATERIAL, EQUIPMENT, COMPONENTS AND RELATED TECHNOLOGY

1. Nuclear material, non-nuclear material, equipment and components may be transferred for applications consistent with this Agreement. Any special fissionable material transferred under this Agreement shall be low enriched uranium, except as provided in paragraph 5.
2. Sensitive nuclear technology, heavy water production technology, sensitive nuclear facilities, heavy water

production facilities and major critical components of such facilities may be transferred under this Agreement pursuant to an amendment to this Agreement. Transfers of dual-use items that could be used in enrichment, reprocessing or heavy water production facilities will be subject to the Parties' respective applicable laws, regulations and license policies.

3. Natural or low enriched uranium may be transferred for use as fuel in reactor experiments and in reactors, for conversion or fabrication, or for such other purposes as may be agreed to by the Parties.
4. The quantity of nuclear material transferred under this Agreement shall be consistent with any of the following purposes: use in reactor experiments or the loading of reactors, the efficient and continuous conduct of such reactor experiments or operation of reactors for their lifetime, use as samples, standards, detectors, and targets, and the accomplishment of other purposes as may be agreed by the Parties.
5. Small quantities of special fissionable material may be transferred for use as samples, standards, detectors, and targets, and for such other purposes as the Parties may agree.
6. (a) The United States has conveyed its commitment to the reliable supply of fuel to India. Consistent with the July 18, 2005, Joint Statement, the United States has also reaffirmed its assurance to create the necessary conditions for India to have assured and full access to fuel for its reactors. As part of its implementation of the July 18, 2005, Joint Statement the United States is committed to seeking agreement from the U.S. Congress to amend its domestic laws and to work with friends and allies to adjust the practices of the Nuclear Suppliers' Group to create the necessary conditions for India to obtain full access to the international fuel market, including reliable, uninterrupted and continual access to fuel supplies from firms in several nations.

(b) To further guard against any disruption of fuel supplies, the United States is prepared to take the following additional steps:

(i) The United States is willing to incorporate assurances regarding fuel supply in the bilateral U.S.-India agreement on peaceful uses of nuclear energy under Section 123 of the U.S. Atomic Energy Act, which would be submitted to the U.S. Congress.

(ii) The United States will join India in seeking to negotiate with the IAEA an India-specific fuel supply agreement.

(iii) The United States will support an Indian effort to develop a strategic reserve of nuclear fuel to guard against any disruption of supply over the lifetime of India's reactors.

(iv) If despite these arrangements, a disruption of fuel supplies to India occurs, the United States and India would jointly convene a group of friendly supplier countries to include countries such as Russia, France and the United Kingdom to pursue such measures as would restore fuel supply to India.

(c) In light of the above understandings with the United States, an India-specific safeguards agreement will be negotiated between India and the IAEA providing for safeguards to guard against withdrawal of safeguarded nuclear material from civilian use at any time as well as providing for corrective measures that India may take to ensure uninterrupted operation of its civilian nuclear reactors in the event of disruption of foreign fuel supplies. Taking this into account, India will place its civilian nuclear facilities under India-specific safeguards in perpetuity and negotiate an appropriate safeguards agreement to this end with the IAEA.

ARTICLE 6—NUCLEAR FUEL CYCLE ACTIVITIES

In keeping with their commitment to full civil nuclear cooperation, both Parties, as they do with other states with advanced nuclear technology, may carry out the following nuclear fuel cycle activities:

(i) Within the territorial jurisdiction of either Party, enrichment up to twenty percent in the isotope 235 of uranium transferred pursuant to this Agreement, as well as of uranium used in or produced through the use of equipment so transferred, may be carried out.

(ii) Irradiation within the territorial jurisdiction of either Party of plutonium, uranium-233, high enriched uranium and irradiated nuclear material transferred pursuant to this Agreement or used in or produced through the use of non-nuclear material, nuclear material or equipment so transferred may be carried out.

(iii) With a view to implementing full civil nuclear cooperation as envisioned in the Joint Statement of the Parties of July 18, 2005, the Parties grant each other consent to reprocess or otherwise alter in form or content nuclear material transferred pursuant to this Agreement and nuclear material and by-product material used in or produced through the use of nuclear material, non-nuclear material, or equipment so transferred. To bring these rights into effect, India will establish a new national reprocessing facility dedicated to reprocessing safeguarded nuclear material under IAEA safeguards and the Parties will agree on arrangements and procedures under which such reprocessing or other alteration in form or content will take place in this new facility. Consultations on arrangements and procedures will begin within six months of a request by either Party and will be concluded within one year. The Parties agree on the application of IAEA safeguards to all facilities concerned with the above activities. These arrangements and procedures shall include provisions with respect to physical protection standards set out in Article 8, storage standards set out in Article 7, and environmental protections set forth in Article 11 of this Agreement, and such other provisions as may be agreed by the Parties. Any special fissionable material that may be separated may only be utilized in national facilities under IAEA safeguards.

(iv) Post-irradiation examination involving chemical dissolution or separation of irradiated nuclear material transferred pursuant to this Agreement or irradiated nuclear material used in or produced through the use of non-nuclear material, nuclear material or equipment so transferred may be carried out.

ARTICLE 7—STORAGE AND RETRANSFERS

1. Plutonium and uranium 233 (except as either may be contained in irradiated fuel elements), and high enriched uranium, transferred pursuant to this Agreement or used in or produced through the use of material or equipment so transferred, may be stored in facilities that are at all times subject, as a minimum, to the levels of physical protection that are set out in IAEA document INFCIRC 225/REV 4 as it may be revised and accepted by the Parties. Each Party shall record such facilities on a list, made available to the other Party. A Party's list shall be held confidential if that Party so requests. Either Party may make changes to its list by notifying the other Party in writing and receiving a written acknowledgement. Such acknowledgement shall be given no later than thirty days after the receipt of the notification and shall be limited to a statement that the notification has been received. If there are grounds to believe that the provisions of this sub-Article are not being fully complied with, immediate consultations may be

called for. Following upon such consultations, each Party shall ensure by means of such consultations that necessary remedial measures are taken immediately. Such measures shall be sufficient to restore the levels of physical protection referred to above at the facility in question. However, if the Party on whose territory the nuclear material in question is stored determines that such measures are not feasible, it will shift the nuclear material to another appropriate, listed facility it identifies.

2. Nuclear material, non-nuclear material, equipment, components, and information transferred pursuant to this Agreement and any special fissionable material produced through the use of nuclear material, non-nuclear material or equipment so transferred shall not be transferred or re-transferred to unauthorized persons or, unless the Parties agree, beyond the recipient Party's territorial jurisdiction.

ARTICLE 8—PHYSICAL PROTECTION

1. Adequate physical protection shall be maintained with respect to nuclear material and equipment transferred pursuant to this Agreement and nuclear material used in or produced through the use of nuclear material, non-nuclear material or equipment so transferred.
2. To fulfill the requirement in paragraph 1, each Party shall apply measures in accordance with (i) levels of physical protection at least equivalent to the recommendations published in IAEA document INFCIRC/225/Rev.4 entitled "The Physical Protection of Nuclear Material and Nuclear Facilities," and in any subsequent revisions of that document agreed to by the Parties, and (ii) the provisions of the 1980 Convention on the Physical Protection of Nuclear Material and any amendments to the Convention that enter into force for both Parties.
3. The Parties will keep each other informed through diplomatic channels of those agencies or authorities

having responsibility for ensuring that levels of physical protection for nuclear material in their territory or under their jurisdiction or control are adequately met and having responsibility for coordinating response and recovery operations in the event of unauthorized use or handling of material subject to this Article. The Parties will also keep each other informed through diplomatic channels of the designated points of contact within their national authorities to cooperate on matters of out-of-country transportation and other matters of mutual concern.

4. The provisions of this Article shall be implemented in such a manner as to avoid undue interference in the Parties' peaceful nuclear activities and so as to be consistent with prudent management practices required for the safe and economic conduct of their peaceful nuclear programs.

ARTICLE 9—PEACEFUL USE

Nuclear material, equipment and components transferred pursuant to this Agreement and nuclear material and by-product material used in or produced through the use of any nuclear material, equipment, and components so transferred shall not be used by the recipient Party for any nuclear explosive device, for research on or development of any nuclear explosive device or for any military purpose.

ARTICLE 10—IAEA SAFEGUARDS

1. Safeguards will be maintained with respect to all nuclear materials and equipment transferred pursuant to this Agreement, and with respect to all special fissionable material used in or produced through the use of such nuclear materials and equipment, so long as the material or equipment remains under the jurisdiction or control of the cooperating Party.
2. Taking into account Article 5.6 of this Agreement, India agrees that nuclear material and equipment

transferred to India by the United States of America pursuant to this Agreement and any nuclear material used in or produced through the use of nuclear material, non-nuclear material, equipment or components so transferred shall be subject to safeguards in perpetuity in accordance with the India-specific Safeguards Agreement between India and the IAEA [identifying data] and an Additional Protocol, when in force.

3. Nuclear material and equipment transferred to the United States of America pursuant to this Agreement and any nuclear material used in or produced through the use of any nuclear material, non-nuclear material, equipment, or components so transferred shall be subject to the Agreement between the United States of America and the IAEA for the application of safeguards in the United States of America, done at Vienna, November 18, 1977, which entered into force on December 9, 1980, and an Additional Protocol, when in force.
4. If the IAEA decides that the application of IAEA safeguards is no longer possible, the supplier and recipient should consult and agree on appropriate verification measures.
5. Each Party shall take such measures as are necessary to maintain and facilitate the application of IAEA safeguards in its respective territory provided for under this Article.
6. Each Party shall establish and maintain a system of accounting for and control of nuclear material transferred pursuant to this Agreement and nuclear material used in or produced through the use of any material, equipment, or components so transferred. The procedures applicable to India shall be those set forth in the India-specific Safeguards Agreement referred to in Paragraph 2 of this Article.
7. Upon the request of either Party, the other Party shall report or permit the IAEA to report to the requesting Party on the status of all inventories of material subject to this Agreement.

8. The provisions of this Article shall be implemented in such a manner as to avoid hampering, delay, or undue interference in the Parties' peaceful nuclear activities and so as to be consistent with prudent management practices required for the safe and economic conduct of their peaceful nuclear programs.

ARTICLE 11—ENVIRONMENTAL PROTECTION

The Parties shall cooperate in following the best practices for minimizing the impact on the environment from any radioactive, chemical or thermal contamination arising from peaceful nuclear activities under this Agreement and in related matters of health and safety.

ARTICLE 12—IMPLEMENTATION OF THE AGREEMENT

1. This Agreement shall be implemented in a manner designed:

   (a) to avoid hampering or delaying the nuclear activities in the territory of either Party;
   (b) to avoid interference in such activities;
   (c) to be consistent with prudent management practices required for the safe conduct of such activities; and
   (d) to take full account of the long-term requirements of the nuclear energy programs of the Parties.

2. The provisions of this Agreement shall not be used to:

   (a) secure unfair commercial or industrial advantages or to restrict trade to the disadvantage of persons and undertakings of either Party or hamper their commercial or industrial interests, whether international or domestic;
   (b) interfere with the nuclear policy or programs for the promotion of the peaceful uses of nuclear energy including research and development; or

(c) impede the free movement of nuclear material, non nuclear material and equipment supplied under this Agreement within the territory of the Parties.

3. When execution of an agreement or contract pursuant to this Agreement between Indian and United States organizations requires exchanges of experts, the Parties shall facilitate entry of the experts to their territories and their stay therein consistent with national laws, regulations and practices. When other cooperation pursuant to this Agreement requires visits of experts, the Parties shall facilitate entry of the experts to their territory and their stay therein consistent with national laws, regulations and practices.

ARTICLE 13—CONSULTATIONS

1. The Parties undertake to consult at the request of either Party regarding the implementation of this Agreement and the development of further cooperation in the field of peaceful uses of nuclear energy on a stable, reliable and predictable basis. The Parties recognize that such consultations are between two States with advanced nuclear technology, which have agreed to assume the same responsibilities and practices and acquire the same benefits and advantages as other leading countries with advanced nuclear technology.
2. Each Party shall endeavor to avoid taking any action that adversely affects cooperation envisaged under Article 2 of this Agreement. If either Party at any time following the entry into force of this Agreement does not comply with the provisions of this Agreement, the Parties shall promptly hold consultations with a view to resolving the matter in a way that protects the legitimate interests of both Parties, it being understood that rights of either Party under Article 16.2 remain unaffected.

3. Consultations under this Article may be carried out by a Joint Committee specifically established for this purpose. A Joint Technical Working Group reporting to the Joint Committee will be set-up to ensure the fulfilment of the requirements of the Administrative Arrangements referred to in Article 17.

ARTICLE 14—TERMINATION AND CESSATION OF COOPERATION

1. Either Party shall have the right to terminate this Agreement prior to its expiration on one year's written notice to the other Party. A Party giving notice of termination shall provide the reasons for seeking such termination. The Agreement shall terminate one year from the date of the written notice, unless the notice has been withdrawn by the providing Party in writing prior to the date of termination.
2. Before this Agreement is terminated pursuant to paragraph 1 of this Article, the Parties shall consider the relevant circumstances and promptly hold consultations, as provided in Article 13, to address the reasons cited by the Party seeking termination. The Party seeking termination has the right to cease further cooperation under this Agreement if it determines that a mutually acceptable resolution of outstanding issues has not been possible or cannot be achieved through consultations. The Parties agree to consider carefully the circumstances that may lead to termination or cessation of cooperation. They further agree to take into account whether the circumstances that may lead to termination or cessation resulted from a Party's serious concern about a changed security environment or as a response to similar actions by other States which could impact national security.
3. If a Party seeking termination cites a violation of this Agreement as the reason for notice for seeking termination, the Parties shall consider whether the action was caused inadvertently or otherwise and

whether the violation could be considered as material. No violation may be considered as being material unless corresponding to the definition of material violation or breach in the Vienna Convention on the Law of Treaties. If a Party seeking termination cites a violation of an IAEA safeguards agreement as the reason for notice for seeking termination, a crucial factor will be whether the IAEA Board of Governors has made a finding of non-compliance.

4. Following the cessation of cooperation under this Agreement, either Party shall have the right to require the return by the other Party of any nuclear material, equipment, non-nuclear material or components transferred under this Agreement and any special fissionable material produced through their use. A notice by a Party that is invoking the right of return shall be delivered to the other Party on or before the date of termination of this Agreement. The notice shall contain a statement of the items subject to this Agreement as to which the Party is requesting return. Except as provided in provisions of Article 16.3, all other legal obligations pertaining to this Agreement shall cease to apply with respect to the nuclear items remaining on the territory of the Party concerned upon termination of this Agreement.
5. The two Parties recognize that exercising the right of return would have profound implications for their relations. If either Party seeks to exercise its right pursuant to paragraph 4 of this Article, it shall, prior to the removal from the territory or from the control of the other Party of any nuclear items mentioned in paragraph 4, undertake consultations with the other Party. Such consultations shall give special consideration to the importance of uninterrupted operation of nuclear reactors of the Party concerned with respect to the availability of nuclear energy for peaceful purposes as a means of achieving energy security. Both Parties shall take into account the potential negative consequences of such termination on the on-going contracts and projects initiated under

this Agreement of significance for the respective nuclear programmes of either Party.

6. If either Party exercises its right of return pursuant to paragraph 4 of this Article, it shall, prior to the removal from the territory or from the control of the other Party, compensate promptly that Party for the fair market value thereof and for the costs incurred as a consequence of such removal. If the return of nuclear items is required, the Parties shall agree on methods and arrangements for the return of the items, the relevant quantity of the items to be returned, and the amount of compensation that would have to be paid by the Party exercising the right to the other Party.
7. Prior to return of nuclear items, the Parties shall satisfy themselves that full safety, radiological and physical protection measures have been ensured in accordance with their existing national regulations and that the transfers pose no unreasonable risk to either Party, countries through which the nuclear items may transit and to the global environment and are in accordance with existing international regulations.
8. The Party seeking the return of nuclear items shall ensure that the timing, methods and arrangements for return of nuclear items are in accordance with paragraphs 5, 6 and 7. Accordingly, the consultations between the Parties shall address mutual commitments as contained in Article 5.6. It is not the purpose of the provisions of this Article regarding cessation of cooperation and right of return to derogate from the rights of the Parties under Article 5.6.
9. The arrangements and procedures concluded pursuant to Article 6(iii) shall be subject to suspension by either Party in exceptional circumstances, as defined by the Parties, after consultations have been held between the Parties aimed at reaching mutually acceptable resolution of outstanding issues, while taking into account the effects of such suspension on

other aspects of cooperation under this Agreement.

ARTICLE 15—SETTLEMENT OF DISPUTES

Any dispute concerning the interpretation or implementation of the provisions of this Agreement shall be promptly negotiated by the Parties with a view to resolving that dispute.

ARTICLE 16—ENTRY INTO FORCE AND DURATION

1. This Agreement shall enter into force on the date on which the Parties exchange diplomatic notes informing each other that they have completed all applicable requirements for its entry into force.
2. This Agreement shall remain in force for a period of 40 years. It shall continue in force thereafter for additional periods of 10 years each. Each Party may, by giving 6 months written notice to the other Party, terminate this Agreement at the end of the initial 40 year period or at the end of any subsequent 10 year period.
3. Notwithstanding the termination or expiration of this Agreement or withdrawal of a Party from this Agreement, Articles 5.6(c), 6, 7, 8, 9, 10 and 15 shall continue in effect so long as any nuclear material, non-nuclear material, by-product material, equipment or components subject to these articles remains in the territory of the Party concerned or under its jurisdiction or control anywhere, or until such time as the Parties agree that such nuclear material is no longer usable for any nuclear activity relevant from the point of view of safeguards.
4. This Agreement shall be implemented in good faith and in accordance with the principles of international law.
5. The Parties may consult, at the request of either Party, on possible amendments to this Agreement. This Agreement may be amended if the Parties so agree. Any amendment shall enter into force on the date on

which the Parties exchange diplomatic notes informing each other that their respective internal legal procedures necessary for the entry into force have been completed.

ARTICLE 1—ADMINISTRATIVE ARRANGEMENT

1. The appropriate authorities of the Parties shall establish an Administrative Arrangement in order to provide for the effective implementation of the provisions of this Agreement.
2. The principles of fungibility and equivalence shall apply to nuclear material and non-nuclear material subject to this Agreement. Detailed provisions for applying these principles shall be set forth in the Administrative Arrangement.
3. The Administrative Arrangement established pursuant to this Article may be amended by agreement of the appropriate authorities of the Parties.

IN WITNESS WHEREOF the undersigned, being duly authorized, have signed this Agreement.

DONE at, this day of , 200 , in duplicate.

FOR THE GOVERNMENT OF THE UNITED STATES OF AMERICA:	FOR THE GOVERNMENT OF INDIA:

AGREED MINUTE

During the negotiation of the Agreement for Cooperation Between the Government of the United States of America and the Government of India Concerning Peaceful Uses of Nuclear Energy ("the Agreement") signed today, the following understandings, which shall be an integral part of the Agreement, were reached.

PROPORTIONALITY

For the purposes of implementing the rights specified in Articles 6 and 7 of the Agreement with respect to special fissionable material and by-product material produced through the use of nuclear material and non-nuclear material, respectively, transferred pursuant to the Agreement and not used in or produced through the use of equipment transferred pursuant to the Agreement, such rights shall in practice be applied to that proportion of special fissionable material and by-product material produced that represents the ratio of transferred nuclear material and non-nuclear material, respectively, used in the production of the special fissionable material and by-product material to the total amount of nuclear material and non-nuclear material so used, and similarly for subsequent generations.

BY-PRODUCT MATERIAL

The Parties agree that reporting and exchanges of information on by-product material subject to the Agreement will be limited to the following:

(1) Both Parties would comply with the provisions as contained in the IAEA document GOV/1999/19/ Rev.2, with regard to by-product material subject to the Agreement.

(2) With regard to tritium subject to the Agreement, the Parties will exchange annually information pertaining to its disposition for peaceful purposes consistent with Article 9 of this Agreement.

FOR THE GOVERNMENT OF THE UNITED STATES OF AMERICA:

FOR THE GOVERNMENT OF INDIA:

Note and Reference

1. Government of USA, Department of State, Office of the Spokesman, **Media Note 2007/658**, Washington D.C., 3 August 2007; http://www.state.gov/r/pa/prs/ps/2007/aug/90050.htm

APPENDIX III

MISSILE IMPORTS AND EXPORTS OF INDIA AND PAKISTAN[1]

I. India: Imports

Year/Date	Exporters	Items (s)	Remarks
(1)	(2)	(3)	(4)
Early 1960s	United States	Technical assistance	NASA trains Indian scientists from the Indian National Committee on Space Research (INCOSPAR) in the assembly, launch, and tracking of sounding rockets. India launches its first sounding rocket in 1963.
Early 1960s	France	Radars and sounding rockets	Centre National d'Etudes Spatiales (CNES) signs agreement with INCOSAPR in 1962 to supply radars and sounding rockets.
1962-1970	Undisclosed	Facilities for machining, tool-making, injection, molding, assembly, inspecting, carpentry, and electroplating	These facilities, acquired from undisclosed sources, give India the technological capability to produce anti-tank missiles.
1964-1965	France	Centaure sounding rocket technology	Agreement with Sud Aviation to produce Centaure sounding rockets in India under license.
1965-1969	France	Technical assistance	As part of the Centaure licensing agreement with Sud Aviation, Indian scientists receive practical training in

(Contd.)

Appendix 3 (*Contd.*)

(1)	(2)	(3)	(4)
			France. They also obtain a list that specifies the equipment needed for building rocket facilities.
1967	Soviet Union	Squadrons of SA-2 surface-to-air missile (SAM) batteries	These air-defense missiles were deployed around New Delhi and key airfields in northern India.
1969-1970	United States and France	Equipment for a solid-propellant space booster plant (SPROB)	India purchases equipment for the SPROB directly from US and French suppliers and constructs the facility itself.
1970	France	License to produce SSIIBI anti-tank missiles	M/s Aerospatiale (Nord Aviation) and India sign a licensing agreement in 1970. Bharat to produce 1,000 SSIIBI anti-tank missiles annually for 10 years.
Early 1970s	West Germany	Technical assistance	The West German Space Agency Deutsche Forschungs und Versuchsanstalt fuer Luft und Raumfahrt (DFVLR) helps the Indian Space and Research Organization (ISRO) design and build a high-altitude test facility that simulates near-vacuum conditions in space for testing the performance of upper stages of satellite launch vehicles.
1970-1972	France	Technical assistance	The French company Societe Europeene de Propulsion (SEP) helps ISRO build facilities and the six-component test stand for the Static Test & Evaluation Complex (STEX) in Sriharikota.
1970-1972	United Kingdom	16-ton vibration table and other machinery	The equipment was used to complete the STEX complex at Sriharikota.

1971	France, Western Europe, United States	Technical assistance	Sud Aviation of France trains Indian scientists in production of composite nozzles for Centaure sounding rockets. Indian scientists also visit other manufacturers and facilities in Western Europe and the United States to gain expertise in the manufacture of composites.
1972	United States	Missile gyros and calibrating equipment	The Defense Research and Development Laboratory (DRDL) imports gyros and equipment for the Valiant ballistic missile's inertial navigation system.
1973-1975	West Germany	Technical assistance	Indian scientists receive training from the West German space agency, DFVLR, in high-altitude testing, remote sensing techniques, microwaves, pulse code modulation (PCM) telemetry, and wind tunnel testing.
1973-1975	France	Technical assistance	Indian scientists study satellite launcher technology at facilities of the French Space Agency, CNES.
Mid-1970s	USA	Filament-winding machine	The DRDL imports this machine to aid in the manufacture of fiber-reinforced plastics for the Valiant ballistic missile's re-entry vehicle.
1978	France	Technical assistance	The French firm SEP provides blueprints and specifications for Viking [Indian designation "Vikas"] rocket engines. CNES agreed to share this information with ISRO in 1974.
February 1980	Soviet Union	Pechora surface-to-air missile batteries	India decides to procure Pechora missiles after canceling Project Devil, a program to reverse-engineer the SA-2 surface-to-air missile.
1982	West Germany	Technical assistance	West Germans assist India in constructing Viking liquid-engine test facilities.

(Contd.)

APPENDIX 3 (*Contd.*)

(1)	*(2)*	*(3)*	*(4)*
1982-1989	West Germany	Technical assistance	India acquires technical assistance for building a navigation system for satellites based on the Motorola microprocessor.
Late 1984	United States and United Kingdom	Valves, chips, and microprocessors (IGMDP).	Anticipating supplier controls, India purchases these stocks for the Integrated Guided Missile Development Program
Late 1984	France and Sweden	Gyros	Gyros are purchased for the IGMDP.
Late 1984	France	Hydraulic actuators	Hydraulic actuators are purchased for the IGMDP.
Late 1984	United States and West Germany	Computers, motion simulators, and three-axis machines	These materials are purchased for the IGMDP.
1985	United States	Six super minicomputers	The Reagan administration approves this sale but refuses India's request for two supercomputers due to fears of technology leakage.
1985	France	License agreement to produce Milan 2 anti-tank guided missiles (ATGM)	Production of the Milan 2 missile commences at Bharat Dynamics Limited (BDL) under license from M/s Euromissile.
Mid-1980s	Soviet Union	Elbrus computer system, computers	The Soviet Union agrees in 1984 to deliver a $20 million Elbrus computer system by 1985. Two high-powered computers are also ordered for defense and nuclear facilities.
Mid-1980s	West Germany	Six-axis filament-winding machine with computer controllers	Using a textile company as a front, India imports this machine to weave carbon fibers for the Agni Technology Demonstrator's re-entry vehicle.

Mid-1980s	United States	Equipment for impregnating graphite into carbon fibers	Using a front company, India purchases the equipment to develop carbon fibers for the Agni's re-entry vehicle.
September 1986	Soviet Union	12 SS-21 Tochka ballistic missiles with transporter-erector launchers	The CIA reports that a Soviet ship carrying this cargo was docked in an Indian port. India dismisses the allegation as "highly imaginative."
Late 1986	United States	Missile test range equipment	India signs contracts worth $6-7 million in October with the US companies Vitro and Scientific Atlanta.
Late 1987	United Kingdom	Sea-Eagle anti-ship missiles	India signs a contract on 26 November 1987 to procure Sea-Eagle missiles from the United Kingdom.
Late 1987	United States	Two Cray XMP 14 supercomputers	India plans to install one supercomputer in New Delhi and the other in Karnataka for meteorological forecasting purposes.
Early 1988	United States	Equipment for missile test range in Orissa	The United States clears the sale of equipment for India's missile test range in Orissa.
1989	Soviet Union	License to produce Konkurs ATGMs	India begins production of Konkurs ATGMs at BDL in Hyderabad.
1990s	Soviet Union/ Russia	Cryogenic engines for the Geo-synchronous Satellite Launch Vehicles (GSLV) and technical assistance	In January 1991, Glavkosmos agrees to supply ISRO with two cryogenic engines and the technology to make additional stages for Rs. 235 crore. By 1992 the United States imposes sanctions against both entities saying the deal violates the Missile Technology Control Regime (MTCR). Although Glavkosmos suspends the contract in 1993, ISRO claims that substantial cryogenic technology has already been transferred. A revised Glavkosmos-ISRO deal in the mid-1990s includes two cryogenic engines minus the technology transfer (two flight-worthy stages, two ground

(Contd.)

APPENDIX 3 (*Contd.*)

(1)	(2)	(3)	(4)
			models, and an option for three more cryogenic engines are also added to the contract). In addition, Glavkosmos modifies the payment amount to $128 million. By September 1998, the first cryogenic stage arrives in India.
1993	United States	One hot isostatic press	This press is exported by a US company through a Scottish subsidiary in violation of US export control laws. The press can be used to shape composites for missile nose cones.
Mid to Late 1990s	Russia	Technical assistance	The United States first accuses Russia of aiding India's "Sagarika" sea-launched ballistic missile program. Russia claims quasi-public research institutes are only providing underwater launch technology. As of April 1998, US sources were divided on whether Russian assistance violated the MTCR.
August 1997	Germany	1,000 kg consignment of aluminum-vanadium master alloy	Alloy used for building rockets and missiles. The consignment, originally ordered in 1994, is stolen in Mumbai after receipt.
Late 1990s-2003	Russia	Klub-S anti-ship cruise missiles	Russia completes the overhaul of two Indian Kilo-class submarines in 1999 and 2002. They are both refitted with Klub-S cruise missiles. A third Kilo-class submarine is currently being refitted.
1999	Israel	Eight Searcher-2 Unmanned Aerial Vehicles (UAV)	The Indian Army acquires UAVs from Israel for high-altitude reconnaissance.

1999-2003	Russia	Technology for PJ-10/ BrahMos supersonic cruise missile.	India and Russia sign an accord in 1999 to co-develop the BrahMos. The missile is currently undergoing flight trials.
Late 2000	Russia	ZM-54E Klub anti-ship cruise missiles	India reportedly buys 3M-54E Klub cruise missiles for $ 30 million.
2001-2003	Israel	Searcher-2 and Heron UAVs	India acquires an unspecified number of UAVs for approximately $300 million.
March 2001	Israel	One Green Pine Radar System	The radar is used to detect and track ballistic missile launches.
August 2001	Germany	Eight hydraulic cylinders missile launch vehicle.	These cylinders will likely be used for the Agni ballistic
September 2001	Israel	Barak anti-missile system	Following a two-year refitting, the aircraft carrier *INS Viraat* is declared combat ready. It is armed with the newly acquired Barak anti-missile system.
October 2002-2003	Israel	Eight Barak anti-missile systems	Delivery of these missiles is still in progress. The Barak anti-missile system will be deployed on naval vessels, in lieu of the canceled Trishul short-range SAM program.
December 2002	Russia	Pending: S-300V SAM system	Russia renews its offer to sell India S-300V SAMs. The sale has yet to materialize.
February 2003	Israel	Pending: Arrow II anti-missile system	The status of the sale is unclear due to opposition from the United States.
February 2003	Israel	Arrow II anti-missile system	India reportedly agrees in principle to invest $150-million in Israel's Arrow anti- missile program.

(*Contd.*)

APPENDIX 3 (Contd.)

(1)	(2)	(3)	(4)
March 2003	Former Soviet Union and other unnamed countries	Millimeter range wave image sensors	India reportedly attempting to recruit foreign scientists especially from the former Soviet Union to develop wave image sensors to be used in precision targeting systems for missiles.
March 2003	Germany	Hydraulic cylinders	German prosecutors order arrest of Peter L. and Michael L. of Montanhydraulik for violating German laws by illegally exporting nine consignments of hydraulic cylinders to India between 1997 and 2000. The cylinders, which were declared as bridge laying equipment, are used in the mobile launchers for the Agni-I and Agni-II missiles.
May 2003	United States	Patriot air defense system	India discusses potential purchase of the Patriot anti-missile system during visit of US Assistant Secretary of State for Arms Control Stephen G. Rademaker.
May 2003	Israel	Barak anti-missile system	India's Defense Ministry reportedly plans on purchasing 10 Barak anti-missile systems during next two years.
June 2003	United States	Missile defense systems	India discusses sale of high-technology equipment and modules of the missile defense shield with the United States.
June 2003	Unknown	Gravimeter	This imported device is capable of accurately measuring the gravitational pull 'g' to parts per billion and can be used in the development of missiles.

August 2003	United States	Patriot air defense system	Indian government requests technical information concerning the Patriot anti-missile system from the United States.
August 2003	United States; Israel	Arrow anti-missile system	India seeks US approval for participation in Israel's Arrow anti-missile system.
November 2003	United States	Master Information Exchange Agreement	India and the United States sign a Master Information Exchange Agreement that will allow the sharing of classified and technical information, including data on US experiments with anti-missile technology.
November 2003	Israel	Barak missile system	India and Israel sign $100 million deal for the transfer of third consignment of Barak missile system to India.
February 2004	United States	Accelerometers	US investigators uncover evidence that Asher Karni, the South African businessman facing felony charges for attempting to export nuclear bomb triggers to Pakistan, also tried to export accelerometers to an Indian company, Foretek Marketing Pvt. Limited. Accelerometers can be used in missile guidance systems.

(Contd.)

Appendix 3 (Contd.)

India: Exports

Year/Date	*Exporters*	*Items (s)*	*Remarks*
(1)	*(2)*	*(3)*	*(4)*
1975	France	Seventy 21U transducers	India delivers transducers for the French Ariane launch vehicle program under an agreement signed in 1974.
June 1992	Indonesia	One ton of ammonium perchlorate	This chemical is an oxidizing agent used in solid-propellant formulas. The ammonium perchlorate is sold to the Indonesian Space Agency.
April 1994	Global Tender	The following items are offered for sale: SAM-II guidance systems, 126 serviceable missiles, 35 SAM-II launchers, 92 liters of "O" fuel (nitric acid), 53, 124 liters of "G" fuel, and 20,785 liters of "IPN"	The Indian Air Force advertises these items for sale in international aviation journals. Although there is no indication that any such sale takes place, an Indian Air Force officer expresses concern that the sales would violate India's export policy.
September 1998 to February 2001	Iraq	10 consignments of prohibited materials including titanium vessels, spherical aluminum powder, titanium centrifugal pumps, and industrial cells with platinum anodes	The Indian company NEC Engineers Private Ltd. reportedly sells materials that could be used for the production of rocket solid fuel. The consignments' worth is estimated at $ 791,343.
December 1998	Politically friendly countries	Proposed: Trishul and Akash surface-to-air missiles (SAM)	Dr. A.P.J. Abdul Kalam, the principal scientific advisor to the Indian government, tells reporters that India will be

		and Nag anti-tank guided missiles (ATGM)	ready to sell tactical missiles in two years to "political friends." The short-range Prithvi ballistic missile, however, will not be exported.
April 2002	Friendly third-world countries	Proposed: PJ-10/BrahMos supersonic cruise missile	The BrahMos is expected to enter production by late 2003 or early 2004. Indian government officials say Brahmos exports will be restricted to "friendly third-world countries."
February 2003	Unspecified	Proposed: ATGMs, SAMs, and air-to-air missiles (AAAM)	BDL announces plans to jointly manufacture missiles for export with the European Aeronautical Defense and Space Company (EADS). The joint venture will produce ATGMs, SAMs, and AAAMs.
February 2003	Israel	Proposed: Lakshya unmanned aerial vehicle (UAV)	Israel and India are reportedly involved in price negotiations regarding the export of Lakshya UAVs. Israel has expressed interest in using the UAV as a targeting drone.
March 2003	International Defense Exhibition, Abu Dhabi (United Arab Emirates)	BrahMos supersonic anti-ship cruise missile	DRDO's Chief Controller of R&D Dr. Sivathanu Pillai says that India is exploring West and East Asian markets for exporting the BrahMos.
May 2003	New Delhi	Proposed: Exports of anti-tank missiles and sub-systems of the Prithvi ballistic missile	Indian government reportedly exploring possibilities of missile sales abroad. Some reports suggest that India may have already exported Prithvi ballistic missile sub-systems.

(*Contd.*)

Appendix 3 (*Contd.*)

(1)	*(2)*	*(3)*	*(4)*
October 2003	Iraq	Ten shipments of equipment that included titanium vessels and centrifugal pumps at an estimated value of $800,000	Indian police arrest Hans Raj Shiv, Director of NEC Engineers Pvt. Limited.
April 2004	Russia	Ship- and aircraft-borne versions of BrahMos supersonic cruise missile	The Indo-Russian joint-venture company BrahMos Aerospace Ltd. signs agreement with Russia's main arms export agency Rosoboronexport to market the BrahMos cruise missile in international markets.
September 2004	South Africa Defense Exposition	BrahMos supersonic cruise missile	India displays BrahMos supersonic cruise missile at the South African Defense Exposition.

(*Contd.*)

Appendix 3 (*Contd.*)

Pakistan: Imports

Year/Date	*Exporters*	*Items (s)*	*Remarks*
(1)	(2)	(3)	(4)
1992	China	Training M-11 ballistic missile and its accompanying transporter-erector-launcher vehicle	The transfer of a training missile suggests that operational missiles will follow. See entry for 1992.
31 January 1992	China	Guidance systems for M-11 ballistic missiles	Allegations concerning the transfer are refuted by China. See entries for 31 January 1992 and 5 February 1992.
1992	China	24 M-11 ballistic missiles	US intelligence agencies suggest that China might have transferred short-range missiles or modified the M-11 missiles to make them incapable of delivering nuclear warheads. See entries for 4 December 1992 and 6 May 1993.
March-May 1995	China	Components for missile systems	China denies reports of such transfers. See entries for June 1995 and 22 June 1995.
First week of March 1996	North Korea	15 tons (200 barrels) of ammonium perchlorate	Taiwanese officials discover the shipment at Kaohsiung harbor. The shipment is destined for Pakistan's Space and Upper Atmosphere Research Commission (SUPARCO). See entry for 12 March 1996.
Spring 1996	North Korea (Changowang Sinyong	Key components of either Nodong or Taepodong missiles, 12 to 25 Nodong	The items are supplied to the Khan Research Laboratories. See entry for Spring 1996.

(*Contd.*)

APPENDIX 3 (*Contd.*)

(1)	(2)	(3)	(4)
	Corporation)	missiles, and at least one transporter-erector-launch vehicle	
29 April 1996	North Korea	200 boxes of ammonium perchlorate	Hong Kong officials say the shipment's destination is SUPARCO. The shipment is sent by Lyongaksan, a North Korean firm controlled by the military. The shipment originated in North Korea and was shipped through China. See entries for 29 April 1996 and 13 December 1996.
1996	China (China Precision Machinery Import-Export Corporation)	Materials for building a missile factory, including crates suspected of containing machine tools for rocket motors, sophisticated equipment such as gyroscopes, accelerometers and on-board computers; technical assistance from engineers from the China Precision Machinery Import-Export Corporation	The missile factory is built at the Kala Chata mountain range near Fatehjung, 40 km west of Islamabad. The missile factory is designed as a "turn-key" facility to produce complete M-11 missiles. The agreement to build the factory was most likely reached between China and Pakistan in the late 1980s. See entries for last week of August 1996 and 27 August 1996.
13 December 1996	Unknown	10 tons of ammonium perchlorate	The shipment is destined for SUPARCO. Pakistan denies that the shipment's destination is SUPARCO. See the entry for 13 December 1996.

1997	North Korea	Maraging steel	A North Korean diplomat in Pakistan brokers a deal with a Russian firm to deliver maraging steel to Pakistan. The shipment is intercepted at Gatwick airport, London. See entry for 1997.
February-March 1998	North Korea, Changowang Sinyong Corporation	Nodong ballistic missiles	See entry for Fall 1997.
Mid-June 1998	North Korea	Missile warhead canisters and missile production components	See entry for Mid-June 1998.
Fall 1998	North Korea	Weapons-grade Russian steel	The shipment is made by North Korea's Changowang Sinyong Corporation. See entry for 20 September 1998.
March 1999	China	Metal-working presses and a special furnace	China's Poly Ventures Co. transferred the US-manufactured equipment to a missile production facility in Pakistan's National Development Complex. See entry for March 1999.
25 June 1999	North Korea	Ten sets of "rolled steel metal frustum" for reinforcing missile nose cones, "plate bending machines" that can be used to roll plates needed for making rocket motor casings, a heavy-duty press along with sophisticated lathes, torroidal air bottles that can be used to produce	The North Korean ship, *Ku Wol San*, carrying the equipment is seized by Indian authorities at Kandla port in Gujarat, India. Indian authorities allege that the shipment is destined fro Pakistan. See entries for 25 June 1999, 4 July 1999, 6 July 1999, 7 July 1999 and 10 July 1999.

(*Contd.*)

APPENDIX 3 (*Contd.*)

(1)	(2)	(3)	(4)
		maneuverable warheads, two sets of theodolites, a digital micron soldering device, water refining and filtration machinery that can be used for making nuclear weapons and also washing missile cones, equipment needed for precision welding, and 1.5 mm forged steel bars	
2000	China	Missile command system (CT-101) and fuel improvement ventilation system	The equipment will be useful for ensuring better control and guidance for Ghauri-II and Shaheen-II missiles. See entry for 2000.
January 1999 to June 2000	China	Specialty steel, guidance systems, and technical expertise	US officials claim that Chinese assistance continues despite China's assurances of stopping its missile-related assistance to Pakistan. See entry for Last Week of June 2000.
July 2001	North Korea	Ballistic missile parts	The missile parts are shipped using a Pakistani C-130 aircraft. US officials are not sure whether the aircraft brought nuclear materials from Pakistan. See entry for July 2001.
January-June 2001	China	Missile parts for Shaheen I and Shaheen-II missiles	China sends a dozen shipments of missile parts. See entry for 6 August 2001.

January 2002	China	Military hardware including missiles	See entry for 8 January 2002.
2002	China	Guidance and control systems, solid fuel, and M-4X missile variants	See entry for 12 January 2002.

Pakistan : Export: N.A.

*_Source_ : Government of India, Department of Space, Annual Reports of Various Years; Government of India, Ministry of Defence, Annual Reports of Various Years; Natural Resources Defense Council, New York;http://www.nrdc.org/nuclear/southasia.asp; Anupam Srivastava and Seema Gahlaut, "Curbing Proliferation from Emerging Suppliers: Export Controls in India and Pakistan", _Arms Control Today_, September 2003, http://www.armscontrol.org/; Shishir Gupta, "The Indian Connection", _India Today_, 14 October 2002, http://www.india-today.com/; and Bill Gertz, Betrayal: How the Clinton Administration Undermined American Security, Regnery Publishing Inc., Washington DC, 1999.

Bibliography

Primary Sources

A.K. Antony, Defence Minister of India, *Security Dynamics in South East Asia: Emerging Threats and Responses,* (Special Address at 9th Security Conference), IDSA Auditorium, New Delhi, 9 February 2007; http://www.idsa.in/speeches_at_ idsa/DefenceMinisterSpeech090207.htm

Abdul Sattar, Pakistani foreign minister, (Address) Carnegie International Non-proliferation Conference, Washington D.C., 18-19 June 2001, *Disarmament Diplomacy,* Issue No. 58, June 2001; http://www.acronym.org.uk/www.acronym.org.uk/dd/dd58/58 docs6.htm

Agreement on the Prohibition of Attack Against Nuclear Installations and Facilities, Signed on December 31, 1988, Islamabad. Instrument of Ratification Exchanged in December 1990; http://www.indianembassy.org/South_Asia/Pakistan/Prohibition_ Attack_Nuclear_Dec_31_1988.html

Air Chief Marshall S. Krishnaswamy, *Challenges to National Security over the Next Decade: A Perspective,* (Speech), IDSA Auditorium, New Delhi, 11 November 2004; http://www.idsa.in/speeches_at_idsa/krishnaswamy lecture foundationday2004.htm

Birla, N.C. and Murthy, B.S., eds., *Indian Defence Technology: Missile Systems,* DRDO, Ministry of Defence, Government of India, New Delhi, December 1998.

Brasstacks and Beyond : Perception and Management of crises in South Asia", *Acids Research Report,* Programmes in Arms

Control, Disarmament of International Security, University of Illinois at Urbana-Champaign, Urbana, 1995.

Central Intelligence Agency, *Acquisition of Technology Relating to Weapons of Mass Destruction and Advanced Conventional Munitions,* Unclassified Report to Congress, 1 July-31 December 2003.

Central Intelligence Agency, *Acquisition of Technology Relating to Weapons of Mass Destruction and Advanced Conventional Munitions,* Unclassified Report to Congress, 1 January-30 June 2001.

Davis, William A. Jr., *Regional Security and Anti-Tactical Ballistic Missiles: Political and Technical Issues,* Special Report, Institute for Foreign Policy Analysis, Inc. Cambridge, 1986.

Feickert, Andrew and Kronstadt, K Alan, "Missile Proliferation and the Strategic Balance in South Asia", *CRS Report RL 32115,* 17 October 2003.

Foreign Affairs, Vol. XLVII, No. 6, June 1998.

Foreign Affairs, Vol. XLLVII, No. 7-8, June-August, 1998.

Foreign Affairs, Vol. XLVII, No. 9-10, September, 1998.

George Fernandes, Indian Defence Minister, *Asian Security in the 21st Century,* (Address) 2nd International Conference, Institute for Defence Studies and Analysis, New Delhi, 24-25 January 2000.

George W. Bush, US President, *New Measures to Counter the Threat of WMD,* (Remarks) Fort Lesely J. McNair National Defense University, Washington D.C., 11 February 2004; http://www.whitehouse.gov/news/releases/2004/02/20040211-4.html

Glasstone, Samuel and Dolan, Philip, *The Effects of Nuclear Weapons,* US Department of Defense, 1977.

Government of India, Ministry of Defence. *IGMDP Update,* New Delhi, 1996.

Government of India, Department of Space, *Annual Reports, 1998-99 to 2006-07,* New Delhi, Respective Years.

Government of India, Department of Space, *Space Programme till 2000 A.D.,* New Delhi, 1988.

Government of India, *Draft Nuclear Doctrine,* National Security Advisory Board, 17 August 1999; http://www.indiagov.org/govt/indnucld.htm.

Government of India, *Lok Sabha Debates,* 1998-2006.

Government of India, Ministry of Defence, *Annual Financial Statement,* Expenditure Budget: Various Years.

Government of India, Ministry of Defence, *Annual Reports, 1998-99 to 2006-07,* New Delhi, Respective Years.

Government of India, Ministry of Defence, *Report of the Comptroller and Auditor General,* March 1997.

Government of India, Ministry of Defence, Standing Committee on Defence, *Report of various years.*

Government of India, Ministry of External Affairs, Annual Reports 1998-99 to 2006-07, New Delhi, Respective Years.

Government of India, Ministry of External Affairs, *Joint Statement, India-Pakistan Expert-Level Talks on Nuclear CBMs,* 20 June 2004, at http://meaindia.gov.in

Government of India, *Rajya Sabha Debates,* 1998-2006.

Government of Pakistan, Ministry of Defence, *Defence Year Book,* 2003-04.

Government of Pakistan, *National Assembly Debates,* 1998-2006.

Government of USA, *Imposition of Missile Proliferation Sanctions Against a North Korean Entity,* Federal Register, Department of State, Vol. 68, No. 63, 2 April 2003.

Government of USA, *Imposition of Missile Proliferation Sanctions Against Entities in Iran and North Korea,* Federal Register, Department of State, Volume 61, Number 114, 12 June 1996.

Government of USA, *Imposition of Missile Proliferation Sanctions Against Entities in North Korea and Pakistan,* Federal Register, Department of State, Volume 63, Number 85, 4 May 1998.

Government of USA, *Proliferation Threat and Response,* Office of the Secretary of Defense, US Department of Defense, January 2001.

Government of USA, *Understanding Radiation: Health Effects,* US Environmental Protection Agency, 3 December 2002.

India's Nuclear Weapons Update 2003, The Risk Report, prepared by Wisconsin Project on Nuclear Arms Control, Vol. 9, No. 5, September-October 2003.

International Military and Defence Encyclopedia, Brassy, Inc., various years

Jonathan Medalia, *Nuclear Terrorism: A Brief Review of Threats and Responses*, CRS Report for Congress, Congressional Research Services, RL 32595, September 22, 2004.

K. Natwar Singh, External Affairs Minister of India, *India and the NPT*, (Speech), India International Center Auditorium, New Delhi, 28 March 2005; http://www.idsa.in/speeches_at_idsa/NatwarSingh280305.htm

Kargil Review Committee Report, Tabled in Parliament on 23 February 2000; http://nuclearweaponarchive.org/India/KargilRCB.html

Kofi Annan, UN Secretary General, *Nuclear Non-Proliferation Treaty Faces Crises of Compliance and Confidence*, (Address) SG/SM/10466, University of Tokyo, Tokyo, 18 May, 2006; http://www.un.org/News/Press/docs/2006/sgsm10466.doc.htm

Koonin, Steven E., *"Radiological Terrorism"*, Prepared Statement before the Senate Foreign Relations Committee, USA, 6 March 2002.

Kristensen, Hans M. and Handler, Joshua, "World Nuclear Forces", in Armament, Disarmament and International Security: *SIPRI Year Book*, OUP, Oxford, 2002.

Margaret Bccket, Secretary of State for Foreign and Commonwealth Affairs, United Kingdom, *A World Free from Nuclear Weapons?* (Key Note Address), Carnegie Endowment for International Peace, 25 June 2007. http://www.carnegieendowment. org/events/index.cfm?fa=eventDetail&id=1004&&prog=zgp&proj=znpp

Norris, Robert S. and Arkin,William M., "Tables of Nuclear Forces", in Armament, Disarmament and International Security: *SIPRI Year Book*, OUP, Oxford, 1999.

Nuclear safety, nuclear stability and nuclear strategy in Pakistan, A concise report of a visit by Landau Network, Arms control Italian Institution Landau Network-Centro Volta, Como, Italy, Draft version January 14, 2002; http://lxmi.mi.infn.it/~landnet /Doc/pakistan.pdf

Paul Keating, former Prime Minister of Australia, *Eliminating Nuclear Weapons: A survival Guide for the Twenty first Century*, (Speech) Issue No. 32, University of New South Wales, Sydney, 25 November 1998.

Shyam Saran, Foreign Secretary of India, *Nuclear Non-Proliferation in International Security*, (Speech), India Habitat Center, New Delhi, 24 October 2005; http://www.idsa.in/speeches_at_idsa/ShyamSaran241005.ht

Sipri Armament and Disarmament Year Books, 1998 to 2006.

The Military Balance, 2003-04, IISS, London, 2003.

U.N., Comprehensive Test Ban Treaty Organisation, *Annual Report, 2006*, Vienna, 2007.

UN, *General Assembly Resolution 3265 (XXIX)*, 9 December 1974, 2309th Plenary Meeting, 29th Session of the UN General Assembly.

UN, *Illicit Trafficking and Theft of Nuclear Material: A Persistent Problem"*, UN Report, 12 September, 2007.

UN, *India and Pakistan's Nuclear Test*, UN Security Council Resolution, S/RES/1172, 6 June 1998.

UN, Mohamed El Baradei, IAEA Director General, *Putting Teeth in the Nuclear Non-Proliferation and Disarmament Regime*, (Statement) Karlsruche Lecture, IAEA, Vienna, 25 March, 2006;http://www.iaea.org/News Center/Statements/2006/ebsp 2006n004.html

UN, *Security Council Resolution*, S/RES/1737, Adopted by Security Council at its 5612th meeting, 23 October, 2006.

UN, *The Radiological Accident in Goiania*, International Atomic Energy Agency, Vienna, 1988.

Secondary Sources

Books

Adams, Benson D., *Ballistic Missile Defense*, American Elsevier Publishing Co., New York, 1971.

Ahmad, Samina and Cotright, David, *South Asia at Nuclear Crossroad*, Fourth Freedom Forum, Joan B. Kroach Institute for International Peace Studies, Managing the project at Harvard University, March 2001.

Ahmed, Samrina and Cortright, David, ed., *Pakistan and the Bomb: Public Opinion and Nuclear Options*, University of Notre Damma Press, Notre Dame, 1998.

Alam, Mohammed B., ed., *Essays on Nuclear Proliferation*, Vikas, New Delhi, 1995.

Albright, David, "India's and Pakistan's Fissile Materials and Nuclear Weapons Inventories, end of 1999", *Institute for Science and International Security*, 11 October 2000.

Armstrong, David and Trento, Joseph, *America and the Islamic Bomb: The Deadly Compromise*, Steerforth, 2007.

Arnett, Eri H., ed., *Proliferation of Ballistic Missiles: Policy Options for the Future*, New Orbans, Louisiana, 1990.

Ashraf, Tariq Mahmud, *Aerospace Power : The Emerging Strategic Dimension*, PAF Book Club, Peshawar, 2003.

Ashraf, Tariq Mahmood "Air Power Imbalance and Strategic Instability in South Asia", *Conference on Strategic Stability in South Asia*, National Postgraduate School, Monterey, CA, 30 June-1 July, 2004, Cooperative Monitoring Centre, Sandia National Laboratory, Albuquerque, 2005 http://www.cmc.sandia.gov/cmc-papers/ sand2005-4957.pdf

Banerjee, Jyotirmoy, *Nuclear World: Defence and Politics of Major Powers*, Manas, New Delhi, 2002.

Barnaby, C.F. and Boserup, A., eds., *Implications of Ballistic Missile Systems*, Souvenir Press, London, 1969.

Barnaby, Frank, eds., *Plutonium and Security—The Military Aspects of Plutonium Economy*, Macmillan, London, 1992.

Basanaby, Frank and Bory, Marlies, ed., *Emerging Technologies and Military Doctrine—A Political Assessment*, Macmillan Press, Houndmills, 1986.

Battle, Joyce, *India and Pakistan on Nuclear Threshold*, Electronic Book, No. 6, US documents, National Security Archive, 1998.

Beg, Aslam, *India and Pakistan Security Perspective*, Foundation for Research on National Development and Security, Rawalpindi, 1994.

Behera, Ajay Darshan, and Mathew Joseph C., eds., *Pakistan in a Changing Strategic Context*, Knowledge World, New Delhi, 2004.

Belons, Vladimir, *Star Wars or Star Peace*? Allied Publishers, New Delhi, 1988.

Bernstein, Jermy, *Nuclear Weapons: What You Need to Know*, Cambridge University Press, London, 2007.

Bhatia, Shyam, *India's Nuclear Bomb*, Vikas Publishing House, Sahibabad, 1979.

Bidwai, Praful and Vanaik, Achin, *South Asia on a Short Fuse*, Oxford University Press, New Delhi, 2002.

Bior, Plund Elis, *International Atomic Policy*, George Allen and Unwin, London, 1956.

Birtles, Philip and Beaver, Paul, *Missile Systems*, Ian Allan Ltd. Shepperton, 1985.

Blair, Bruce, *The Logic of Accidental Nuclear War*, Brookings Institution Press, Washington DC, 1993.

Blair, Bruce G., *Global Zero Alert for Nuclear Forces*, Brookings Institution Press, Washington DC, 1995.

Bottome, Edgar N., *The Missile Gap: A Study of the Formulation of Military and Political Policy*, Fairleigh Dickinson University Press, Rutherford, 1971

Bracken, Paul J., *The Command and Control of Nuclear Forces*, Yale University Press, New Haven, 1983.

Brennan, Donald G., ed., *Arms Control and Disarmament*, Janathan Cape, London 1961.

Bundy, McGeorge, *Danger and Survival*, Affiliated East-West Press, New Delhi, 1989.

Carter, Ashton B. and Schwartz, David N., eds., *Ballistic Missile Defense*, The Brookings Institutions, Washington DC, 1984.

Carter, Ashton B. *et al.*, eds., *Managing Nuclear Operations*, The Brooking Institution, Washington DC, 1987.

Chand, Attar, *Global Nuclear Politics*, Udh Publishers, Delhi, 1983.

Chanin, David and Murfin, Walter, *Site Restoration: Estimation of Attributable Costs From Plutonium-Dispersal Accidents*, Sandia National Laboratory Report, SAND96-0957, May 1996.

Chawla, Sudershan and Sardesai, D.R., ed., *Changing Patterns of Security and Stability in Asia*, Prayer Publishers, New York, 1980.

Charles D. Ferguson *et al.*, *Commercial Radioactive Sources: Surveying the Security Risks*, Monterey Institute of International Studies, Monterey, California, January 2003; http://cns.miis.edu/pubs/opapers/op11/op11.pdf

Chayes, Abram and Wigner, Jerome, B., eds., *ABM: An Evaluation*, Harper and Row Publishers, New York, 1969.

Chengappa, Raj, *Weapons of Peace : The Secret Story of India's Quest to be a Nuclear Power*, Harper Collins, New Delhi, 2000.

Cirincione, Joseph, *Bomb Scare: The History and Future of Nuclear Weapons*, Columbia University Press, Columbia, 2007.

Cirincione, Joseph, *Deadly arsenals : Tracking Weapons of Mass Destruction*, Carnegie Endowment for International Peace, Washington D.C., 2002.

Cochran, Thomas B. and Paine, Christopher, E., *Hydronuclear Testing and The Comprehensive Test Ban: Memorandum to Participants*, Natural Resources Defense Council, Washington D.C. *Summer 1994*.

Colonel, Guy, and B., Roberts, *Elegant Irrelevance: The Anti-Ballistic Missile Treaty in the New World Disorder*, New War College, New Port, November, 1994.

Das, Jita, *National and International Perceptions of India's Guided Missile Programme*, Unpublished, CPS/SSS, JNU, New Delhi, 1990.

Davis, Jacquelyn K., *et. al.*, eds., *Air/Missile Defense, Counter-proliferation and Security Policy Planning*, The Emirates Centre for Strategic Studies and Research, Abu Dhabi, 1999.

Dixit, J.N., *India's Foreign Policy 1947-2003*, Picus Books, New Delhi, 2003.

Dixit, J.N., *India-Pakistan in War and Peace*, Book's Today, New Delhi, 2002.

Dunn, David H., *The Politics of Threat*, Macmillan Press, London, 1997.

Feld, B.T., *et. al.*, eds., *Impact of New Technologies on the Arms Race*, MIT Press, Massachusetts, 1971.

Ferguson, Charles, *et al.*, *Commercial Radioactive Sources: Surveying the Security Risks*, Monterey Institute of International Studies, January 2003.

Findlay, Trevor ed., *Chemical Weapons and Missile Proliferation*, Lynne Thenner Publishers, Colorado, 1991.

Frey, Karsten, *India's Nuclear Bomb and National Security*, Routledge, New York, 2006.

Ganguly, Sumit, *Conflict Unending : Indo-Pakistan Tensions Since 1947*, Columbia University Press, New York, 2001.

Garnell, P. and East, D.J., *Guided Weapon Control Systems*, Pergamon Press, Oxford, 1977

Gertz, Bill, *Betrayal: How the Clinton Administration Undermined American Security*, Regnery Publishing, Inc., Washington, DC 1999.

Goldstein, Joshna S., *International Relations*, Pearson Education, New Delhi, 2003.

Gregory, Shaun, *The Hidden Cost of Deterrence: Nuclear Weapons Accidents*, Brassey's, London, 1990.

Gupta, Rakesh, ed., *SDI: Aims, Implications and Response*, Panchsheel Publishers, New Delhi, 1988.

Halperin, Morton H., *Contemporary Military Strategy*, Faber and Faber, London, 1968.

Hegerty, Devin T., *The Consequences of Nuclear Proliferation: Lessons from South Asia*, The MIT Press, Cambridge MA, 1998.

Holst, Johan J. and Schneider, William, Jr., eds., *Why ABM?* Pergamon Press, New York, 1969.

Jacob, Lt. Gen. J.F.R., *Surrender at Dacca: Birth of a Nation*, Manohar, New Delhi, 1997.

Jain, B.M. and Hexamer, Eva-Maria, eds., *Nuclearisation in South Asia: Reactions and Responses*, Rawat Publications, Jaipur, 1999.

Jain, Tariq, ed., *Pakistan's Security and the Nuclear Option*, Institute of Policy Studies, Islamabad, 1995.

Jastrow, Robert, *How to Make Nuclear Weapons Obsolete*, Little Brown and Co., Boston, 1983.

Jensen, Gordon E. and Netzer, David W., eds., *Tactical Missile Propulsion*, Vol. 170, American Institute of Aeronautics and Astronautics, Inc., Virginia, 1996.

Johnstone, Diana, *The Politics of Euro-Missiles*, Verso, London, 1984.

Jones, Rodney W., *et. al.*, *Tracking Nuclear Proliferation: A Guide in Maps and Charts, 1998*, Carnegie Endowment for International Peace, Washington DC, 1998.

Jones, Rodney W., "Force Modernization Trends: India and Pakistan", *Conventional Arms Modernization in Asia and the Pacific*, Asia Pacific Centre for Security Studies, Honolulu.

Jones, Rodney W., "*Minimum Nuclear Deterrence Postures in South Asia—An Overview*", Final Report by Policy Architects International for DTRA/ASCO, October 2001.

Jones, Rodney W., "Military Asymmetry and Instability in Emerging Nuclear States: India and Pakistan", *Fourth Nuclear Stability Round Table on 'Strategic Stability and Global Change*, Policy Architects International, Washington D.C, 12-13March 2002.

Joseph, Carleon, ed., *Tactical Missile Warheads*, Vol. 155, American Institute of Aeronautics and Artonautics, Inc., Washington DC, 1993.

Kalam, A.P.J. Abdul, *Wings of Fire: An Autobiography*, Universities Press (India) Limited, Hyderabad 1999.

Karp, Aaron, *Ballistic Missile Proliferation—The Politics and Technique*, Oxford University Press, New York, 1996.

Kaushik, Brij Mohan and Mehrotra, O.N., *Pakistan's Nuclear Bomb*, Sopan, New Delhi, 1980.

Khera, S.S., *India's Defence Problem*, Orient Longmans, Bombay, 1968.

Kothari, Smitu and Mian, Zia, eds., *Out of the Nuclear Shadow*, Lokayan and Rainbow Publishers, New Delhli, 2001.

Krepon, Michael and Gagne, Chris, eds., *The Stability-Instability Paradox : Nuclear Weapons and Brinkmanship in South Asia*, The Henry, L. Stimson Centre, Washington D.C., June 2001.

Krepon, Michel *et al.*, eds., *Escalation Control and Nuclear Option in South Asia*, The Henry, L. Stmson Center, Washington D.C., November 2004.

Krishna, Ashok and Chari, P.R., eds., *Kargil : The Tables Turned*, Manohar, New Delhi, 2001.

Kumar, A. *et. al.*, *Safety and Security of Radioactive Materials—The Indian Scenario*, Bhabha Atomic Research Center, Trambay, Mumbai, 1998.

Lavoy, Peter, *et. al.*, ed., *Planning The Unthinkable*, Cornell University Press, Ithaca, New York, 2000.

LeGalley, Donald P., ed., *Ballistic Missile and Space Technology*, Academic Press, New York, 1960.

Levi, Barbara G., *et. al.*, *The Future of Land Based Strategic Missiles*, American Institute of Physics, New York, 1989.

Lewis, William H. and Johnson, Stuart E., eds., *Weapons of Mass Destruction : New Perspective on Counter-proliferation*, National Defence University Press, Washington D.C., 1995.

Long, Franklin A., *et. al.*, eds., *Weapons in Space*, W.W. Norton and Company, New York, 1986.

Lowell, Dittmer, ed., *South Asia's Nuclear Security Dilemma: India, Pakistan and China*, M.E. Shape, New York, 2005.

Luongo, Thenneth, N., ed., *Advances in the SDI Programme: Prospects for Development and Implications for the ABM Treaty*, The Proceedings from a Congressional Seminar, AAAS Programme on Science, Arms Control and National Security, Washington DC, May 14, 1987.

Malhothra, Shikha, *Challenges to India's Security : A Study of Its Perceptions and Nuclear Response*, unpublished, Ph.D. Thesis, Department of Political Science, University of Jammu, Jammu, 2004.

Malhotra, Vinay Kumar, *Nuclear and Missile Race in South Asia*, Wisdom House Publications Ltd., Leeds, 2001.

Matto, Amitab, ed., *India's Nuclear Deterrent: Pokhran-II and Beyond*, Har Anand, New Delhi, 1999.

Melkote, Rama S., ed., *Indian Ocean—Issues for Peace*, Manohar Publishers, New Delhi, 1995.

Mian, Zia, *Pakistan's Atomic Bomb and the Search for Security*, Gautam Publishers, Lahore, 1995.

Mukunda, H.S and Krishnamurty, A.V, eds., *Recent Advances in Aerospace Sciences and Engineering*, Interline Publishing, Bangalore, 1992.

Nair, Vijay, *Nuclear India*, Spencer and Lancer, Hartford, WI, 1992.

Navias, Martin S., *Going Ballistic: The Build of Missiles in the Middle East*, Brassey's Ltd., London, 1993.

Nolan, Janne E., *Trappings of Power: Ballistic Missiles in the Third World*, Washington DC, 1991.

Oberg, James E., *Uncovering Soviet Disasters*, Random House, New York, 1988.

Palit, D.K. and Namboodri, P.K.S., *Pakistan's Islamic Bomb*, Vikas, New Delhi, 1979.

Pelmar, Norman, *Strategic Weapons: An Introduction*, Russak and Co., New York, 1982.

Perkovich, George, *India's Nuclear Bomb : The Impact on Global Proliferation*, OUP, New Delhi, 2000.

Perrow, Charles, *Normal Accidents: Living with High-Risk Technologies*: Basic Books, New York, 1984.

Pfaltzgraff, Jr., Robert, L., ed., *Security Strategy and Missile Defence*, Institute for Foreign Policy Analysis, Brassy's, Virginia, 1996.

Pierre, Andrew J., *Nuclear Politics*, Oxford University Press, London, 1972.

Podvig, Pavel, ed., *Russian Strategic Nuclear Forces*, MA: The MIT Press, Cambridge, 2001.

Potter, William C. and Jencks, Harlen, eds., "*The International Missile Bazaar: The New Suppliers Network*, Westview Press, Boulder, Colorado, 1993.

Rajan, Arpit, *Nuclear Deterrence in Southern Asia: China, India and Pakistan*, Sage, New Delhi, 2005.

Rajgopalan, Rajesh, *Second Strike: Arguments about Nuclear War in South Asia*, Penguine, New Delhi, 2005.

Ramana, M.V., *Bombing Bombay: Effects of Nuclear Weapons and a Case Study of a Hypothetical Explosion*, International Physicians for the Prevention of Nuclear War, Cambridge, U.S.A., 1999.

Ramnusino, Polo Cotta and Martellini, Maurizio, *Nuclear Safety, Nuclear Stability and Nuclear Strategy in Pakistan*, Landau, Network, Como, January 2002.

Rao, P.V.R., *Defence Without Drift*, Popular Prakashan, Bombay, 1970

Ray, J.K., *Security in the Missile Age*, Allied Publishers, Bombay, 1967.

Raza, Maroof, *Three Wars and No Peace over Kashmir*, Lancers, New Delhi, 1996.

Sachdev, A.K., *Space Age Gladiators: Surface to Surface Missiles and Air Strategy: An Indian Viewpoint*, Knowledge World in Association with IDSA, New Delhi, 2000.

Sagan, Scott D. and Waltz, Kenneth N., *The Spread of Nuclear Weapons: A Debate*, W.W. Norton, New York, 1995.

Sagan, Scott, *The Limits of Safety: Organizations, Accidents and Nuclear Weapons*, Princeton University Press, Princeton, 1993.

Sardesai, D.R. and Thomas Raju G.C., eds., *Nuclear India in the Twenty First Century*, Palgrave-Macmillan, New York, 2002.

Shah, A.B., ed., *India's Defence and Foreign Policies*, Manaktalas, Bombay, 1966.

Shaker, Mahmed I., *The Nuclear Non-Proliferation Treaty : Origin and Implementation, 1959-79*, 3 Vols., Oceana, New York, 1980.

Shneydor, N.A., *Missile Guidance and Pursuit: Kinematics, Dynamics and Control*, Harwood Publishing Ltd., Chichester, 1998.

Simon, Jeffrey, ed., *Security Implications of SDI*, National Defense University Press, Washington, DC. 1990.

Singh, Jasjit, ed., *Kargil 1999: Pakistan's Fourth War for Kashmir*, Knowledge World, New Delhi, 1999.

Singh, Jasjit, ed., *Nuclear India*, Knowledge World, New Delhi, 1998.

Singh, Jasjit, *The Balance of Power in South Asia*, Emirates Center for Strategic Studies and Research, Abu Dhabi, 2002.

Singh, Lt. Gen. Harbaksh, *War Dispatches : Indo-Pak Conflict, 1965*, Lancers, New Delhi, 1991.

Sinha, K.K., ed., *Problems of Defence of South and East Asia*, Manaktalas, Bombay, 1969.

Sood, V.K. and Sawhney, Pravin, *Operation Prakram: The War Unfinished*, Sage, New Delhi, 2003.

Subrahmanyam, K., *Perspectives in Defence Planning*, Abhinav Publications, New Delhi, 1972.

Subrahmanyam, K., ed., *Nuclear Myths and Realities*, ABC Publishing House, New Delhi, 1981.

Sutton, George P., *Rocket Propulsion Elements: An Introduction to the Engineering of Rockets*, John Wiley and Sons, New York, 1992.

Swicker, Charles C., *Theater Ballistic Missile Defense From the Sea*, The New Port Papers, 14th in Series, Naval War College Press, New Port, Rhode Island, 1998.

Syed, Fashar H., ed., *Nuclear Disarmament and Conventional Arms Control Including Light Weapons*, Friends, Rawalpindi, 1997.

Tellis, Ashley J., *India's Emerging Nuclear Posture : Between Recessed Deterrent and Ready Arsenal*, RAND, Santa Monica, 2001.

Tellis, Ashley J., *Stability in South Asia*, CA: RAND, Santa Monica, 1997.

Thomas, Raju G.C. and Gupta, Amit, eds., *India's Nuclear Security*, Vistaar Publications, New Delhi, 2000.

Vasil, Yev, B.A., *Long Range Missile Equipped: A Soviet Review*, Published under the Auspices of The United States Air Force, Moscow, 1972.

Wiberg, H., Petersen, I.D. and Smoker P., eds., *Inadvertent Nuclear War: The Implications of the Changing Global Order*, Pergamon Press, Oxford, 1993.

Yost, David S., *Soviet Ballistic Missile Defense and the Western Alliance*, Harvard University Press, Cambridge, 1988.

Zarchan, Paul, ed., *Tactical and Strategic Missile Guidance*, American Institute of Aeronautics and Astronautics Inc., Vol. 176, Virginia,1997.

Articles

Abrams, Herbert L., "Human Reliability and Safety in the Handling of Nuclear Weapons", *Science and Global Security*, Vol. 2, 1991.

Ahmad Khan, Munir, "Nuclearisation of South Asia and its Regional and Global Implications", *Regional Studies*, Vol. 16, No. 4, Autumn, 1998.

Ahmad, Babar, "Pakistan: Tests May Not Include Cruise Missile Tests", *Defencetalk*, September 8, 2004.

Ahmadullah, Mohammad, "Prithvi and Beyond: India's Ballistic Missile Programmes", *Military Technology*, Vol. 23, No. 4, 1999.

Ahrari, Whson, "South Asia Faces the Future with a Clean Strategic State", *Jane's Intelligence Review*, Vol. 18, No. 2, December 1998.

Alam, Aftab, "Nuclearisation in South Asia", *Third Concept*, Vol. 11, No. 127, September 1997.

Allison, Graham T. Jr. *et. al.*, eds., "A Primer for the Nuclear Age", *Occasional Paper*, No. 6, Center for Science and International Affairs, Harvard University, Cambridge, 1990.

Anderson, Jack; and Van Atta, Dale, "North Korea Aids Iran's War of Terror", *The Washington Post*, February 3, 1986.

Arkin, William and Handler, Joshua, "Naval Accidents, 1945-1988", *Neptune Paper*, No. 3, Greenpeace and The Institute for Policy Studies, Washington, D.C., 1989.

Ayoob, Mohammed, "India and South Asia: The Quest for Regional Predominance", *World Policy Journal*, Vol. 7, No. 1, Winter, 1989-90.

Bailey, Kathleen, "Can Missile Proliferation Be Reversed?", *Orbis*, Winter, 1991.

Banerjee, Jyotirmoy, "Pokharan-II: Fallout and Implications", *World Affairs*, Vol. 3, No. 3, July-September 1999.

Banerjie, Indranil, "Integrated Guided Missile Development Programme", *Indian Defence Review*, July 1990.

Baskaran, A., "Export Control Regimes and India's Space and Missile Programme", *India Quaterly*, Vol. LVIII, Nos. 3&4, July-December 2002.

Basrur, Rajesh M. and Rizvi, Hasan-Askari, "Nuclear Terrorism and South Asia", Cooperative Monitoring Centre, *Occasional Paper SAND 98-0505/25*, Sandia National Laboratories, 2003.

Basrur, Rajesh M., "Nuclear Weapons and Indian Strategic Cultural", *Peace Research*, Vol. 38, No. 2, March 2001.

Baveja, Harinder, "Ghauri-Fire in the Sky", *India Today*, Vol. 23, No. 16, 14-20 April 1998.

Bedi, Rahul, "Agni-II IRBM: Built to Carry Nuclear Warhead", *Jane's Defence Weekly*, Vol. 31, No. 17, 28 April 1999.

Bedi, Rahul, "India Pressured to Halt Prithvi Production", *Jane's Defence Weekly*, 15 April 1995.

Bedi, Rahul, "Pakistan's First Test of its New Ballistic Missile", *Jane's Defense Weekly*, Vol. 29, No. 15, 15 April 1998.

Beri, Ruchita, "Challenges of Proliferation and the Existing Control Regimes", *Strategic Analysis*, 19 January 1994.

Beri, Ruchita, "Ballistic Missile Proliferation", *Asian Strategic Review, 1991-92*, August 1992.

Beri, Ruchita, "Why does Missile Proliferation Matter?" *Strategic Analysis*, November 1992.

Bermudez, Joseph S., "A History of Ballistic Missile Development in the DPRK", *Occasional Paper*, No. 2, Center for Non-proliferation Studies, Monterey, 1999.

Bermudez, Joseph S., "A History of Ballistic Missile Development in the DPRK", *Monterey Institute of*

International Studies, Center for Non-proliferation Studies, Occasional Paper, No. 2, 1999.

Bermudez, Joseph, "Silent Partner: North Korea is a Significant Partner in Pakistan's Growing Missile Capabilities", *Jane's Defense Weekly,* Vol. 29, No. 20, May 1998.

Bhaskar, Udai, C., "New Challenges in the Spread of Weapons of Mass Destruction: One Year after the South Asian Nuclear Tests", *Strategic Analysis,* Vol. 23, No. 8, November 1999.

Bilver, S., "India Fires into the Missile Age", *Asian Defence Journal,* September 1989.

Bobb, Dilip and Menon, Amarnath, K., "Agni: Chariot of Fire", *India Today,* New Delhi, 1-15 June 1989.

Chandrashekar, S., "An Assessment of Pakistan's Missile Capability", *Missile Monitor,* No. 3, Spring 1993.

Chandrashekar, S., "The Origins and Antecedents of the Ghauri Missile—An Assessment", *Current Science,* Vol. 76, No. 3, 10 February 1999.

Chellaney, Brahma, "India Demonstrates to Missile Prowess", *The Hindustan Times,* 12 April 1999.

Chellaney, Brahma, "India's Missile Programme: Behaving like a Wimp", *The Indian Express,* 12 October 1995.

Chellaney, Brahma, "Missiles India's Pusillanimity, China's Wall", *The Pioneer,* 7 May 1997.

Chellaney, Brahma, "Misguided Missiles", *The Hindustan Times,* 11 Sept 1996.

Chengappa, Raj, "Nuclear Policy: Making Compromises", *India Today,* New Delhi, 30 April 1995.

Chengappa, Raj, "Boom for Boom", *India Today,* New Delhi, 26 April 1999.

Cherian, John, "Missiles Under Fire", *Frontline,* 3 June 1994.

Coach, Andrew, "India, Pakistan: Nuclear Arms Race Gets Off to a Slow Start", *Jane's Intelligence Review,* 13 January 2001.

Datt, Savita, "Pakistan Series of Missiles: A Review", *Mainstream,* Vol. 36, No. 25, June 13, 1998.

Dhanjal, Gursharan Singh, "Agni: A deterrent", *Mainstream,* 12 August 1989.

Dhanjal, Gursharan, "Gauri Missile: The External Connection", *Mainstream,* Vol. 36, No. 17, April 18, 1998.

Dixit, Abha, "Missile Race in South Asia: Linear Progression Required to Cap Race", *Strategic Analysis*, Vol. XXI, No. 6, September, 1997.

Donnelly, John, "Congress Warns Bush, Israel on Arrow Exports", *Defense Week*, Vol. 24, No. 22, 2 June 2003.

Drell, Sidney and Peurifoy, Bob, "Technical Issues of a Nuclear Test Ban", *Annual Reviews of Nuclear and Particle Science*, Vol. 44, 1994.

Erlanger, Steven, "U.S. Wary of Punishing China For Missile Help to Pakistan", *New York Times*, 27 August 1997.

Farzana, Shakoor, "Nuclearisation of South Asia and the Kashmir Dispute", *Pakistan Horizon*, Vol. 51, No. 4, October 1998.

Feller, Steve, "Ballistic Missiles and Weapons of Mass Destruction", *International Security*, Summer, 1991.

Fetter, Steve and Hippel, Frank Von, "The Hazard from Plutonium Dispersal by Nuclear-warhead Accidents", *Science and Global Security*, Vol. 2, No. 1, 1990.

Foss, Christopher F., "Pakistan Extends its Missile Capabilities", *Jane's Intelligence Review*, Vol. 9, No. 3, March 1997.

Frost, Roger, "Pakistan's New Defence Minister: On Missiles, Self-Reliance and Afghanistan", *International Defence Review*, Surrey, UK, April 1989.

Ganguly, Sumit, "India to Build Nuclear-Proof Bunkers for Leadership", *Global Security Newswire*, 22 September, 2003.

Gaurav Kampani, "Stakeholders' Analysis in the Indian Strategic Missile Program", *Non-proliferation Review*, Fall/ Winter 2003.

Gerardi, Greg, "India's 333rd Prithvi Missile Group", *Jane's Intelligence Review*, Vol. 7, No. 8, 1995.

Gertz, Bill. "Iran-Bound Mystery Freighter Carried Parts for Missiles", *The Washington Times*, 16 July 1992.

Ghosh, C.N., "Directed Energy Weapons", *Strategic Analysis*, Vol. XXIV, No. 11, February 2001.

Ghosh, P.K., "Emerging Trends in the Nuclear Triad", *Strategic Analysis*, Vol. XXV, No. 2, May 2001.

Gizeneski, Peter, "Managed Proliferation in South Asia: Implications for Regional Security and the Non-proliferation", *International Journal*, Vol. 56, No. 2, Spring, 1999.

Gopalakrishnan, A., "Disturbing Lack of Safety", *Frontline,* 23 August 1996.

Gopalakrishnan, A., "Issues of Nuclear Safety", *Frontline,* 26 March 1999.

Gupta, Amit, "Nuclear Forces in South Asia: Prospects for Arms Control", *Security Dialogue,* Vol. 38, No. 3, September 1999.

Harvey, John R., "Regional Ballistic Missiles and Advanced Strike Aircraft", *International Security,* 1992.

Hegerty, Devin T., "South Asia's Nuclear Balance", *Current History,* Vol. 95, April 1996.

Heisbounz, Francois, "The Prospects for Nuclear Stability Between India and Pakistan", *Survival,* Winter, 1998-99.

Hermann, Wilfried, A., "Missile Proliferation in Asia", *Military Technology,* Vol. 24, No. 3, March 2000.

Huntley, Wade, L., "Alternate futures After the South Asian Nuclear Tests: Pokhran as Prologue", *Asian Survey,* Vol. 39, No. 3, May/June 1999.

Iqbal, Muhammad, "Missile Proliferation in South Asia", *Regional Studies,* Spring 1990.

Iranzo, E., *et. al.,* "Air Concentrations of 239Pu and 240Pu and Potential Radiation Doses to Persons Living near Pu-contaminated Areas in Palomares, Spain", *Health Physics,* Vol. 52, No. 4, April 1987.

Ishaq Ilahi Choudhary, "Security Challenges of South Asian Countries in the Coming Decade", *BIIS,* Vol. 21, No. 1, January 2000.

Jain, B.M., "Post Test Scenario in South Asia: Global and Regional Implications", *Indian Journal of Asian Affairs,* Vol. 11, Nos. 1-2, June and December 1998.

Jehl, Douglas, "China Breaking Missile Pledge, U.S. Aides Say", *The New York Times International,* 6 May 1993.

Jindal, Nirmal, "Paradox of a Nuclearised South Asia", *Journal of Peace Studies,* Vol. 7, No. 2, March-April 2000.

Joeck, Neil, "Maintaining Nuclear Stability in South Asia", *Adelphi Paper,* No. 312, International Institute for Strategic Studies, London, 1997.

Jones, Rodney W., "Minimum Nuclear Deterrence Postures in South Asia: An Overview", *Journal of South Asian and Middle Eastern Studies,* Villanova, Vol. XXV, No. 5, Summer, 2002.

Joshi, Manoj, "From Technology Demonstration to Assumed Retaliation", *Strategic Analysis,* January 1999.

Kak, Kapil, "Missile Proliferation and International Security", *Strategic Analysis,* Vol. XXIII, No. 3, June 1999.

Kanwal, Gurmeet, "India's National Security Strategy in a Nuclear Environment", *Strategic Analysis,* Vol. XXIV, No. 9, December, 2000.

Kanwal, Gurmeet, "India's Nuclear Doctrine and Policy", *Strategic Analysis,* Vol. XXIV, No. 11, February 2001.

Kanwal, Gurmeet, "India's Nuclear Force Structure", *Strategic Analysis,* Vol. XXIV, No. 6, September 2000.

Kanwal, Gurmeet, "Safety and Security of India's Nuclear Weapons", *Strategic Analysis,* Vol. XXV, No. 1, April 2001.

Kanwal, Gurmeet, "Command and Control of Nuclear Weapons", *Strategic Analysis,* Vol. 23, No. 10, January 2000.

Karp, Aaron, "Ballistic Missiles in the Third World", *International Security,* Winter, 1984-85.

Kartha, Tara, "Ballistic Missile Defences: The Debate in United States", *Strategic Analysis,* Vol. XXIV, No. 1, April 2000.

Katyal, K.K., "A Crucial Step in Missile Technology", *The Hindu,* April 12, 1999.

Kesavan, K.V., "Japan's Nuclear Policy and the Nuclearisation of South Asia", *International Studies,* Vol. 37, No. 4, October-December, 2000.

Khan, Ayaz Ahmad, "Air Accidents in Spite of High Efficiency", *Defence Journal,* August 1998.

Khan, Feroz Hasan, "Challenges to Nuclear Stability in South Asia", *Non-proliferation Review,* Vol. 10, No. 1, Spring 2003.

Kibria, Ruksana, "US Non-Proliferation Policy and the Nuclearisation of South Asia", *BIIS,* Vol. 28, No. 4, October. 1999.

Koblentz, George, "Viewpoint: Theater Missile Defense and South Asia: A Volatile Mix", *The Non-proliferation Review,* Spring–Summer 1997.

Koch, Andrew "Pakistan Persists with Nuclear Procurement", *Jane's Intelligence Review,* Vol. 9, No. 3, March 1997,

Koch, Andrew, "South Asia Rivals Keep Test Score Even", *Jane's Intelligence Review,* Vol. 11, No. 8, August 1999.

Lennox, Duncan, "Hatf-6 (Shaheen 2)", *Jane's Strategic Weapon Systems,* 15 June 2004.

Lenox, Duncal, "Comparing India's and Pakistan's Strategic Weapons Capabilities", *Jane's Strategic Weapon Systems,* 30 May 2002.

Litwak, Robert S., "The New Calculus for Pre-emption", *Survival,* No. 44, Winter, 2002-03.

Lodhi, Maleeha *et. al.*, "Pakistani Media Reports on the Ghauri Missile: Testing Times in the Sub-Continent", *Strategic Digest,* Vol. 28, No. 6, June 1998.

Mahapatra, Chintamani, "The US, China and the Ghauri Missile", *Strategic Analysis,* June 1998.

Mama, Hormuz, "Improved Prithvi Missile Launched", *International Defense Review,* 1 August 1992.

Mannshaiya, Harbir K., "India's Prithvi", *International Defense Review,* August 1995.

Mehta, Ashok K., "Missiles in South Asia : Search for an Operational Strategy", *South Asian Survey,* Vol. 11, No. 2, July-December 2004.

Menon, Prakash, "Nuclear Deterrence in South Asia: Limited War and Arms Race", *Trishul,* Vol. 12, No. 2, Spring 2000.

Milhollin, Gary, "India's Missiles With a Little Help from Our Friends", *Bulletin of the Atomic Scientists,* November 1989.

Milhollin, Gary, "Asia's Nuclear Nightmare: The German Connection", *The Washington Post,* 10 June 1990.

Mohan, Raja, C., "Agni and Sino-Indian Ties", *The Hindu,* 16 April 1999.

Mohanty, Pratap, "India tests nuclear capable missile", *Agence France Presse,* 4 July 2004.

Murthy, Padamja, "India and Its Neighbours: The 1990s and Beyond", *Strategic Analysis,* Vol. XXIV, No. 8, November 2000.

Nair, Nijai, K., "Nuclear Terrorism: The South Asian Scene", *Aakrosh,* Vol. 4, No. 10, January 2001.

Nalupat, M.D., "DRDO has a long way to Go", *Times of India,* 10 December 1998.

Nayam, Rajiv, "India and the Agni Missile", *Deccan Herald,* 29 January 1997.

Norris, Robert S. and Arkin, William", Soviet Nuclear Testing, August 29, 1949-October 24, 1990", *The Bulletin of the Atomic Scientists,* May/June 1998.

Norris, Robert S., Arkin, William and Others, "India's Nuclear Forces 2002", *Bulletin of The Atomic Scientists,* Vol. 58, No. 2, March/April 2002.

Palevit, Marc, "Beyond Deterrence; What the US Should do about Ballistic Missiles in the Third World", *Strategic Review,* Summer, 1990.

Pande, Savita, "Missile Technology Control Regime Impact Assessment", *Strategic Analysis,* Vol. XXIII, No. 6, September 1999.

Pandey, Savita, "India's Missile Programme", *World Focus,* Vol. 18, No. 3, March 1997.

Panneerselvan , A.S., "Nuclear Safety: Radioactivity", *Outlook,* 19 June 2000.

Panwar, Sango, "India's Missiles: A New Dimension in South Asia", *Vayu Aerospace Review,* VI/1989.

Parasannan, R., "Stealing a March", *Week,* Vol. 18, No. 30, July 9, 2000.

Parthsarthy, Anand, "For a Weapons Delivery System", *Frontline,* June 19, 1998.

Patel, Sujatha, "Balijal Agitation: Socio-Economic Background", *Economic and Political Weekly,* 25 March 1989.

Podvig, Pavel, "History and Current Status of the Russian Early Warning System", *Science and Global Security,* Vol. 10, No. 1, 2002.

Podvig, Pavel, "The Operational Status of the Russian Space-based Early Warning System", *Science and Global Security,* Vol. 4, No. 3, 1994.

Pyne Keith, "Past Cold War Deterrence and Missile Defence", *Strategic Digest,* April 1996.

Raghavan, V.R., "Beyond Missile Machismo", *Outlook,* 26 April 1999.

Raghuvanshi, Vivek, "India To Develop Extensive Nuclear Missile Arsenal", *Defense News,* 24 May 1999

Raghvan, V.R., "Limited War and Nuclear Escalation in South Asia", *The Non-proliferation Review,* Vol. 8, No. 3, Fall-Winter 2001.

Rahul Bedi, "Missile Test is 'Partial Success', says India", *Jane's Defence Week,* 19 April 2000.

Ramana, M.V., "Risks of Launch on Warning Posture", *Economic and Political Weekly,* 1 March 2003.

Rashid, Ahmed, "Pakistan Announces First Successful Test of its Own Missile", *Independent*, London, 6 February 1989.

Raza, Maroof, "To Achieve Non-Weaponised Nuclear Deterrence in South Asia", *Peace Initiatives*, Vol. III, No. IV, July-August, 1997.

Rehbein, Robert E., "Managing Proliferation in South Asia : A Case for Assistance to Unsafe Nuclear Arsenals", *The Nonproliferation Review*, Vol. 9, No. 1, Spring 2002.

Rethinaraj, T.S. Gopi, "Going Global : India aims for a Credible Nuclear Doctrine", *Jane's Intelligence Review*, Vol. 13, No. 2, February 2001.

Rome, Barbara Opall, "Israel Boosts Arrow Arsenal as War Looms", *Defense News*, 25 November–1 December 2002.

Sachdeva, A.K., "India's Surface to Suface Missiles: The Doctrinal and Strategic Framework", *Strategic Analysis*, Vol. XXIV, No. 2, May 2000.

Sachdeva, A.K., "Pakistan's Missile Capability", *Pertinence of Pakistani Ballistic Missiles in the Indo-Pak Conflict*, Delhi Papers-14, IDSA, New Delhi, 2000.

Sachdeva, A.K., "Surface to Surface Missiles and International Law", *Strategic Analysis*, Vol. XXIII, No. 3, June 1999.

Sahgal, Arun, "Comparative Analysis of Indo-Pak Nuclear Capabilities", *Combat Journal*, Vol. 30, No. 1, March 2001.

Sanger, David E. and Schmitt, Eric, "Reports Say China is Aiding Pakistan on Missile Project", *New York Times*, 2 July 2000.

Sawhney, Pravin, "Army Organizes First Prithvi Missile Unit", *Asian Age*, New Delhi, 29 April 1995.

Sawney, Pravin "Standing Alone : India's Nuclear Imperative", *Jane's International Defense Review*, November 1996.

Sethi, Manpreet, "CTBT and India's Options", *Strategic Analysis*, Vol. XXIV, No. 6, September, 2000.

Sethi, Manpreet, "Dangers From Weapons of Mass Destruction: Any Different in South Asia", *Strategic Analysis*, Vol. XXIV, No. 11, February 2001.

Shahi, Agha, "Command and Control of Nuclear Weapons in South Asia", *Strategic Issues*, No. 3, March 2000.

Shepard, Ben, "South Asia Nears Nuclear Boiling Point", *Jane's Intelligence Review*, Vol. 11, No. 7, July 1999.

Siddiqa-Agha, Ayeesha, "South Asia: Nuclear Navies?" *Bulletin of Atomic Scientists*, Vol. 56, No. 5, September-October 2000.

Singh, Bulbul, "BrahMos Cruise Missile Test-Fired from Destroyer", *Aerospace Daily*, Vol. 208, No. 42, 1 December 2003.

Singh, Bulbul, "India to Build Missile Stocks While Seeking Missile Defense", *Aerospace Daily*, 17 July 2003.

Singh, Jasjit, "Civilian Space Efforts and the MTCR", *Frontline*, 20 August 1994.

Singh, Jasjit, "Nuclear Command and Control", *Strategic Analysis*, Vol. XXV, No. 2, May 2001.

Singh, Jaswant, "Against Nuclear Aparthied", *Foreign Affairs*, Vol. 77, No. 5, 1998.

Singh, Swaran, "Ghauri: Pakistan's First IRBM", *Strategic Analysis*, Vol. 31, No. 12, March 1998.

Smith, R. Jeffrey, "China Linked to Pakistani Missile Plant", *The Washington Post*, 25 August 1996.

Smith, R. Jeffrey, "China Said to Sell Arms to Pakistan; M-11 Missile Shipment May Break Vow to U.S.", *Washington Post*, 4 December 1992

Smith, R. Jeffrey, 'China Linked To Pakistani Missile Plant; Secret Project could Renew Sanctions issue", *Washington Post*, 25 August 1996.

Smith, R. Jeffrey, "Dozens of U.S. Exports went to Iraqi Arms Projects", *The Washington Post*, 22 July 1992.

Soundhi, Sunil, "India's Quest for Autonomous Capability in Space Technology", *UP Journal of Political Science*, January-December 1993.

Srivastava, Anupam and Gahlaut, Seema, "Curbing Proliferation from Emerging Suppliers: Export Controls in India and Pakistan", *Arms Control Today*, September 2003.

Srivastava, Anupam, "India's Growing Missile Ambitions: Assessing the Technical and Strategic Dimensions", *Asian Survey*, Vol. XL, No. 2, March/April 2000.

Subrahmanyam, K., "Challenges to Indian Security", *Strategic Analysis*, Vol. XXIV, No. 9, December 2000.

Subramanian, T.S., "Issues of Safety: Former AERB Chairman Speaks Out", *Frontline*, 23 August 1996.

Subrahmanyam, K., "Agni-II Modes Divya Astra", *Economic Times*, 14 April 1999.

Swaine, Michael D. and Loren H. Runyon, "Ballistic Missile Development", *Strategic Asia, 2001-02*.

Thomas, Mahnken, "Why Third World Space Systems Matter", *Orbis,* Fall 1991.

Urayama, Kori J., "Chinese Perspectives on Theater Missile Defence: Policy Implications for Japan", *Asian Survey,* Vol. XI, No. 4, July/August, 2000.

Verma, Virendra Sahai, "Fallacy of Nuclear Deterrence", *Journal of Peace Studies,* Vol. 7, No. 2, March-April 2000.

Vishwakarma, Arun and Maharaj, Sanjay Badri, "Evaluating India's Land-based Missile Deterrent", *Indian Defense Review,* Vol. 19, No. 4, Lancer Publishers, New Delhi, October-December 2004.

Wallace, Michael D. *et. al.,* "Accidental Nuclear War: A Risk Assessment", *Journal of Peace Studies,* Vol. 23, No. 1, March 1986.

Weirr, Kenneth G., "Danger and Opportunity: The United States, Non-Proliferation and South Asia", *Comparative Strategy,* Vol. 18, No. 2, April-June 1999.

Wright, David and Kadyshev, Timur, "An Analysis of the North Korean Nodong Missile", *Science and Security,* Vol. 7, No. 2, 1998.

Zaitseva, Lyudmila and Hand, Kevin, "Nuclear Smuggling Chains, Suppliers, Intermediaries, and End-Users", *American Behavioral Scientist,* Vol. 46, No. 6, February 2003.

Zaloga, Steven, "Ballistic Missiles in the Third World: Scud and Beyond", *Interrfational Defence Review,* Nov. 1998.

Zimmerman, Peter D. and Loeb, Cheryl, "Dirty Bombs: The Threat Revisited", *Defense Horizons,* No. 38, January 2004.

Zook Darren C., "A Culture of Deterrence: Nuclear Myths and Cultural Chauvenism in South Asia", *World Policy Journal,* Vol. 17, No. 1, Spring 2000.

Zuberi, Matin, "Soviet and American Technology Assistance and Pace of Chinese Nuclear Tests", *Strategic Analysis,* Vol. XXIV, No. 7, October 2000.

Newspapers

Dawn (Pakistan)
Deccan Herald
Economic Times
Hindustan Times
Indian Express

International Herald Tribune (New York)
National Herald (New Delhi)
Space Daily (Banglore)
The Hindu
The New York Times (New York)
The Pakistan Observer
The Pioneer
The Statesman
The Times of India
The Tribune
The Washington Times
Washington Post

Magazines

Chronicle
Frontline
India Today
News week
Outlook

Internet Sources

http://www.janes.com/security/international_security/ new/janes/janes020530_1_n.shtml
http://www.world-nuclear.org/info/reactors.htm
http://www.isis-online.org/publications/southasia/ch-indpak.html
http://www.janes.com/security/international_security/news/jsws/jsws020530_1_n.shtml
http://www.iaea.org.at/worldatom/About/Policy/GC/GC39/Documents/gc3919.html
http://www.jang.com.pk/thenehes/mar2002-daily/06-03-2002/oped/04.htm.
http://www.ipcs.org/issues/700/788-mikrishna.htm
http://times of India.indiatimes.com/articleshow/616847.cms
http://www.dtra.mil/about/organisation/south_asia.pdf
http://www.fas.org/nuke/guide/pakistan/missile/hatf-I.htm.
http://www.fas.org/nuke/guide/china/theater/df-11.htm.
http;//www.pakmilitary.com/army/missles/ghauri.html.
www.policyarchitects.org/pdf/ForceModern_indiapakistan2.pdf

www.policyarchitects.org/pdf/NucStability_indiapakistan.pdf.
http://www.globalsecurity.org/military/world/israel/phalcon.htm
http://www.dawn.com/2002/01/23/nat1.htm_.
http://www.afghanbooks.com/beartrap/
http://www.the-week.com/21jan21/events6.htm.
http://www.ceip.org/files/projects/npp/resources/Conference%202001/sattar.htm.
http://www.cnn.com/2002/US/06/10/ashcroft.announcement/.
http://www.nrpb.org/faq/epidemiology/epid2.htm.
http://www.nrpb.org/faq/epidemiology/epid2.htm.
http://www.nbcme.dorg/SiteContent/MedRef/OnlineRef/CaseStudies/csgoiania.html
http://www.fas.org/nuke/intro/nuke/blast.htm.
http://www.fas.org/nuke/guide/usa/nuclear/nv209nar.pdf.
http://nuclearweaponarchive.org/Russia/Sovtestsum.html.
http://www.cdi.org/Issues/NukeAccidents/accidents.htm
http://www.indiagov.org/govt/indnucld.htm.
http://www.defencejournal.com/aug98/airaccidents.htm.
http://plutoniumerl.actx.edu/restoration.html
http://www.space.com/Space
http://timesofindia.indiatimes.com/articleshow/901642.cms
http://www.drdo.com/pub/techfocus/aug04/missile13.htm
http://www.nti.org/e_research/profiles/India/Missile/1931_4696.html
http://www.nti.org/e_research/profiles/India/Missile/1931_4696.html
http://www.nti.org/e_research/profiles/India/Missile/1931_4696.html
http://www.drdo.com/pub/techfocus/oct2001/propulsion.htm
http://www.hindu.com/2004/10/28/stories/2004102807641300.htm
http://www.drdo.com/pub/techfocus/oct2001/propulsion.htm
http://web.lexis-nexis.com/
http://www.aeronautics.ru/archive/wmd/ballistic/
http://www.deccanherald.com/deccanherald/dec202005/state1861820051219.asp

www.tribuneindia.com/1998/98sep07/head6.htm

http://www.bharat-rakshak.com/

http://www.hinduonnet.com/.

http://www.nti.org/e_research/profiles/India/Missile/1931_2023.html

http://www.hindustantimes.com/

http://www.india-today.com/>.

http://www.telegraphindia.com/1040830/asp/nation/story_3694401.asp

http://www.telegraphindia.com/1040830/asp/nation/story_3694401.asp

http://www.ias.ac.in/currsci/feb102004/372.pdf

http://www.nytimes.com/

http://www.cia.gov/.

http://www.armscontrol.org/

http://www.fas.org/nuke/guide/pakistan/missile/hatf-1.htm

http://www.globalsecurity.org/wmd/world/pakistan/hatf-2.htm

http://www.pakistanidefence.com/images/AbdaliPictures.htm

http://www.pakdirectory.net/hatf_missiles.asp.

http://www.fas.org/nuke/guide/pakistan/missile/hatf-3.htm

http://www.fas.org/nuke/guide/pakistan/missile/shaheen-2.htm

http://www.defencetalk.com/news/publish/article_001868.shtml

http://www.sas.upenn.edu/casi/reports/RiedelPaper051302.htm

http://www.cia.gov/cia/reports/721_reports/july_dec2003.htm#15

http://www.cnn.com/ALLPOLITICS/1997/06/23/time/missiles. html.

http://www.cns/pubs/opapers/op2/index.htm

http//www.dtra.mil/abut/organiza tion/souty_asia.

http//www.janes.com/security/international_security/news/jsnes020530_1_n.shtml.

Index